AN INTRODUCTION TO PENTECOSTALISM

Global Charismatic Christianity

Global Pentecostalism and (
sity is the fastest expanding r
Allan Anderson, a former Pt
global Pentecostalism, aims to   ..1-western'
nature of Pentecostalism withou   .. importance of the
movement emanating from Nor   ...ica. Offering an innovative
interpretation of Pentecostalism, he takes seriously the contributions
of the Majority World to its development and, concentrating on its
history and theology, reflects on the movement's development and significance throughout the world. Anderson also examines those theological issues that helped form a distinctive spirituality and how this
relates to different peoples and their cultures. Finally, Anderson discusses the development of Pentecostal and Charismatic Christianity
in the different countries from its origins at the beginning of the twentieth century to its theological emphases in the present day, together
with the impact of the processes of globalization.

ALLAN ANDERSON is Reader in Pentecostal Studies at the University
of Birmingham. He is the author of six books, including *Moya: The
Holy Spirit in an African Context* (1991), *Zion and Pentecost* (2000) and
African Reformation (2001), and has edited two collections, *Pentecostals
after a Century* (1999) and *Asian and Pentecostal* (2004).

AN INTRODUCTION TO PENTECOSTALISM

Global Charismatic Christianity

ALLAN ANDERSON

CAMBRIDGE
UNIVERSITY PRESS

CAMBRIDGE UNIVERSITY PRESS
Cambridge, New York, Melbourne, Madrid, Cape Town, Singapore, São Paulo,
Delhi, Tokyo, Mexico City

Cambridge University Press
The Edinburgh Building, Cambridge, CB2 8RU, UK

Published in the United States of America by Cambridge University Press, New York

www.cambridge.org
Information on this title: www.cambridge.org/9780521825733

© Allan Anderson 2004

First published 2004
6th printing 2011

Printed in the United Kingdom at the University Press, Cambridge

A catalogue record for this publication is available from the British Library

ISBN 978-0-521-82573-3 hardback
ISBN 978-0-521-53280-8 paperback

Contents

List of illustrations   *page* vii
Acknowledgements   viii
List of abbreviations   x
Preface   xii

1   Identifying Pentecostals and Charismatics   1

PART ONE: HISTORICAL DEVELOPMENT OF PENTECOSTAL
DISTINCTIVES

2   Historical and theological background   19

3   North American Classical Pentecostalism   39

4   Pentecostalism in Latin America and the Caribbean   63

5   Pentecostalism in Europe   83

6   African Pentecostalism and 'Spirit' churches   103

7   Pentecostalism in Asia, Australia and the Pacific   123

8   The Charismatic Movement and the New Pentecostals   144

9   The writing of Pentecostal history   166

PART TWO: PENTECOSTAL AND CHARISMATIC THEOLOGY
IN CONTEXT

10 A theology of the Spirit   187

11 Mission, evangelism and eschatology   206

12 The Bible and the 'full gospel'   225

Contents

13   Pentecostal education and ecumenism   243

14   Pentecostals and Charismatics in society   261

15   Globalization and the future of Pentecostalism   279

Bibliography   287
Index   298

Illustrations

1. Worshippers inside Yoido Full Gospel Church, Seoul, Korea, 2002. *Yoido Full Gospel Church.*   *page* 3
2. William Seymour (seated centre right) with leaders including Florence Crawford (left), Jennie Moore (later Mrs Seymour, third from left, back row), Azusa Street, Los Angeles, c. 1911. *Flower Pentecostal Heritage Center.*   41
3. Azusa Street building, Los Angeles before its demolition, c. 1928. *Flower Pentecostal Heritage Center.*   42
4. Willis C. Hoover, Valparaiso, Chile, c. 1910. *Flower Pentecostal Heritage Center.*   66
5. (from left) Lewi Pethrus, Mrs Barratt, T. B. Barratt, and the Bjørners, Stockholm, Sweden, c. 1913. *Flower Pentecostal Heritage Center.*   87
6. First Executive Council with James McKeown, Church of Pentecost, Accra, Ghana, 1963. *Church of Pentecost.*   119
7. James McKeown and Ghanaian President General Acheompong at Church of Pentecost convention, Accra, Ghana, 1978. *Church of Pentecost.*   120
8. Pandita Ramabai (centre), Minnie Abrams (front centre) and staff, Pune, India, 1907. *Flower Pentecostal Heritage Center.*   125
9. Mark Buntain and Indian children at the Mission of Mercy, Calcutta, India, 1988. *Flower Pentecostal Heritage Center.*   126
10. Tent where Yonggi Cho started his church, Taejo-dong, Seoul, Korea, c. 1959. *Yoido Full Gospel Church.*   138
11. David Yonggi Cho, Seoul, Korea, 2002. *Yoido Full Gospel Church.*   139
12. Church of Pentecost women dancing at Easter convention, Nsawam, Ghana 2003. *Photograph by author.*   275

Acknowledgements

This book is the result of two processes in particular over the past eight years. First, my appointment to what was then The Selly Oak Colleges in October 1995 gave me the opportunity to do research in a stimulating environment and the space to develop teaching programmes in Pentecostal and Charismatic Studies. This was further stimulated by personal interaction with Professor Walter J. Hollenweger in June 1996 during a seminar I coordinated at Selly Oak. The resulting postgraduate lectures I began the following year are the foundation of this study and have been developed every subsequent year. I want to thank colleagues Andrew Kirk, Werner Ustorf, Sugirtharajah and Edmond Tang for their participation, encouragement and commitment to my personal development.

Second, my involvement in postgraduate supervision at the Graduate Institute for Theology and Religion of the University of Birmingham has been one of the great learning experiences of my life and an immense privilege. I want to express my appreciation to those first seven doctoral candidates (now graduated) whose research I supervised: Drs Robert Beckford, Jeri Jehu-Appiah, Jeong Jae Yong, Jeong Chong Hee, Opoku Onyinah, Clifton Clarke and John Padwick. Their pioneering work and that of those who are following them has opened me up to some of the unexplored areas in Pentecostal Studies. Then there are those fine scholars whose work I have drawn on both consciously and unconsciously, and here in particular I think of Walter Hollenweger, Harvey Cox, Cecil Robeck, David Bundy and Bill Faupel, whose work I have leaned on considerably. I am also immensely grateful to Stanley Burgess, whose encyclopaedic *New International Dictionary of the Pentecostal and Charismatic Movements* was invaluable in the preparation of this book.

My first meeting with Kevin Taylor from Cambridge and his subsequent urging me to formulate a book proposal was the formal beginning of this project, and his encouragement and that of his successor Kate Brett have given me further motivation to complete it. Permission by the Yoido Full

Gospel Church in Seoul, Korea, the Church of Pentecost in Accra, Ghana and the Flower Pentecostal Heritage Center in Springfield, Missouri to publish the photographs in the pages of this book is gratefully acknowledged. I am particularly grateful to the Yoido Full Gospel Church and Pastor David Yonggi Cho for permission to use the photograph on the cover. I am also thankful to the Donald Gee Centre in Mattersey, England and its director David Garrard who allowed me to peruse the early periodicals housed there, and the Flower Center's website and digital copies of early periodicals were extremely useful.

The book is dedicated to my octogenarian Salvation Army officer parents Keith and Gwenyth Anderson who first taught me to love and serve God, to my loving partner of twenty-five years Olwen from whose classical Pentecostal spirituality and that of her parents Leonard and Ruth Brooke I have learned so much, and to my creative son Matthew and vivacious daughter Tami who have grown up too quickly while this book was gestating. Finally, I hope that the many friends and scholars I have been closely associated with over the past thirty-five years in the Pentecostal and Charismatic movements in Zimbabwe, South Africa and the UK, and those in the other countries I have visited more recently in Europe, Africa, Asia and the Americas will recognize something of their dynamic spiritual heritage in this modest offering.

Abbreviations

ACFCJ	Apostolic Church of the Faith in Christ Jesus (Mexico)
AFC	Apostolic Faith Church (UK)
AFM	Apostolic Faith Mission (South Africa)
AG	Assemblies of God
AGBI	Assemblies of God in Great Britain and Ireland
AIC(s)	African Independent/Initiated Church(es)
AICN	Africa Israel Church Nineveh (Kenya)
AJPS	*Asian Journal of Pentecostal Studies*
BFC	Brazil for Christ
BP	Brotherhood of Pentecostal Assemblies (Netherlands)
CAC	Christ Apostolic Church (Nigeria)
CBN	Christian Broadcasting Network
CC	Christian Congregation (Brazil)
CGC	Church of God (Cleveland, TN)
CGP	Church of God of Prophecy (USA)
CMS	Church Missionary Society (Anglican)
COGIC	Church of God in Christ (USA)
COP	Church of Pentecost (Ghana)
CPM	Ceylon Pentecostal Mission (South Asia)
DRC	Democratic Republic of the Congo
EPC	Evangelical Pentecostal Church (Chile)
FG	Full Gospel Assemblies (Netherlands)
FGBMFI	Full Gospel Business Men's Fellowship International
HTB	Holy Trinity Church, Brompton (UK)
ICFG	International Church of the Foursquare Gospel (USA)
IMC	International Missionary Council
IPCG	Indian Pentecostal Church of God
IPHC	International Pentecostal Holiness Church (USA)
JAG	Jesus Assemblies of God (Korea)
JEPTA	*Journal of the European Pentecostal Theological Association*

JPT	*Journal of Pentecostal Theology*
KAG	Korean Assemblies of God
MPC	Methodist Pentecostal Church (Chile)
NAE	National Association of Evangelicals (USA)
NIDPCM	Burgess and van der Maas (eds.), *New International Dictionary of Pentecostal and Charismatic Movements*
PAC	Pentecostal Assemblies of Canada
PAW	Pentecostal Assemblies of the World (USA)
PCC	Pentecostal Church of Chile
PCI	Pentecostal Church of Indonesia
PCJC	Pentecostal Church of Jesus Christ (Mexico, USA)
PHC	Pentecostal Holiness Church (USA)
PMU	Pentecostal Missionary Union (UK)
Pneuma	*Pneuma: The Journal of the Society for Pentecostal Studies*
SJC	Spirit of Jesus Church (Japan)
SPS	Society for Pentecostal Studies
TBN	Trinity Broadcasting Network
TJC	True Jesus Church (China)
TSPM	Three Self Patriotic Movement (China)
UCKG	Universal Church of the Kingdom of God (Brazil)
UK	United Kingdom of Great Britain and Northern Ireland
UPC	United Pentecostal Church (USA)
US(A)	United States (of America)
WCC	World Council of Churches
YFGC	Yoido Full Gospel Church (Korea)
ZCC	Zion Christian Church (South Africa)

Preface

This study concentrates on the history and theology of Pentecostal and Charismatic Christianity and its origins, development and significance throughout the world. The book traces connections between a maze of movements and leaders and the various ideas and controversies that constitute Pentecostalism. In the process of tracing the historical background to its early twentieth century emergence and its subsequent influence on older churches, the book examines those theological issues that helped form a distinctive spirituality and the creation of what was in effect a reformation and renewal of the church. It also shows how this emerging spirituality related to peoples and their cultures in different parts of the world. The book discusses Pentecostalism in the different continents from its earliest origins and development to the present day, and the relationship between Pentecostals and Charismatics and their religious, political and social contexts. It aims to provide a global, non-parochial and contextual perspective on the history and theology of Pentecostalism.

I write as a sympathetic yet critical insider, having had my own experience of 'baptism in the Spirit' in 1968, and having spoken in tongues since that time. I have been a Pentecostal and Charismatic minister in South Africa for twenty-three years, a theological educator for much of that time and involved in classical Pentecostal and Charismatic churches for thirty-five years, all my adult life. After seventeen years of teaching theological students in South Africa, I have taught postgraduate and undergraduate theological students at the University of Birmingham for the past eight years and have supervised over thirty doctoral and masters research students from half as many nations studying different aspects of Pentecostalism in different parts of the world. I am indebted to the stimulating interactions with these co-learners, from whom I have gained much. I have travelled and observed Pentecostalism in four continents and these experiences, together with my experiences as a Pentecostal and Charismatic minister, will be reflected in this study. In addition, academic studies, archival material and early Pentecostal publications and popular literature are all used to illustrate that from its beginning, Pentecostalism has consisted of a variety of local movements with particular contextual responses to imported forms of Christianity. This study approaches Pentecostalism from two main perspectives. First it places the movements within their historical contexts; and second, it does this by drawing out their theological emphases as they developed.

Identifying Pentecostals and Charismatics

The Pentecostal and Charismatic movements in all their multifaceted variety constitute the fastest growing group of churches within Christianity today. According to some often-quoted estimates there are over five hundred million adherents worldwide,[1] found in almost every country in the world. If these figures are not wild guesses, they indicate that in less than a hundred years, Pentecostal, Charismatic and associated movements have become the largest numerical force in world Christianity after the Roman Catholic Church and represent a quarter of all Christians. Pentecostalism began just over a century ago and the movements continue to expand into the twenty-first century. Although the term 'Pentecostalism' is used here in an all-embracing way to include the Charismatic movement and new Pentecostal or 'neocharismatic' churches of many different descriptions, the subtitle of this book includes 'Charismatic Christianity' because we must sometimes distinguish between denominational or 'classical' Pentecostalism on the one hand, and those other movements like Charismatic movements within the older churches, autochthonous prophetic churches in the Majority World and the neocharismatic independent churches on the other. But before we introduce this phenomenon and define our terms, here are descriptive vignettes from five cities in different continents of Sunday worship services in Pentecostal and Charismatic churches.

SEOUL, KOREA

My first visit to the Yoido Full Gospel Church in Seoul, South Korea, the largest Christian congregation in the world, was in May 1998. This bustling congregation of some 700,000 members defies superlatives. I remember watching in awe as I stood outside the building half an hour before the third

---

[1] David B. Barrett and Todd M. Johnson, 'Annual Statistical Table on Global Mission: 2003', *International Bulletin of Missionary Research* 27:1 (2003), 25.

service of the day at 11.00 am. Ushers in cream jackets linked arms together to prevent the thousands of people who were waiting from going up the steps into the main sanctuary. All are dressed in their 'Sunday best'. If they were not in early they would have to sit in one of the overflow chapels and watch the service on a large video screen. But first, the 25,000 worshippers who had attended the 9.00 am service had to get out. Eventually the outgoing throng subsided and the ushers let the incoming crowds in. Thousands of people armed with Bibles and hymnbooks pressed on up the stairs, and after finishing my camcorder recording my Korean host and I joined them. The transition was carried out smoothly and quickly with remarkable Korean efficiency.

Yonggi Cho and his future mother-in-law, Jashil Choi, started this congregation in 1958 in a slum area of Seoul. This is by no means the only mega-church in Seoul but it is the largest, now situated in Yoido, the area of the most expensive real estate in the country and the capital's equivalent of New York's Manhattan. Cho acquired the property before the present high-rise development. The building with an illuminated white cross is a prominent landmark in the city and can be seen from the motorway on the other side of the Han River.

I have attended three Sunday morning services in Yoido, and apart from the content of the sermon they were much the same. Korean Pentecostalism is generally more formal than most other Pentecostal types I am familiar with. Their liturgy is influenced by the Presbyterian churches in Korea, by far the largest group of churches in the country, who in turn have been influenced by the 'Korean Pentecost', the Korean Revivals of 1903–10. Hymns born in the revivals and in the USA Holiness movements of the late nineteenth century are easily recognized in their Korean translations used by all Protestant and Pentecostal churches.

As we enter the 11.00 am service in September 2002, a performance of the highly professional orchestra and the about 200-voice choir is going on. The church has a different choir and orchestra for each service. Women dance gracefully in traditional costumes in front of the large platform. We are seated on the balcony of the ornate, circular sanctuary where earphones for simultaneous translations in English, Japanese, Chinese, Spanish, French and Russian are available. The view is overwhelming. To the left of us is the blue-robed choir, behind them the enormous pipes of the organ, below is the orchestra, ahead is the large platform, which seems strangely empty, adding to the aura surrounding one pastor sitting on the left and Pastor David Yonggi Cho kneeling in prayer on the right, with

Figure 1. Worshippers inside Yoido Full Gospel Church, Seoul, Korea, 2002.

the pulpit in the centre. When the choir finishes, the pastor reads a Psalm and the vast congregation sings 'Praise God from whom all blessings flow'. In common with all Korean Protestants and unlike most Pentecostals in the rest of the world, the congregation then recites the Apostles' Creed. When this is done, we sing a hymn as the music director turns around from facing the choir and conducts us, baton in hand. Then an elder prays while the congregation assents by punctuating his prayer with many 'Amens'. One woman cries out in tongues during this prayer, but she is mostly unnoticed. The whole congregation then reads together the text for the sermon, Matthew 11:12, and the choir sings an anthem. We are then presented with a video presentation on two large screens concerning the recent typhoon that has devastated areas of south-east Korea leaving some 200 dead and many more homeless, said to be the greatest natural disaster in recent Korean history. This church has been involved in extensive relief work, collecting 700 million won (over half a million US dollars) to provide food, clothing, medical supplies and volunteers to work in the affected areas.

After the video presentation Dr Cho goes to the pulpit and welcomes all people watching on satellite and internet links, including churches in several Japanese cities that he mentions by name. His sermon, of which foreigners are given an English outline, is 'Drive Out the Seven Enemies'. He declares that just as the Israelites had to drive out seven nations from Canaan, so Christians have to drive out the seven enemies of sin, worldliness, sickness, poverty, hatred, fear and despair. He preaches for a little less than an hour. Sometimes he asks the congregation to read a key Bible verse aloud; sometimes he exhorts the congregation to 'tell the people next to you' that they are eternally saved, that they have power over the devil, or that they are blessed. In characteristic fashion, he gives testimonies of people helped during his ministry spanning five decades. He describes the Korean War and the failings of Communism. The sermon ends with Cho leading the people in responsive prayer and the audience applauds warmly. The choir and orchestra strike up 'Because He lives, I can face tomorrow', followed as quickly by 'Chio' ('Lord') prayer. This may be the most moving part of the service, as 25,000 voices swell in simultaneous audible prayer. Just as quickly it ceases to the single high-pitched peal of a bell, and again the choir leads the congregation in the refrain 'God is so good, He's so good to me'. Again applause, followed by the offering while the choir sings 'Tell me more about Jesus'. Announcements are made, after which Pastor Cho again takes the microphone and encourages people to continue their work in the storm relief. After prayer the entire congregation sings 'The Lord's Prayer' (another moving moment); Cho gives a benediction and the choir sings a short 'Hallelujah' anthem. The service has taken exactly an hour and a half and we disperse with the crowd.

LAGOS, NIGERIA

Lagos is arguably the most Pentecostal city in the world. It has a long history of independent African churches emphasizing spiritual gifts, dating back to the time of the great influenza epidemic of 1918. Then, those who left the mission churches and sought God in prayer for healing became known as 'Aladura', a Yoruba word meaning 'possessors of prayer'. The whiterobed, often bare-footed Aladura are still found in thriving churches, but in Lagos one cannot fail to notice hundreds of relatively new churches with signboards on every street corner, as I did in May 2001 on a visit to this teeming African city. Pentecostals are everywhere: they preach in buses, at market places and in massive campgrounds, tents, stadiums, churches and auditoriums. They dominate the media. Pentecostalism has profoundly affected all forms of Christianity in Nigeria. On one Sunday we visited five different churches, including a Charismatic Anglican church, two Aladura churches, and two independent Charismatic churches. Some of the largest gatherings of Christians in the world occur in the campgrounds of these Nigerian churches, where literally hundreds of thousands of people attend all-night Friday meetings in places with names like Redemption Ground and Canaan Land. The older churches are struggling to keep pace with the jet-setting entrepreneurs who head up these new organizations. One that is managing to do so is the Christ Apostolic Church, the biggest of Nigeria's older Pentecostal churches sitting somewhat half way between Aladura and classical Pentecostal churches.

We attend a service of this church in a church building that has only a platform, steel structure and a roof with no walls. This makes it easier for the two thousand or so people who have gathered, cramming around the sides of the property. Unlike their white-robed Aladura compatriots, the CAC members wear ordinary clothes, and they too have dressed up for church, thus belying the poverty all around them in this part of Lagos. Men and women are separated on either side of the aisle but as is usually the case throughout the world, there are many more women than men present. When the congregation are invited to pray there is a roar of simultaneous prayer in unison. Pastor Samuel Abiara is dressed in a dark pinstriped business suit with coattails almost reaching his knees. His is a commanding presence, and the people have obviously come with eager expectation to hear him preach. He preaches from the Gospel of John on the power of the Word of God for protection against spiritual enemies, and his long sermon is interspersed with readings from the Bible in English and Yoruba. As he preaches from hand-written notes the pastor walks around the congregation with a microphone and a video camera operator in hot pursuit. At the end of the preaching he reads letters from people who have been helped by the preaching in the church. One woman has been abused by her husband, and the pastor uses this as an occasion to give counselling to the many women in similar situations. Come and listen to the Word of God, he says, for you cannot control your husband with violence. The service ends with an offering, in which large plastic bins are used.

BUENOS AIRES, ARGENTINA

A Christian worker in Argentina from Northern Ireland attended the church of one of the city's best-known Pentecostal pastors, Claudio

Freidzon, and gave the following graphic, somewhat tongue-in-cheek account of her experience.[2]

It was just about to start. My hope for a seat evaporated instantly; the old cinema was completely full and people were already standing at the back. A smartly suited young man took centre stage and suddenly the hall erupted into applause. A deep drum roll led into the bouncy beat of 'La única razón para vivir'. The floor vibrated with hundreds of tapping feet and a few energetic youth jumping to rhythm. The rock music electrified the air, raising excitement and expectation; the people sang with hot Latin enthusiasm. The song finished to instant applause and another song even more vibrant than the first started up. The first had only been a warm up, now we were really getting into it. The song leader paced the stage like a pop star holding the microphone close to his mouth. Everyone knew the words, and they sang without restraint, punching the air with clenched fists, then with pointed fingers. The floor vibrated, the air tingled, the beat pulsated through the body and excitement grew. 'We are part of history', he shouted. Everyone cheered. 'Argentina is part of history'. Excited clapping and screaming erupted.

Freidzon arrived to more applause. He took the microphone, a stream of incomprehensible words followed, people joined in with praise tongues, the loud music continued, the auditorium was filled with music and the hum of human voices praising God. Slowly he walked back and forth with hands in the air continuing to speak in tongues into the mike, and then he started clapping. In a loud voice he declared, 'You reign over all the earth'. The people cheered and clapped. 'Manifiesta, manifiesta', he commanded. He started to pray. 'Flames, flames', he called while wafting his hands over the front rows. People stretched their hands high as if trying to catch the flames. The deep drum roll continued while he prayed in tongues then moved into the music for the next song, as he started singing 'Rise up Lord'.

With the lively beat everyone burst into fiesta mode once more. The worship leader took over, he sang a line and everyone responded, 'huye, huye' (flee or get out) while pushing their hands over their shoulders. After five minutes of this I reckoned that any demons present should have known that they weren't welcome. Ecstatic clapping and cheering followed. We watched a video on how the tragic nation of Uganda is being changed by God. The video emphasized how the Ugandan people had turned to God in prayer, even publicly dedicating their nation to God on Millennium night. 'The key, which the world doesn't know, is prayer', explained Pastor Freidzon. 'We are aware that Argentina is passing through a spiritual awakening . . . our God is God of the impossible . . . We have access to the most important decisions of the government because the King of Kings hears us'. Applause. 'We are in His presence'. Applause. 'This is a supernatural convocation'. Applause. 'I call all the churches of the nation to prayer . . . [I call the nation to] renounce witchcraft and give place to Jesus. Our reaction in

---

[2] Adapted from a report by Wilhelmina (Wilma) Davies, Buenos Aires, May 2002 (PhD candidate at the University of Birmingham, England researching Argentinean Pentecostalism).

these adverse times must be to pray to God with our whole heart'. He paces the platform while praying. 'You know and you liberate from every kind of sickness and difficulty, . . . giving prosperity, . . . we pray for those in the midst of this testing. Some among the people of God are still captives of the enemy. . . . Resist the devil, submit yourselves to God, resist the lie. . . . How does one break the curses that have held generations? Jesus! . . .' Applause. 'Let's pray individually but together'.

Five hundred people, having been moved by what they have seen and heard, turn and kneel at the chairs they had been sitting on. The soft hum of prayer fills the hall. Those without chairs kneel heads to the floor. Some pray quietly, some loudly; the lady in front of me weeps audibly, a man nearby trembles gently. Freidzon walks down the aisle touching people's heads; as he touches the trembling man saying 'more fire, more fire' he shakes all over. A boy of about nine carrying a bundle of clothing goes to him and asks for prayer. He falls backwards but is caught and soon recovers and takes the blessed clothing back to his mother. People prayed for their families, for the nation, for the government. Surely if God can change Uganda he can change Argentina! Certainly no one else has an answer.

BIRMINGHAM, ENGLAND

My family and I enter the South Birmingham Vineyard at 10.30 in the morning on a warm summer's day in July 2002. This is one of the 'Third Wave' churches in the UK that began in the early 1990s and is part of the Association of Vineyard Churches founded by John Wimber in Anaheim, California. The service is held in a school hall and about 250 chairs have been put out. Doughnuts and coffee are served at the back, and as we enter we are warmly greeted and handed a weekly bulletin. The congregation is mostly English middle class, casually dressed and rather youthful by church standards in this country, although there are a number of grey hairs around. The service begins on time and first a pastor dressed in Bermuda shorts and a tee shirt welcomes everyone and says that we are going to get intimate with the Lord. The congregation murmurs approvingly. A young man in a tee shirt and jeans on the electronic keyboard leads the worship, accompanied by two young women on vocals, a bass guitarist and a drummer. There is no rhythm guitar this morning. The young man begins singing 'He brought me to his banqueting table and his banner over me is love . . . We can feel the love of God in this place . . .' and we sing this several times through. We pass on to a softer and more 'worshipful' song and people raise their hands in praise. For about forty minutes we sing about four songs and listen as various people share the revelations they have received. One woman describes a solid heavy wooden door that we must open and go through if we are to worship God correctly. Another says that we must push the door the right way to 'enter in' to God's intimate presence.

Next, the senior pastor Andrew McNeil, mounts the stage and apologizes for being absent the previous Sunday, as he was north in Leeds helping a new Vineyard church recently planted there. He is in his thirties, quietly spoken and refined in speech. He begins to teach from 2 Corinthians 9 about generous giving. He speaks about two couples going out from this 'church family' in the next two months to work in Lebanon among Palestinian refugees, work that is being done in Malawi for the poor and an organization called 'Christians Against Poverty' that someone in the congregation will talk about after the sermon. After he has finished speaking for about half an hour people are invited to go forward for prayer, and several people pray for those who respond. The service ends with announcements and people begin to disperse.

CHICAGO, ILLINOIS

African American church historian David D. Daniels III and I arrive at about midday at the St Luke Church of God in Christ in March 1999, as snowstorms in Missouri had delayed our flight to Chicago from the annual meeting of the Society for Pentecostal Studies. At his gracious invitation I am visiting his home church in downtown Chicago, a congregation of the largest African American Pentecostal denomination in the USA, founded in 1897 by Charles H. Mason, who remained its presiding bishop until 1961. I later learn from David Daniels and PhD student Eric Williams that activities at their church start at 6.00 am, when the doors are opened for 'prayer warriors' to pray for the Spirit's presence and moving in the coming service that begins at 7.45 am. The church 'Mothers' lead the prayer service, and most kneel around the altar, with a unique musical chant-like quality infusing their prayer accompanied by tears, praise and ecstatic speech. During the main service, especially during the lively praise singing led by the choir, many of the church members will break into 'holy dancing', speaking in tongues, or loud and spontaneous praises. The service also includes formal hymn singing, Scripture readings, community announcements and the offering. The church is packed with some two hundred people all dressed in their Sunday best, men in suits and women in modestly conservative dresses with hats. Somebody makes room for us and hands us a printed order of service as we sit in the front row; the preacher is in full swing. His preaching is dialogical, punctuated with exclamations from members of the congregation, 'Yes, Lord!', 'Thank you Jesus!', 'Hallelujah!', 'Glory!', 'Amen!', and other similar expressions of appreciation. The organist sounds arpeggios at appropriate times during the sermon. The preaching is not just a sermon – it is a spontaneous poem, a vivid illustration and a hymn of praise at the same time. Towards the close of his message the preacher begins to sing an exhortation and the congregation are taken up with the elation of it. When the congregation sings, it is an intensely soul-like chant in harmonious unity with bodily movements like exuberant dancing, rhythmic clapping and uplifted hands. People are invited to come to the altar at the front to respond to the preacher's invitation for prayer. After a benediction the service ends and the congregation melts into groups for social interaction and communion.

UNDERSTANDING TERMS

In the study of global 'Pentecostal' and 'Charismatic' Christianity, it is very important to understand what we mean by these terms. The sampling of different Pentecostal and Charismatic church services given above demonstrates several common features, but there are many differences too. All demonstrate what Suurmond has called 'the Word and Spirit at play', where everyone has a contribution to make to the service, much like the creative combination of spontaneity and order in a jazz performance.[3] All would emphasize the immediate presence of God in the service, all would expect some sign of miraculous intervention (often called 'gifts of the Spirit'), and would encourage congregational participation, especially in prayer and worship. There is usually a leading preacher, and an appeal for a response. But these similarities are only the tip of the iceberg. There are as many different types of Pentecostal and Charismatic churches as there are thousands of organizations. Although an oral liturgy is still part of most Pentecostal and Charismatic services, in the larger celebrations a written order of service has become necessary, which limits the spontaneity and participation of all in the liturgy. This is often offset in the opportunities given to members to pray simultaneously, to dance and sing during the 'praise and worship', to exercise gifts of the Spirit, to respond to the 'altar call', and to call out their approval of the preaching with expletives like 'Amen!' and 'Hallelujah!' and with applause and laughter.

---

[3] Jean-Jacques Suurmond, *Word and Spirit at Play: Towards a Charismatic Theology* (London: SCM, 1994), pp. 22–3, 85.

But because of the great diversity within Pentecostal and Charismatic movements, it is very difficult to find some common unifying features or distinctiveness by which they might be defined. It is an extremely precarious task in the first place, as it gives the person who attempts it a tremendous responsibility to see that justice is done to those who might not fit precisely into this definition. Pentecostals have defined themselves by so many paradigms that diversity itself has become a primary defining characteristic of Pentecostal and Charismatic identity. It is now probably better to speak of a whole 'range of Pentecostalisms'.[4] Scholars have attempted various and divergent ways of defining Pentecostalism, some of which are ambiguous and of little use, while others attempt to demonstrate 'distinctiveness' and create unnecessarily strained relationships with other Christians as a result. These typically argue for the 'purity' of the term 'Pentecostal' and adopt a particular theological position over and even against others, implicitly linking the term to the doctrines of 'subsequence' and 'initial evidence'. These doctrines, which will be discussed in more detail later, originated in the USA at the beginning of the twentieth century and refer to the experience of the baptism with (or in) the Holy Spirit. This is a primary defining characteristic of US Pentecostalism, where it is believed that those who have this post-conversion experience will speak in strange tongues as 'initial physical evidence'. Although this reflects the doctrinal position of most 'classical' Pentecostals (but by no means all), this way of defining Pentecostalism narrows to include only what we call 'classical' Pentecostals of the North American type, or those who speak in tongues. Too limited a definition of 'Pentecostal' and 'Charismatic', however, cannot be supported from a global perspective, as this excludes those multitudes of Christians whose equally authentic experience of the Spirit is different from those who speak in tongues. Even Donald Dayton's well-known exposition of a 'common four-fold pattern' to distinguish what 'Pentecostalism' is,[5] although broader, can only neatly be applied to 'classical Pentecostalism' in North America. In this book I will adopt an inclusive definition to avoid both the bigotry of excluding those who do not agree with a particular understanding of the Bible and the triumphalism of those who boast about the growth of their own movement.

A look at some statistics may help us understand the diversity of this phenomenon and the controversy surrounding definitions. The numbers

[4] Cecil M. Robeck, Jr. 'Making Sense of Pentecostalism in a Global Context', unpublished paper presented at the 28th Annual Meeting of the Society of Pentecostal Studies (Springfield, MI, March 1999), p. 18.
[5] Donald W. Dayton, *Theological Roots of Pentecostalism* (Metuchen, NJ: Scarecrow Press, 1987), p. 21.

of Pentecostals and Charismatics in the world, as with any global statistics, are not easily arrived at. David Barrett's statistics (now produced in conjunction with Todd Johnson) on world Christianity are well known, widely quoted and broadly accepted – and for good reason. They are quoted at the beginning of many a scholarly work on Pentecostalism, particularly to underline the strength of Pentecostal and Charismatic movements. They have been produced with considerable effort and painstaking research, suggesting that there were over 523 million 'Pentecostal/ charismatics' in the world in 2001.[6] Recent statistics from Johnstone and Mandryk are much more conservative: 345 million 'Charismatic', including 115 million 'Pentecostal' in 2000. This considerable difference is easily explained. Barrett and Johnson include in their category of 'Pentecostal/charismatic' a 'megabloc' of 394 million 'Independents', which is about three quarters of the total. To add to the confusion, the 'Independents' are further defined as having the 'synonymous alternate terms' of 'postdenominationalists' and 'neo-apostolics'. They are clearly distinguished from classical Pentecostals, but share with them an emphasis on the power of the Spirit. The writers say that one of the hallmarks of this movement is the emphasis on 'gifts of the Spirit' and 'a desire to receive more of God's empowering for the Christian life'. They explain that this new 'megabloc' includes the 'non-white indigenous' category in their earlier statistics. Johnstone and Mandryk don't include this latter group in their use of the term 'Charismatic', saying that their figures are at best reasonable estimates and 'more cautious' than Barrett and Johnson's. Unpacking Barrett and Johnson's terminology even further reveals that among many other groups, the majority of the 'non-white indigenous' churches are the 'Han Chinese churches' with an estimated 80 million members, and the 'African Independent Churches' (AICs) with 55 million members. In comparison, Johnstone and Mandryk have estimated 78 million adherents of AICs, a fifth of African Christians, and these are not included in their 'Charismatic' category. Another reason for the discrepancies between the two sets of statistics lies in the 'more cautious' approach of Johnstone and Mandryk, who define 'Charismatics' as 'those who testify to a renewing experience of the Holy Spirit and present exercise of the gifts of the Spirit'. 'Pentecostals' are defined as 'those affiliated to specifically Pentecostal denominations committed to a Pentecostal theology usually including a post-conversion experience of a baptism in the Spirit'.[7] It is clear these days that classical Pentecostals cannot be universally classified

---

[6] Barrett and Johnson, 'Annual Statistical Table', 25.

[7] Patrick Johnstone and Jason Mandryk, *Operation World: 21st Century Edition* (Carlisle, UK: Paternoster Press, 2001), pp. 3, 21, 755, 757, 762.

on the basis of the 'initial evidence' teaching, which is not in the official doctrines of some of the oldest Pentecostal denominations in Europe and South America; and even where it is, classical Pentecostals are by no means unanimous about its interpretation.

The obvious difficulty with Barrett and Johnson's broad classification of 'Pentecostal/Charismatic' greatly affects our understanding of the terms. The figures for 'Han Chinese churches' and 'African Independent Churches' are speculative and probably not very accurate. The global statistics are conditioned by the authors' interpretations of the meaning of their own categories and cannot be taken as the final word. But as these statistics are all we have, they have to be taken into consideration, and how 'Pentecostal/ Charismatic' is defined is crucial to understanding them. As sociologist David Martin has recently observed, 'How you estimate the overall numbers involved depends on the criteria you apply', and his own 'fairly conservative estimate' puts 'Pentecostalism and its vast charismatic penumbra' at 'a quarter of a billion people'.[8] However, many classical Pentecostals do not feel comfortable with a broad classification, especially those who would see themselves more squarely as 'evangelicals'.[9] Unfortunately, a widespread and uncritical use of statistical speculations for drawing conclusions about the rapid progress of Pentecostalism promotes triumphalism and ignores crucial issues affecting our understanding of these phenomena.

In spite of these dangers, many who want to demonstrate the global strength of the movement have adopted the inclusive definition and quote Barrett's statistics in support without always recognizing its wide diversity. Scholars of Pentecostalism both within and without the movement quote Barrett's figures with abandon to claim that Pentecostalism is the second largest force in world Christianity. They do not always point out that most of the half a billion people are not classical Pentecostals at all and are predominantly Africans, Latin Americans and Asians. It is in these three continents where the greatest expansion has occurred, despite the obvious significance of Pentecostalism in North America and in parts of Europe.[10] The statistics appear indiscriminately in many theses, books and other academic works on Pentecostalism written in the past decade. Such grandiose conclusions would not be such a problem if there were an adequate recognition of the diversity of the forms of 'Pentecostalisms', and that this did

---

[8] David Martin, *Pentecostalism: The World Their Parish* (Oxford: Blackwell, 2002), p. 1.

[9] Gary B. McGee, 'Pentecostal Missiology: Moving Beyond Triumphalism to Face the Issues', *Pneuma* 16:2 (1994), 276–7.

[10] Vinson Synan, *The Holiness-Pentecostal Tradition: Charismatic Movements in the Twentieth Century* (Grand Rapids: Eerdmans, 1997), pp. ix–x, 281, 296.

not refer to a single movement like 'classical Pentecostalism', which is only a fraction of the total.

Nevertheless, Barrett and Johnson's categories do illustrate that Pentecostal and Charismatic movements have many different shapes and sizes all over the world. But we can't use their figures without also accepting their inclusive definition of 'Pentecostal/charismatic'. Walter Hollenweger, founding father of academic research into Pentecostalism, is one who does this. He mentions 'the stupendous growth of Pentecostalism/ Charismatism/ Independentism from zero to almost 500 million in less than a century' and sees 'Pentecostalism' as having three distinct forms in the global context: (1) Classical Pentecostals; (2) the Charismatic renewal movement; and (3) Pentecostal or 'Pentecostal-like' independent churches in the Majority World.[11] Although there is some danger of reductionism in this threefold classification, it is a useful starting-point.

Without minimizing the numerical strength of the first two categories and remembering that the majority in the second category are Catholic Charismatics, it is the third category that is particularly significant in the global statistics. In many parts of the world, Pentecostalism has taken forms quite distinct from those of North America. For example, the largest Pentecostal denomination in Chile, the Methodist Pentecostal Church, practises infant baptism and uses Methodist liturgy. Many Pentecostal groups, including some churches in Europe and Latin America and most of the Charismatics, do not insist on the 'initial evidence' of tongues. But in Africa and Asia even greater divergences are to be found. Some churches, like the Pentecostal-type, 'Spirit' or so-called 'prophet-healing' AICs use more ritual symbolism in their liturgy than other Pentecostals do, including the use of holy water, oil and other symbols in healing services. Chinese grassroots churches, perhaps the majority of Christians in China, are mainly of a Pentecostal type, although most of them would not describe themselves as 'Pentecostal'. The largest of these, the True Jesus Church, espouses Oneness theology and practises Sabbath observance on Saturday as essential for salvation.[12]

I think that the term 'Pentecostal' is appropriate for describing globally all churches and movements that emphasize the working of the gifts of the Spirit, both on phenomenological and on theological grounds – although

[11] Walter J. Hollenweger, *Pentecostalism: Origins and Developments Worldwide* (Peabody: Hendrickson, 1997), p. 1.

[12] Deng Zhaoming, 'Indigenous Chinese Pentecostal Denominations', Allan Anderson and Edmond Tang (eds.), *Asian and Pentecostal: The Charismatic Face of Christianity in Asia* (Kuala Lumpur and Oxford: Regnum, 2004).

not without qualification. A broader definition should emphasize Pentecostalism's ability to 'incarnate' the gospel in different cultural forms. This broad use of 'Pentecostal' will often include the terms 'Charismatic' and 'Neopentecostal'; but there will be times when 'Charismatic' will refer more narrowly to Pentecostal experience in 'mainline' churches. However, even here there are difficulties, as there are several examples of 'Charismatics' who preceded the 'Charismatic Movement' in the western world by several decades. The debate about the meaning of 'Pentecostal' and 'Pentecostalism' must conclude that it is a definition that cannot be prescribed. Perhaps it is appropriate to follow Robert Anderson, who observes that whereas western classical Pentecostals usually define themselves in terms of the *doctrine* of 'initial evidence', Pentecostalism is more correctly seen in a much broader context as a movement concerned primarily with the *experience* of the working of the Holy Spirit and the *practice* of spiritual gifts.[13] Because Pentecostalism has its emphasis in experience and spirituality rather than in formal theology or doctrine, any definition based on the latter will be inadequate. In this book we will usually use the terms 'Pentecostal' and 'Pentecostalism' in this broad sense to include all the different forms of 'spiritual gifts' movements; often we will refer to them as 'Pentecostal and Charismatic' movements; and on occasions we will use the terms 'classical Pentecostal' and 'Charismatic' when a narrower definition is required.

A word about my use of other terms in this book. The central idea of classical Pentecostalism, 'baptism with (or in) the Holy Spirit' I have usually termed 'Spirit baptism' for brevity's sake and not for any other reason. I have retained the words 'western' and 'the West' but have avoided the ideological use of words like 'Third World' or 'Two-Thirds World', and instead have opted for the term 'Majority World' or 'developing world' to describe Africa, Asia, Latin America and the Pacific. I have avoided the use of 'indigenous', and have substituted 'autochthonous', 'national' or 'inculturated' (depending on the context), and whenever possible have tried to use local terms. I have also tried not to use the term 'American' when it means 'US American', or 'North American' when it excludes 'Canadian'.

What may be the fastest expanding religious movement in the world today has contributed to the reconfiguration of the nature of Christianity itself in the present century. The Pentecostal and Charismatic movements

---

[13] Robert Mapes Anderson, *Vision of the Disinherited: The Making of American Pentecostalism* (Peabody, MA: Hendrickson, 1979), p. 4.

have indeed become globalized in every sense of the word; this has enormous ecumenical implications, and adherents are often on the cutting edge of encounter with people of other faiths. All this demonstrates how important it is to study these movements. As Pentecostal and Charismatic churches continue to expand, scholarly works on these movements in different parts of the world have arisen in the past forty years, particularly sociological studies, but also historical and theological ones. Most of these studies, however, are limited in scope to particular regions or continents. This book seeks to introduce the phenomenon of Pentecostalism in all its global variety in an accessible form, particularly for students of theology and religion. Furthermore, although much has been written on the strength of Pentecostals and Charismatics in the Americas, relatively little has been written on their significance in Africa and Asia. The main aim of this book is to bring a perspective on Pentecostalism that challenges existing presuppositions and paradigms. One of the fundamental problems in the academic study of Pentecostalism has been a misinformed interpretation of Pentecostal and Charismatic history and theology, where the role players are mainly white North Americans and western Europeans. This study seeks to challenge this interpretation by pointing to the dynamics of religious change in the world and to make more visible and accessible the 'non-western' nature of Pentecostalism without overlooking the international importance of the movement emanating from North America. The book offers an interpretation of Pentecostal and Charismatic movements that takes seriously the contributions of the Majority World to the development of a form of Christianity that can be described as a new reformation of the church.

PART ONE

Historical development of Pentecostal distinctives

2

Historical and theological background

CHARISMATA IN THE EARLY CHURCH

The Early Church was a community of the Holy Spirit, and the freedom of expression and spontaneity of its worship may not have been very different from that of many Pentecostal and Charismatic churches today. Some of the characteristic features and ecstatic phenomena of Pentecostalism like prophecy, healing and speaking in tongues were common. Although not all scholars agree on their frequency, the New Testament at least bears witness to unusual manifestations of the Spirit, especially in the book of Acts and the first letter of Paul to the Corinthians. Speaking in tongues, prophecy and miraculous healings are among other 'spiritual gifts' or *charismata* mentioned several times in Acts, and although their frequency is less noticeable in the epistles of Paul, he gives directions for their use in 1 Corinthians 12 and 14. Christian worship in the first century was quite different from what the experience is for most people today. Nevertheless, throughout the two thousand year history of Christianity there have been reports of charismata and other phenomena associated with the emergence of Pentecostalism in the early twentieth century. Some of these reports are discussed in this chapter.

It seems that the decline in the practice of spiritual gifts began quite early, as the Montanist movement in the second century believed that the gifts of the Spirit had been restored to their former importance in their movement. Monasticism itself was originally a charismatic movement that reacted to what seemed to be cold orthodoxy, claiming the sympathies and probably the allegiance of the famous African theologian Tertullian (c.155–220). Speaking in tongues and prophecy were common among Montanus and his disciples; and they believed in 'progressive revelation', so distasteful and destabilizing for the church seeking to establish itself and even more so as it became increasingly identified with the heresy of Gnosticism and millennialist excesses. Most of the surviving sources for information on Montanism, however, come from opponents like Eusebius, who said that Montanus was 'wrought up into a certain kind of frenzy and irregular ecstasy, raving, and speaking and uttering strange things'.[1] If these biased reports are to be believed, the Montanists saw the spiritual gifts as the exclusive possession of the prophets. No less a person than Tertullian in his challenge to Marcion affirmed that gifts of the Spirit such as prophecy (which he defined as prediction and revelation), visions, ecstasy and interpretation of tongues were 'forthcoming from my side without any difficulty'; and elsewhere he writes that healing, revelation and exorcism were among the joys available to Christians.[2]

Among other early Christian writings are scattered references to charismatic gifts. Bishop Ignatius of Antioch (d.107) wrote about an ability to understand heavenly things and his special gift, which he must 'restrain with humility'. The *Didache* and the *Shepherd of Hermas* recognized that the prophet speaks in the Spirit, and the author of *Hermas* was 'carried away in the Spirit' when he saw visions. Bishop Clement of Rome tells the Corinthians that 'a full outpouring of the Holy Spirit was upon you all', and Justin Martyr writes 'Now it is possible to see among us women and men who possess gifts of the Spirit of God' and mentioned exorcism practised by Christians in his time. Bishop Irenaeus of Gaul (c.130–202) wrote of prophecy, casting out demons, healing through the laying on of hands and even the raising of the dead – all taking place at that time, but he implied that these gifts should be located in the bishop's office. The pseudonymous apocryphal *Acts of the Apostles* provides further evidence of an expectation of the miraculous in the early church, and Pseudo-Barnabas suggested that prophecy was normative in the church of his time. Clement of Alexandria (d.c.215) stated that a 'perfect man' is characterized by his reception of the charismata of 1 Corinthians 12.[3] The Church Fathers never suggested that any of the gifts of the Spirit had ceased.

But the established church's repudiation of Montanism quenched any similar tendencies within the church for centuries. The charismatic gifts came to be localized in the office of the bishop and in popular legends surrounding individual saints, martyrs and ascetics. For example, Martin of Tours was reported by his disciple Sulpicius to have been remarkably used in

---

[1] John V. Taylor, *The Go-Between God: The Holy Spirit and the Christian Mission* (London: SCM, 1972), p. 219.

[2] Morton Kelsey, *Tongue Speaking: The History and Meaning of Charismatic Experience* (New York: Crossroad, 1981), pp. 37–8; Ronald A. N. Kydd, *Healing through the Centuries: Models of Understanding* (Peabody: Hendrickson, 1998), pp. 21, 24, 30.

[3] Kelsey, *Tongue Speaking*, pp. 35–7; Kydd, *Healing*, pp. 23, 28–9, 65–9; S. M. Burgess, 'Holy Spirit, Doctrine of: The Ancient Fathers', *NIDPCM*, pp. 730–1, 734–5.

healing and exorcism in the fourth century. After the time of Origen (c.184–254), most western church writers seemed to think that charismatic gifts were for biblical times and had now ceased. Origen denied that prophecy still occurred in the church and implied that Paul's speaking in tongues was the ability to speak Greek and Latin, although he saw spiritual gifts like healing and exorcism as evidence of the validating power of Christ, as did Novatian (d.258), another third century writer who said that the church is perfected by gifts of the Spirit. Cyprian of Carthage (c.200–58) said that the charismata were the sole prerogative of the bishop. John Chrysostom (347–407) said that spiritual gifts no longer were needed. Augustine (354–430) was somewhat ambiguous on the subject. He said that occasions of speaking with tongues in the New Testament were 'signs adapted to the time' that had passed away, and he posed a rhetorical question: 'For who expects in these days that those on whom hands are laid that they may receive the Holy Spirit should forthwith begin to speak with tongues'? (Nobody!) But he acknowledged that the miraculous was necessary to bring into the church 'ignorant men and infidels', although this was the prerogative of God alone.[4]

The subject of gifts of the Spirit had almost become a closed book in western Christianity, although eastern Christianity remained more other-worldly, individual and mystical. Egyptian monk Pachomius (d. 346) was reported to have spoken in tongues of angels. Basil of Caesarea (330–79) wrote of the working together of the charismata through individual members of the body of Christ, and his friend Gregory of Nazianzus (c.329–90) mentioned instances of divine healing in his family and of the diversity of the Spirit's gifts. The Orthodox churches have always recognized, expected and controlled the charismata, including speaking in tongues, which has been a continuing experience throughout all the ages among them, though confined mainly to the monasteries.[5]

CHARISMATA IN THE MIDDLE AGES

The eastern churches continued to practise gifts of the Spirit in their monasteries throughout the medieval period. Pneumatology has always been at the centre of their theology, and they have always been open to the charismata. Perhaps one of the most outstanding eastern writings on the Holy

[4] Kydd, *Healing*, pp. 21–2, 29, 71–4, 79; Burgess, 'Ancient Fathers', p. 735.
[5] Kelsey, *Tongue Speaking*, pp. 39–46; Burgess, 'Ancient Fathers', p. 739–40; Léon Joseph Cardinal Suenens, *A New Pentecost?* (London: Darton, Longman and Todd, 1975), pp. 27–8.

Spirit was that of exiled mystic Symeon the New Theologian (949–1022), who had ecstatic experiences, spoke in tongues and wrote about 'baptism of the Holy Spirit' as a separate experience from water baptism. Gregory Palamas (1296–1359) wrote of experiencing the transcendent God through the Spirit, and of receiving the charismata through the laying on of hands, including healing, miracles, tongues and interpretation of tongues.[6]

But in the West, the situation was very different. The Catholic Church in western Europe officially continued to deny the possibility of spiritual gifts. By the year 1000, the liturgy book *Rituale Romanorum* explained to a priest when exorcism from demons was necessary:

Signs of possession are the following: ability to speak with some facility in a strange tongue or to understand it when spoken by another; the faculty of divulging future and hidden events; display of powers which are beyond the subject's age and natural condition; and various other indications which, when taken together as a whole, pile up the evidence.[7]

Charismatic gifts were now seen as signs of the demonic in the official church, which was dominated by the scholasticism of this period. There were, however, isolated reports of the continued presence of unusual and ecstatic manifestations in the western church; and there were even cases where speaking in tongues (or at least, the miraculous ability to speak a language that had not been learned) was regarded as one of the evidences of sainthood. The German abbess Hildegard of Bingen (1098–1179) was known for her fearless prophesies and miracles, and she was reported to be able to speak and interpret an entirely unknown language after ecstatic religious experiences that included a long series of visions and singing in tongues. Other mystical women saints of the thirteenth and fourteenth centuries included Gertrude of Helfta, Brigitta of Sweden and Catherine of Siena, all of whom had ecstatic experiences and spiritual gifts. But Thomas Aquinas (1224–74) in his *Summa Theologica* said that the original purpose of the gift of tongues was to enable the apostles to teach all nations and that the same gift of tongues could only be gained now through diligent language study. However, he also distinguished between ordinary gifts and the charismata of 1 Corinthians 12 as revelatory gifts of God to both believers and unbelievers. Bonaventure (1217–74), disciple and biographer of Francis of Assisi, wrote about Christian growth in the Spirit, of being healed from a serious illness through the prayers of Francis, and of Francis' ministry of the miraculous. Dante in *The Divine Comedy* spoke of his own experiences

---

[6] S. M. Burgess, 'Holy Spirit, Doctrine of: The Medieval Churches', *NIDPCM*, pp. 747, 750–2.
[7] Cited in Kelsey, *Tongue Speaking*, p. 46.

of ecstatic and unintelligible speech. Vincent Ferrer, a Spanish missionary in western Europe around 1350, was famed for his gifts of prophecy and healing, and was reported to have been able to speak and be understood in the many different languages of the different peoples he was evangelizing. Missionaries Francis Xavier and Louis Bertrand were said to have spoken in foreign languages they had never learned, and Xavier had the language of angels and a ministry of healing. Among the Jansenists (French Catholic reformers), gifts of the Spirit began to manifest in 1731, halted by Jesuits and French state authorities.[8] But all these were isolated and unusual events in the lives of saints and mystics, certainly not expected to be part of 'normal' church life.

THE PROTESTANT REFORMATION AND SUBSEQUENT REVIVALS

During the Reformation, gifts of the Spirit seem to have been virtually unknown, apart from occasional reports in the Anabaptist movement that brought such occurrences into further disrepute. Martin Luther (1483–1546) said that tongues were given as a sign to the Jews and had ceased, and that Christians no longer needed miracles. He used 1 Corinthians 12 and 14 to develop his case for preaching in German. John Calvin (1509–64) likewise said that speaking in tongues facilitated the preaching of the gospel in foreign languages, but God had removed it from the church and miracles had long since ceased. Unfortunately, as far as the radical wing of the Reformation, the Anabaptists were concerned, spiritual gifts were associated with Thomas Müntzer and the apocalyptic fringes, whose alleged excesses and immoralities resulted in Luther and other Reformation leaders totally rejecting the entire Anabaptist movement.[9] The established Protestant churches were even more firmly opposed to 'religious enthusiasm' than the Catholic Church had ever been, and it took over four centuries for this to change. Spiritual gifts would continue to appear, mainly in the radical periphery of Protestantism, and were almost always regarded as sectarian movements at the time.

The early Quakers (Society of Friends) founded by George Fox (1624–90) in England emphasized 'Inner Light' through the Holy Spirit and all kinds of manifestations of the Spirit's work were evident: trembling (hence their name), jerking spasms, weeping, visions, prophecy and faints, and

---

[8] Burgess, 'Medieval Churches', pp. 755–7, 759; Kelsey, *Tongue Speaking*, pp. 47–50.
[9] Robert H. Culpepper, *Evaluating the Charismatic Movement: A Theological and Biblical Appraisal* (Valley Forge, PA: Judson Press, 1977), pp. 41–3.

speaking in tongues, witnessed by one early Quaker writer. After the French revocation of the Edict of Nantes in 1685, which had given religious freedom to Protestants, most Huguenots left France. Among those who remained was a group of young people and children in the Cévennes Mountains of southern France, where a revival movement began with many ecstatic phenomena; and these Cévenol revivalists were known as the 'little prophets of Cévennes'. The movement lasted for ten years, during which time many came from far to hear miraculous prophesying, after which persecution ensued and many of the group were imprisoned and killed. Later this became a political movement known as the Camisards, which after two years of withstanding the French army, was finally crushed in 1711. Some Cévenol refugees in London made converts there and John Wesley, founder of Methodism, countered a critic who said that speaking in tongues had ceased by referring favourably to these 'little prophets'. One of the early Methodist preachers, Thomas Walsh, recorded in his diary in 1750, 'the Lord gave me a language I knew not of, raising my soul to him in a wondrous manner'.[10]

These sporadic outbursts of charismata continued into the nineteenth century. In the Scottish Presbyterian church in 1830–1, through the preaching of controversial minister Edward Irving (1792–1834), charismatic gifts including prophecy and speaking in tongues, broke out in Glasgow, in London in Irving's church and in several other places, and were practised and recorded in the subsequently formed Catholic Apostolic Church until about 1879. The New Apostolic Church, which seceded from this church in Germany in 1863, continued the charismatic tradition for longer; and the Irvingite movement is an important precedent for Pentecostalism. In Sweden in 1841, a revival with frequent speaking in tongues was reported. In Germany, Johann Blumhardt (1805–80) operated a 'healing home' to which people flocked for healing and exorcism for almost thirty years. North American Shakers practised speaking in tongues, healing, prophecies and ecstatic dancing from the late eighteenth to the mid nineteenth centuries. Mormons practised speaking in tongues in the early years, but discouraged its practice later. A revival began in Russia and Armenia in 1855, with people speaking in tongues, but was soon limited to a group in the Black Sea area who called themselves Pentecostal Christians. In 1880, an experience of Spirit baptism was received by a group of Armenian Presbyterians who began to fellowship with the Russian Pentecostals. An eleven-year-old Russian boy had prophesied in the 1855 revival about coming Turkish

[10] Taylor, *Go-Between God*, p. 219.

invasions and the Russian and Armenian Pentecostals started leaving for North America from 1900 to 1912. They formed Pentecostal congregations there that had predated the classical Pentecostal denominations in origin by fifty years.[11]

METHODISM AND THE HOLINESS MOVEMENT

Although the established Christian churches knew of these early manifestations of Charismatic phenomena, those who practised charismata were regarded at best as eccentric 'enthusiasts' and at worst as heretics and demonized fanatics. Modern Pentecostalism's more immediate background was in the nineteenth century Holiness movement, which was itself based on a particular interpretation of the teaching of the founder of Methodism, John Wesley (1703–91) and especially that of Wesley's theologian, John Fletcher (1729–85). Fletcher differed subtly with Wesley on issues that were to be important in the shaping of Pentecostal theology, but the earlier German Pietism influenced both of them. The Pietist movement in seventeenth and eighteenth century Lutheranism stressed the importance of a personal experience of God or 'new birth' by the Holy Spirit, over and above what they saw as mere head-knowledge. Pietism, which also drew inspiration from Catholic mysticism, gave emphasis to the importance of emotion in Christian experience and encouraged a personal relationship with God. It encouraged a restoration of the Reformation's doctrine of the priesthood of all believers, and the working of the Spirit to bring about a changed, morally ascetic Christian life separated from 'the world'. The Pietist movement in turn spawned the Moravian movement of Count Nicolaus von Zinzendorf (1700–60) and his community at Herrnhut, when in 1727 it was said that the Spirit had been outpoured, and a continuous round-the-clock prayer meeting lasted for a hundred years thereafter.

The Moravian Church had a profound effect upon Wesley and the Methodist revival. Wesley's contact with Moravian missionaries in Georgia who challenged him about his personal experience of Christ during his return voyage to England, led him to his Aldersgate conversion experience in 1738 when, as he wrote, 'I felt my heart strangely warmed'. Wesley himself later visited the Herrnhut community, and in some early Methodist revivals there were unusual manifestations of the Spirit. Wesley said that charismatic gifts were withdrawn when dry, formal, orthodox men had begun to ridicule them, and that these gifts had returned to some of his fellow Methodists. But

---

[11] Kelsey, *Tongue Speaking*, pp. 52–9, 65–8; D. D. Bundy, 'Irving, Edward', *NIDPCM*, pp. 803–4.

a central emphasis of early Methodism was Wesley's doctrine of a 'second blessing', a crisis experience subsequent to conversion that he called sanctification, 'Christian perfection' or 'perfect love'. It was this 'second blessing' doctrine that had a significant influence on Pentecostalism, but only as this doctrine was transmitted and reinterpreted through the US American Holiness movement in the nineteenth century. Evangelical Protestantism, especially of the Methodist variety, was the dominant subculture in the USA in the nineteenth century. Early Methodism in the USA was the frontier religion *par excellence*; it stressed personal liberty and allowed the emotional element of popular religion, and it extended its offer of religious power and autonomy to the 'dispossessed', to women, African Americans and the poor. Eventually there was a polarization within Methodism in the West between those who believed what they saw as Wesley's 'Christian perfection' teaching (who subsequently formed the Holiness movement) and those who did not, who remained in mainstream Methodism. There was some ambiguity as to what Wesley actually meant by his 'perfect love' doctrine, and this caused some confusion for his later interpreters. John Fletcher took the doctrine a step further when he spoke of the subsequent experience of sanctification as the 'baptism with the Holy Ghost', linking the 'second blessing' with an experience of receiving the Spirit. Wesley found this idea unacceptable and seemed to have taught that the Spirit was received at conversion.[12] But his doctrine of entire sanctification and the possibility of spiritual experiences subsequent to conversion undoubtedly constituted the egg that hatched the Holiness movement and its offspring, Pentecostalism.

One of the most prominent Holiness leaders, Phoebe Palmer, stressed 'perfection' (sanctification) as an instantaneous experience for every Christian from 1835 onwards, and she led the Holiness revival as editor of *Guide to Holiness* and as an international travelling preacher. After the Civil War, one of the most important vehicles for the Holiness movement was the National Camp Meeting Association for the Promotion of Holiness, which began regular camp meetings from 1867. There was a gradual separation between the Reformed and Wesleyan wings of the Holiness Movement resulting in the 'Keswick solution' from England that swept through Reformed theology but caused a breach with Wesleyan Perfectionism.[13]

---

[12] Dayton, *Theological Roots*, pp. 44–5, 49–50; Harvey Cox, *Fire from Heaven: The Rise of Pentecostal Spirituality and the Reshaping of Religion in the Twenty-first Century* (London: Cassell, 1996), p. 91.

[13] D. William Faupel, *The Everlasting Gospel: The Significance of Eschatology in the Development of Pentecostal Thought* (Sheffield: Sheffield Academic Press, 1996), pp. 59, 64, 66, 68–9; Dayton, *Theological Roots*, pp. 64–5.

Developments within the Holiness movement itself resulted in it becoming less Methodist and Wesleyan in orientation in the late nineteenth century, and the term 'Pentecostal' became more prominent. A revival in 1857–8 in the Northeast USA created a new expectancy throughout the Holiness movement linking the 'second blessing' experience of sanctification with a worldwide revival, the 'latter rain' that would precede the return of Christ. At the same time, the experience of the Spirit was linked with a search for the 'power' of Pentecost, a new development that was to gain momentum and overtake the earlier emphasis on 'perfection'. Phoebe Palmer herself began to refer to holiness as 'the full baptism of the Holy Spirit', and Asa Mahan wrote in 1870 of 'the baptism of the Holy Ghost' with the main consequence being 'power'.[14] The early Pentecostals continued this eschatological and pneumatological emphasis. Towards the end of the century, prominent Holiness teachers began to say that spiritual gifts were connected to the power of the Spirit and should still be in operation, and some spoke of Spirit baptism as a 'third blessing' to be sought, separating Spirit baptism from sanctification – this idea was rejected by most Holiness leaders.

The Holiness movement was a reaction to liberalism and formalism in established Protestant churches and stood for Biblical literalism, the need for a personal and individual experience of conversion and the moral perfection (holiness) of the Christian individual. The major churches, which had by this time become middle class establishments and rather nervous of the vast numbers of new, enthusiastic converts from the working classes, did not really support these principles or emphasize them any longer. Methodist leaders in particular, from whom most of the Holiness associations had sprung, began to denounce the 'second blessing' teaching. The result was that gradually, separate Holiness churches were created, characterized by revivalism and accompanied by ecstatic phenomena and camp meetings across the continent. A revival in 1896 in a group called the Christian Union in North Carolina was accompanied by healings and, according to some reports, speaking in tongues by 130 people. Church of God (Cleveland) historians link this event with the emergence of their denomination. Between 1895 and 1905 over twenty Holiness denominations were set up including the Church of God (1886), the Christian and Missionary Alliance (1887), the Church of the Nazarene (1895) and the Pilgrim Holiness Church (1897) – thus creating a precedent for the further fragmentation that was to occur in Pentecostalism.

---

[14] Dayton, *Theological Roots*, pp. 74, 88–9; Faupel, *Everlasting Gospel*, pp. 73–5.

REVIVALISM AND KESWICK

Lederle has pointed out that the Methodist-Holiness movement is not the only important influence on early Pentecostalism.[15] US American revivalism was a different and more Reformed stream that stressed the role of the emotions in changing lives. The understanding of Wesley's doctrine in North American Methodism and the Holiness Movement was further shaped by the emphasis on experience in the Reformed revivalism of Jonathan Edwards and the 'Oberlin Perfectionism' of revivalists Charles Finney and Asa Mahan. Methodism was the largest denomination in nineteenth century North America and as a result, ideas of sanctification as a distinct experience were also prevalent in Reformed revivalism. Charles Finney (1792–1876) had an experience in 1821 in his law office which he described as 'a mighty baptism of the Holy Spirit', when the Spirit descended on him 'in waves and waves of liquid love' – although it seems that, unlike the Holiness movement, Finney did not equate the 'baptism of the Holy Spirit' with the experience of sanctification. But Finney's dependence on the presence of the Spirit gave his message a profound emotional impact. His revivalist theology was another great influence on the Keswick movement and on the major part of North American Pentecostalism, as was the impact of Finney's spiritual successors, well known evangelists Dwight L. Moody and Reuben A. Torrey.

The Keswick Convention, which began with annual gatherings in the English Lake District in 1875, recognized two distinct experiences of the 'new birth' and the 'fullness of the Spirit' and represented another major influence on Pentecostalism. Although the 'fullness of the Spirit' was seen in terms of 'holiness' or the 'higher Christian life', the Keswick movement was more influenced by Reformed teachers like the South African Andrew Murray, Jr. who taught that sanctification was a possible, but progressive experience. Increasingly in the Holiness movement, the phrase 'baptism with the Spirit' came to be used to indicate the 'second blessing'. Towards the end of the nineteenth century, Spirit baptism in Keswick and elsewhere was no longer understood in terms of holiness, but as empowering for service. In particular, this change in emphasis was taught by evangelist Torrey, Moody's associate and successor, who wrote that 'the Baptism with the Holy Spirit' was a definite experience separate from regeneration and 'always connected with testimony and service', and implied that it had nothing to do with sanctification. Torrey went on to say that the form of

[15] Henry I. Lederle, *Treasures Old and New: Interpretations of 'Spirit-baptism' in the Charismatic Renewal Movement* (Peabody, MA: Hendrickson, 1988), p. 15.

the power received during Spirit baptism varied according to different gifts of the Spirit. By the end of the nineteenth century, the idea of a 'baptism with the Spirit' as a distinct experience giving power for service was the major theme in North American revivalism. The groundwork was laid for the birth of Pentecostalism.[16]

And so, by the turn of the century there were three distinct groups of Holiness adherents: (1) the Wesleyan position, which said that 'entire sanctification' or 'perfect love' was the 'second blessing' or baptism with the Spirit; (2) the Keswick position, which held that the baptism with the Spirit was an enduement with power for service; and (3) the 'third blessing' position, which had both the 'second blessing' of sanctification and a 'third blessing' of 'baptism with fire' – again an enduement with power. The first US Pentecostals were to follow this position, but equated the 'third blessing' with 'baptism in the Spirit', usually evidenced by speaking in tongues.[17]

A particular kind of eschatological expectation was also to become a dominant theme in North American Pentecostalism. The shift from the optimism of the postmillennialism that prevailed in early nineteenth century Protestantism to a pessimistic premillennialist 'secret rapture' dispensationalism occurred gradually in the Holiness movement during this period as a result of several factors, precipitated by the teaching of John Nelson Darby of the Plymouth Brethren in Britain. A monthly periodical *The Prophetic Times* commenced in 1863 and prophetic conferences like D. L. Moody's annual Northfield Prophecy Conference from 1880, prominently advocated Darby's eschatological views. Premillennialism was also expounded by popular preachers A. B. Simpson and A. J. Gordon, eventually accepted by a majority of US American Evangelicals, and became a prominent theme of Keswick conventions. The differences between these various interpretations of biblical apocalyptic literature amounted to divergent worldviews. Postmillennialists held that Christ would return after a thousand-year period, whereas premillennialists believed that his return could be imminent, and before the thousand-year period. With a few exceptions, most of the Holiness movement, and subsequently most early Pentecostals, accepted Darby's eschatology – although several prominent Methodist and Holiness leaders of the Wesleyan persuasion were actively opposed to it. The reasons for the acceptance of premillennialism are complicated and include a pessimistic reaction to theological liberalism and the 'social gospel' that

[16] Faupel, *Everlasting Gospel*, pp. 84–7; Culpepper, *Evaluating*, pp. 46–7; Dayton, *Theological Roots*, pp. 95–100, 103.

[17] Robert Mapes Anderson, *Vision of the Disinherited: The Making of American Pentecostalism* (New York: Oxford University Press, 1979), pp. 28–46.

increasingly came to identify the main Protestant denominations. But more significantly, this eschatology was based on the same modernistic assumptions as those of the emerging 'liberalism' that Evangelicals were trying to counteract. Because the Keswick movement was at first an expression of Reformed Evangelicalism, it accepted premillennialism early. As most other Holiness groups gradually accepted the pneumatological centre of the Keswick position through exposure to Keswick teachers, they also accepted its eschatology with its stress on the coming of a new Pentecost to usher in the return of Christ.[18] The idea of a revival that would precede the 'soon coming King' became a prominent theme in early Pentecostalism. Early North American Pentecostalism received most of its leaders and many of its members from the Holiness movement.

THE HEALING MOVEMENT

Another very important movement linked to the Holiness movement and the consequent emergence of Pentecostalism was the divine healing movement. Most Pentecostals and Charismatics agree on the possibility of healing through prayer and faith in the name of Jesus Christ. Prayer for divine healing is perhaps the most universal characteristic of the many varieties of Pentecostalism and perhaps the main reason for its growth in the developing world. Gifts of healing are listed among the charismata of 1 Corinthians 12 and healing through faith has been practised at different times in the history of the church, miracles of healing being attributed especially to the activities of Catholic saints. Reformation churches tended to believe that healings were part of Catholic 'superstition' and had ceased, and the rationalism of the eighteenth and nineteenth centuries strengthened these convictions. Once again, radical groups like Anabaptists and Quakers made claims of healings. John Wesley reported occasional miracles of healing in his journal, and healing through prayer was part of the tradition of Pietism.

The nineteenth century brought healing into sharper focus. Johann Christoph Blumhardt (1805–80), from a Pietist background, operated a healing centre in Bad Boll, Germany for thirty years. His reputation as a healer and exorcist was known internationally, as was his Christological emphasis 'Jesus is Victor'. Blumhardt also linked the healing ministry of Christ with the power of the Spirit. In Männedorf, Switzerland, Dorothea Trudel (1813–62) and her successor Samuel Zeller (1834–1912) operated a similar centre for healing through prayer called Elim. The fame of

---

[18] Faupel, *Everlasting Gospel*, pp. 99, 104–5, 110–12.

Blumhardt and Trudel began to reach the English-speaking world by the middle of the century. One of the earliest healing ministries in North America was that of the African American woman Elizabeth Mix, who was to have a formative influence on the later healing ministry of Carrie Judd Montgomery. Charles Cullis, an Episcopalian physician in Boston and major figure in the Holiness movement, visited Männedorf in 1873 and began to pray for the sick in healing conventions, where he linked forgiveness of sin and healing from sickness. Cullis influenced a Presbyterian minister, A. B. Simpson, who was a founding figure in the Christian and Missionary Alliance. Simpson began a healing home in 1884 and wrote about healing provided for in the atonement of Christ. Other figures in the divine healing movement were Boston Baptist minister and associate of Cullis, A. J. Gordon, Presbyterian W. E. Boardman, who moved to England, the Episcopalian woman Carrie Judd Montgomery, who taught that healing was part of the gospel of Christ, and Maria Woodworth-Etter, who added a message of healing to her evangelistic ministry after 1885, her meetings being characterized by people who were 'slain in the Spirit' – another feature of early Pentecostalism, when people would fall to the ground as if unconscious – and speaking in tongues occurred in her meetings once in 1888 and in St Louis, Missouri in 1890, and on several occasions since, prior to the commencement of Pentecostalism. Both Montgomery and Woodworth-Etter later joined the Pentecostal movement. Many leaders in the healing movement taught that divine healing was possible without medical assistance, and some rejected the 'use of means' (medical science). This too was a feature of early Pentecostalism. Divine healing had become a prominent teaching in the Holiness movement by the beginning of the twentieth century.[19]

John Alexander Dowie (1847–1907) had an important influence on the emerging Pentecostal movement. He was a prominent healer at the close of the nineteenth century, but was alienated from those associated with the Holiness movement because of his outspoken criticisms. Born and educated in Scotland and at first a Congregational minister then an independent healing evangelist in Australia, he immigrated to the USA in 1888 to found the Divine Healing Association in 1890 and then the Christian Apostolic Church in 1895 as his following grew. He set up the first of several healing homes in Chicago and began publishing a periodical, *Leaves of Healing*, that was sent all over the world with testimonies of healing from Dowie's

[19] Dayton, *Theological Roots*, pp. 119–29; Kydd, *Healing*, pp. 33–45, 142–53; Maria Woodworth-Etter, *Signs and Wonders* (New Kensington, PA: Whitaker House, 1997), pp. 58, 105, 135, 141, 471–2.

meetings in Zion Tabernacle, the spacious auditorium he had built. In 1900 he set up a city called Zion as a 'theocracy' near Chicago, Illinois, which grew in a few years to about eight thousand residents, with some 200,000 members in his church worldwide. This 'theocracy' sought to be a classless, pacifistic society, was committed to racial and gender equality, sent missionaries overseas, encouraged interracial marriages and supported the disadvantaged. These were revolutionary ideas at the turn of the century in North America. Dowie with his Reformed roots was in the Keswick tradition, with a 'Full Gospel' that included 'Salvation, Healing and Holy Living'. Healing for Dowie was part of the atonement, and his followers were to shun medicine, medical doctors and the eating of pork. His stress on holiness had a strong social dimension, modelled by the creation of the city of Zion. In 1903 while on a tour in Australia he castigated King Edward VII of Britain for his vices, and in *Leaves of Healing* he denounced Britain's colonial treatment of Africans. His was a realized eschatology, however, as from 1901 Dowie placed himself in the centre and announced that he was the 'Messenger of the Covenant' prophesied by Malachi and 'Elijah the Restorer'. In 1904 he declared himself 'First Apostle' of a new end-times church, renamed the Christian Catholic Apostolic Church in Zion. In 1905 Zion City went bankrupt; Dowie suffered a stroke and died in disgrace within two years.

Faupel sees Dowie as making a significant impact on Pentecostalism in four areas: first by giving the Keswick motif 'its most radical eschatological expression' including a strong missionary orientation and an emphasis on healing; second, many leaders of the early Pentecostal movement came from his organization with his worldview; third, he formed the link between Pentecostalism and the Irvingite movement with which he had much in common, even taking a similar name; and fourth, he gave Pentecostalism an alternative between liberalism and fundamentalism.[20] Dowie's end-time restorationism and his acceptance of people from all walks of life became prominent motifs in Pentecostalism. His Zionist movement was one of the most important formative influences on the growth of 'Spirit' African independent churches in southern Africa, where the largest denomination today is called the Zion Christian Church, and millions of 'Zionists' attend large celebrations at African 'Zion Cities'. We will return to this in chapter 6.

Another influential revivalist and healer at the turn of the twentieth century was Frank Sandford (1862–1948), a former Baptist pastor in Maine who

---

[20] Faupel, *Everlasting Gospel*, pp. 121, 123, 127, 132–5; E. L. Blumhofer, 'Dowie, John Alexander', *NIDPCM*, pp. 586–7.

came to an experience of sanctification through the Holiness movement and a belief in divine healing through contact with A. B. Simpson. In 1894 he received an experience of Spirit baptism that he described as an enduement of power. He founded the Holy Ghost and Us Bible School the following year, where several future Pentecostal leaders were trained and he published his first periodical called *Tongues of Fire*. He established a large community called Shiloh whose residents had to give over all their possessions, and he purchased ships for the evangelization of the world. Like Dowie, he believed that the end time was brought nearer by divine/human co-operation, he motivated his followers into world evangelization through 'signs, wonders, and mighty deeds', and in 1901 he too called himself 'Elijah the Restorer' and 'First Apostle', six months after Dowie's declaration. But he added an emphasis on the imminent premillennial return of Christ, 'spiritual warfare' (intercessory prayer) and a belief in Anglo-Israelism, the racist theory that the White Anglo-Saxon Protestant nations (especially Britain and the United States) were descended from the 'lost tribes' of Israel. Sandford also advocated circumcision, observance of Saturday as the Sabbath, and abstinence from pork. 'Israel' was to be a blessing to all nations, which reinforced his missionary zeal. Although opposed to Pentecostalism, his main impact was the formative influence he had upon Charles Parham, who imbibed many of his teachings. He died in relative obscurity.[21]

CHARLES FOX PARHAM

Charles Parham (1873–1929) was an independent Kansas preacher who resigned from the Methodist Church in 1895, experienced healing from the consequences of rheumatic fever in 1898 and began a healing ministry thereafter. He relocated to Topeka, Kansas where he opened a healing home and began publishing his periodical *The Apostolic Faith*. There he propounded his views of healing in the atonement of Christ, premillennialism with the belief in a worldwide revival (the 'latter rain') to precede the imminent coming of Christ, and a third blessing beyond 'entire sanctification'. In January 1900 he met emissaries from Frank Sandford's Shiloh, and Sandford himself came to Topeka in June that year. Parham was so impressed that he decided to accompany Sandford to Shiloh and enrol in his Bible school, and he accepted Sandford's views including his Anglo-Israelism and the possibility of foreign tongues given by the Spirit to

---

[21] Faupel, *Everlasting Gospel*, pp. 149–50, 157–8; C. M. Robeck, Jr., 'Sandford, Frank', *NIDPCM*, pp. 1037–8.

facilitate world evangelization. En route he visited Dowie's Zion City and Simpson's Bible and Missionary Training Institute, among others. After six weeks of attending Sandford's lectures and accompanying him on another preaching trip, Parham returned to Topeka convinced that God had called him to enter a new phase of ministry. He opened Bethel Gospel School in a newly leased building known as Stone's Folly and enrolled thirty-four students in a short-term school to train for world evangelization, where the only textbook was the Bible. Before leaving on a three-day preaching trip, Parham gave the students the assignment to discover in the Book of Acts 'some evidence' of the baptism with the Spirit. He convinced them that they had yet to receive the full outpouring of a second Pentecost, and he called them to seek this with fasting and prayer. They reached the conclusion that the biblical evidence of Spirit baptism was speaking in tongues, which they told Parham on his return. They set aside 31st December 1900 for praying for this experience. A 'watch-night' service was held with great expectation. Throughout 1st January they prayed and waited until finally at 11pm, a student named Agnes Ozman asked Parham to lay hands on her to receive the gift of the Spirit. She was the first to speak in tongues, described later by Parham as 'speaking in the Chinese language', and followed by others including Parham 'in the Swedish tongue' three days later.

Although this revival attracted the sceptical curiosity of the local press, for two years there was little acceptance of this experience. After the death of his son and the Parhams' move to Kansas City, Parham preached at Holiness missions in Kansas and Missouri in 1903–4, where there were again experiences of tongues and healings. By 1905 Parham was at the height of his influence, and several thousand people were said to have received Spirit baptism in this new movement known as the 'Apostolic Faith'. Parham began meetings and a three-month Bible school in Houston, Texas, where an African American Holiness preacher, William Joseph Seymour, was to hear his doctrine of evidential tongues and take it far beyond Parham's orbit. Parham's theology, unlike Dowie's and Sandford's, was in the 'Third Blessing' framework. He formulated the 'evidential tongues' doctrine that became the hallmark of North American Classical Pentecostals, but unlike them his theology insisted on the belief that tongues were authentic languages (*xenolalia*) given for the proclamation of the gospel in the end times. These tongues were the second Pentecost that would usher in the end, achieve world evangelization within a short period, and seal the Bride of Christ, the Church. Although some authors consider Parham to be the founding father of Pentecostalism and he is given this honour in white Pentecostal mythology, he was ultimately rejected from this position by almost the entire North American Pentecostal movement. His doctrine of *xenolalia* for the proclamation of the gospel was quite different from the doctrine of evidential tongues that later emerged in classical Pentecostalism, although belief in *xenolalia* was widespread in their early years and was never repudiated.[22] Some of Parham's other beliefs like Anglo-Israelism and the annihilation of the 'wicked' were also at variance with later Pentecostal doctrine. Unlike his predecessors Dowie and Sandford, Parham did not actively engage in world evangelization and his efforts did not constitute the driving force that resulted in Pentecostalism being quickly transformed into an international movement. That role was left to Parham's one-time disciple, William Seymour. After his failure to gain control of either Zion City or the Asuza Street revival in 1906 and his arrest in the unproven scandal of 1907, when he was charged with homosexuality, Parham lost most of his supporters and spent the last two decades of his life in relative obscurity in Baxter Springs, Kansas, where he continued to lead his Apostolic Faith. Parham continued to embrace Anglo-Israelism and became increasingly racist in his views, supporting racial segregation. He also had the ignominy of speaking to gatherings of the Ku Klux Klan, who he thought had 'high ideals for the betterment of mankind'.[23] But there can be no doubt that it was probably Parham more than any other person who was responsible for the theological shift in emphasis to glossolalia as the 'evidence' of Spirit baptism in early North American Pentecostalism.

THE ROLE OF INTERNATIONAL REVIVALS

We noted earlier in this chapter revival movements happening in different parts of the European and North American world during the nineteenth century that indirectly prepared the ground for the Pentecostal revival of the twentieth century, such as the Irvingite movement in the 1830s in Britain, the revivals in Sweden, Germany, Russia and Armenia, and those associated with the Holiness movement. But there were also revivals with charismatic phenomena in Asia, Africa and Latin America not directly related to the events in North America. Some of these will be dealt with in later chapters, but those that were to have special significance for international Pentecostalism were those in Wales, India and Korea at the beginning of the twentieth century. These set off a chain of events that influenced each

---

[22] Grant Wacker, *Heaven Below: Early Pentecostals and American culture* (Cambridge, MA and London: Harvard University Press, 2001), pp. 44–51.
[23] Faupel, *Everlasting Gospel*, pp. 158–80, 185; J. R. Goff Jr., 'Parham, Charles Fox', *NIDPCM*, pp. 955–7; Anderson, *Vision*, pp. 87, 190.

other. Significantly, Frank Bartleman, participant in the Azusa Street revival wrote, 'The present world-wide revival was rocked in the cradle of little Wales. It was 'brought up in India, following; becoming full-grown in Los Angeles later'.[24] As we shall see, however, the Indian revival was at least as 'full-grown' a Pentecostal revival as the Azusa Street one was.[25]

The Welsh Revival (1904–5) was centred mainly among the Welsh-speaking mining community, where there were at least 32,000 converts throughout Wales. During this revival, the Pentecostal presence and power of the Holy Spirit was emphasized, and meetings were hours long, spontaneous, seemingly chaotic and emotional, with 'singing in the Spirit (using ancient Welsh chants), simultaneous and loud prayer, revelatory visions and prophecy, all emphasising the immediacy of God in the services and in personal experience. Revival leader Evan Roberts (1878–1951) taught a personal experience of Holy Spirit baptism to precede any revival. The revival was declared to be the end-time Pentecost of Acts 2, the 'latter rain' promised by biblical prophets that would result in a worldwide revival. Charismatic Baptist pastor in Los Angeles Joseph Smale visited the Welsh revival, and Frank Bartleman corresponded with Evan Roberts, asking for prayer for a similar revival in Los Angeles. These and other contacts encouraged people to expect a revival there. Several early British Pentecostal leaders, including George Jeffreys, founder of the Elim Pentecostal Church and his brother Stephen, and Daniel Williams, founder of the Apostolic Church, were converted in the Welsh revival. The first leader of Pentecostalism in Britain, Anglican vicar Alexander Boddy, visited it. Although Evan Roberts, influenced by his mentor Jesse Penn-Lewis, later discouraged the use of tongues, and although Pentecostalism's emphases were found in the radical and less common manifestations of the Welsh revival, early Pentecostal leaders drew inspiration from the revival and saw their movement as the continuation of it. Interestingly, both movements made use of ancient cultural forms to express their experiences and liturgy, the Welsh revival encouraging a resurgence of the Welsh language, particularly in the singing of hymns and chants.[26]

Indian Christians had heard of the Welsh Revival, but Pentecostal-like revival movements had been known in South India since 1860, when glossolalia and other manifestations of the Spirit's presence were reported. In

---

[24] Frank Bartleman, *Azusa Street* (S. Plainfield, NJ: Bridge Publishing, 1980), p. 19.

[25] Gary B. McGee, '"Latter Rain" Falling in the East: Early-Twentieth-Century Pentecostalism in India and the Debate over Speaking in Tongues', *Church History* 68:3 (1999), p. 650.

[26] Eifon Evans, *The Welsh Revival of 1904* (Bridgend, UK: Evangelical Press of Wales, 1969), pp. 190–6; D. D. Bundy, 'Welsh Revival', *NIDPCM*, pp. 1187–8.

1905 a revival broke out in the Khasi Hills in North-East India where Welsh Presbyterian missionaries were working.[27] Hot on the heels of this revival was another at Pandita Sarasvati Ramabai's Mukti Mission for young widows and orphans in Pune near Bombay (Mumbai), commencing in 1905 and lasting two years. Speaking in tongues and other ecstatic phenomena were reported in other parts of India in April and June 1906, the same time as the Azusa Street revival was starting and before any news of it had reached India. But in India tongues were not regarded as essential for Spirit baptism, as they were in most of the North American Pentecostal movement. Young women at Mukti were reported to have been baptized in the Spirit and to manifest various ecstatic phenomena, including speaking in tongues in December 1906. These young women fanned out into the surrounding areas spreading the revival message wherever they went. Some of Ramabai's missionary assistants, including American Methodist Minnie Abrams, also received Spirit baptism in this revival. Abrams spread the news to her friends the Hoovers in Chile; and Mukti thus became a catalyst for the beginning of Pentecostalism there. Bartleman also documents the influence reports of the Indian revivals had on their expectations for Los Angeles.[28]

The 'Korean Pentecost' of 1907–8 commenced at a convention in Pyongyang, and followed an earlier revival that began among Methodist missionaries in Wonsan in 1903. These revivals, like those in Wales and India, were characterized by emotional repentance with loud weeping and simultaneous praying. Eyewitness William Blair likened the 1907 revival to the Day of Pentecost in Acts 2. The 'Korean Pentecost' soon spread throughout Korea, Blair recording that 'Christians returned to their homes in the country taking the Pentecostal fire with them'.[29] The features of the revival still characterize Protestant churches in Korea today, and are a feature of Pentecostal churches too: daily early morning prayer meetings and all-night prayer, simultaneous prayer, Bible study, and an emphasis on evangelism and missions. But beyond this are more characteristically Pentecostal practices like healing the sick, miracles and casting out demons. As was the case in India, national evangelists, especially the Presbyterian pastor Ik Doo Kim, famous for his healing and miracle ministry,[30] probably took the

---

[27] T. Nongsiej, 'Revival Movement in Khasi-Jaintia Hills', O. L. Snaitang (ed.), *Churches of Indigenous Origins in Northeast India* (Delhi: ISPCK, 2000), pp. 32–4.

[28] Bartleman, *Azusa Street*, p. 35; McGee, 'Latter Rain', pp. 649, 653–9.

[29] William N. Blair and Bruce Hunt, *The Korean Pentecost and the Sufferings which Followed* (Edinburgh: The Banner of Truth Trust, 1977), pp. 71, 75.

[30] Young Hoon Lee, 'The Holy Spirit Movement in Korea: Its Historical and Doctrinal Development' (PhD thesis, Temple University, 1996), pp. 80–90.

revival movement into a more 'Pentecostal' and 'contextual' direction than the missionaries would have been comfortable with.

This chapter has demonstrated that charismata or 'spiritual gifts' and ecstatic or 'enthusiastic' forms of Christianity have been found in all ages, albeit sometimes at the margins of the 'established' church. Their incidence increased during the nineteenth century, especially in the Methodist and Holiness movements and those radical Protestants who espoused similar ideas. The many and various revival movements at the turn of the twentieth century had the effect of creating an air of expectancy and longing for Pentecostal revival in many parts of the Protestant world. The signs that this revival had come would be based on the earlier reports: intense desire to pray, emotional confession of sins, manifestations of the coming of the Spirit, successful and accelerated evangelism, and spiritual gifts to confirm that the power of the Spirit had come. Bolstered by earlier revival movements in the nineteenth century, especially in the Holiness and healing movements, this coming of the Spirit was linked to a belief that the last days had come, and that the gospel was to be preached to all the nations of earth before the soon coming of the Lord. Although at first predominantly a northern movement, the stage was set for the coming of a new Pentecost to spread across the world in the new (twentieth) century.

3

North American Classical Pentecostalism

When Charles Parham started preaching in Houston, Texas in 1905 and began a short-term Bible school there, William Joseph Seymour (1870–1922), an African American preacher and the son of freed slaves, was allowed to listen to Parham's lectures for about a month through a half-opened door (in keeping with the segregation of the southern states), and was persuaded by Parham's views on the baptism in the Spirit. Seymour was invited to pastor a small African American Holiness church in Los Angeles in 1906; but his sermon saying that tongues was a sign of Spirit baptism caused the church building to be locked against him. Members of this church, soon joined by others, continued meeting with Seymour in prayer in Richard and Ruth Asberry's house in North Bonnie Brae Street. At the house where Seymour was staying, his host Edward Lee asked the preacher to lay hands on him, after which he fell to the floor as if unconscious and began speaking in tongues. Later that evening at the meeting at Bonnie Brae Street, seven others including Seymour and his future wife Jennie Moore received the same experience. For three days and nights the house was filled with people praying and rejoicing, continuously and loudly. A few whites joined this group and the house became too small. Within a week they had rented and moved into an old building used for storage at 312 Azusa Street, a former African Methodist Episcopal church, where the Apostolic Faith Mission was born. With sawdust-sprinkled floors and rough planks as benches, daily meetings commenced at about ten in the morning and usually lasted until late at night. They were completely spontaneous and usually emotional, without planned programmes or speakers. Singing in tongues and people falling to the ground 'under the power' or 'slain in the Spirit' were common phenomena.[1] The racial integration in these meetings

---

[1] Faupel, *Everlasting Gospel*, pp. 194–7, 200–2.

was unique at that time, and people from ethnic minorities discovered 'the sense of dignity and community denied them in the larger urban culture'.[2] Seymour's core leadership team was fully integrated with black and white men and women being responsible for various aspects of the work (more than half were women), but Seymour remained in charge. He was described as a meek and gracious man of prayer, even allowing his critics to speak to his congregation and advertising the meetings of his rivals.[3] Such was the impression that Seymour made on people that healing evangelist John G. Lake, meeting him for the first time in 1907, commented that Seymour had 'more of God in his life than any man I had ever met'.[4] Seymour was spiritual father to thousands of early Pentecostals in North America.

For the next three years the revival in Azusa Street was the most prominent centre of Pentecostalism, further promoted by Seymour's periodical *The Apostolic Faith*, which reached an international circulation of 50,000 at its peak in 1908. People affected by the revival started several new Pentecostal centres in the Los Angeles area, so that by 1912 there were at least twelve in the city. Hundreds of visitors from all over the continent and internationally came to see what was happening and to be baptized in the Spirit. Many of these began Pentecostal centres in various US and Canadian cities and eventually further afield. Hostile local press reports helped publicize the revival with glaring headlines like 'Whites and Blacks Mix in a Religious Frenzy'. A local white Baptist pastor said that Azusa Street was a 'disgusting amalgamation of African voodoo superstition and Caucasian insanity'.[5] Parham came to 'control' this revival in October 1906 and was disgusted particularly by the interracial fellowship and what he termed 'hypnotism' and the 'freak imitation of Pentecost'. 'Horrible, awful shame!' he cried. Years later, Parham referred to Azusa Street as making him 'sick at my stomach . . . to see white people imitating unintelligent, crude negroism of the Southland, and laying it on the Holy Ghost'.[6] Among other things, these racist remarks at least made the correct assumption that Azusa Street's Pentecostalism owed much of its manifestations of the Spirit to the broader African American religious milieu. Parham was rejected by Azusa Street as overseer, was never reconciled with Seymour and went into relative obscurity. A year later he was arrested on unproven charges of sodomy and disgraced. His role in the formation of the classical Pentecostal doctrine of

[2] Anderson, *Vision*, p. 69.
[3] Cecil M. Robeck, Jr., 'Azusa Street Revival', *NIDPCM*, pp. 344–50; Robeck, 'Seymour, William Joseph', *NIDPCM*, pp. 1053–8.
[4] John G. Lake, *Adventures in God* (reprinted, Tulsa, OK: Harrison House, 1981), p. 19.
[5] Faupel, *Everlasting Gospel*, pp. 202–5, 208.   [6] Anderson, *Vision*, p. 190.

Figure 2. William Seymour (seated centre right) with leaders including Florence
Crawford (left), Jenny Moore (later Mrs Seymour, third from left, back row),
Azusa Street, Los Angeles, c. 1911.

baptism in the Spirit was all but forgotten as Pentecostal leaders dissociated
themselves from him.

The leadership of the movement passed to William Seymour and took on
international dimensions never realized in Parham's work. Perhaps because
of all the hurt Seymour suffered from white Pentecostals, he later repudiated Parham's 'initial evidence' doctrine and was later himself rejected as
leader by white Pentecostals, who were unable to allow a sustained role for
black leadership. After Parham's foiled attempt to take over the work, in
1908 Seymour's workers Clara Lum and Florence Crawford left Azusa Street
with the mailing list of *The Apostolic Faith*, objecting to Seymour's marriage;
and Crawford commenced the Apostolic Faith in Portland, Oregon. Several
competing white missions in Los Angeles drew away members from Azusa
Street. In 1911 Chicago preacher William Durham, who had received Spirit
baptism at Azusa Street, came to Los Angeles and tried to take over the mission while Seymour was away on a preaching trip, until Seymour returned
to lock the church against him. Glenn Cook, Seymour's business manager,
left with Durham at this time and they started a rival congregation nearby.
By 1912 Seymour's Apostolic Faith Mission at Azusa Street had become a
small black congregation, and a constitution ruled in 1915 that leadership of

Figure 3.   Azusa Street building, Los Angeles before its demolition, c. 1928.

the movement was to remain with a 'man of color'. After Seymour's death his wife Jenny became 'bishop' of the church, until in 1931 the building was demolished. But at least twenty-six different denominations trace their Pentecostal origins to Azusa Street, including the two largest: the Church of God in Christ and the Assemblies of God. In a real sense, the Azusa Street revival marks the beginning of classical Pentecostalism and as we will see, the revival reached to many other parts of the world.

From its beginning, North American Pentecostalism placed an emphasis on evangelism and missions. People came from as far away as Europe and went back there with the 'baptism', and Pentecostal missionaries were sent out all over the world from Azusa Street, reaching over twenty-five nations in two years, including places as far away as China, India, Japan, Egypt, Liberia, Angola and South Africa.[7] This was no mean achievement and the beginning of what is arguably the most significant global expansion of a Christian movement in the history of Christianity.

The story of the Azusa Street revival raises the complex question of the origins of Pentecostalism. One theory of the origins cannot be emphasized to the exclusion of others. Pentecostal historian Augustus Cerillo has outlined at least four approaches to the subject: (1) *providential*, the belief that the movement came 'from heaven' through a sudden, simultaneous

---

[7] Faupel, *Everlasting Gospel*, pp. 182–6, 208–9, 212–16.

and spontaneous outpouring of the Spirit, the 'latter rain' foretold in the Bible (this view was held by many early Pentecostals); (2) *historical*, where the movement is seen as continuous with nineteenth century revivalist Christianity, especially the Methodist and Holiness movements; (3) *multicultural* (the view explained below); and (4) *functional* or *sociological*, which looks at the functions of Pentecostalism in a given social context to provide an explanation for its emergence.[8]

However, although all of these approaches must be taken into consideration, I prefer the multicultural approach for several reasons. Although it is clear that several centres of Pentecostalism emerged in the first decade of the twentieth century, the movement was first given national and international impetus at Azusa Street. Some scholars have referred to the 'myth' of Azusa Street that has overlooked the importance of other centres and have suggested that its role was not as central as has been generally accepted.[9] There were other important early centres of Pentecostalism independent of Azusa Street, in particular Marie and Robert Brown's Glad Tidings Tabernacle in New York City (which commenced in 1907), William H. Piper's Stone Church in Chicago (which became Pentecostal in 1907), and Ellen and James Hebden's Queen Street Mission in Toronto (the Hebdens were baptized in the Spirit in 1906). But what cannot be denied is that for three years, Seymour's Apostolic Faith Mission was the most prominent and significant centre of Pentecostalism on the continent. That this was a predominantly black church and leadership, rooted in the African American culture of the nineteenth century, is really significant. Many of the early manifestations of Pentecostalism came from African American Christianity and were also found in the religious expressions of the slaves. These expressions were a reflection of the African religious culture from which slaves had been abducted and Seymour himself was deeply affected by black slave spirituality.[10] Walter Hollenweger says that the main features of this African American spirituality were an oral liturgy, a narrative theology and witness, the maximum participation of the whole community in worship and service, the inclusion of visions and dreams into public worship, and an understanding of the relationship between body and mind manifested by healing through prayer.[11] Other examples of African American Christian

---

[8] Augustus Cerillo, Jr., 'Interpretative Approaches to the History of American Pentecostal Origins', *Pneuma* 19:1 (1997), 29–49.

[9] Joe Creech, 'Visions of Glory: The Place of the Azusa Street Revival in Pentecostal History', *Church History* 65 (1996), 405–24.

[10] Douglas J. Nelson, 'For Such a Time as This: The Story of William J Seymour and the Azusa Street Revival' (PhD thesis, University of Birmingham, 1981), pp. 157–8.

[11] Hollenweger, *Pentecostalism*, pp. 18–19.

liturgy include rhythmic hand clapping, the antiphonal participation of the congregation in the sermon, the immediacy of God in the services and baptism by immersion, which are all practices common to Pentecostal churches worldwide.[12] These expressions were a fundamental part of early Pentecostalism and remain in the movement to this day.

Harvey Cox describes William Seymour and his band of followers as 'praying that God would renew and purify a Christianity they believed was crippled by empty rituals, dried-up creeds, and the sin of racial bigotry'. He says 'when the fire finally did fall' at Azusa Street, 'a spiritual fire roared forth that was to race around the world and touch hundreds of millions of people with its warmth and power'. The hundreds of millions were not to emerge for almost a century, but the early Pentecostals saw themselves on the edge of a new dispensation. The revival was 'a new Pentecost, a mighty gathering together of the tribes and nations that had been scattered and confounded at the foot of the ill-fated Tower of Babel'. The early Pentecostals believed that something had gone wrong with the church after the 'original fire from heaven' on the Day of Pentecost, and that Christianity had degenerated or had 'lapsed into writing meticulous creeds and inventing lifeless rituals'. The Pentecostal revival was believed to be the 'latter rain' promised by God through the prophet Joel, and would be characterized by a 'worldwide resurgence of faith', and 'healings and miracles' that were 'a prelude to the second coming of Jesus Christ'. It is impossible to understand the origins of North American Pentecostalism without reference to Seymour and the Azusa Street revival.[13]

Hollenweger suggests that the founder of Pentecostalism is either Parham or Seymour and that the choice between the two depends on what the essence of Pentecostalism is. Either it is found in a particular doctrine of a particular experience (speaking in tongues as languages), or else it lies in its oral, missionary nature and its ability to break down barriers, emphases of the Azusa Street revival. For Hollenweger, his choice of Seymour as founder of Pentecostalism is not based as much on historical sequence (which shows the earlier work of Parham) as it is on theological principles, which become the basis on which the Pentecostal message spreads around the world.[14] Although Parham was indeed influential in the early formation

---

[12] Iain MacRobert, *The Black Roots and White Racism of Early Pentecostalism in the USA* (Basingstoke, UK: Macmillan, 1988), p. 29.

[13] Cox, *Fire*, pp. 46–8.

[14] Walter J. Hollenweger, 'The Black Roots of Pentecostalism', Allan Anderson and Walter J. Hollenweger (eds.), *Pentecostals after a Century: Global Perspectives on a Movement in Transition* (Sheffield, UK: Sheffield Academic Press, 1999), pp. 42–3.

of Pentecostalism, Seymour and Azusa Street eclipsed him in significance and play a major role in the ways most Pentecostals and Charismatics define themselves. In a certain sense, early North American Pentecostalism typified by Azusa Street was a revolutionary movement where the marginalized and dispossessed could find equality regardless of race, gender or class. The primary purpose of the coming of the Spirit as it was practised in Azusa Street was to bring a family of God's people together on an equal basis. We must not underestimate the importance of this revival. Although events have moved a long way from these heady days, this formative period of North American Pentecostalism should be seen as its fundamental essence and not merely as its infancy. This means that if the movement is to continue to be strong in the twenty-first century, it must consider its Azusa Street prototype to be the source of inspiration for theological and spiritual renewal.[15]

SCHISM: 'FINISHED WORK' AND 'ONENESS' PENTECOSTALISM

Racial, doctrinal and personal issues simultaneously caused the divisions that erupted in early Pentecostalism. Some Pentecostals had come from churches outside the Holiness movement and were more influenced by the Keswick view of progressive sanctification, which tended to deny a second instantaneous experience of holiness. William Durham in Chicago was one of these. A former Baptist turned Holiness preacher, Durham was undoubtedly one of the most influential of the Pentecostal preachers and the cause of the first major doctrinal schism in the movement. Durham received his Spirit baptism at Azusa Street in March 1907 and returned to Chicago transformed. His Gospel Mission Church (better known as the North Avenue Mission) became a revival centre that rivalled and ultimately exceeded Azusa Street in influence, and indirectly resulted in the creation of several European immigrant Pentecostal congregations in Chicago, especially Italian and Scandinavian ones. Unlike Azusa Street, where the emphasis was on the experience of the Spirit and anyone under the guidance of Seymour could share testimonies or preach as the Spirit directed, people came primarily to the nightly revival meetings in Chicago to hear Durham's persuasive preaching. In 1911 Durham, once so influenced by Seymour and the Azusa Street revival, went to Los Angeles to preach against them both in the Azusa Street Mission. The issue was his 'Finished Work' doctrine, not unusual in Durham's old Baptist church, but it had already greatly

---

[15] Robeck, 'Pentecostal Origins', p. 179; Faupel, *Everlasting Gospel*, p. 309.

influenced many white Pentecostals, the majority of whom had Holiness and Wesleyan backgrounds. Seymour, who itinerated often, was preaching on the East Coast at this time, and on his return to Los Angeles he asked Durham to stop teaching his doctrine. When Durham refused to do so, Seymour locked the Azusa Street Mission against him. Durham continued in a nearby hall with about two-thirds of Seymour's workers who had been convinced by him, including Frank Bartleman, recently returned from a round the world trip, who wrote of Durham's meetings, 'God's glory filled the place. "Azusa" became deserted'.[16] At issue was the Holiness teaching of 'entire sanctification', which had been embraced by Seymour and most early Pentecostals, but which in 1910 Durham had declared to be unscriptural. Durham taught that sanctification was not a 'second blessing' or a 'crisis experience', but that Christ had provided for sanctification in his atonement and that this was received at conversion by identification with Christ in an act of faith. He therefore taught a 'two-stage' work of grace (justification and Spirit baptism) instead of a 'three-stage' one.

Durham's influence was enormous. Up until 1910 the 'three stage' view that had evolved from the Holiness movement was the accepted teaching of most Pentecostals, even though many of them came from Baptist, Presbyterian and Christian and Missionary Alliance churches, who did not share the Holiness position. Many of those who became major leaders of the Pentecostal movement came to Durham in Chicago to embrace his 'Finished Work of Calvary' doctrine. They included E. N. Bell (who was to be the first general superintendent of the Assemblies of God, AG), A. H. Argue (a Canadian Pentecostal leader), Andrew Urshan (Iranian born and early 'Oneness' leader), Luigi Francescon (or Francisconi, founder of Italian Pentecostalism in the USA, Argentina and Brazil), Giacomo Lombardi (pioneer of Pentecostalism in Italy), Daniel Berg and Gunnar Vingren (Swedish missionaries who founded the AG in Brazil), Howard Goss (AG and later 'Oneness' leader), F. A. Sandgren (a Norwegian elder in Durham's church who published a Norwegian periodical) and Aimee Semple McPherson, founder of the International Church of the Foursquare Gospel, who was instantly healed of a broken ankle when she visited Durham's church in 1910. After Durham's premature death from tuberculosis in 1912 (an event that had been prophesied by Parham, perhaps Durham's severest critic), his doctrine became the basis upon which the AG, the later 'Oneness' churches, and several other smaller Pentecostal denominations were formed. Durham's assistant minister, Frank Ewart, who also became one of

[16] Bartleman, *Azusa Street*, p. 151.

the leaders of 'Oneness' Pentecostalism took over the North Avenue Mission after his death. Those who resisted Durham's teaching and remained in the 'three-stage' camp were Seymour, Crawford and Parham, and Bishops Charles H. Mason, A. J. Tomlinson and J. H. King, respectively leaders of the Church of God in Christ, the Church of God (Cleveland) and the Pentecostal Holiness Church. Tomlinson and King each issued tirades against the 'finished work' doctrine in their periodicals, but by 1914 some 60 per cent of all North American Pentecostals had embraced Durham's position.

But there were several other factors at work in this division, which had never been a monolithic movement anyway. Nelson suggests that Durham was obsessed with becoming leader of the whole Pentecostal movement and that his 'Finished Work' doctrine was a means to that end. Most of the 'Finished Work' supporters were white, and only whites were invited to the convention that launched the AG in 1914, including those that held the 'three-stage' position. The first address in this convention was entitled 'The Finished Work of Calvary'. To some extent, therefore, this division in the Pentecostal movement was also a racial one. But although this major division was caused by a variety of factors of which Durham's theology was only one, the theological factor was still the main cause. Durham himself said he did not proclaim the 'Finished Work' doctrine because of his Baptist roots, but because of his experience of Spirit baptism.[17] His influence on the theology of the majority of Pentecostals was certainly immense and the division in US American Pentecostalism on this issue remains today, although with less rancour than in the first three decades.

The 'Finished Work' controversy was only the first of many subsequent divisions in North American Pentecostalism. Not only did Pentecostal churches split over the question of sanctification as a distinct experience, but a more fundamental and acrimonious split erupted in 1916 over the doctrine of the Trinity. Several Pentecostal groups arose with a type of theological modalism called 'New Issue', 'Jesus' Name' or 'Oneness' by its proponents, and 'Jesus Only' by its opponents. The 'New Issue' was a schism in the ranks of the 'Finished Work' Pentecostals that began as a teaching that the correct formula for baptism is 'in the name of Jesus' and developed into a dispute about the doctrine of the Trinity. It confirmed for the Holiness Pentecostals that they should have no further fellowship with the 'Finished Work' Pentecostals, who were in 'heresy'. The 'Finished Work' Pentecostals had an increasing expectation that God would continue to bring 'further

---

[17] Faupel, *Everlasting Gospel*, pp. 230, 232–43, 251–2, 256, 260–3, 268; Anderson, *Vision*, pp. 169–73.

revelation' and that God was going to do a 'new thing'. Remarkable revival meetings, especially those conducted by the 68-year-old female evangelist Maria Woodworth-Etter in Dallas in 1912 and in Arroyo Seco, near Los Angeles in 1913, encouraged this heightened expectation but failed to unite Pentecostalism. William Seymour was not accorded any leadership role in these meetings. In the Arroyo Seco camp meeting, the Canadian evangelist Robert McAlister began to preach about baptism 'in the name of Jesus Christ' from Acts 2:38, which he said was the common practice of the early church, rather than the triune formula of Matthew 28:19. Baptism was to be 'in the name of Jesus' because Jesus was the 'name' of God, whereas 'Father, Son and Holy Spirit' were different titles for the singular name of Jesus Christ. This new teaching not only resulted in calls for rebaptism, but also developed into a theology of the name of God based on a combination of the Keswick emphasis on Jesus and the Old Testament names of God, and leading ultimately to what became known as the 'Oneness' doctrine.[18]

Early leaders in the Oneness movement included Durham's assistant and successor Frank Ewart (1876–1947), Seymour's former business manager Glenn Cook (1867–1948), prominent African American pastor Garfield T. Haywood (1880–1931) and Parham's former field superintendent Howard Goss (1883–1964). Ewart was credited with first formulating the distinctive Oneness theology on the nature and the name of God to accompany the new baptismal practice. This he first announced in a public sermon in 1914, when he and Cook rebaptized each other. The new doctrine spread through evangelistic meetings and in Indianapolis, Cook baptized Haywood together with 465 members of his congregation. The 'New Issue' became a schism especially in the AG. Goss, a disciple of Parham, was one of the organizing founders of the AG in 1914. The AG was split on this 'New Issue' in 1916, when 156 ministers, including Goss, Ewart and Haywood, were barred from membership over the doctrine of the Trinity, which became a condition for membership. The AG emerged thereafter as a tightly structured, centralized denomination with a 'Statement of Fundamental Truths' affirming the Trinity. The split also meant that the AG lost its black membership and became an all-white denomination, especially with the departure of Haywood, the only prominent black leader associated with the AG. The AG's stand for 'orthodoxy' at this time was to ease their later acceptance by evangelicals. Oneness Pentecostalism in contrast was destined to remain isolated from the rest of Pentecostalism

---

[18] Anderson, *Vision*, pp. 166, 176; Faupel, *Everlasting Gospel*, pp. 273–80, 283–8, 301.

and Christianity in general, particularly through its practice of rebaptism and rejection of Trinitarian beliefs.

In January 1917, a Oneness organization called the General Assembly of Apostolic Assemblies was formed and joined Haywood's Pentecostal Assemblies of the World (PAW) in 1918. This remained a racially integrated church until 1924, after which most of the whites withdrew and the PAW adopted episcopal government, with Haywood as presiding bishop. After an abortive attempt to unite under the umbrella of the newly formed Pentecostal Church of Jesus Christ (PCJC) in 1931, the PAW has since been predominantly an African American church. The largest Pentecostal denomination in Canada, the Pentecostal Assemblies of Canada (PAC) was first organized as a Oneness denomination and planned to unite with the PAW, but in 1920 repudiated Oneness and joined the AG, later in 1925 to become independent. The Oneness members of the PAC formed the Apostolic Church of Pentecost in 1921. The United Pentecostal Church (UPC) is now the largest Oneness group in North America, a white denomination formed in 1945 from a union of the PCJC and the Pentecostal Church, Incorporated. Howard Goss was the first general superintendent of the UPC. Goss was involved in the discussions leading to the formation of the Pentecostal Fellowship of North America in 1948, but the Trinitarian doctrinal statement drawn up excluded the UPC. Oneness Pentecostals have been excluded from fellowship with Trinitarian Pentecostals ever since, except in the Society for Pentecostal Studies, where they have participated since 1973.

In the UPC were included those who believed that baptism in the name of Jesus and baptism in the Spirit with the sign of speaking in tongues constituted the new birth, also a doctrine held by the PAW. There are also a large number of smaller organizations usually having the word 'Apostolic' in their names, many of which formed a loose association called the Apostolic World Christian Fellowship in 1971. Oneness Pentecostals are found all over the world and may account for up to a quarter of all classical Pentecostals. The UPC operates in over a hundred nations, and its biggest work is now in Ethiopia. In Canada, the Apostolic Church of Pentecost is unique in that it is a Calvinistic denomination that accommodates both 'Oneness' and 'Triunity' believers. Most, if not all, of the black British Apostolic groups are Oneness in doctrine with roots in the Caribbean. The largest Chinese Pentecostal church and the largest Oneness denomination in the world is the True Jesus Church, which also observes the Sabbath. There are significant autochthonous Oneness Pentecostal churches in Indonesia and Japan, where the Spirit of Jesus Church may be the largest Christian denomination in the nation. Several Oneness denominations, including the True Jesus Church, the UPC and the PAW, practise foot washing.[19]

The essence of Oneness teaching as it has developed is a rejection of the traditional Christian concept of 'separate but equal' Persons in the Trinity. Oneness Pentecostals hold that Jesus is the revelation of God the Father and that the Spirit proceeds from the Father (Jesus). Unlike the traditional idea that Jesus is the human name of Christ, in Oneness teaching Jesus is the New Testament name of God, and this name reveals His true nature. The one God of the Old Testament (Yahweh) reveals His immanence in the incarnation of Jesus, and His transcendence in the presence of the Spirit. God has now permanently taken up His abode in the human body of the Son. The Spirit indwells Jesus in fullness as God (the Father) incarnate, and thus an attempt is made to resolve the intricacies of Trinitarian theology. Oneness Pentecostals charge that Trinitarians have embraced tritheism because they assume that Trinitarians believe in three separate and distinct 'Persons' in the Godhead. Instead, Oneness teaching affirms that Jesus is fully God and not one divine being out of three. They prefer to refer to Father, Son and Spirit as 'modes' or 'manifestations' of God, all of which are present in the manifestation of each one. It follows that they also reject the traditional Christian teaching of the eternal Sonship of Christ, and that Oneness teaching on the dual nature of Christ tends towards a separation of the divine and the human. A prominent section of Oneness Pentecostalism teaches a threefold soteriology based on Acts 2:38 – repentance, baptism in the name of Jesus Christ and the gift of the Spirit, all as essential to salvation. Oneness Pentecostalism is not a homogeneous movement, as today there are several varieties and hundreds of denominations. It emerged as an alternative to the Trinitarian doctrine and baptismal practice of early Pentecostalism, and was possibly the unavoidable outcome of the Christocentric 'Finished Work' theology of William Durham.[20]

By 1916, North American Pentecostalism was doctrinally divided into three competing groups: 'Second Work' (Holiness) Trinitarians, 'Finished Work' (Baptistic) Trinitarians and 'Finished Work' Oneness Pentecostals, divisions that remain to this day.[21] Other issues that divided Pentecostals were the authority of spoken prophecy (some held that there should be set apostles and prophets in the church), different eschatological interpretations, church polity, personality conflicts and racial differences. The process

---

[19] Talmadge L. French, *Our God is One: The Story of Oneness Pentecostalism* (Indianapolis, IN: Voice and Vision Publications, 1999).
[20] French, *Our God is One*, p. 15; Faupel, *Everlasting Gospel*, pp. 304–6.
[21] Lederle, *Treasures Old and New*, p. 16.

of schism and the proliferation of new sects that had commenced in the nineteenth century Holiness movement was multiplied and perpetuated in the global expansion of Pentecostalism, and remains a feature of the movement to this day. In addition to these doctrinal differences, within two decades the US American Pentecostal movement had divided on racial lines. In 1914 the nucleus of the AG was formed from white preachers, many of whom had been issued credentials by Bishop Mason of the Church of God in Christ. Mason was one of the earliest and most effective Pentecostal leaders whose denomination became the largest Pentecostal and African American church in the USA. The Oneness schism in 1916 effectively meant that no black leaders remained in the AG. Charles Parham was well known for his racist views, which became more prominent after his rejection by Seymour, further creating conflict. Racial divisions continued and proliferated. In 1921 the Church of God (Cleveland) was reorganized by segregating the black and white churches, and by 1937 even Oneness Pentecostals, the most integrated of all early Pentecostal groups, were split on racial lines.

Another major controversy split the Pentecostal movement in 1948, when the 'Latter Rain' revival movement arose in which several leading ministers in Pentecostal denominations resigned to be part of a movement purporting to 'restore' a fallen and 'cold' Pentecostalism to its former glory. This movement emphasized the restoration of the 'ministry gifts' of apostles and prophets to the church, spoken prophecies, and the independence of the local church, tending to shun 'denominationalism'. Many of the independent Charismatic churches that constitute a large portion of Pentecostalism in North America today have roots in the Latter Rain movement. And yet, despite all these divisions, the Pentecostal movement continued to grow and as a whole probably retained as much friendly contact across racial divides as any other religious group in North America.[22] 'Finished Work' Trinitarian Pentecostalism is probably the most prominent expression of the movement today, particularly as this is the position adopted by the largest classical Pentecostal denominations.

TRINITARIAN PENTECOSTAL DENOMINATIONS

During its first fifty years, Pentecostalism consolidated in North America and formed segregated denominations. There are hundreds of Pentecostal denominations today, most of them, including Parham's Apostolic Faith

---

[22] R. M. Riss, 'Latter Rain Movement', *NIDPCM*, pp. 830–3; Anderson, *Vision*, pp. 155, 160, 190–3.

(Baxter Springs) being small; but others are now among the largest denominations on the continent. The largest classical Pentecostal churches in the USA today are the Church of God in Christ (COGIC, originally formed in 1885) and the AG (founded in 1914), followed by the Church of God (Cleveland) (CGC, 1886), the International Church of the Foursquare Gospel (ICFG, 1927), the International Pentecostal Holiness Church (IPHC, 1895), the United Pentecostal Church (UPC, 1931), and the Pentecostal Church of God (1919). Denominations first began as associations for fellowship and accreditation that with the passing of time became increasingly institutionalized.

One of the leading figures in early Pentecostalism was African American Bishop Charles H. Mason (1866–1961), who led COGIC for over fifty years with headquarters in Memphis, Tennessee. COGIC was founded in 1897 by Mason and C. P. Jones, who were former Baptist ministers who had embraced the Holiness position of entire sanctification. Mason visited Azusa Street in 1907 and received Spirit baptism there. The denomination split in 1908 over the issue of tongues as evidence of Spirit baptism, when Mason's co-founder C. P. Jones and more than half the members left to reorganize themselves as the Church of Christ (Holiness), while the remainder elected Mason as overseer of COGIC. Because COGIC was already an officially registered church in 1907, Mason issued credentials to preachers in the entire US Pentecostal movement from that time. Many of the first white leaders in the AG had Mason's credentials, and COGIC had an equal number of white ministers and members until the founding of the AG in 1914. Mason had considerable abilities and organized his church with bishops and overseers in most regions of the USA, the church growing tenfold between 1930 and 1960. After a seven-year dispute following his death, Mason was eventually succeeded as presiding bishop by his son-in-law J. O. Patterson in 1968, who remained in office until his death in 1989. During his period of office, the church again grew tenfold to become the largest Pentecostal church and largest black church in the USA, with some four million members by 1990. Since 1995 Bishop Chandler Owens has been presiding bishop. A major schism in 1969 resulted in fourteen bishops leaving to form the Church of God in Christ, International. Secessions from COGIC have resulted in at least five small Pentecostal church organizations, and there are many other black Holiness-Pentecostal denominations in the USA today. COGIC had an estimated five and a half million members in 2001.[23]

---

[23] S. S. DuPree, 'Church of God in Christ', *NIDPCM*, pp. 535–7; I. C. Clemmons, 'Mason, Charles Harrison', *NIDPCM*, pp. 865–7.

The AG was organized in 1914 in Hot Springs, Arkansas under the leadership of Eudorus N. Bell (1866–1923), the first chairman. Having an emphasis on local and regional government, the AG was created to counter the extreme individualism developing in Pentecostalism. The invitation to attend the founding convention was only issued to white Pentecostal leaders, with the exception of G. T. Haywood. Bishop Mason attended as a guest and preached to the gathering of over four hundred white preachers. The new organism (most of its adherents would not call it an organization, which they disdained) did not adopt either a constitution or a statement of faith. Two early doctrinal controversies split the AG: the 'Oneness' controversy in 1916, and the debate over 'initial evidence' in 1918 in which healing evangelist F. F. Bosworth was forced to resign. Bosworth argued that speaking in tongues was one of the gifts of the Spirit but did not necessarily constitute the 'initial evidence' of Spirit baptism. As a result of these and other disputes the AG became more rigid on doctrinal issues and formulated a 'Statement of Fundamental Truths' in 1916, enshrining the doctrine of the Trinity and (later) 'initial evidence' as essential teachings of the denomination. Gradually there was a shift to centralization at the headquarters in Springfield, Missouri (from 1918). In 1929 the denomination adopted its first constitution and Ernest Swing Williams (1885–1981), former member of Azusa Street, became first general superintendent, a post he held until 1949. In 1942 the AG joined the newly formed National Association of Evangelicals (NAE), a move that was to identify them increasingly with conservative evangelicalism. Another highly influential AG leader was J. Roswell Flower (1888–1970), who held various executive positions in the denomination from its inception and was general secretary until 1959. Thomas Zimmerman (1912–91), general superintendent from 1959 to 1985, was one of the most significant AG leaders in recent years. Zimmerman stressed church growth, identification with Evangelicalism, and presided over the AG's transition to a middle American popular denomination.

Hollenweger traces four stages in the AG's transition to full denominational status: (1) the decline of enthusiasm, as the economic and social status of members improved, ministers were expected to be Bible school trained and leadership was restricted to pastors; (2) the break with the healing evangelists in the 1950s, who were increasingly criticised by AG ministers for their alleged moral lapses, egotism and overemphasis on healing and prosperity (see below); (3) the relaxation of ethical rigors, such as early taboos against dress, make-up, the theatre, cinema and higher education; (4) an elaborate structure for Sunday schools wherein the whole family is given regular teaching and an increasing number of Bible schools, universities and seminaries for the training of pastors and missionaries. The AG had over two and a half million members in the USA in 2001.[24] The main areas of growth in the AG today are among Hispanic and Korean congregations, whereas many white congregations are in a state of stagnation or decline.

The second largest predominantly white Pentecostal denomination, the CGC, had its roots in the Christian Union founded by R. G. Spurling in 1886 in Tennessee, and in the revival in Cherokee County, North Carolina in 1896 (see chapter 2). In 1902 the church was renamed the Holiness Church, and in 1907 this was organized as the Church of God and the headquarters moved to Cleveland, Tennessee, under Ambrose J. Tomlinson (1865–1943) as leader. In 1908 the CGC became Pentecostal when G. B. Cashwell, who had received Spirit baptism at Azusa Street, brought the experience to Cleveland. Seated on the stage at Cashwell's meeting, Tomlinson fell off his chair and was 'slain in the Spirit', and the whole denomination eventually became Pentecostal. In 1909 Tomlinson became the CGC's first General Overseer, the church's first missionaries were sent to the Bahamas the following year and to Jamaica in 1918. In 1920 the denomination's Assembly accepted the proposal that Tomlinson, 'General Overseer for Life' since 1914, be given unrestricted control. The resulting tensions led to Tomlinson's expulsion from the church and his founding the Tomlinson Church of God in 1923. The leadership of the CGC passed to Flavius J. Lee. A protracted legal battle between the two Churches of God in Cleveland over property and the name of the church only ended in 1952, when Tomlinson's faction was to be known as the Church of God of Prophecy (CGP). When A. J. Tomlinson died in 1943, his son Milton A. Tomlinson (1906–95) became general overseer of the CGP, a position he held until 1990. This church has been possibly the most integrated classical Pentecostal denomination in the USA and has remained true to the conservative ethical principles of the Tomlinsons, resulting in the withdrawal of many middle class white US Americans in the 1990s. In contrast to the CGP, in 1926 the black and white congregations in the CGC were segregated. Hollenweger's assessment of the CGC is probably true of many North American Pentecostal denominations. The church adopted the patriotic values of the US American middle class and has consequently changed from being a protesting 'church of the poor' to 'a conservative middle-class force'.[25] The CGC and CGP underwent further splits, so that ten separate

---

[24] E. L. Blumhofer and C. R. Armstrong, 'Assemblies of God', *NIDPCM*, pp. 333–40; Walter J. Hollenweger, *The Pentecostals* (London: SCM Press, 1972), pp. 33–40.
[25] Hollenweger, *The Pentecostals*, p. 59.

Pentecostal denominations emerged. As a result of the extensive work of both the CGC and the CGP in the Caribbean, in Britain the CGC is called the New Testament Church of God, which, along with the Church of God of Prophecy, have become the largest black-led churches in Britain. The CGC joined the NAE at its inauguration in 1942, but the CGP has not joined this organization.[26]

The International Pentecostal Holiness Church (IPHC) is a Holiness Pentecostal church formed as a result of a merger in 1911 between the Fire-Baptized Holiness Church (founded by Benjamin Irwin in 1895) and the Holiness Church of North Carolina (founded by Ambrose Crumpler in 1898). A further merger took place in 1915 when the Tabernacle Pentecostal Church (founded in 1898 by N. J. Holmes) joined what was by then the Pentecostal Holiness Church (PHC). When Irwin resigned suddenly from his church leadership in 1890 over 'gross sin', his assistant Joseph H. King (1869–1946) took over. G. B Cashwell, a minister in Crumpler's church, travelled to Azusa Street in 1906 and began preaching the Pentecostal message to all three groups, who rapidly accepted it. Crumpler did not, and he resigned from the Holiness Church, after which Cashwell became leader. In 1909 the name of the Holiness Church was changed to Pentecostal Holiness Church, and discussions on the merger with the Fire-Baptized Holiness Church began, the merger completed in 1911. Like other Holiness Pentecostal churches, the PHC has five 'cardinal doctrines' corresponding to the 'fivefold gospel': justification by faith, sanctification as a 'second definite work of grace', the baptism in the Spirit evidenced by speaking in tongues, divine healing in the atonement of Christ, and the imminent, premillennial second coming of Christ. J. H. King was general superintendent of the church from 1917 until his death in 1945, and in 1937 his title was changed to Bishop. A split occurred in 1920 over the use of medicine and church polity (the PHC being against medicine at that time, and episcopal in government). The secession of the Congregational Holiness Church was the result. The PHC joined the NAE in 1943. Bishop J. A. Synan (father of the Pentecostal historian Vinson Synan) was leader of the church from 1950 to 1969. One of the best-known ministers in the church was the evangelist Oral Roberts, who began his tent campaigns in 1948. Roberts left the PHC in 1969 to join the United Methodist Church. The church became the IPHC in 1975.[27]

---

[26] C. W. Conn, 'Church of God (Cleveland, TN)', *NIDPCM*, pp. 530–5; H. D. Hunter, 'Church of God of Prophecy', *NIDPCM*, pp. 539–42.

[27] H. V. Synan, 'International Pentecostal Holiness Church', *NIDPCM*, pp. 798–801.

The Pentecostal Church of God commenced as the Pentecostal Assemblies of the USA in 1919 after a group of AG ministers under John Sinclair left in protest against the formation of a statement of faith in 1916. The name changed to Pentecostal Church of God in 1922. The church succumbed to pressure to formulate its own statement of faith in 1933, similar to those of other 'Finished Work' Trinitarian Pentecostals. The headquarters of the church since 1951 is in Joplin, Missouri. The church has joined with other white Trinitarian Pentecostal churches in the NAE (1942), the Pentecostal Fellowship of North America (1948) and the inter-racial Pentecostal/Charismatic Churches of North America (1994).[28]

Probably the most remarkable and certainly the most prominent of the many North American Pentecostal women involved in church leadership was the colourful and controversial Aimee Semple McPherson (1890–1944), founder of the ICFG in 1927, another 'Finished Work' denomination. Born into a Canadian Salvation Army family, she became a Pentecostal in 1907 and was ordained by William Durham with her evangelist husband Robert Semple in 1909, first to accompany Durham on his preaching tours and then to go to Hong Kong as missionaries in 1910. When Semple died of malaria after two months in Hong Kong, his twenty-year-old widow Aimee returned to Los Angeles, remarried Harold McPherson in 1911 and began an ecumenical, interdenominational preaching and healing career of the 'Foursquare Gospel' (Christ the Saviour, Baptizer in the Holy Spirit, Healer and Coming King). In mass meetings all over the country, she used bold and innovative methods including flamboyant advertising techniques, showering handbills from an aeroplane, driving a 'gospel auto' on which slogans were painted, using dramatic illustrations in her partially acted sermons, and becoming the first woman to preach on the radio. 'Sister Aimee', as she was known, was an enormously talented public speaker, writer, musician and administrator, and a media star. She was ordained in the AG in 1919, but left in 1922 over the question of ownership of church property. She and McPherson were divorced in 1921. In 1923 she opened a 5,300 seat building in Los Angeles called Angelus Temple with red carpets and provision for two large choirs and an orchestra, a building still in use and recently (2001) renovated. She opposed racism, fought against crime and poverty, encouraged women to enter the ministry, and began a crusade against drug trafficking that resulted in her disappearance through kidnapping to Mexico in 1926 and her spectacular reappearance a month later – an event shrouded in controversy and great media publicity. Even

---

[28] W. E. Warner, 'Pentecostal Church of God', *NIDPCM*, pp. 965–6.

her death in 1944 of an overdose of a medical prescription was controversial. She left behind a membership of 22,000 in over four hundred churches and two hundred overseas mission stations, and a Bible college founded in 1923 that had trained 3,000 preachers. Aimee McPherson was the prototype of a new kind of US American Pentecostalism that was able to use and adapt the prevailing popular culture of its day for its own purposes. Aimee's son, Rolf McPherson (1913–) took over as president of the ICFG, a post he held until 1988. During his time in office the church continued to expand throughout the world and has become one of the fastest growing Pentecostal denominations. Large ICFG congregations like Angelus Temple and the Church on the Way led by Jack Hayford have continued their founder's vision of changing with the times, especially in adapting to the challenge of the rapidly growing new Charismatic churches with their modern worship styles. It joined the NAE in 1952, and it has maintained its founder's commitment to mission, helping the poor, disaster relief, and the ministry of women. Over 40 per cent of the ICFG's ministers today are women, probably a higher proportion than any other Pentecostal denomination.[29]

GLOBAL EXPANSION AND HEALING EVANGELISTS

Charles Parham, William Seymour and many of the first North American Pentecostals believed that they had been given foreign languages through Spirit baptism so that they could preach the gospel throughout the world. Hundreds did just that. The first North American missionaries that went out only five months after the Azusa Street revival had begun were self-supporting, and the majority were women. Alfred and Lillian Garr, the first white pastors to be baptized in the Spirit at Azusa Street, believed they had spoken in Bengali and left Los Angeles for India, arriving in Calcutta in 1907. Although they were disillusioned about their language abilities, they persevered, and were invited to conduct services in a Baptist church there and a Pentecostal revival began. Quite independently of this event and eight kilometres away, a revival broke out in a girls' orphanage run by Fanny Simpson, a Methodist missionary from Boston, who was thereupon dismissed and sent back to the USA. She returned to India as a Pentecostal missionary in 1920 and set up another orphanage in Purulia. The Garrs went on to minister for a short time in Hong Kong before returning to pastor a church in the USA. African American evangelist Lucy Farrow was also

---

[29] C. M. Robeck, Jr., 'International Church of the Foursquare Gospel', 'McPherson, Aimee Semple', *NIDPCM*, pp. 793–4, 856–9.

one of the first missionaries from Azusa Street, arriving in Liberia in 1907. Also from Azusa Street, Canadian evangelist and former elder in Dowie's Zion City, John G. Lake, travelled to South Africa in 1908 with Thomas Hezmalhalch and established the Apostolic Faith Mission there. Others left for the Bahamas in 1910 and for British East Africa in 1911. Kathleen Miller and Lucy James left for India from Britain under the Pentecostal Missionary Union in 1909, followed by four others a year later, one of whom, John Beruldsen, spent thirty-five years in North China. Pentecostal phenomena broke out in a missionary convention in Taochow, China in 1912 when William Simpson (1869–1961), missionary in China and Tibet from 1892–1949, became a Pentecostal. Simpson travelled throughout China, much of the time by foot, assisted in the training of Chinese ministers, and became one of the best-known missionaries in Pentecostalism. Another well-known pioneer Pentecostal missionary was H. A. Baker (1881–1971), missionary to Tibet and China from 1912–50 and in Taiwan for sixteen years until his death in 1971. He worked among tribal peoples and established an orphanage in Yunnan. In 1909 the Pentecostal message was taken from Chicago to Italian communities in Argentina and Brazil by Luigi Francescon, and in 1910 two Swedish immigrants influenced by Durham in Chicago, Gunnar Vingren and Daniel Berg, began what became the AG in Brazil, now the largest non-Catholic denomination in Latin America and the largest AG in any nation. These events will be discussed in the next chapter.[30]

Healing was part of the 'foursquare' or 'fivefold' gospel, and healing evangelists have always been part of the Pentecostal movement, from Maria Woodworth-Etter, John G. Lake and Aimee Semple McPherson in the earlier years of the movement to Kathryn Kuhlman in the 1960s and 1970s, and to Benny Hinn and German evangelist Reinhard Bonnke in the 1980s and 1990s. The healing campaigns of North American evangelists, which contributed to the growth of western forms of Pentecostalism in many parts of the world, developed after the Second World War and had their peak in the 1950s. At first, the evangelists enjoyed support from most Pentecostal denominations. Leading independent healing evangelists at this time were William Branham (1909–65), T. L. Osborne (1923–), Oral Roberts (1918–) and Tommy Hicks (1909–73), and remarkable healings and miracles were reported in their campaigns. First Branham and then Roberts were probably the best known and most widely travelled. Branham's sensational healing services, which began in 1946, are well documented and he was the

---

[30] Entries: 'Baker, H. A.'; 'Farrow, Lucy F.'; 'Garr, Alfred Goodrich, Sr.'; 'Simpson, William Wallace'; *NIDPCM*, pp. 352, 632–3, 660–1, 1070–1.

pacesetter for those who followed before he became involved in doctrinal controversies. Hicks was responsible for a revival in Argentina in 1954 resulting in accelerated growth among Pentecostal churches there. Osborne had large crowds at his crusades in Central America and the Caribbean, Indonesia and East Africa. By 1960, Oral Roberts had become the leading healing evangelist, increasingly accepted by 'mainline' denominations, and one of the most influential Pentecostals in the emergence of the Charismatic movement.[31] His moving from the PHC to the United Methodist Church in 1969 marked the end of the relationship that had existed between healing evangelists and denominational Pentecostals, who were becoming increasingly critical of the evangelists' methods (particularly their fundraising) and often lavish lifestyles. Sometimes the emphasis on the 'miraculous' has led to shameful showmanship and moral decadence, exaggerated and unsubstantiated claims of healing, and a triumphalism that betrays the humility of the cross.

Hispanic Pentecostalism is undoubtedly the fastest growing form of Pentecostalism in the USA today, with some 20 per cent of Hispanics found in Pentecostal churches, some six million people. The larger Pentecostal denominations, especially the AG and the CGC, have substantial Hispanic congregations and Hispanics also constitute a tenth of the Anglo congregations in the AG. About a third of Hispanic Pentecostals belong to ethnic denominations founded by Latinos either in the USA or those that have been imported from Latin America. The largest of these are the Puerto Rican denomination Iglesia de Dios Pentecostal (Pentecostal Church of God) and the Mexican Oneness denomination Asamblea Apóstolica de la Fe en Cristo Jesús (Apostolic Assembly of the Faith in Christ Jesus). Hispanic congregations often have a large majority of women and children in attendance and consist of marginalized people from the lower strata of US society. Churches are planted by Hispanics on their own initiative, even when they are within established Anglo-dominated denominations. Like Pentecostals everywhere, they have been subject to the ravages of fission, racism and diversity. But they have been in the forefront of social concern and community enhancing projects. Their increasing numbers, improving economic status and political power in society make them a force to be reckoned with in the changing face of North American Pentecostalism.[32]

---

[31] Entries: 'Branham, William Marrion'; 'Hicks, Tommy'; 'Osborne, Tommy Lee'; 'Roberts, Granville Oral'; *NIDPCM*, pp. 440–1, 713, 950–1, 1024–5.
[32] E. A. Wilson and J. Miranda, 'Hispanic Pentecostalism', *NIDPCM*, pp. 715–23.

In its beginnings, Pentecostalism in the western world was an ecumenical movement of people claiming a common experience rather than a common doctrine. But we have traced some of the main doctrinal and administrative differences that soon began to appear in different Pentecostal groups in the USA. Leaders became concerned over the apparent decline in the movement there at the same time that great expansion was taking place in many other parts of the world. After the demise of Parham, Seymour and other early leaders also lost influence, and Pentecostalism was no longer centred in Los Angeles with any one particular leader, although it continued to have its impetus in the 'Sunbelt' states. Denominations like the AG and different Church of God groups began to arise. The distinct and central teaching of most of these Pentecostals that speaking in tongues was the 'initial evidence' of Holy Spirit baptism alienated them and brought fierce opposition from other Christian churches. In particular, Holiness and emerging fundamentalist groups from which Pentecostalism had come derided what they termed the 'tongues movement' as 'Satanic', 'heresy' and 'sorcery'.[33] But within Pentecostal groups themselves there was antagonism and controversy that continued for many years, including differences over the 'initial evidence' doctrine. Most (but not all) Pentecostal groups baptized believers by immersion, but differed on the methods and formulae of such baptism, which eventually resulted in more serious doctrinal differences, particularly the Oneness schism.

William Faupel has identified four interrelated terms used by early North American Pentecostals to refer to themselves, which together describe the essence of early Pentecostalism: (1) *Full Gospel*, which included the five (or four) cardinal doctrines of justification, sanctification (for Holiness Pentecostals), healing, the second coming (usually premillennialism) and Spirit baptism, usually believed to be evidenced by speaking in tongues; (2) the *Latter Rain*, a dispensational philosophy that believed in the restoration of the 'lost' power of the Spirit at what was now seen as the culmination of salvation history; (3) *Apostolic Faith*, a sharpened view of seeing Pentecostalism as a movement of restoration of apostolic doctrine: the 'full gospel'; apostolic power: gifts of the Spirit and 'signs and wonders'; apostolic authority: the 'gift ministries' of apostles, prophets, evangelists, pastors and teachers; and apostolic practice: restoring a New Testament church based on the model of the church in the book of Acts. Finally, the term

---

[33] Wacker, *Heaven Below*, p. 44.

that has gained ascendancy over the others: (4) *Pentecostal*, with a twofold significance: the dispensational aspect, whereby the Pentecostal experience is seen as the inauguration of a new era; and the spiritual aspect, whereby Pentecost is both an event and a lifestyle to be repeated in the experiences of believers.

The strengths of this early North American Pentecostalism included two things in particular. First, the eschatological message of hope offered by the Azusa Street mission was particularly important for people displaced and disillusioned by poverty. William Seymour's message that this was the climax of history, with 'signs and wonders to prove it' gave hope to a people downtrodden and marginalized. Second, the unusual racial inclusiveness in a time when the USA was sharply and increasingly becoming a segregated society was in itself an astounding achievement. Frank Bartleman exclaimed, 'The color line was washed away by the blood'. Not only did blacks and whites mix freely at Azusa Street; so did Hispanics and other ethnic minorities. Seymour's vision of Pentecost breaking down human barriers was significantly different from Parham's because it was based on his black experience. Not only did he encourage people to remain in their churches after they had received Spirit baptism, but he saw the Pentecostal experience as that which dissolved distinctions of race, class and gender and created one common family. Seymour was greatly disturbed when divisions began to appear in the movement, because of his ecumenical vision.[34] Harvey Cox describes the many different ecstatic experiences characteristic of the reports of early Pentecostalism ('signs and wonders tumbling out of the pages'), and says that these experiences of Spirit baptism were 'not just an initiation rite' but a 'mystical encounter' in which Pentecostals were convinced that they were already living in 'a whole new epoch in history'. Cox says that the essence of Pentecostalism cannot be understood through 'dogma and doctrines' but through the experience of God, a 'narrative theology whose central expression is the testimony'. He thinks that this emphasis on experience is 'so total it shatters the cognitive packaging'.[35]

But early Pentecostalism had many weaknesses, including the fact that when the expected 'last days' did not occur, people were left struggling with the realities of a harsh world. Internal divisiveness soon occurred, beginning with an attack on Seymour from Parham, then from Crawford and Durham, but which paradoxically ultimately stimulated further growth. As Cox put it, 'the more they fought, the more they multiplied', and the movement

[34] Faupel, *Everlasting Gospel*, pp. 28–41, 198, 208.   [35] Cox, *Fire*, pp. 58, 68–71.

thrived on division as much as it did on opposition.[36] The main reason for the split between Parham and Seymour was Parham's opposition to both the ecstatic manifestations at Azusa Street and the inter-racial mingling. Faupel thinks that the paternalistic Parham failed to understand the expressions of black spirituality and disagreed with Seymour's understanding of Spirit baptism that encouraged emotionalism and ecstatic phenomena, and included the dimension of racial equality in the family of God.[37] Although blatant racism was more clearly evident in Parham's later years, accounts of his immediate reaction to the Azusa Street revival and his treatment of Seymour show his racism to be already obvious. His Anglo-Israelism was incipiently racist to the core, and he had absorbed this from Sandford much earlier than 1906. The divisions within Pentecostalism that began after his clash with Seymour were to become a feature of the movement from that time onwards, all over the world.

In North America, Pentecostals started as a reaction against dogma and creeds, but were soon engaged in doctrinal haggling, as subsequent history was to prove. The fact that the Pentecostals were isolated, rejected and ridiculed by established churches, especially by fundamentalists, eventually resulted in an anti-ecumenical attitude. These Pentecostals saw no reason to co-operate with what they perceived as the old and corrupt churches that had ridiculed them. At the forefront of this attack were leading contemporary fundamentalist preachers like Benjamin Warfield, Henry Ironside and Campbell Morgan, who reportedly called Pentecostals 'the last vomit of Satan'.[38] Nevertheless, the early Pentecostal movement expanded rapidly and Cox suggests that this was because of its heady and spontaneous spirituality, 'like the spread of a salubrious contagion'. It touched people emotionally, and its emphasis on experience was spread through testimony and personal contact. He warns, however, that the Pentecostal movement in the USA 'might lose touch completely with its humble origins and become the righteous spiritual ideology of an affluent middle class'.[39] This is a warning that must be taken seriously in the richest and most powerful nation on earth for if unheeded, Pentecostalism there might no longer be a movement following the example of Christ.

---

[36] Ibid., p. 77.   [37] Faupel, *Everlasting Gospel*, pp. 209–12.
[38] Anderson, *Vision*, p. 193; Cox, *Fire*, pp. 61, 74–5.   [39] Cox, *Fire*, pp. 71, 297.

4

Pentecostalism in Latin America and the Caribbean

The growth of Pentecostalism in Latin America has been one of the most remarkable stories in the history of Christianity. Pentecostalism in this region (as elsewhere in the world) is extremely diverse with many schisms, and any assessment must beware of making generalizations. Statistics are imprecise and vary enormously between the different sources – but it is quite possible that half of the classical Pentecostals in the world are found in Latin America. Statisticians Barrett and Johnson estimated that there were 141 million Latin American Pentecostals/Charismatics/Neo-Pentecostals in 2000, half of whom were in Brazil.[1] This is a higher number than in any other continent, although Africa and Asia are not far behind. According to present growth rates, some Latin American countries could have a majority of 'evangelicals' (mostly Pentecostals) by 2010. Scholars recognize this as a mass popular movement that is transforming the religious landscape of the region, a viable religious alternative for those seeking security in the face of an uncertain socio-economic future. The success of Pentecostalism has been threatening for the Roman Catholic Church, whose traditional dominance in Latin America is weakening. Pope John Paul II warned against the 'invasion of the sects' and the 'ravenous wolves' that were threatening the Catholic hold – yet Pentecostalism, more than Catholicism, is fundamentally a Latin American phenomenon. Recent studies show that Catholicism has proportionately far more foreign priests in Latin America (an astonishing 94 per cent in Venezuela) than Pentecostal churches have foreign missionaries.[2]

Some Pentecostal denominations were established in Latin America several years before the major ones in the USA were founded from which they are sometimes erroneously presumed to have emerged. The origins of Latin American Pentecostalism took place at a time when North American

---

[1] D. B. Barrett and T. M. Johnson, 'Global Statistics', *NIDPCM*, p. 287.
[2] E. A. Wilson, 'Latin America (Survey)', *NIDPCM*, pp. 157–8; Cox, *Fire*, p. 168.

Pentecostalism was still emerging. The movement in the South, therefore, is distinctly different from that of the North, and we should not regard it as a North American creation or importation. This is particularly true of the countries of Chile, Argentina and Brazil, which together account for some two thirds of all Pentecostals in this region. There is more North American involvement and influence in Pentecostalism in Central America and the Caribbean. Their geographical proximity to the USA makes this inevitable; but even here, there are many characteristics and emphases that have formed in these particular contexts that are distinct from North American forms of Pentecostalism. The diversity and schismatic fragmentation of Pentecostal groups make it difficult, if not impossible to categorize Pentecostalism in Latin America, and categories created in the North simply will not fit.

CHILEAN PENTECOSTALISM

The first Pentecostals in Latin America were Chileans. Their origins are associated with Willis Collins Hoover (1858–1936), a US American revivalist minister in Valparaiso, a former medical doctor who had been in Chile since 1889, pastor of the largest Methodist congregation in Chile and a district superintendent. In 1907, the Hoovers learned of the Pentecostal revival taking place in the home for young widows of Pandita Ramabai, in Pune, India through a former classmate in Chicago of Mrs Hoover, Minnie Abrams, who sent them her pamphlet *The Baptism of the Holy Ghost and Fire.* The Hoovers corresponded with Abrams and others, including Thomas B. Barratt, Methodist pioneer of Pentecostalism in Europe, about the revivals taking place in various parts of the world. The Valparaiso church was stirred to pray for and expect such a Holy Spirit revival until April 1909, when it happened. Then many unusual and ecstatic manifestations occurred, including weeping, laughing uncontrollably, groaning, prostration, rolling on the floor, people repenting and confessing sin (more than two hundred conversions in a year), seeing revelatory visions, singing and speaking in tongues.[3] Those baptized in the Spirit felt compelled to rush out onto the streets to tell of their experiences, and together with the noise generated, there was a hostile reaction from the authorities, the local press and eventually the Methodist Church itself. In Santiago, some of the revivalists were arrested, including a young woman from Valparaiso,

[3] Willis Collins Hoover, *History of the Pentecostal Revival in Chile* (Santiago, Chile: Imprenta Eben-Ezer, 2000), pp. 9, 18–20, 29–32, 36, 68–73.

Nellie (Elena) Laidlaw, who had been refused permission to prophesy in two Santiago Methodist churches. Spirit baptized Methodists were asked to leave their congregations and they began holding meetings in their homes. In 1910, the Methodist Conference (which met in Hoover's own Valparaiso church building in the presence of his members) charged Hoover with conduct that was 'scandalous' and 'imprudent', and with propagating teachings that were 'false and anti-Methodist . . . contrary to the Scriptures and irrational'. Reminiscent of Parham's denunciation of the Azusa Street revival, the manifestations of this revival were derided as being 'offensive to decency and morals' and involving 'hypnotism'.[4]

Hoover was removed as district superintendent and he agreed to travel to the New York headquarters. But he then realized that he could not leave Chile at this crucial time, which he told the bishop the next day. He was told that either he had to leave Chile or leave the church. In the meantime, the Santiago revivalists had decided to form a new church called the Iglesia Metodista Nacional (National Methodist Church) and the Valparaiso congregation officials and two-thirds of its members joined them. Hoover finally resigned from the Methodist Episcopal Church in April 1910, stating that he was not separating himself either from Wesley or from Methodism. He was invited to become superintendent of the new church, whose name he suggested be changed to Iglesia Metodista Pentecostal, the Methodist Pentecostal Church (MPC), to make it clear that the division did not come out of nationalism. To the present day, the MPC has maintained its Methodist doctrines and practices, including infant baptism and other Methodist (episcopal) structures.[5] This closeness to Methodism differentiates Chilean Pentecostalism from classical Pentecostalism from North America. Significantly, the Chilean movement was not connected to North American Pentecostalism and Hoover became founder of an autochthonous Chilean church. In addition, Chilean Pentecostalism did not follow North American Pentecostalism's doctrine of 'initial evidence', but since Hoover's time it has seen speaking in tongues as one of many of the manifestations of Spirit baptism. Hoover later resigned from the MPC in 1933 over the question of leadership and the use of popular music and guitars in the church (Hoover opposed these).[6] Manuel

---

[4] D. D. Bundy, 'Hoover, Willis Collins', *NIDPCM*, pp. 770–1; Edward L. Cleary and Juan Sepúlveda, 'Chilean Pentecostalism: Coming of Age', E. L. Cleary and H. W. Stewart-Gambino (eds.), *Power, Politics and Pentecostals in Latin America* (Boulder, CO: Westview Press, 1997), pp. 99–100, 112.

[5] Hoover, *History*, pp. 74–100, 240–7.

[6] Juan Sepúlveda, 'Indigenous Pentecostalism and the Chilean Experience', Anderson and Hollenweger, *Pentecostals After a Century*, pp. 116–17, 132.

Figure 4. Willis C. Hoover, Valparaiso, Chile, c. 1910.

Umaña Salinas became General Superintendent, a post he held until his death in 1964 (his title changing to 'Bishop' in 1950). Umaña had been a leader in the original Santiago church forced out of the Methodist Church in 1910, and had been its pastor since 1911. The Santiago congregation was soon the largest in the MPC, and in 1928 it moved to Jotabeche. After Hoover's death in 1936 his supporters formed the Iglesia Evangélica Pentecostal (EPC, Evangelical Pentecostal Church), the first of many subsequent schisms.

There are now over thirty Pentecostal denominations deriving from the MPC forming some 95 per cent of the Protestants in Chile, which have at least a thousand other denominations. The MPC and the EPC are the two largest, followed by the Iglesia Pentecostal de Chile (PCC, Pentecostal Church of Chile), accounting together for over a million Christians in 2000, while the original Methodist Church had thirty thousand.[7] The PCC was formed after a schism in the MPC in 1946. The PCC and the smaller Misión Iglesia Pentecostal, which split from the EPC in 1952, joined the WCC in 1961, the first Pentecostal churches ever to do so. The MPC entered into a 'fraternal relationship' with the IPHC in the USA in 1967, based on their common Holiness (Wesleyan) and Pentecostal heritage. The Jotabeche Cathedral in Santiago under Pastor Javier Vásquez Valencia since 1965, with some 80,000 members in 1999 is the MPC's biggest congregation and one of the largest in the world. The Chilean dictator Augusto Pinochet officially opened this edifice in September 1975, and a 'Protestant Te Deum' followed the opening. A few months earlier Vásquez with 2,500 other evangelical leaders had placed an advertisement in the national newspaper supporting the Pinochet regime. Vásquez has been presiding Bishop of the MPC since 1982. Questions have been raised about the MPC leaders' friendly relationship with the Pinochet government, as Pinochet's presence at Pentecostal functions in the face of Catholic opposition seemed to legitimize his repressive regime. But the vast majority of Pentecostal members in Chile represent the lower, working classes and did not follow their leaders' example; most of them opposed Pinochet and supported the popular, socialist politics of Salvador Allende before his overthrow in 1973. Young Pentecostals who later resisted Pinochet's regime were harassed, tortured and even killed. Pentecostal churches in the WCC like the PCC were particularly targeted for persecution by the military junta.[8]

Both the MPC and the EPC have established work in neighbouring Argentina and Bolivia. Pentecostals in Chile have been especially successful in reaching the Amerindian tribes of the Mapuche (in the south) and the Aymara (in the north), who have joined Pentecostal churches in their thousands. Chilean Pentecostal churches, together with African independent churches, were among the first churches in the Majority World in the twentieth century to flourish without any assistance from western agencies. Chilean Pentecostal churches were also the first Pentecostal groups ever to join the WCC, although the largest ones remain aloof.[9]

[7] Johnstone and Mandryk, *Operation World*, p. 156.   [8] D. D. Bundy, 'Chile', *NIDPCM*, pp. 55–7.
[9] Cox, *Fire*, p. 170; Mike Berg and Paul Pretiz, *Spontaneous Combustion: Grass-Roots Christianity, Latin American Style* (Pasadena, CA: William Carey Library, 1996), pp. 83–4.

Pentecostalism arrived in Argentina early in 1909, the first western mission-aries being Berger Johnson from Norway and Alice Wood from Canada. Italian Pentecostals from Chicago, Luigi Francescon, Giácomo Lombardi and Lucía Menna followed them in the same year and founded the Iglesia Asamblea Cristiana (Christian Assembly Church) among Italian immi-grants. Swedish Pentecostal missionaries from the Swedish Free Mission began work in Argentina in 1920, and today their Assemblies of God (not connected to the AG, USA) is perhaps the largest Pentecostal denomina-tion in the country. The second largest, Unión des las Asambleas de Dios, was formed in 1948 through a merger of the churches of the AG (USA), the PAC and a few smaller organizations.[10] David Martin has contrasted the early growth of Protestantism in Chile with that of Argentina until 1930. In Argentina, Protestant churches increased as a result of immigra-tion from Europe and were fundamentally European in character. In Chile the situation was entirely different, as there was no large-scale immigra-tion from Europe and autochthonous Pentecostal churches grew by con-versions, as working class Chileans evangelized their own people in large cities.[11] The situation began to change in Argentina after the 1954 cam-paign of USA evangelist Tommy Hicks with the patronage of President Juan Perón and the Argentine authorities. Pentecostal churches began to grow slowly thereafter. In the late 1960s a Charismatic movement in the established churches began, and one of its main leaders was Juan Carlos Ortiz (a former AG pastor), whose books on radical discipleship became international bestsellers. In 1962, a Pentecostal mass revival among the Toba, one of Argentina's minority Amerindian peoples, led to the formation of an autochthonous Toba church, the Iglesia Evangélica Unia Toba. This church and one of the larger Pentecostal churches, the Church of God in Argentina, led by Dr Gabriel Viccaro, are members of the WCC.

Argentinean Pentecostalism made its most rapid progress in the 1990s, and by 2000 had 3.5 million or 9 per cent of the population, compared with Chile's 1.8 million or 12 per cent of the population, according to one source. These recent statistics suggest that the proportion of 'Charismatics' in the population of Chile is about 24 per cent and that of Argentina 19 per cent. Pentecostal churches are rapidly expanding in Argentina. There are

[10] D. D. Bundy, 'Argentina', *NIDPCM*, pp. 23–5; Johnstone and Mandryk, *Operation World*, pp. 77, 156.
[11] David Martin, *Tongues of Fire: The Explosion of Protestantism in Latin America* (Oxford: Basil Blackwell, 1990), p. 76.

over a million AG members. New Pentecostal and Charismatic churches have more recently arisen, like Omar Cabrera's Visión del Futuro (Vision of the Future) with 112,000 people in 300 centres in 2000. Cabrera began this work in 1972 and focuses on the need for afflicted people to be healed, delivered from demons and protected by angels. Visión del Futuro also has social outreaches and support for destitute children and abused women, although his organization has become increasingly middle class. Cabrera wears a clerical collar and a bishop's purple vest, unusual among Latin American Pentecostals. Héctor Giménez's Ondas de Amor y Paz (Waves of Love and Peace) with 340,000 affiliates, concentrates more on the lower and underprivileged classes and had one of the largest Christian congregations in the world. Giménez, a former drug addict, began this church in 1986, and by 2000 it had over 300 preaching centres in Argentina, and abroad in Uruguay, Brazil, Chile and the USA. In 1998 Giménez was involved in controversy over financial and moral irregularities and has been disowned by other Pentecostals. Perhaps the highest profile Argentine Pentecostal is the evangelist Carlos Annacondia, whose big tent campaigns since 1981 calling people to conversion, healing and exorcism have taken him all over the country and internationally. His organization is known as Mensaje de Salvación (Message of Salvation). Another high profile Pentecostal pastor, Claudio Freidzon is an example of a new Pentecostal who remains within a classical Pentecostal denomination, the (Union) AG, but whose Rey de Reyes (King of Kings) operates as a separate organization with hundreds of relating churches.[12]

BRAZILIAN PENTECOSTALISM

Brazil has one of the highest numbers of Pentecostals in the world. In a survey conducted in greater Rio de Janeiro, 61 per cent of all churches (congregations) in the city were Pentecostal and 710 new churches had been founded between 1990 and 1992, 91 per cent of which were Pentecostal – in contrast, one new Catholic parish was formed in this period. There are probably more Pentecostals in church on Sundays throughout Brazil than Catholics, and more Pentecostal pastors (all Brazilians) than Catholic priests, who are often foreigners.[13] The growth of Pentecostalism must also be seen in the light of the significance of Brazilian spiritism. Movements

[12] Berg and Pretiz, *Spontaneous Combustion*, pp. 92–7; Cleary and Sepúlveda, 'Chilean Pentecostalism', pp. 106, 110.
[13] Phillip Berryman, *Religion in the Megacity: Catholic and Protestant Portraits from Latin America* (New York: Orbis, 1996), pp. 26, 42.

like Umbanda (the largest), Candomblé and Macumba (with more African elements) have combined European (Kardecian) spiritualism with West African and Amerindian traditional religion to create something uniquely Brazilian. Estimates are that some 60 per cent of Brazil's population is involved in some form of spiritualism. Pentecostals, who accept the reality of the popular spirit world, are diametrically opposed to this and routinely exorcize Umbanda and other Brazilian 'demons' from their converts.

The two earliest forms of Pentecostalism in Brazil have their roots in the Chicago ministry of William Durham, who had prophesied that his associate since 1907, Luigi Francescon (1866–1964), a former Waldensian, would preach the Pentecostal message to Italian people. Francescon established Italian congregations throughout the USA and in Argentina in 1909. In 1910, he went to São Paulo to begin work among the large Italian community there, at the time more than a million strong. He preached on the baptism in the Spirit to Italian Presbyterians and was expelled from the church. The result was the formation of a Pentecostal denomination, Congregacioni Christiani (the Italian name), the first Pentecostal church in Brazil. In about 1935 it began to adopt Portuguese in its services and to attract native Brazilians, and is now known by its Portuguese name as Congregação Cristã (Christian Congregation, CC).[14] In 2000 the CC had some 1.4 million affiliates (some say over two million), the second largest Pentecostal denomination in the country.[15] Unlike other Brazilian Pentecostal churches, the CC uses elders and deacons ('co-operators') instead of a full-time ordained ministry, has no prepared sermons (the leader will ask if anyone in the congregation has a message), does not insist on a tithe, take offerings or ask for money from members, does not engage in street preaching nor publicize itself by printed matter or radio programmes – which makes its growth the more remarkable. Men and women are separated in worship, women wear head coverings (but are allowed jewellery and make-up), prayers are said kneeling, and testimonies given at the front of the church are encouraged – although the liturgy in the CC is much more formal and subdued than in most Brazilian Pentecostal churches. The three-time repetition of the exclamation 'Gloria!' ('Glory!') has earned members the nickname 'Glorias'. The church has a weekly distribution of financial and practical help to members in need. Although its main concentration is in São Paulo, the CC has spread to other parts of Brazil, Argentina,

---

[14] Hollenweger, *The Pentecostals*, pp. 85–92; Cox, *Fire*, pp. 168, 175.
[15] Johnstone and Mandryk, *Operation World*, p. 120.

Chile and Bolivia, and has sent missionaries to Italy and Portugal. It has a rigid conservative morality and dress code, stresses family relationships, and because it does not associate with other churches it gives the impression that it regards itself as the only true church.[16]

The Assembléias de Deus (Assemblies of God, AG) in Brazil is today the largest Protestant church in Latin America, with over four million affiliates in 2000 (some say five to eight million), among the forty million Brazilian 'Charismatics' that form 23 per cent of the total population.[17] The formation of the AG began with two Swedish immigrants to the USA, Gunnar Vingren and Daniel Berg, associated with William Durham and a related Swedish Pentecostal church in Chicago. Vingren, a Baptist pastor in South Bend, Indiana and Berg received separate prophecies that they should go to 'Pará'. When they discovered where that was, they went to Belém in the northern Brazilian state of Pará in 1910, the same year that Francescon had gone to São Paulo. Unable to speak Portuguese, they began prayer meetings in the cellar of a Baptist church pastored by a Swedish missionary, and they waited for revival. Some received Spirit baptism and began evangelism in their neighbourhood. A group of eighteen, a majority of members, was expelled from the Baptist church in June 1911 and Vingren became their pastor. The resulting church was first called the Apostolic Faith Mission but registered in 1918 as the Assembléia de Deus (Assembly of God). The church grew rapidly, particularly through its practice of prayer for healing. Vingren left Brazil in 1932 with stomach cancer and the work quickly became autochthonous. Brazilian Pentecostals from Belém began evangelizing the Amazonas region, sent missionaries to Portugal in 1913 and spread to the big cities of Recife, Rio de Janeiro, São Paulo and Pôrto Alegre. They emphasized healing and establishing churches in cities, which experienced remarkable growth. In São Paulo 10,000 converts a year were baptized and the city now has a thousand AG congregations.[18]

In 1930 the AG headquarters transferred from Belém to Rio de Janeiro, the Swedish leaders handed over to Brazilians (although the 'pastor-president' was Swedish until 1950), and the AG became a national church independent of foreign missions. The church spread to every state in Brazil,

---

[16] R. Andrew Chesnut, *Born Again in Brazil: The Pentecostal Boom and the Pathogens of Poverty* (New Brunswick: Rutgers University Press, 1997), p. 30; Berg and Pretiz, *Spontaneous Combustion*, pp. 85–8.

[17] Johnstone and Mandryk, *Operation World*, p. 120.

[18] Hollenweger, *The Pentecostals*, pp. 75, 78; Chesnut, *Born Again*, pp. 26–7; Berryman, *Religion in the Megacity*, p. 22; Cox, *Fire*, pp. 163–7.

an autochthonous movement with no support of finance or personnel from the USA or anywhere else (apart from Vingren's early support from the USA and Sweden). The church considers itself an independent church within the worldwide AG fellowship of churches. Members were recruited initially from the lower strata of society, and Pentecostalism appealed to black, mixed race and Amerindian Brazilians. Mulattos (mixed race African and European) are still the majority in the AG – and there are more black Brazilians in Pentecostal churches than in any other denomination. The AG has education and literacy programmes for members, provident funds for unmarried mothers, the sick and the orphaned; abundant printed literature from their own publishing house, and community projects like community centres, factories, schools, hospitals, old age homes, libraries and day nurseries. Until 1952 the AG and the CC were the only significant Pentecostal denominations in Brazil.[19] All that was to change dramatically.

It is estimated that a second phase of twenty to thirty new Brazilian Pentecostal denominations arose during the 1950s (the so-called 'modern' phase), the most important being the third largest Pentecostal church Igreja Evangélica Pentecostal 'Brasil para Cristo' (BFC, Brazil for Christ Evangelical Pentecostal Church), the Igreja Pentecostal Deus É Amor (God is Love Pentecostal Church) and the Igreja do Evangelho Quadrangular (Foursquare Gospel Church). The Foursquare Gospel Church was founded in 1955 as a result of a tent campaign by North American healing evangelists from Aimee McPherson's church in Los Angeles led by Harold Williams, a former Hollywood actor. The church now has more members in Brazil than it has in the USA and significantly, more than a third of its pastors are women. Brazil for Christ was also commenced in 1955, the first major Pentecostal church to be founded by a Brazilian, former AG evangelist and member of Williams' tent campaign, Manoel de Mello. De Mello was well known for miraculous healings in meetings, with Brazilian folk music as a medium. His congregation in São Paulo built a new temple that was razed to the ground by a demolition crew (it is thought on government orders). It was rebuilt into what may be the largest church building in the continent, with crowds of 30,000 attending on occasions. By 2000 BFC had some 1.2 million affiliates in 4,500 congregations.[20] BFC developed good relations with other churches and Catholic Charismatics, and became a

---

[19] Chesnut, *Born Again*, p. 30; Berryman, *Religion in the Megacity*, p. 17.
[20] Johnson and Mandryk, *Operation World*, p. 120.

member of the WCC in 1969. Besides the attraction of its enormous and lavish headquarters temple, it became known for its use of modern communications and its participation in national politics, thus also attracting the middle class. On the death of Manoel de Mello in 1970 his son Paul Lutero de Mello became leader of the church, eventually withdrawing BFC's membership of the WCC. He began a Bible college and took the church into a more revivalist emphasis with weekly healing services. BFC sees speaking in tongues as only one of the signs of the receiving of the Spirit.

God is Love Church is another vigorous Brazilian movement founded in São Paulo in 1962 by a 26-year-old preacher from BFC, Manoel de Mello's brother-in-law David Miranda, with an estimated 600,000 members by 2000. This church also emphasizes healing and exorcism, consists largely of poor and unschooled blacks or mulattos, has detailed and highly restrictive rules for its members, and has planted churches throughout Latin America. Brazilian Pentecostals in general, but in particular BFC, God is Love and the UCKG (below) have received considerable attention because of their sociological and political significance.[21]

After about 1975, a third type of Pentecostal movement began in what sociologists call the 'postmodern' era, by far the largest being the Igreja Universal do Reino de Deus (UCKG, Universal Church of the Kingdom of God), with over 2,000 congregations in Brazil. This is a prosperity-oriented healing and deliverance movement founded in 1977 in Rio de Janeiro by Bishop Edir Macedo, a former state lottery official. By the early 1990s the UCKG was the fastest growing church in Brazil with 1,000 churches, some estimate well over a million members (some suggest many more), a television station costing 45 million US dollars (now the third largest TV network in the country), about 30 radio stations, a newspaper, highly entrepreneurial business dealings, a political party participating in national politics and a 'Cathedral of Faith' seating 10,000 worshippers in Rio de Janeiro. The UCKG emphasizes healing, prosperity, collective exorcisms from Umbanda spirits and other demons from Brazilian popular spiritualism and a dramatic display of the power of the Holy Spirit. Members, who are mostly poor people, are encouraged to bring cash to church in order to receive the blessings of God. Holy oils, anointed handkerchiefs, fig paste, water from the Jordan River and other sacred objects are sold as healing accessories. Different coloured flowers, particularly roses, are used

---

[21] Martin, *Tongues of Fire*, p. 66; Chesnut, *Born Again*, pp. 35–8; Berg and Pretiz, *Spontaneous Combustion*, pp. 101–9.

to symbolize prosperity (yellow) and health (red). Macedo himself is one of the most controversial religious leaders in Brazil. He emphasizes giving money to the church, attacks all forms of theology and draws large crowds to stadiums. He is accused by other church leaders of getting rich at the expense of believers, of running the church like a highly organized business, and bringing disgrace to the whole Protestant church. He has been arrested and imprisoned in 1992 for illegal financial dealings and in 1995 he created controversy when he kicked an image of the patron saint of Brazil on his own TV programme. He has rejected all forms of puritanical rules common to most Pentecostals in Brazil, and has a declared policy of individual freedom. The UCKG has expanded its operations into over fifty countries worldwide, with particular success in Portugal, South Africa and Argentina. In the USA, the church made little headway until it switched from English to Spanish, and it now works exclusively with the Hispanic population. In the UK, Macedo's son-in-law runs the church as bishop. Although services are held in English, here the church has targeted the black population, and has become a black church (the majority of African Caribbean descent) with white Brazilian pastors.[22]

OTHER SOUTH AMERICAN COUNTRIES

The countries of Brazil, Chile and Argentina have the biggest Pentecostal churches on the continent, but nearly every other South American country has also been affected by this phenomenon, often with the aid of western missions mainly from North America and Sweden. The United Pentecostal Church of Colombia, which broke away in 1967 from its parent organization in the USA, may now be the largest Pentecostal church in that country. Swedish Canadian Oneness missionary Verner Larsen started this work in 1936, and the church had sustained and severe persecution from the authorities with the collusion of the Catholic Church until the 1960s. The Catholic Charismatic movement is now strong in Colombia, having first appeared in 1967 in Bogota, the same year it commenced in the USA. In Venezuela the AG is the largest non-Catholic denomination, and has a significant presence in all other countries on the continent. Pentecostalism

---

[22] Richard Shaull and Waldo Cesar, *Pentecostalism and the Future of the Christian Churches: Promises, Limitations, Challenges* (Grand Rapids, MI: Eerdmans, 2000), pp. 15–17, 44; Paul Freston, 'The Transnationalisation of Brazilian Pentecostalism: The Universal Church of the Kingdom of God', Corten and Marshall-Fratani, *Between Babel*, pp. 196–215.

began in Venezuela through the work of a German missionary from the USA, Frederick Bender (who had been associated with Mebius in El Salvador, below), who arrived in 1914 followed by many others from the USA and Sweden. When Bender retired in 1947 he encouraged the churches he had helped establish to affiliate with the AG (USA). A subsequent influx of US American AG missionaries resulted in tensions with national leaders and the creation of a new denomination in 1957, Unión Evangélica Pentecostal Venezolana, led by Exeario Sosa, a disciple of Bender. This church affiliated with the ecumenical movement in Latin America and joined the WCC. The Mexican originated Oneness movement Luz del Mundo (below) and the UPC are respectively the second and third largest Pentecostal churches in Venezuela. There is also a large Catholic Charismatic movement there.

In Peru, Bolivia, Uruguay and Paraguay the AG is the largest Pentecostal denomination among several others. Pentecostalism began in Peru when US missionaries Howard and Clara Cragin arrived in 1911, to be followed by others, including the first AG missionaries in 1922. Willis Hoover from Chile held a revival campaign in Callao and Lima in about 1928 resulting in the first congregations led by Peruvian pastors. The first of several schisms in the AG took place in 1936 over the issues of local autonomy and financial dependency. This resulted in the founding of the first Peruvian independent Pentecostal denomination, La Iglesia Evangélica de Cristo del Perú, to spread all over the country within a few years. In 1956 Melvin Hodges, then missions secretary in the AG (USA), visited the Peruvian AG, gave autonomy to the Peruvians and withdrew most of the missionaries, whose tight control had caused schisms. There are now more than fifty-five Pentecostal denominations in Peru, but the AG is the largest, strongly Peruvian in emphasis and with the distinction of producing scholars, particularly historians and theologians. In Ecuador the ICFG (Foursquare Gospel) is the largest Pentecostal work, possibly followed by the UPC. A Peruvian evangelist, Fernando Moroco, founded the AG there in 1956. Pentecostal work began in Bolivia in 1914 with missionaries from the USA. In Uruguay, the complex history of Pentecostalism follows the pattern of several other Latin American countries of numerous small Pentecostal denominations and independent congregations, and foreign missionaries vying for influence and having little to do with each other.[23]

---

[23] Wilson, 'Latin America', *NIDPCM*, pp. 161–4; D. D. Bundy, 'Colombia', 'Peru', 'Uruguay', 'Venezuela', *NIDPCM*, pp. 65–6, 198–200, 277–8, 279–81; French, *Our God is One*, pp. 138–9.

PENTECOSTALS IN CENTRAL AMERICA AND MEXICO

Dramatic Pentecostal growth has taken place in Central America, especially in Guatemala, which has over two million Pentecostals and Charismatics, half of whom are Amerindian Maya. The largest non-Catholic denomination in Central America is the AG, with closer links to the AG, USA than the Brazilian AG has. But this is not a dependent relationship, for there is only one foreign missionary for every 25,000 members. Pentecostalism was introduced to El Salvador in 1904 by the Canadian Frederick Mebius, who was influenced by Parham's Apostolic Faith, and who established a church among coffee workers in a remote area, by 1927 growing to several hundred members in twenty-four congregations, each with an 'apostle' and a 'prophet'. From these rural beginnings began the two largest Salvadoran Pentecostal denominations, the AG and the Church of God, as well as several independent churches in El Salvador, Guatemala, Nicaragua and Honduras. About half of the early Salvadoran Pentecostals led by Francisco Arbizú, disaffected with Mebius' leadership, sent a delegation to the USA to ask for the assistance of a foreign missionary. They met the Welshman Ralph Williams, who thereafter came to El Salvador. His role was primarily motivational and he worked with Arbizú. On the church board of each autonomous congregation there were to be men and women, the only stipulation being that the number of women was not to exceed that of men. The organization of the AG seems to have taken place in 1932. Other strong Pentecostal movements in El Salvador include a Oneness denomination also developing from the Mebius churches, Los Apóstoles y Profetas (The Apostles and Prophets). The Church of God in Guatemala took over Mebius' remaining congregations in 1940.

El Salvador was the centre for the spread of Pentecostal movements in Central America, first to Honduras and Guatemala. Although the AG and Church of God in Guatemala have somewhat tenuous links with the USA, they have developed contextual forms of leadership as a result of their emphasis on spontaneity and spiritual authority. Some of the largest churches in the country were founded by Guatemalans without foreign patronage, such as the Elim Church founded by Otoniel Rios in 1962, and the Iglesia del Principe de Paz (Church of the Prince of Peace), founded in 1955. These churches have in turn spread to neighbouring countries like El Salvador. As in other parts of Latin America, new Pentecostals have been active in Guatemala since the late 1970s and are the most rapidly growing churches there. They have a greater appeal to the more affluent middle class and are usually centred in a dominant, central urban church, such as the Verbo (Church of the Word) in Guatemala City to which former Guatemalan president (and dictator) José Efraín Ríos Montt belongs.[24]

Pentecostals also have significant numbers in Nicaragua, Costa Rica and Panama. As in other Central American countries, in Panama the AG is the largest non-Catholic denomination. Costa Rica, with its large European population has always been fertile ground for a North American style of evangelism, and by 1997 an estimated 18 per cent of the population was evangelical. Pentecostalism arrived in Costa Rica from El Salvador in 1949 and the AG is now the largest non-Catholic denomination followed by the Seventh Day Adventists and the CGC. T. L. Osborne and Billy Graham led evangelistic campaigns in Costa Rica in the 1950s, to be followed by many others. The US classical Pentecostal denominations AG, CGC, IPHC and ICFG together account for two thirds of all Protestants there. Whereas most of the early Pentecostal growth was the direct result of North American initiatives, since the 1970s new Pentecostal organizations have been founded by Costa Ricans, several of which now have congregations of over a thousand members. With this development has occurred the Latinization of Pentecostalism, use being made of several daily services, public processions and Latino music and rhythms in worship. At the same time, these are presented with modern marketing strategies and electronic media. In Nicaragua, Pentecostalism was introduced by North Americans, but during the Sandanista government (1982–91) Pentecostals became strong and nationalistic, with some involvement in the political arena.[25]

There are over 150 Pentecostal denominations in Mexico. Romanita Carbajal de Valenzuela, a Mexican woman converted to Pentecostalism in Los Angeles in 1912, founded what was probably the earliest denomination, Iglesia Apostólica de la Fe en Cristo Jesús (Apostolic Church of the Faith in Christ Jesus, ACFCJ) in northern Mexico in 1914. This Oneness church spread all over Mexico, and has sent missionaries to many parts of Latin America and the USA since the 1950s. For some years the ACFCJ worked with African American missionaries from the PAW like Manuel Walker. Although founded by a woman, the ACFCJ does not ordain women for ministry. In common with some other Oneness groups, the ACFCJ teaches speaking in tongues and baptism as essential to salvation and has strict moral and dress codes. There have been several schisms from this church,

[24] Johnstone and Mandryk, *Operation World*, p. 288; Douglas Petersen, *Not by Might nor by Power: A Pentecostal Theology of Social Concern in Latin America* (Oxford: Regnum, 1996), pp. 62, 68, 70–3.
[25] Berg and Pretiz, *Spontaneous Combustion*, pp. 41–2, 69, 74–9; Martin, *Tongues of Fire*, p. 51.

the most significant taking place in 1926, when Eusebio Joaquín (who changed his name to Aarón) founded Luz del Mundo (Light of the World), perhaps now the largest Oneness church in Central America. He built a community called Hermosa Provincia (Beautiful Province) with a temple seating 3,000, sending missionaries out from there to other parts of Latin America. The members of Luz del Mundo are known as Aaronistas, and some observers suggest that 'Aarón', whose body now rests in Hermosa Provincia, has become a messiah figure. After his death in 1966, Aarón's son, Samuel Joaquín, led the organization. From this movement a signif-icant schism took place in 1942, resulting in a new movement under José Maria Gonzalez called Le Buen Pastor (The Good Shepherd).

Two large Pentecostal movements in Mexico, Iglesia Cristiana Inde-pendiente Pentecostés and Fraternidad Pentecostal Independiente resulted from the efforts of Swedish missionaries Axel and Esther Andersson, who worked in Mexico from 1919 until Axel's death in 1981. The Iglesia Cris-tiana Independiente Pentecostés was founded by Andrés Ornelas Martínez and Raymundo Nieto in 1922, and it amalgamated with the Anderssons' churches. From these churches came many schisms and further amalgama-tions, including the largest Pentecostal denomination in Mexico, Unión de Iglesias Evangelicas Independientes (Union of Independent Evangeli-cal Churches), which mainly consists of Otomi Amerindians, with origins in the work of Venancio Hernández in the 1930s. The AG is the second largest Pentecostal denomination in Mexico, established as an indepen-dent district of the USA church in 1929, mainly through the efforts of missionaries Henry Ball and Alice Luce, who operated from Texas among Mexicans there. There have been several schisms from the AG, mainly over the question of autonomy. A significant schism took place in 1922 when Francisco Olazábal, a Mexican American, founded the Concilio Latino-Americano de Iglesias Cristianas (Latin American Council of Christian Churches). He was one of the most effective Pentecostal preachers and orga-nizers of the time, establishing Hispanic churches all over the USA, Puerto Rico and Mexico. The CGC is the third largest Pentecostal denomination in Mexico, linked to the pioneering work of a Mexican woman, Maria Atkinson, who had founded four congregations among Amerindians and Hispanics in her home state by 1931. She joined the CGC in 1932 when con-tact was made with the missionary James H. Ingram, and her congregations became the Iglesia de Dios (Evangelio Completo). As in other parts of Latin America, Mexican Pentecostals have encountered severe persecution until relatively recently. There is now a strong Catholic Charismatic movement in Mexico, and several large independent Charismatic congregations in the cities.[26]

There has also been remarkable Pentecostal growth throughout the Caribbean. In Puerto Rico, Jamaica and Haiti Pentecostals represent over a quarter of the population with denominations often having North American connections, but with significant local character. The history of Pentecostalism in the Caribbean is a complicated one, each island having its own particular history. But this history reveals the importance of local preachers and women leaders and missionaries, who pervade the stories of Pentecostal churches in the region. The development of Pentecostalism in Puerto Rico is attributed to Puerto Rican preachers beginning with Juan L. Lugo (1890–1984). Converted in Hawaii in 1907 by missionaries from Azusa Street, Lugo went to Puerto Rico in 1916 as a missionary with the AG. Like Pentecostal missionaries everywhere, he had little regard for Protestant comity arrangements and evangelized all over the island, being told by Protestant pastors that he lacked the training and was 'putting the gospel on too humble a level'. In 1921 he founded what is now the largest non-Catholic denomination in the island, the Pentecostal Church of God of Puerto Rico. This church affiliated with the AG in the USA but withdrew in 1956, nine years after it had been refused the status of an independent district. In 1929 Lugo went to New York to pastor the first Puerto Rican Pentecostal church there, which now flourishes in the north-east USA as the Latin American Council of the Pentecostal Church of God of New York. The Pentecostal Church of God of Puerto Rico has sent missionaries all over Latin America and to the USA, Spain and Portugal. The AG is the second largest Pentecostal denomination, followed by the Iglesia Defensores de la Fe (Defenders of the Faith), a Puerto Rican denomination founded in 1934 by Juan Francísco Rodríguez Rivera.

Puerto Rican missionaries have played a vital role in the development and character of Pentecostalism throughout the Caribbean. These missionaries also established a vigorous Pentecostalism in the Dominican Republic. Lugo's friend Salomón Feliciano Quiñones, who had become a Pentecostal in Hawaii in 1913, was the first, arriving in the Dominican Republic in 1917.

---

[26] G. Espinosa, 'Apostolic Church of Faith in Jesus Christ', *NIDPCM*, pp. 323–4; D. D. Bundy, 'Mexico', *NIDPCM*, pp. 175–8; French, *Our God*, pp. 133–5.

His work and that of several other Puerto Rican missionaries was eventually taken over by the AG (USA) in 1941. The AG and the CGP, which began there in 1940, are the largest Pentecostal churches in the Dominican Republic. Pentecostalism arrived in Cuba with the visit of two women missionaries in 1920. One of these, May Kelty, returned in 1931 and worked together with a Puerto Rican couple, Esther and Francisco Rodríguez, in the AG. The AG is now the largest non-Catholic denomination in Cuba and Pentecostalism is expanding rapidly there in many forms. Some of the other prominent Pentecostal churches are members of the ecumenical Council of Churches of Cuba. In Haiti the CGC is the largest Pentecostal denomination and has been established there since 1934, when a Haitian pastor, Vital Herne, was accepted into this church. The CGP (since the 1930s), the AG (1957) and the UPC (1968) have all established significant work in Haiti.[27]

In the Anglophone Caribbean, the Church of God (Cleveland) is the largest Pentecostal denomination, followed by the Church of God of Prophecy. The PAC has also been influential in the eastern and southern Caribbean. Rebecca and Edmund Barr were probably the first African Caribbean Pentecostal believers, who received Spirit baptism in Florida in early 1909 and returned to their home church in the Bahamas. Later that year the CGC sent its first missionaries to the Bahamas, R. M. and Ida Evans, who joined up with the Barrs. A. J. Tomlinson came to the island for an evangelistic tour at this time. When Evans, the only US American in the church on the island, returned to the USA in 1913 because of a shortage of funds, leadership passed to William Franks, appointed overseer in 1918 and having a ministry in the Bahamas of some sixty years. Most of the Bahamian churches joined Tomlinson in his new church in 1923 (to become the CGP). The CGC sent emissaries to the Bahamas to re-establish their work, and although they appointed a black overseer in 1928, in 1931 a white overseer from the US church was appointed, a position that has only recently been reversed.

The CGC missionary leader James Ingram had his first assignment in Bermuda, arriving there in 1921. However, the CGC was not established in Bermuda until 1938, when Ingram made a further visit there while working in Mexico. Ingram was a highly influential figure in the development of the CGC in the Caribbean and Central American regions. Canadian

[27] D. D. Bundy, 'Cuba', 'Dominican Republic', 'Haiti', 'Puerto Rico', *NIDPCM*, pp. 77–9, 81–3, 115–17, 209–10; Berg and Pretiz, *Spontaneous Combustion*, pp. 70–3.

missionaries Robert and Elizabeth Jamieson brought Pentecostalism to Trinidad in 1923, affiliating with the PAC in 1926, and their work became known as the Pentecostal Assemblies of the West Indies. This church sent Trinidadian missionaries to Montserrat, Barbados and Martinique. The CGC has worked mainly with Trinidadians of Indian descent, led by Edward Hasmatali. Hasmatali also led a mission to Grenada and established the CGC there in 1958. There are many other Pentecostal churches in Trinidad and Tobago.

Jamaica already had a number of independent churches by 1917 whose origins are uncertain. The PAW had established itself on the island by 1914. The CGC sent an evangelist to Jamaica in 1918, J. Wilson Bell, who only stayed a few months, handing over the work to Jamaicans Rudolph Smith, Henry Hudson and Percival Graham. From 1924 to 1935 US American overseers were appointed, but a split occurred in 1935, after which Hudson became overseer of the CGC and Smith overseer of the CGP. The UPC started on the island in 1947, building on the earlier PAW work, especially that of the Jamaican woman Nina Ryan Russell. The CGC is now the largest Pentecostal denomination in Jamaica, known as the New Testament Church of God, followed by the CGP and the UPC. Some 30 per cent of all Jamaicans are now members of Pentecostal churches. Jamaican immigrants took their denominations to England in the 1950s, and the New Testament Church of God and the CGP are the largest black-led denominations there. These churches attracted other African Caribbean people in the UK who had belonged to older churches, but who had not been made welcome in these churches.[28]

The twentieth century has seen the emergence of dynamic Pentecostal movements of such considerable variety and creativity in Latin America and the Caribbean that they have fundamentally transformed the religious and social landscapes of the region. Both national and expatriate pioneers have established hundreds of different Pentecostal denominations to make South America the most Pentecostal continent on earth, with its own distinct character. With all their human frailties and often limited and inconsistent impact, these many movements continued to arise, splinter and reform themselves into churches that challenged the status quo often represented by a conservative Catholicism. In the process these new communities sometimes filled the gaps created by socio-economic and religious

[28] D. D. Bundy, 'Caribbean Islands (Survey)', 'Jamaica (II)', 'Trinidad and Tobago', *NIDPCM*, pp. 51–3, 146–7, 272–3.

disintegration and offered full participation and supportive structures for marginalized and displaced people. Thus they have become catalysts of social change and may eventually become instruments of political clout. Whether Pentecostals proactively oppose reactionary structures or bolster the forces of conservativism remains to be seen.

5

Pentecostalism in Europe

THE CASE OF 'SECULAR' EUROPE

Europe has a very different and less developed Pentecostalism than Latin and North America. According to one statistician, Portugal is the only country in Europe where more than 2 per cent of its population is of a 'Pentecostal' denomination and ten European countries have more than 1 per cent. Only three countries (Ireland, Finland and Norway) have more than 5 per cent of the population as 'Charismatic', and only four countries (Ukraine, Britain, Romania and Russia) have Pentecostal populations of more than 400,000.[1] Barrett and Johnson, however, give a rather different picture. Their statistics, which include 'neocharismatics', put Russia, Britain, Italy and Ukraine respectively in front with over four million each, and most countries with much higher numbers of 'Charismatics'.[2] The actual figures probably lie somewhere in between.

Pentecostalism began in Europe very soon after the Azusa Street revival, but differed from the North American movement in several important aspects. Although like its North American counterpart it had roots in the Holiness Movement, there were stronger influences from the Keswick movement (and its position on sanctification), Pietism in the state churches and the Welsh Revival. Most European Pentecostals would have identified with a 'Finished Work' position in keeping with the influence of Reformed theology on the Keswick and Pietistic movements. In contrast to most other parts of the world, the Pentecostal movement in Europe is quite small. David Martin takes issue with the common secularization theories in explaining the 'exceptionalism' of Europe and suggests that there are other, equally as important factors. Pentecostalism is less likely to succeed

---

[1] Countries with more than 1 per cent 'Pentecostals' in 2000 were: Portugal (2.6 per cent), Sweden, Finland, Norway, Iceland, Estonia, Bulgaria and Ukraine (the largest number, with 787,000), Moldova, Romania and Belarus. Johnstone and Mandryk, *Operation World*.

[2] The figures for 'total renewal' are: Russia 6,475,000; Britain 5,820,000; Italy 4,180,000; Ukraine 4,035,000. *NIDPCM*, pp. 42, 132, 217, 277.

in the developed world because it 'represents the mobilization of a minority of people at the varied margins of that world, whereas in the developing world it represents the mobilization of large masses'. The USA is the obvious exception to this, and Pentecostalism flourishes there because of its well-established Protestant pluralism and voluntarism. He suggests further that in Europe, Pentecostalism does not do as well where there is a strong state church, unless there has been a significant minority of 'free churches' like the Baptists, as is the case in Romania and the Ukraine.[3]

NORTHERN EUROPE

Most western European Pentecostal churches have their origins in the revival associated with Thomas Ball Barratt (1862–1940) in Oslo (then Kristiania), Norway. Barratt was a pastor in the Methodist Episcopal Church of Norway who visited the USA in 1906 to unsuccessfully raise funds for his City Mission to the poor of Oslo. In New York he read the first edition of *The Apostolic Faith* from Azusa Street, and he began writing to Los Angeles. Barratt was baptized in the Spirit in an African American congregation and sailed back to Norway via Liverpool together with a party of Azusa Street missionaries to Africa, including Samuel and Ardella Mead on their way back to Angola and African American Azusa Street leader Lucy Farrow, on her way to Liberia. Barratt was now a zealous Pentecostal destined to become the founder and prime motivator of classical Pentecostalism in Europe. His new teachings were unacceptable to his bishops and he was eventually forced to leave the Methodist Church and found what is now the largest non-Lutheran denomination in Norway, a fellowship of independent churches known as *Pinsebevegelsen* (Pentecostal Revival). Starting with a small group of believers, the revival in Barratt's independent Filadelfia Church in Oslo was a place of pilgrimage for people from all over Europe, including Pentecostal pioneers Alexander Boddy from England, Jonathan Paul from Germany and Lewi Pethrus from Sweden. Large crowds attended Barratt's meetings all over Europe. Barratt sent missionaries to Sweden and Germany, and went himself to the Middle East and India. He wrote to the Hoovers in Chile, encouraging them and others wherever he went to establish self-governing, self-supporting and self-propagating churches. Unlike the hierarchical Pentecostalism that was to develop in North America, Barratt's churches were strictly independent and congregational. Barratt

---

[3] Martin, *Pentecostalism*, pp. 67–70.

submitted himself to baptism by immersion through the Swedish Baptist pastor Pethrus in 1913. His ministry also had a social impact by caring for the poor, the homeless, children and the elderly; and he was a prolific writer, especially in his periodicals *Byposten* and *Korsets Seier*. By 1910, Norwegian Pentecostal missionaries had already gone to India, China, South Africa and South America.[4]

From Oslo the Pentecostal movement spread to other parts of Europe. Pentecostals in Sweden, Norway and Finland soon became the biggest churches outside the Lutheran state churches. Barratt made several visits to Sweden. Lewi Pethrus' Filadelfia Church in Stockholm, Sweden was the largest Pentecostal congregation in the world until the 1960s (when churches in Korea and Chile overtook it), with its own aggressive mission programme. Pethrus (1884–1974) was a Baptist pastor who became a Pentecostal after visiting Barrett in Oslo in 1907. Opposition from the Baptist churches only occurred slowly. He became pastor of the Filadelfia Church in Stockholm in 1911, and he and his congregation were expelled from the Baptist denomination in 1913 – not ostensibly because they had become Pentecostal, but for allowing non-Baptists to take communion. Pethrus remained Baptist in ecclesiology, a strong advocate of the independence of the local church with no outside interference or denominational organization. This principle has influenced Scandinavian Pentecostal churches and missions all over the world. With over 6,000 adult members, Pethrus pastored the Filadelfia Church for forty-seven years and his output was prodigious. During that time he established a rescue mission (1911), a publishing house (1912), Bible school (1915) and a secondary 'folk' school (1942); he edited a daily Christian newspaper *Dagen* (1945), wrote some fifty books and established a bank (1952) and a radio station broadcasting in twenty-three languages from North Africa (1955). He was probably the most influential Pentecostal in Europe during his lifetime. In 1949 Pethrus gave support to the new Latter Rain movement that had arisen in North America, but withdrew three years later. He retired from the pastorate of the Filadelfia Church in 1958, but remained active until his death in 1974. Swedish Pentecostal churches, though strictly autonomous, meet together in annual conventions and thereby maintain their unity.[5] One of the largest Charismatic

---

4 David Bundy, 'Thomas Ball Barratt: From Methodist to Pentecostal', *JEPTA* XIII (1994), 19–40; David Bundy, 'Historical and Theological Analysis of the Pentecostal Church in Norway', *JEPTA* XX (2000), 66–92.

5 D. D. Bundy, 'Pethrus, Petrus Lewi', *NIDPCM*, pp. 986–7; Joseph R. Colletti, 'Lewi Pethrus: His Influence upon Scandinavian-American Pentecostalism', *Pneuma* 5:2 (1983), 18–29.

congregations in Europe today is the Word of Life (*Livets Ord*) church in Uppsala, a prosperity and faith oriented Charismatic church founded in 1983 by Ulf Ekman, a former Swedish Lutheran minister trained in theology at the University of Uppsala and later at Kenneth Hagin's Rhema Bible Training Center in Tulsa, Oklahoma. This church's influence extends to a network of some ninety congregations in Sweden, and, through its Bible School, much further in Europe.[6]

Pentecostal ideas grew slowly in Finland, founded on a long tradition of charismatic manifestations in the Finnish Lutheran church, including speaking in tongues in the 'Awakened' movement since 1796 and in the Laestadians since 1889. The latter groups heard of the Pentecostal revival in Norway and invited T. B. Barratt to visit Finland. Barratt made the first of several visits in 1911, had two weeks of meetings in Helsinki and left behind a group of Pentecostal believers. The first Pentecostal baptismal service was held in 1912, after which a revival broke out, and the movement consisted of people of various denominations. Eventually Pentecostals were ostracized from their churches and came together in association, but as in other Scandinavian countries, they formed autonomous churches and rejected any ideas of a set apart clergy. The grouping of Pentecostal believers was known as Pentecostal Revival (like Barratt's Norwegian fellowship), and this became the largest church group in Finland after the state Lutheran church. Finnish Pentecostal missionaries were sent out from 1912, when Emil Danielsson went to Kenya. These and other Scandinavian missionaries have been very influential in spreading Pentecostalism to many parts of the world. The Finnish Free Foreign Mission was formed by the Pentecostal churches in 1927 and missionaries sent out to Manchuria, India, Burma, Tanzania, South Africa and Argentina before the Second World War. These days, the annual summer conference in Finland attracts attendances of over 30,000, one of the largest gatherings of Pentecostals in Europe.[7]

Barratt first visited Denmark in June 1907 at the invitation of several Danish ministers who had seen the revival in Oslo. The meetings in Copenhagen were crowded and the movement began as an ecumenical group of people who remained affiliated to their churches. On Barratt's second visit in 1908 the famous Danish actress Anna Larsen and her husband Sigur Bjørner were converted to Pentecostalism, which publicized

---

[6] Simon Coleman, *The Globalisation of Charismatic Christianity: Spreading the Gospel of Prosperity* (Cambridge University Press, 2000), pp. 87–92, 97.

[7] L. Ahonen, 'Finland', *NIDPCM*, pp. 103–5; Veli-Matti Kärkkäinen, 'From the ends of the earth to the ends of the earth' – the expansion of the Finnish Pentecostal Missions from 1927 to 1997, *JEPTA* XX (2000), 116–31.

Figure 5. (from left) Lewi Pethrus, Mrs Barratt, T. B. Barratt, and the Bjørners, Stockholm, Sweden, c. 1913.

the movement significantly. Larsen gave up acting in the prime of her career to become a leading personality in the Danish Pentecostal movement. The first Pentecostal church was started in Copenhagen in 1912, followed by several others that together formed a loose association called the Pentecostal Revival. In 1924 a split occurred in these churches, when the Apostolic Church of Wales appointed Sigur Bjørner an apostle for Denmark. With a centralized government, the Apostolic Church of Denmark continues to this day, but was reconciled with the Pentecostal Revival churches in 1998. Pentecostalism has not flourished in Denmark as it has elsewhere in Scandinavia.[8] Barratt introduced Pentecostalism to Iceland in 1920, and the Pentecostal Church of Iceland is the largest movement there, with the Filadelfia Church in Reykjavik being the largest Pentecostal congregation.[9]

German Pietists were expecting revival since hearing of the Welsh and Indian revivals. North American evangelist R. A. Torrey visited Germany in 1906 and taught on the baptism in the Spirit. Lutheran pastors and prominent leaders in the German Holiness movement Jonathan Paul and Emil Meyer visited Oslo early in 1907 and received Spirit baptism there. Two Norwegian women, Dagmar Gregersen and Agnes Thelle, took the Pentecostal message to Hamburg in June 1907, where they worked together with the Hamburger Strandmission of Emil Meyer and then accompanied evangelist Heinrich Dallmeyer to Kassel. As a result of the controversial and reportedly tumultuous meetings held there (but stopped by police), the movement received wide publicity in both the secular and religious press. Dallmeyer rejected Pentecostalism and Gregersen and Thelle moved on to Zürich, Switzerland in August 1907, starting a Pentecostal group there. Barratt visited Zürich the following year and appointed Anglican minister C. E. D. Delabilière as leader of the group. The first Pentecostal conference was held in 1910 with the participation of Barratt, and the consequent revival drew the attention of the press. Swiss Pentecostalism has been small but influential. The first World Pentecostal Conference was held in Zürich in 1947. The leading scholar of Pentecostalism in the twentieth century, Walter J. Hollenweger, was raised in Swiss Pentecostalism and was a pastor in the *Pfingstmission* (Pentecostal Mission) until 1958. The two main Swiss Pentecostal groups are the *Pfingstmission* and *Gemeinde für Urchristentum* (Apostolic Assemblies). Some twenty Swiss Pentecostal groups have now formed the Fellowship of Pentecostal Free Churches.

---

[8] Nils Bloch-Hoell, *The Pentecostal Movement* (Oslo: Universitetsforlaget; London: Allen and Unwin, 1964), pp. 77–9; T. Jacobsen *et al.*, 'Denmark', *NIDPCM*, pp. 80–1.
[9] L. Ahonen and T. Birgisson, 'Iceland', *NIDPCM*, pp. 117–18.

The first Pentecostal conference in Germany was held in Mülheim/Ruhr in July 1909 under the leadership of Emil Humburg (1874–1965), and continued annually thereafter. Pentecostal leaders met annually at such meetings in Mülheim and in Sunderland, England, until the outbreak of the First World War. Opposition to Pentecostalism was mounting, and in September 1909 the 'Berlin Declaration' of German evangelicals set itself firmly against the Pentecostal movement. Pentecostalism was condemned as 'demonic spiritualism' and speaking in tongues as 'not from above, but from below'. The Berlin Declaration isolated the Charismatic Lutheran and Reformed ministers in the German state churches and greatly hindered the expansion of the movement. Two weeks after this Jonathan Paul (1853–1931) called another conference, which led to the founding in 1913 of an ecumenical Pentecostal group known as the *Mülheimer Verband* (Mülheim Association) of Christian Fellowships, with Humburg its first president. This is the oldest group within German Pentecostalism and emphasizes the spiritual gifts and holiness of life. Eventually becoming an independent denomination, both infant and adult baptism are recognized and there is no doctrine of 'initial evidence'. The Mülheim Association made an unsuccessful attempt in 1934 to have the Berlin Declaration reversed. The Pentecostal churches in Germany grew very slowly with increasing opposition by the state church and especially from the Nazi regime, but in 1995 Pentecostals and Evangelicals in Germany came together to reconcile and declare that the Berlin Declaration had no contemporary relevance. Jonathan Paul has been a most prolific writer, remained a Lutheran minister and was responsible with five others for the first modern German translation of the Bible in 1914. Another Pentecostal association in Germany is called *Bund Freier Pfingstmeinden* (Federation of Free Pentecostal Churches), formed after the Second World War. Evangelist and former missionary in Lesotho, Reinhard Bonnke, came from this movement. His Christ for All Nations crusades in Africa since the mid 1970s have attracted enormous crowds and have had a significant effect on the popularizing of Pentecostalism in Africa.[10]

Gerrit Polman (1868–1932) joined the Salvation Army in the Netherlands in 1890 and worked as an officer there with William Booth's son-in-law Arthur Booth-Clibborn. He left the Army with Booth-Clibborn in 1902 to join Dowie's Zionist movement near Chicago and Polman and his wife Wilhelmine went to live in Zion City from 1903–5. They returned to

---

[10] Bloch-Hoell, *Pentecostal Movement*, pp. 79–81; W. J. Hollenweger, 'Switzerland', *NIDPCM*, pp. 257–9; Lynne Price, *Theology Out of Place: A Theological Biograghy of Walter J. Hollenweger* (London and New York: Sheffield Academic Press, 2002), pp. 6–8.

Amsterdam to start the Christian Catholic Church in Holland, but on receiving news of the Azusa Street revival, began prayer meetings for a similar revival in the Netherlands. Wilhelmine Polman was the first to receive Spirit baptism in October 1907 (the date of the Polmans' break with Zionism), and Gerrit Polman followed in June 1908 while attending the first Sunderland conference in England. By 1909 there were 150 Pentecostal believers in Amsterdam, and the movement began to spread around the Netherlands. Ada Esselbach, originally from England, received Spirit baptism in 1909 and became a Pentecostal worker in Antwerp, Belgium. Polman had regular meetings in Antwerp from 1920–24. A Dutch evangelist, Cornelis Potma, worked in Belgium with the Elim movement from Britain from 1920–29 and George Jeffreys had meetings there in 1926. The Belgian Pentecostal churches have remained small, and the two largest groups merged in 1993 to form the Union of Flemish Pentecostal Churches. The first Dutch Pentecostal missionaries were sent to China in 1910, working with the British Pentecostal Missionary Union until 1920, when Polman formed the *Nederlands Pinksterzendings-genootschap* (Netherlands Pentecostal Missionary Society). In 1912 Immanuel Hall was opened in Amsterdam and a training school for missionaries started. On Polman's death in 1932, former missionary to China Piet Klaver led the Amsterdam congregation and Pieter van der Woude, who became a prominent leader in the movement, started a new congregation in Rotterdam. Visits by North American evangelists, especially that of T. L. Osborne in 1958, and the Dutch healing evangelist Johan Maasbach helped spread the movement thereafter.

There are many different Pentecostal groups in Holland that have divided and amalgamated into new groups, including the *Broederschap van Pinkster-gemeenten* (BP, Brotherhood of Pentecostal Assemblies) formed in 1952 and associated with the American AG, and the *Volle Evangelie Gemeenten* (FG, Full Gospel Assemblies) founded in 1978. But the majority of Holland's Pentecostals are in independent churches and new Charismatic churches have emerged in recent years. Immigration to the Netherlands from Africa, Asia and Latin America has resulted in a large number of vibrant ethnic Pentecostal churches. In 2002 the BP and the FG amalgamated to form the largest Pentecostal grouping in the Netherlands, the *Verenigde Pinkster- en Evangeliegemeenten* (United Pentecostal and Gospel Assemblies).[11]

---

[11] Cornelis van der Laan, 'Discerning the Body: An Analysis of Pentecostalism in the Netherlands', *JEPTA* XIV (1995), 34–53; C. van der Laan, 'Netherlands', *NIDPCM*, pp. 184–6; C. van der Laan, 'Belgium', *NIDPCM*, pp. 32–3; David D. Bundy, 'Pentecostalism in Belgium', *Pneuma* 8:1 (1986), 41–56.

BRITISH PENTECOSTALISM

There were several factors at work preparing the way for Pentecostalism to enter Britain. England was the home of the Keswick Conventions, which had taught a distinct baptism in the Spirit as 'endeument with power'. The 1904–5 Welsh Revival brought an estimated 100,000 people into Christian churches, and its leader Evan Roberts had an ecstatic experience of 'baptism in the Spirit'. Many leading British Pentecostals like George and Stephen Jeffreys and Donald Gee were converted through this revival, and Anglicans Alexander Boddy and Cecil Polhill visited it. Although a rift developed between Pentecostal groups and Holiness groups, especially through the opposition and writings of the influential Jessie Penn-Lewis, the influence of Keswick and the Welsh Revival on the emergence of British Pentecostalism was considerable, creating an expectation for revival throughout Britain and Europe. The first recorded instance of Pentecostal meetings in Britain with speaking in tongues was at the home of Catherine Price in London in January 1907, apparently unrelated to subsequent events.

Alexander A. Boddy (1854–1930), Anglican vicar at All Saints in Monkwearmouth, Sunderland since 1886, visited T. B. Barratt's church in Oslo in March 1907 and commented that he had 'never witnessed such scenes' in Wales. He invited Barratt to preach in his parish in September that year. Barratt did so, and many of the people who had gathered received Spirit baptism at his meetings. Boddy's Anglican church became the most significant early Pentecostal centre in Britain, and Boddy provided leadership and direction that shaped its future. Annual Whitsun (Pentecost) conventions from 1908 to 1914 drew Pentecostals from all over Britain and continental Europe, including Barratt, Jonathan Paul and Gerrit Polman. Boddy edited the widely influential periodical *Confidence* (1908–26), which reported on the Pentecostal revivals all over the world and expounded the doctrine of Spirit baptism and spiritual gifts. Although Boddy was acknowledged leader of British Pentecostalism before the First World War, he remained an Anglican minister until his death. He appears to have shifted from an 'initial evidence' position to a more flexible view of Spirit baptism. His ecumenical stance was evident in the words he penned about the revival in *Confidence* in September 1908, 'Denominationalism has melted away and the barriers disappeared as the Holy Spirit came in full possession'. The Sunderland conventions became known as 'international' conventions and there were increasing contacts between the northern European Pentecostal leaders who met during the conventions at Sunderland and at Mülheim, beginning at the Hamburg conference in 1908. In 1912 Barratt proposed a 'Consultative International Pentecostal Council', which was formed to protect from 'false teachers' in the movement. This Council met four times (thrice at Sunderland and once at Amsterdam) before being aborted by the First World War. Leaders from Norway, Germany, Holland and Switzerland joined Boddy and Polhill in the Council, but only Polman and Paul attended all the meetings. J. H. King from the PHC in the USA attended the first meeting, but this was effectively a northern European council.

From Boddy's church the Pentecostal Missionary Union for Great Britain and Ireland (PMU) was formed in 1909, led by Cecil Polhill (1860–1938), a former missionary (since 1885) to south-western China and one of the 'Cambridge Seven' in the China Inland Mission. Through an inheritance, he was now a wealthy landowner and avid supporter of Pentecostal missions. Polhill was baptized in the Spirit during a visit to Los Angeles in early 1908 and he bought a large house in London in which to hold Pentecostal services. He also organized annual conventions in London that lasted through the war years. The PMU was the first organized Pentecostal missionary society, with its own separate training institutions for women and men. Missionaries were almost immediately sent by the PMU to south-western China and India. It joined the Assemblies of God in 1925, when Polhill and Boddy (who opposed Pentecostal denominations being formed) withdrew from its board, no longer to play any leading role in British Pentecostalism. There were several reasons for this break between the Anglican Charismatics and the other Pentecostals; besides the issues of denominationalism and pacifism, doctrinal differences like the role of tongues in Spirit baptism and water baptism had also become contentious issues. All classical Pentecostal churches in Britain today baptize adult believers by immersion.[12]

William Oliver Hutchinson, a Baptist preacher who had received Spirit baptism in Sunderland in 1908, opened the first purpose-built Pentecostal hall in Britain in the same year, the independent chapel Emmanuel Mission in Bournemouth. Hutchinson founded the first Pentecostal denomination in Britain, the Apostolic Faith Church (AFC) in 1911. It is likely that former Congregationalist preacher in the Welsh Revival, George Jeffreys (1889–1962) received Spirit baptism at Emmanuel Mission in 1910. The AFC became increasingly a personality cult around its leader and imbibed

---

[12] Hollenweger, *The Pentecostals*, pp. 184–5; Hollenweger, *Pentecostalism*, pp. 343–5; Cornelis van der Laan, 'The Proceedings of the Leaders' Meetings (1908–11) and of the International Pentecostal Council (1912–14)', *Pneuma* 10:1 (1988), 36–49.

British Israelism and other teachings rejected by most early Pentecostals who distanced themselves from it. Daniel P. Williams led the first secession of most of the Welsh congregations to form the Apostolic Church in 1916. James Brooke was to lead another secession from the AFC in 1926 to form the United Apostolic Faith Church. The AFC was to go into obscurity and the other two British Apostolic denominations were to remain relatively small in Britain, but with significant work overseas, especially in West and southern Africa. The healing evangelist Smith Wigglesworth (1860–1947) received Spirit baptism in Boddy's church and became an international preacher. George Jeffreys was founder of the Elim movement and his brother Stephen Jeffreys became an evangelist in the Assemblies of God. George Jeffreys was trained at the PMU college in Preston in 1912–13 under Polhill's sponsorship and one of his fellow students was William F. P. Burton, founder of the Congo Evangelistic Mission. Successful evangelistic meetings held by George and Stephen Jeffreys in South Wales in 1913 put the Jeffreys brothers on the national stage. George Jeffreys has been described as the greatest British Pentecostal evangelist ever, whose meetings attracted many thousands with remarkable healings and great numbers of conversions, especially in the 1930s. British Pentecostals experienced significant growth during their first forty years.

George Jeffreys founded the Elim Pentecostal Church in Belfast, Northern Ireland in 1915 as the Elim Evangelistic Band – to be renamed the Elim Pentecostal Alliance in 1918, after which a central council governed the organization. Jeffreys remained in Ireland until 1921, only making occasional visits to Britain, and by this time there were twenty-two churches in the region. Jeffreys did not intend to form a denomination and he discouraged proselytizing, but the nature of the movement led inevitably to denominationalism. After 1921 Jeffreys began planting churches in England and Wales, moved his headquarters to London, and a number of churches joined Elim. From 1926 until the 1990s, Elim held its annual Easter Convention in the Royal Albert Hall in London (then seating 10,000), and Aimee McPherson was the first invited guest speaker. In 1929 the Elim name was changed yet again to Elim Foursquare Gospel Alliance, Jeffreys apparently being inspired by Aimee McPherson's movement. From 1934, Jeffreys began to lose his tight control over the Elim leadership and issues of local church government and the British Israel theory (both espoused by Jeffreys) led to his resignation from Elim in 1939 and a schism, when the Bible Pattern Church Fellowship was created. The majority of ministers and members remained in the Elim movement, but it took a long time to recover. In more recent years, the Elim movement has had to adjust to the challenges posed by the Charismatic movement and to the question of the authority of the local church, but has emerged as the largest classical Pentecostal denomination in Britain today, with some 69,000 members in 2000. By far the largest and best-known congregation in Elim is the multi-ethnic Kensington Temple in London, which with its many branch churches accounts for a significant proportion of the national Elim membership – perhaps as much as a quarter of the total.[13]

The Assemblies of God in Great Britain and Ireland (AGBI), unlike its namesake in the USA, emerged in 1924 as a congregational association of autonomous churches under the chairmanship of J. Nelson Parr (1886–1976). These assemblies were highly suspicious of the centralized control that was emerging in the Elim movement and George Jeffreys was not invited to be part of it. Nelson Parr, baptized in the Spirit in Boddy's church in 1910, issued the invitation to a meeting of fourteen leaders in Aston, Birmingham in 1924 when the AGBI was formed, with seventy-four assemblies joining the association guaranteeing autonomy to each local church. The AGBI specifically declared itself to be pacifist, another reason for the break with the patriotic aristocrats Boddy and Polhill, and it also declared the doctrine of the 'initial evidence' of tongues. The following year the PMU joined to become the missionary arm of the AGBI. Donald Gee (1891–1966), a pastor in Leith, Edinburgh, was chairman of the AGBI from 1948 until his death in 1966. His overtures to non-Pentecostal churches and his support of David du Plessis's ecumenical efforts earned him the opposition of the AG, USA. Gee travelled internationally and was the organizer of the European Pentecostal conference held in Stockholm in 1939 (the first such meeting since Amsterdam, 1921) and the first World Pentecostal Conference (PWC) in Zürich in 1947. A prolific author, he was also the first editor of the PWC's periodical *Pentecost* and one of the most influential Pentecostal leaders of his time. Like the AG in the USA, and unlike the Elim movement and most other European Pentecostal churches, the AGBI had always held an officially unyielding position on 'initial evidence' and premillennialism, but as is the case with its US namesake, there are internal voices being raised questioning these positions, particularly from academics. AGBI historian William Kay considers 'evidential tongues' to be the 'core distinctive' of this denomination, although his

---

[13] Malcolm R. Hathaway, 'The Elim Pentecostal Church: Origins, Development and Distinctives', Keith Warrington (ed.), *Pentecostal Perspectives* (Carlisle, UK: Paternoster, 1998), pp. 1–39; Johnstone and Mandryk, *Operation World*, p. 650.

survey during 1996–97 reveals that only 42 per cent of Elim ministers and 81 per cent of AGBI ministers believed in 'initial' evidence, and 72 per cent of Elim ministers believed that Spirit baptism could occur without tongues.[14]

After the mass immigration of people from the West Indies to Britain after 1951, African Caribbean Pentecostal churches were set up and grew remarkably during the 1960s. The main churches had links with the Caribbean and the USA, but many new independent churches were also formed, resulting in a great variety of churches in the African Caribbean and later in the African community in Britain. Later migrations after 1960 resulted in a number of West African Pentecostal churches being established in Britain (especially Nigerian ones) and elsewhere in Europe. The largest 'Black-led' churches in Britain are the New Testament Church of God (part of the CGC), with some 20,000 members, and the Church of God of Prophecy, also the largest Pentecostal churches in the English-speaking Caribbean. Black Pentecostal immigrants were made to feel unwelcome in British churches, partly because of the cultural differences between the community-oriented African Caribbeans and the more reserved and individualistic English, but also due to the incipient racism present in British society. The formal Christianity encountered in England was so different from what people were used to in the Caribbean. The first New Testament Church of God was formed in Wolverhampton in 1953 by Oliver Lyseight, A. D. Brown and G. S. Peddie. By 1961 there were already eighty African Caribbean churches in Britain, mostly Pentecostal, and this was before the period of their greatest expansion. They have been extremely influential within the British church context. At present, a minister from the New Testament Church of God, Joel Edwards, is general secretary of the Evangelical Alliance.

The fastest growing churches in Britain today are the 'new churches', mostly independent Charismatic churches, sometimes led by former Anglican ministers and forming loose associations. These have probably outstripped the classical Pentecostal churches in influence and extent. Some of the leading new churches, thirty associations that in 2000 had an estimated 406,000 affiliates, are Ichthus, Pioneers, New Frontiers and the Vineyard Association. Pentecostalism has also profoundly affected older churches in Britain, particularly Anglican and Baptist churches, which have a significant

---

[14] William K. Kay, *Pentecostals in Britain* (Carlisle, UK: Paternoster, 2000), p. 74; William Kay, 'Assemblies of God: Distinctive Continuity and Distinctive Change', Warrington, *Pentecostal Perspectives*, pp. 40–63.

proportion of churches considered 'Charismatic', to which we will give attention in chapter 8.[15]

The early history of Pentecostalism in France is obscure and limited to isolated cases of Pentecostal meetings. Hélène Biolley (1854–1947), an important early influence, ran a temperance hotel in Le Havre that was also a gospel mission. She invited several Pentecostal speakers including Boddy in 1909, Wigglesworth in 1920–21, Polman in 1920 and Douglas Scott (1900–67), the English founder of the French AG who first visited Le Havre in 1927. The Apostolic Church of Wales sent Thomas Roberts (1902–83) to Paris in 1926 and a flourishing Pentecostal mission was established. Roberts became an independent Reformed minister in 1936 (still with Pentecostal convictions) and worked closely with Louis Dallière (1897–1976), Reformed Charismatic minister and founder of the Union de Prière in 1946. The Pentecostal message spread among Baptist and Reformed churches, where there was remarkable openness, assisted by the work of Roberts, Scott and Dallière, among others. Scott was converted to Pentecostalism through George Jeffreys and was to become the prime mover in French and Francophone Belgian Pentecostalism, his healing evangelism resulting in numerous conversions. Dallière was convinced by Scott in 1932 and was the leading Reformed Charismatic and apologist for Pentecostalism during the 1930s. Scott founded the AG in France in 1932 in Le Havre, independent of its namesakes in Britain and the USA and by far the most widespread of the Pentecostal groups today. Pentecostalism began among the Roma (Gypsy) people in 1952 when Clément le Cossec began ministry to about thirty Roma people in Brest, Britanny. From 1954 national conventions were held annually, beginning in Brest, and then in Rennes. A revival broke out among Roma people worldwide, and in France and Spain the result has been that about a quarter of the Roma population belongs to a Pentecostal church. The Filadelfia church has been in the forefront of this trend. Le Cossec and his sons have been leaders in the movement known as the International Evangelical Gypsy Mission. An all Roma council now leads the church in France with Djimy Myer as the leader. The largest Pentecostal denominations in France are the AG and the Gypsy Mission.[16]

---

[15] Joel Edwards, 'Afro-Caribbean Pentecostalism in Britain', *JEPTA* XVII (1997), 37–48; Johnstone and Mandryk, *Operation World*, p. 650.

[16] Entries: 'France', 'Biolley, Hélène', 'Gypsies', 'Roberts, Thom', 'Scott, Douglas', *NIDPCM*, pp. 105–7, 417–18, 683–6, 1027, 1045; David Bundy, 'Louis Dallière: Apologist for Pentecostalism in France and Belgium, 1932–1939', *Pneuma* 10:2 (1988), 85–115.

Portuguese Pentecostalism has its roots in Brazil. Among the first converts of Gunnar Vingren and Daniel Berg, Swedish founders of the AG in Brazil, were José Placido da Costa (1869–1965) and José de Mattos (1888–1958), who returned to Portugal in 1913 and 1921 respectively as Pentecostal missionaries. The first congregation was established in the Algarve and pastored by de Mattos until 1938. Daniel Berg founded a congregation in Porto in 1934 and another Swedish missionary Jack Härdstedt started a church in Lisbon. The mission to Portugal from Brazil and Sweden was soon followed in 1931 by Portuguese missionaries going to Portuguese territories and colonies abroad, the first to the Azores. The AG in Portugal was the largest non-Catholic denomination there until recently, for by 2000 the Brazilian church of Edir Macedo, the UCKG, had overtaken it. Portuguese AG congregations were also established wherever Portuguese people had emigrated. The Neocharismatic church Mana Igreja Crista (Manna Christian Church), founded in Lisbon in 1980 now rivals the AG in extent and influence. Another Brazilian church, the Christian Congregation is also significant in Portugal, where Pentecostalism remains among the most vibrant in Europe.

Pentecostalism was planted in Spain in 1923 by Swedish missionaries, but has grown slowly among the Spanish population. The largest Pentecostal denomination and the largest Roma church in the world is the Filadelfia Evangelical Church, founded by Clement le Cossec from France in the 1950s. Spain has several Pentecostal denominations started by missionaries from Latin America, including Puerto Rico (Pentecostal Church of God), Mexico (Good Shepherd Church) and Brazil.[17]

Italy has the second largest population of Pentecostals in western Europe, after Britain. The founder of Italian Pentecostalism was Luigi Francescon, who sent his convert Giacomo Lombardi back to Italy from Chicago in 1908, and Lombardi is recognized as founder of the movement in Italy. The Pentecostal Christian Congregations and the Italian Pentecostal Christian Church trace their origins to Lombardi and practise strict congregationalism with no church hierarchy. Francescon visited Pentecostal churches in Italy many times. Pentecostalism spread rapidly in spite of severe persecution, so that by 2000 Pentecostals had over 300,000 members. Largely drawn from the exploited poor classes, they were twice as many as all other Italian Protestants together. They were only officially recognised in 1960 after great persecution and harassment, especially under Mussolini's Fascist

---

[17] D. D. Bundy, 'Portugal', 'Spain', *NIDPCM*, pp. 208–9, 247; Johnstone and Mandryk, *Operation World*, pp. 529, 583.

government (with the support of the Catholic Church) between 1935 and 1945. Italian Pentecostals were only given government permission to evangelize in 1987. The largest Italian Pentecostal denomination is the AG in Italy (which has been very isolationist), which started in Naples in 1947 and affiliated with the AG in the USA but is independent in government. One of the largest of the new churches is the International Evangelical Church, founded by John McTernan from the USA, becoming a member of the WCC in 1972. Various streams of Italian Pentecostalism came together in 2000 to form the nation's second largest Pentecostal group, the Federation of Pentecostal Churches.[18]

CENTRAL AND EASTERN EUROPE

The Pentecostal movement has been relatively more successful in Eastern Europe, where it has grown (especially since the Second World War) in the face of severe restrictions and persecution from state (or dominant) churches and Communist regimes. During the Soviet years, most Pentecostals were forced to merge with evangelicals and Baptists in state-controlled structures, and those who failed to co-operate were seen as 'anti-revolutionary' and severely punished, often imprisoned and exiled. In the Baltic states and Russia, Pentecostal influence came from neighbouring Scandinavia, the Englishwoman Eleanor Patrick and the Latvian William Fetler (1883–1957), also known by his pen-name Basil Malof. Fetler was a Baptist pastor in St Petersburg, Russia who had graduated from Spurgeon's College in London. He had heard about events at Azusa Street and introduced the baptism in the Spirit to his congregation. He opened a church building in Riga, Latvia in 1927 called the Salvation Temple, with its own prayer tower, by which time he was in contact with Pentecostals internationally. He fought vigorously against what he perceived to be 'liberal' tendencies in the Baptist church, and although he defended the doctrine of Spirit baptism, he remained a Baptist all his life, moving to the USA in 1939 before the outbreak of war. There was a significant Charismatic movement among Latvian Baptists as a result of Fetler's ministry. Organized Pentecostalism in Latvia began with the Latvian American AG missionary James Grevins, who arrived in 1926 and was deported in 1930, leaving behind some 400 members. An early English missionary of Pentecostalism in the region was

---

[18] G. Traetinno, 'Italy', *NIDPCM*, pp. 132–41; Cox, *Fire*, pp. 192–5; Hollenweger, *The Pentecostals*, p. 251; Johnstone and Mandryk, *Operation World*, p. 365.

Eleanor Patrick, and although she mainly worked with Baltic Germans, she visited Russia, Belarus, Estonia and Latvia from 1909 to 1912, reporting back to Alexander Boddy and eventually settling in Russia. Estonian Pentecostalism traces its beginnings to her meetings there. Swedish Pentecostals established the movement in Estonia, Voldemar Ellingson being the main leader and arriving there in 1926. Three Russian Pentecostal women missionaries began a Pentecostal movement in Lithuania in 1923, and in 1940 the Union of Pentecostal Churches in Lithuania was formed. Pentecostals in the Baltics are now divided between those autochthonous churches with links to western Pentecostal denominations, Neopentecostals and 'Eastern Pentecostals', mainly founded by Russians and Ukrainians and resistant to any influence from the West.[19]

Russia was a vast mission field for early Pentecostals. Fetler had established a Russian Missionary Society and travelled extensively throughout Russia. T. B. Barrett had a successful evangelistic campaign in St Petersburg in 1911, leaving behind a sizeable Pentecostal congregation. Ivan Voronaev (1886–c.1940?), who moved to the USA from Russia in 1911, was pastor of a Russian Baptist congregation in New York when baptized in the Spirit. He commenced a Russian Pentecostal church there in 1919. A year later he established eighteen Pentecostal congregations in Bulgaria and travelled to Odessa and St Petersburg, continuing to preach and establish churches. A number of leading Baptists and Evangelicals joined him, and Voronaev's headquarters church in Odessa soon had a thousand members. In 1927 the first Pentecostal Congress for the Soviet Union took place when Voronaev was appointed president of the Union of Christians of Evangelical Faith. By this time there were an estimated 80,000 Pentecostal members, enjoying the favour of the Communist state that had liberated them from Orthodox persecution. But after the passing of the anti-religious laws, Voronaev and 800 pastors were arrested and sent to Siberian concentration camps in 1930, where after a brief release in 1935, Voronaev disappeared and was later presumed dead.

The Pentecostal churches continued to grow in the face of persecution. In 1944 they united with the Baptists to form the All Union Council of Evangelical Christians and Baptists, which joined the WCC in 1961. Tensions within this union over the forbidding of tongues in public worship resulted in a large number of Pentecostals setting up their own organization,

---

[19] Valdis Teraudkalns, 'Pentecostalism in the Baltics: Historical Retrospection', *JEPTA* XXI (2001), 91–108.

the Christians of the Evangelical Faith (Pentecostal), which unsuccessfully approached Soviet leaders Kruschev (in 1957) and Brezhnev (in 1965) for religious freedom. The recognition was finally accomplished in 1991 and they had more than 100,000 members in 2000. Another Pentecostal association of churches in Russia of equal size has refused to register for government recognition. Its leader, Bishop Ivan Fedotov was imprisoned for nineteen years for his faith during the Soviet regime. In the Ukraine the Evangelical Pentecostal Union is probably now the largest Pentecostal denomination in Europe, with some 370,000 members in 2000. These churches continued to grow and expand, and by 2000 there were some 400,000 Russian Pentecostals, and 780,000 in the Ukraine, the highest number of Pentecostals in any European nation. The great majority of the Ukrainian and Russian churches are fiercely independent, have a conservative dress code and morality, and eschew formal links with the West.[20]

According to a conservative estimate, there are over 300,000 Pentecostals in Romania, and some suggest over 800,000, which would make it the most Pentecostal country in Europe. Pentecostalism may have first arrived in Romania in 1918 when a Romanian soldier in the Russian army, Nişu Constantin, returned home having had the Pentecostal experience through Russian believers. The Pentecostal Apostolic Church of God is the largest denomination there, founded in 1922 by George Bradin and later (1929 and 1950) uniting with other groups, on the last occasion at the behest of the Communist government. This was largely a rural phenomenon until the 1950s, when it began to work in urban areas and it now has flourishing city churches. Bradin remained president of this church until 1962, when Pavel Bochian (1918–96), president until 1990, took his place. Bochian negotiated a fraternal agreement with the Church of God (Cleveland) in 1980. Since 1996 the church has simply been known as the Pentecostal Union.[21]

In Poland, always a strongly Catholic country, Pentecostalism has struggled, although it has been there since 1910 through contact between Polish Lutherans and Jonathan Paul in Germany. The first Pentecostal Bible college in this region was opened in 1929 in Gdansk, called the Danzig Bible Institute. This was supported by the AG in the USA, but had teaching

---

[20] Hollenweger, *The Pentecostals*, pp. 267–9, 274, 281; Steve Durasoff, *Bright Wind of the Spirit: Pentecostalism Today* (London: Hodder and Stoughton, 1972), p. 227; Johnstone and Mandryk, *Operation World*, pp. 540, 644.

[21] Johnstone and Mandryk, *Operation World*, p. 536; Rodica Pandrea, 'A Historical and Theological Analysis of the Pentecostal Church in Romania', *JEPTA* XXI (2001), 109–35.

support from all over Europe. From here many of Eastern Europe's leaders emerged in the following years, but the Nazis closed it in 1938. Polish Pentecostals were forced to join the government-registered United Evangelical Church in 1947 and the Pentecostal Church of Poland was only officially recognized in 1987. This autonomous church is in fellowship with the World Assemblies of God Fellowship. Poland also has a strong Catholic Charismatic community.[22]

The Czech and Slovak Republics were early centres of Pentecostalism with separate histories, that in the Czech Republic originating in an independent revival in Tensinsko and the experience of Charismatics in the Free Reformed Church in Prague in 1907–8. The Association of Resolute Christians was a Pentecostal organization officially registered in 1910. In Slovakia, the movement began through Slovaks who had been to Pentecostal meetings in the USA and Norway and through a visit by Swedish missionaries. The first Pentecostal church in Slovakia was opened in 1924. Repressive laws during the Communist era were only lifted in 1989, when the Apostolic Church in the Czech Republic and the Apostolic Church in Slovakia emerged.[23]

Since the disintegration of Communism there has been more freedom for Pentecostals in Eastern Europe, but this has not been without its problems. In particular, new Pentecostal groups from the West have flooded into former Communist countries with aggressive evangelistic techniques, and this has led to opposition from dominant Orthodox churches and even from national governments. Some of the new churches have succeeded in attracting large crowds to their services. But there have been other developments: the institutionalizing of Pentecostal denominations that had been forced to share their identity with evangelicals and Baptists and the creation and expansion of Pentecostal theological colleges has resulted in a more inward-looking Pentecostal movement in some of these countries. The situation is still in a state of flux, and the next few years will determine the direction that Pentecostal Christianity will take in Eastern Europe.

Like its counterpart in Latin America, European Pentecostalism presents a very different picture to that of North America and has maintained its independence and developed its own roots. From the start it has been an

---

[22] Wojciech Gajewski and Krzysztof Wawrzeniuk, 'A Historical and Theological Analysis of the Pentecostal Church of Poland, *JEPTA* XX (2000), 32–48.

[23] Josef Brenkus, 'A Historical and Theological Analysis of the Pentecostal Church in the Czech and Slovak Republics', *JEPTA*, XX (2000), 49–65.

essentially European phenomenon that has (in some countries) shown evidence of growth that belies the general decline of European Christianity in the twentieth century. Independent of expatriate missionaries, the future of European Pentecostalism still looks promising; and it may be that Pentecostal and Charismatic forms of Christianity will help rescue the church from pending oblivion in this post-Christian continent.

6

African Pentecostalism and 'Spirit' churches

Pentecostalism is big business in Africa. Statistics are notoriously difficult to calculate and verify and even more so in Africa. But the estimates we have for Christian affiliation at the beginning of the twenty-first century reveal some amazing trends that any casual observer of Christianity in Africa will not find so incredible. According to one estimate, 11 per cent of Africa's population (including the predominantly Muslim north) was 'Charismatic' in 2000.[1] Even if this figure is only roughly approximate, the Pentecostal and Charismatic movements undoubtedly are fast becoming dominant forms of Christianity on the continent. This has been developing for over a century and Africa now has its own distinct contribution to make to the shape of global Pentecostalism.

Some prominent expressions of Christianity in the sub-Sahara may be called 'African Pentecostal' churches because of a particular emphasis that is common to churches that would otherwise be quite different. Despite inadequacies and the danger of making generalizations, the term 'Pentecostal' in this chapter refers to divergent African churches that emphasize the working of the Spirit in the church, particularly with ecstatic phenomena like prophecy and speaking in tongues, healing and exorcism. These phenomena have been characteristic of Pentecostal and Charismatic churches throughout the world, and are widespread throughout Africa across a great variety of Christian churches. These include thousands of African initiated churches (AICs) known collectively as 'prophet-healing', 'Spirit' or 'spiritual' churches.[2] The term 'African Pentecostal' also includes two other types of churches that are now growing more rapidly than the older AICs: those churches of western, 'classical' Pentecostal origin, and the new independent

---

[1] Johnstone and Mandryk, *Operation World*, p. 21.
[2] Allan Anderson, *Zion and Pentecost: The Spirituality and Experience of Pentecostal and Zionist/Apostolic Churches in South Africa* (Pretoria: University of South Africa Press, 2000), pp. 34–7.

Pentecostal and Charismatic churches and 'ministries' that have arisen since the late 1970s. Classical Pentecostals have been operating in Africa since 1907, when the first missionaries from Azusa Street arrived in Liberia and Angola. The AG in particular has grown in almost every African country, with over four million members estimated throughout Africa in 1994 and now with many more.[3] The several churches emanating from West African revivals linking in the 1930s with the Apostolic Church in Britain are now enormous organizations throughout this region, but especially in Nigeria and Ghana. Classical Pentecostal and new Pentecostal and Charismatic churches are actively growing throughout Africa. This is particularly the case in countries like Zimbabwe, where they were an estimated fifth of the population in 2000; in Kenya, Nigeria, Ghana and Zambia over a tenth, and the Democratic Republic of the Congo (DRC) and South Africa just less than a tenth. If we add the African 'Spirit' churches to this reckoning, then the figures would be considerably higher. More than half of Zimbabwe's population would belong to African Pentecostal churches, almost half of South Africa's, over a third of Kenya's, followed by the DRC, Nigeria, Ghana and Zambia – all over a quarter of the population.[4] These proportions, though speculative and subject to interpretations of how 'Pentecostal' is defined (see chapter 1), nevertheless give an indication of the strength of African Pentecostalism today.

Not everyone is convinced that all these different churches should be considered 'Pentecostal' and I have not presumed that they are anywhere near a homogeneous whole. The variety and creativity in African Christianity is remarkable. Most observers of African Christianity, however, will admit that a great number of AICs are of a Pentecostal type and that these churches have been in the forefront of the contextualization of Christianity in Africa for over a century. Harvey Cox, following Hollenweger, says that the 'Spirit' AICs are 'the African expression of the worldwide Pentecostal movement'. The 'Pentecostalization' of African Christianity can be called the 'African Reformation' of the twentieth century that has fundamentally altered the character of African Christianity, including that of the older, 'mission' churches.[5] The 'Spirit' churches are African expressions of Pentecostalism because of their characteristics, theology and history, as this chapter will reveal. Although the older 'Spirit' AICs might no longer be

---

[3] Everett A. Wilson, *Strategy of the Spirit: J. Philip Hogan and the Growth of the Assemblies of God Worldwide 1960–1990* (Carlisle: Regnum, 1997), p. 119.

[4] Johnstone and Mandryk, *Operation World*.

[5] Cox, *Fire*, p. 246; Allan Anderson, *African Reformation: African Initiated Christianity in the Twentieth Century* (Trenton, NJ and Asmara, Eritrea: Africa World Press, 2001), pp. 4–5.

paradigmatic of African Pentecostalism, they are certainly an important expression of it. No student of global Pentecostalism can afford to ignore this facet of African Christianity. There are thousands of these churches throughout the sub-Sahara, and although they do not usually call themselves 'Pentecostal' or 'Charismatic', many do consider themselves part of Pentecostal and Charismatic Christianity and exhibit a very similar theology and orientation. In southern Africa, the majority are known as 'Zionists' after the Chicago movement of John Alexander Dowie and 'Apostolics' after the classical Pentecostal movement from which they emerged, the Apostolic Faith Mission. In East Africa and in parts of West Africa they originated in African Pentecostal revivals and are called 'churches of the Spirit,' and in western Nigeria 'Aladura' ('people of prayer') churches, after a Charismatic prayer group that formed in an Anglican church but was later influenced by classical Pentecostalism.

In several African countries, independent churches of the older and the newer (Charismatic) varieties form the majority of Christians, an extremely important component of world Christianity. The 'Spirit' churches have much in common with classical Pentecostals and their history is inextricably tied up with them. They practise gifts of the Spirit, especially healing and prophecy and they speak in tongues. Because of their 'Spirit' manifestations and pneumatic emphases and experiences, most earlier studies of these churches misunderstood or generalized about them and branded them 'syncretistic', 'post-Christian' and 'messianic'. Unfortunately, these terms are still used pejoratively by other African Pentecostals, often based on misapprehensions and a lack of communication. Part of the problem that outside observers have had with the 'churches of the Spirit' is that they have often been seen as accommodating the pre-Christian past, and linked with traditional practices like divination and ancestor rituals. More recent studies have shown this to be a fallacious view and certainly not how these churches see themselves.

Although most AICs can be called 'Pentecostal', many of them have few connections with classical Pentecostalism and are very different from it in several ways. There are external differences like the use of healing symbolism including blessed water, many other symbolic ritual objects representing power and protection, forms of government and hierarchical patterns of leadership (sometimes including hereditary leadership, not a stranger to western Pentecostalism!), the use of some African cultural practices and the wearing of distinctive robes or uniforms. They also differ fundamentally in their approach to African religions and culture, in liturgy, healing practices and in their unique contribution to Christianity in a broader African context. This distinct and innovative approach often differs sharply from those Pentecostals and Charismatics who are more heavily influenced by western Pentecostalism. Although there are clear affinities and common historical and theological origins shared by African and western Pentecostals, the passing of time and the proliferation of AICs have accentuated the differences. Pentecostal AICs throughout Africa are often churches that emphasize healing through prophets. One of the largest AICs on the continent, the Church of Jesus Christ on Earth according to the Prophet Simon Kimbangu, better known as the Kimbanguist Church in the DRC and Central Africa, will not be considered in this chapter because it has become so significantly different from most other Pentecostal AICs that it has little in common with them. We will focus here on those African movements with a more definite Pentecostal identity in terms of history, theology and liturgy. Despite the significance of 'classical' Pentecostal denominations throughout Africa today and the brave sacrifices made by their missionaries in remote parts of Africa, most of these missionaries have been well chronicled. African leaders of Pentecostal churches tend not to appear as prominently in the literature, so here we will concentrate more on those Pentecostal and Charismatic movements initiated by Africans.[6]

SOUTHERN AFRICAN CHURCHES

The complex history of Pentecostalism in South Africa cannot be separated from that of the Zionist and Apostolic churches with which Pentecostalism is inextricably entwined. In about 1902, Pieter (P. L.) le Roux (1865–1943), Dutch Reformed missionary in South Africa, together with some 400 Africans in what is now the province of Mpumalanga, joined the Christian Catholic Apostolic Church of John Alexander Dowie in Zion City, near Chicago (see chapter 2), a movement that emphasized divine healing and triune baptism of adult believers by immersion. Le Roux had come to know of the Zionist movement through Dowie's periodical *Leaves of Healing*. This group of Zionists had reached 5,000 believers by 1905, when Dowie sent a missionary to South Africa, Daniel Bryant, who soon returned to the USA. In 1908 several independent Pentecostal missionaries, including John G. Lake (a former elder in Zion City) arrived and took over the Zion building in Johannesburg, calling their new movement the Apostolic Faith Mission, officially constituted in 1913. Le Roux joined the AFM and by 1915, after Lake's return to the USA, he became its president,

[6] Anderson, *Zion and Pentecost*, pp. 27–8; Anderson, *African Reformation*, pp. 69–190.

a post he held until his death in 1943. His African fellow-workers still considered themselves Zionists, while embracing the new doctrine of the Holy Spirit with speaking in tongues and prophecy emphasized by the Pentecostals. The first Pentecostal services in Johannesburg were racially integrated, but as the African leaders continued to work together with the AFM the white leaders passed racist laws and kept all significant positions for themselves. This contributed to the many schisms that took place thereafter, most of the African Zionist leaders leaving the AFM. Daniel Nkonyane broke with le Roux and the AFM as early as 1910, eventually forming the Christian Catholic Apostolic Holy Spirit Church in Zion. In 1917 Elias Mahlangu founded the Zion Apostolic Church of South Africa, Paulo Mabilitsa founded the Christian Apostolic Church in Zion in 1920, and J. C. Phillips (a Malawian migrant worker) commenced the Holy Catholic Apostolic Church in Zion.[7] Out of Mahlangu's Zion Apostolic Church, Edward Lion's Zion Apostolic Faith Mission seceded in 1920. Engenas Lekganyane's Zion Christian Church seceded from the ZAFM in 1925 – now the largest denomination in South Africa, with over four million affiliates in 2000.[8] There are also now thousands of smaller Zionist and Apostolic churches in southern Africa.

Engenas Lekganyane (c.1880–1948) was an evangelist in the Free Church of Scotland when a voice told him that he should join a church baptizing by triune immersion and thus find healing for his longstanding eye problem. He joined Elias Mahlangu in the Zion Apostolic Church, started his own congregation and won many converts, but differences emerged. Mahlangu promoted wearing white robes, growing beards and removing shoes before a service (common among many southern African churches) and Lekganyane objected to these customs. At this time, while praying on a mountain he had a vision that a multitude would follow him and in 1917 he prophesied the defeat of Germany by Britain. When this happened, his prestige as a prophet and his following grew. He left Mahlangu's church in 1920 and joined Edward Lion's ZAFM, where he was appointed bishop for the Transvaal. Edward Lion had also been the AFM's overseer in Lesotho, and John G. Lake in his own writings had commended Lion's ministry of healing and miracles. Differences again emerged between Lion and Lekganyane resulting in the latter founding the Zion Christian Church (ZCC) in 1924–25, with over 900 members at the time. In 1930 Lekganyane

---

[7] B. G. N. Sundkler, *Bantu Prophets in South Africa* (Oxford: Oxford University Press, 1961), pp. 48–9; B. G. N. Sundkler, *Zulu Zion and some Swazi Zionists* (London: Oxford University Press, 1976), pp. 52, 55–6; Anderson, *Zion and Pentecost*, pp. 57–63.
[8] Johnstone and Mandryk, *Operation World*, p. 577.

was able to buy a farm that he called Moria, the place of pilgrimage for ZCC members thereafter. The church grew to over 40,000 members by 1943 and had spread to Zimbabwe, Botswana and the Cape, already one of the biggest AICs in the continent. The early emphasis of Lekganyane's ministry was healing, at first by laying on hands; but as the church developed he began to bless various objects like strips of cloth, strings, papers, needles, walking sticks and water for healing and protective uses by his ministers. After Engenas Lekganyane's death in 1948, his two surviving sons Edward and Joseph disputed the leadership, as it was not clear who Engenas had appointed as his successor. Two separate churches were formed in 1949, the followers of Joseph becoming the St Engenas ZCC, while the majority of Engenas' followers stayed with Edward Lekganyane in the ZCC.

In doctrine there are no significant differences between Zionist and Apostolic churches on the one hand and classical Pentecostal churches on the other, but in rituals the differences are marked. A Zionist becomes a Christian through baptism by triune immersion, which often must take place in running water, in a river often called 'Jordan'. There is an emphasis on healing, although the methods of obtaining it differ. Whereas classical Pentecostals generally practice laying on hands and prayer for the sick, this will usually be accompanied in Zionist and Apostolic churches by the use of symbolic objects appropriated and modified from traditional religion, like blessed water, ropes, staffs, papers, ash and so on. This constitutes one of the obvious differences between these churches and western Pentecostals. Speaking in tongues is also practised in some churches but doctrinal disputes over this issue are unknown. There are strong ethical rules for members, and many churches prohibit alcohol, tobacco and pork (also prohibitions found in early Pentecostalism). The attitude to traditional religious practices is generally ambivalent (particularly when it comes to ancestors), and some churches allow polygyny. For the outsider, the biggest distinguishing feature of these churches is the use of uniform apparel, usually white robes with coloured belts and sashes and other markings, and in the case of the ZCC, mainly khaki, green and gold military-like uniforms. These churches do not have many church buildings and often meet in the open air.[9]

The AFM is one of South Africa's biggest classical Pentecostal denominations. Its white membership is mainly Afrikaner and there is a significant black membership today. David du Plessis (1905–87), who later emigrated to the USA to become leading spokesperson for Pentecostals to the ecumenical

---

[9] Anderson, *Zion and Pentecost*, pp. 70–1, 79–80.

movement, was General Secretary of the AFM from 1936 to 1947. Another of its well-known leaders is Frank Chikane (1951–), Vice-President of the church from 1996 to 2000, when he gave up this position to attend to his post as Director-General in the Office of the President, one of the top government positions in the country. Active in the AFM in Soweto as a young man, Chikane joined German evangelist Reinhard Bonnke's organization 'Christ for All Nations' for a short time. Between 1977 and 1982 he was detained four times by the police – on two occasions for over seven months – although he was never convicted of any crime. His continued involvement in the freedom struggle and his community projects got him into trouble with the AFM leadership, who suspended him from 'full-time service' for one year in 1981, but did not reinstate him until 1990 after intense pressure. For his involvement in youth community projects in Soweto, Chikane had been tortured by police officers, one of whom was a white member of the AFM. Although Chikane's ministerial credentials had been withdrawn, by 1993 he was elected president of the 'Composite Division' of the church (a union of three sections of the church excluding the white section), and vice-president of the newly united church in 1996. He became Director-General of the Office of the President (Thabo Mbeki) in 1999, and retained his office in the church while facing criticism from white delegates to the church governing body. The AFM, like most classical Pentecostal denominations in South Africa, was divided on racial grounds to separate whites from blacks in church affairs (although the black church was controlled by the white section). In 1996 the different 'divisions' of the AFM were united after a painful and protracted period of negotiation.

The same situation pertained in the Full Gospel Church of God, a church founded as the Full Gospel Church in 1910 with origins in white South African initiatives like those of Archibald Cooper, and in affiliation with the CGC since 1951. This church is also the largest Christian church among the South African Indian population in Natal. The first steps towards unity between the different 'associations' in this church were only achieved in 1997. The South African AG has its origins in the work of several early Pentecostal missionaries including Henry Turney, a product of Azusa Street, and Charles Chawner, a Canadian who became a missionary in the PAC. Both these independent missionaries arrived in 1909 and a number of Pentecostal churches were first registered as the AG in 1917. The AG has also been beset by schisms, but these have not been primarily on racial lines. One of its greatest leaders was Nicholas Bhengu (1909–86), whose 'Back to God Crusades' were the means of bringing many thousands of Africans into the church.[10] The South African AG had been separate from the AG, USA since 1932, but the latter has continued to operate in the country. In 2002 the AG achieved a historic unity between three major schisms that may now make it the largest classical Pentecostal denomination in the country.

Pentecostalism and AICs in other parts of southern Africa were greatly influenced by developments in South Africa, from where Pentecostal, Zionist and Apostolic ideas spread to the surrounding countries to the north, mainly through migrant workers from these countries who met Pentecostalism while working in South African mines. Different types of AICs arose simultaneously in these countries, and Zionist and Apostolic churches soon eclipsed other AICs in size and influence. The AFM has been influential in spreading Pentecostal ideas further north in Africa as far as Kenya. The largest Pentecostal church in Zimbabwe, the Zimbabwe Assemblies of God Africa, popularly known by its acronym ZAOGA (pronounced 'za-o-ja'), has its roots in both the AFM and Bhengu's AG. The largest AIC in Zimbabwe, the African Apostolic Church of Johane Maranke, also has roots in the AFM. The largest Pentecostal church in Mozambique, the Evangelical Assemblies of God of Mozambique has its origins in the South African AG and the work of Austin and Ingrid Chawner, with the co-operation of the AG in Portugal and national Mozambican preachers like Laurentino Mulungo. Many other Pentecostal and Charismatic groups are active in Mozambique, particularly South African ones. The same is true of Pentecostal and Charismatic work in Zambia and Malawi. In Angola, the Pentecostal Assembly of God of Angola is the largest evangelical denomination, with roots in the work of CGC missionary Pearl Stark and Portuguese AG missionaries Joaquim and Manuel Martins.[11]

CENTRAL AND EAST AFRICAN CHURCHES

Pentecostalism in the DRC is thriving in many forms, and much of it is fruit of the sacrificial labours of European missionaries in this heart of Africa. Among the earliest Pentecostal missionaries from Britain were William F. P. Burton (1886–1971) and James Salter (1890–1972), who were trained at the PMU college and settled in the southern (Belgian) Congo in 1915. They officially launched the Congo Evangelistic Mission in 1919, Burton remaining in the Congo until 1960, when he retired to South Africa, his wife's home. Burton recruited many European missionaries, the majority from Britain. During the Civil War that began in 1960, two CEM missionaries were

---

[10] Ibid., pp. 89–106.   [11] D. J. Garrard, 'Angola', 'Mozambique', *NIDPCM*, pp. 21–2, 180–1.

killed and most missionaries left the Congo. The church that has resulted from this mission is now called the Communauté Pentecôtiste du Congo (Pentecostal Community of the Congo), found mainly in the south of the country where it has some half a million members. Jonathan Ilunga has led the church since 1960. This church has continued the mission station approach of the CEM, churches being divided into seventy districts, each under a station pastor who has replaced the European missionary. There have been many schisms, especially since the 1980s, and some of these groups have joined Pentecostal movements established elsewhere in the country, including the (US) AG, the AGBI and the churches emanating from the work of Swedish and Norwegian missionaries since the 1920s. Some have formed independent African churches. Swedish missionaries have also been responsible for the beginning of Pentecostalism in Rwanda and Burundi in the 1930s. Another one of the largest Pentecostal and Charismatic churches in the DRC is popularly known as the *Nzambe Malamu* ('God is good') church, founded by Alexander Adini-Abala (c.1927–97) in Kinshasa in the late 1960s. Adini-Abala was converted during a T. L. Osborne campaign in Kenya and throughout his remarkable healing and church-planting ministry he has made selective use of European missionaries. He has planted over 350 churches in Kinshasa alone, and the membership of the church is well over half a million. On Adini-Abala's death in 1997, the leadership passed to his son, Pefa.[12]

Pentecostalism is also thriving in East Africa, where most of the numerous AICs place an emphasis on the Holy Spirit. Various revival movements in the region, especially the 'Holy Spirit' movement that began around the time of the First World War and the later East African Revival have shaped all forms of Protestant Christianity there. The Holy Spirit movement operated outside of and usually with the opposition of European missions and the colonial administration. The influence of this movement on the East African Revival, which enjoyed much more support from established mission churches, may need more consideration. However, the 'official' East African Revival movement in the CMS (Anglican) churches prevented the use of spiritual gifts such as speaking in tongues, prophecy and healing, which often brought it into conflict with those Africans who desired the more tangible evidence of God's presence and power provided by the Pentecostals.

One of the earliest Pentecostal works in the region was that of the Finnish missionary Emil Danielsson who went to Kenya in 1912. Otto

[12] D. J. Garrard, 'Congo, Democratic Republic of', *NIDPCM*, pp. 67–74.

and Marion Keller began a mission station with a school and a church at Nyang'ori near Kisumu in western Kenya in 1918, which in 1924 affiliated with the PAC and became the centre of Pentecostal activity in the region. Many of the Canadian missionaries who arrived thereafter were involved in educational work in PAC schools and colleges, and many were women. The PAC churches became independent in 1965, when they were renamed the Pentecostal Assemblies of God. US American and Scandinavian Pentecostals have also been active in Kenya resulting in a number of different classical Pentecostal denominations of which some, particularly in keeping with the Scandinavian Pentecostal ecclesiology, are associations of autonomous churches. Those Pentecostal denominations with over 100,000 members include the Pentecostal Evangelical Fellowship of Africa (begun by US missionaries in 1944), the Full Gospel Churches of Kenya (founded by Finnish missionaries in 1949) and the Kenya Assemblies of God (founded in 1967 and now in association with the AG, USA).[13]

The Roho ('Spirit') movement was one of the earliest African Pentecostal movements that commenced in 1912 among the Luo people of western Kenya, at first as a popular Charismatic movement among young people within the Anglican church. Roho's founders are Alfayo Odongo Mango (1884–1934) and his nephew Lawi Obonyo (c.1911–34). Mango was an Anglican deacon baptized in the Spirit in 1916, who received a special calling in a vision. As far as we know, he had no contact with Pentecostal missionaries. The English CMS Archdeacon Owen reported that Mango was the 'inspirer and mainstay' of 'a movement characterized by much hysteria and visions'. Mango prophesied the end of colonialism and agitated for the restoration of misappropriated Luo land, but he also preached against certain Luo customs. In early 1933 Lawi began a prophetic ministry, when several remarkable healings and other miracles were reported. Owen and two other European missionaries attended one of Lawi's revival meetings in October 1933, in which they publicly denounced him as a 'deceiver' and ordered the meeting to disperse. In Owen's opinion, Lawi was involved in 'the most extravagant forms of hysteria and emotionalism'. Mango installed new rites of baptism and Communion, and his home became a centre to which people came and from where missionaries, both women and men, fanned out. The peaceful JoRoho ('people of the Spirit') were accused of 'acts of violence' against non-Roho Luo and were banned from attending Anglican churches. Owen reported in 1934 that Mango through his actions had 'broken away' from the Anglican Church. Five days after he made

---

[13] D. J. Garrard, 'Kenya', *NIDPCM*, pp. 150–5.

this report, Mango, Lawi and seven of their followers were murdered by a Wanga mob of several hundred, as Mango's house in Musanda was set alight. The JoRoho thereafter began a vigorous missionary expansion movement called Dini ya Roho ('Religion of the Spirit'), emphasizing the power of the Spirit and dressing in white robes with red crosses. It is thought that Roho churches now claim that Mango's sacrificial death atoned for their sins and opened heaven to Africans. Mango is prayed to as 'our Saviour' and he has inaugurated a new era of the reign of the Holy Spirit in Africa. These churches enjoin monogamy on their leaders and are known for their processions through the streets of towns and villages. The Roho movement has had several schisms.[14]

A Holy Spirit movement also called Dini ya Roho among the Luo's neighbours, the Abaluyia, emerged after a Pentecostal revival in a Friends (Quaker) mission in 1927. The local church leaders and North American mission authorities discouraged the revival and banned public confession of sins and spiritual gifts like prophecy and speaking in tongues. The revivalists, expelled from the Friends mission in 1929, organized themselves into a church, the largest of many churches to emerge being the African Church of the Holy Spirit.[15] The African Israel Church Nineveh (AICN) founded in 1942 by the Pentecostal Luyia evangelist Daudi Zakayo Kivuli (1896–1974), is another prominent church in Kenya. Kivuli associated with the Kellers in the PAC from 1925. He was a supervisor of schools for this mission and after an ecstatic Spirit baptism experience in 1932 embarked on an evangelistic and healing ministry among both the Luyia and the Luo with the initial encouragement of the PAC. In 1940, he founded his own church, took the title 'High Priest' and his home became the headquarters Nineveh, the place to which people flocked. The AICN has many practices similar to those of other Pentecostal AICs in other parts of the continent. Members wear white robes and turbans, practise constant singing and dancing in procession, emphasize Spirit baptism, observe Old Testament dietary and purification taboos, and have a holy place (Nineveh) where the present archbishop resides. The AICN, like other Roho churches, is known for its joyful and colourful processions and open-air meetings in which flags, drums, staffs and trumpets are used in singing to African tunes. Several secessions have occurred in the AICN since the death of the founder, nearly

---

[14] Cynthia Hoehler-Fatton, *Women of Fire and Spirit: History, Faith and Gender in Roho Religion in Western Kenya* (Oxford University Press, 1996), pp. 3–6, 12–18, 58–64; Anderson, *African Reformation*, pp. 153–5.

[15] Ane Marie Bak Rasmussen, *Modern African Spirituality: The Independent Spirit Churches in East Africa, 1902–1976* (London and New York: British Academic Press, 1996), pp. 11–63.

all using the word Israel in their name and looking back to Kivuli as founder. On Kivuli's death in 1974 his wife Rebecca became High Priestess of the church and on her death in 1983 her grandson John Mweresa Kivuli II (1960–) became High Priest. Since 1991 he has been known as Archbishop and has embarked on a process of modernization.

There are many other churches in Kenya, like the Arathi ('Prophets'), also known as 'Watu wa Mungu' ('People of God'), or as now better known, Akurinu. This is a prophet-healing movement among the Gikuyu of central Kenya that selectively rejects western dress, medicine and education, and uses the Bible together with some elements of Gikuyu tradition. This movement started in a Pentecostal revival that began in 1922, with manifestations of the Spirit including speaking in tongues, prophecy, visions and other ecstatic phenomena, and with an emphasis on prayer and the confession of sins. There are now more than thirty Akurinu churches in Kenya, nearly all of which use 'Holy Ghost' in their church title. Like most Roho churches, they do not baptize with water but practise a 'baptism of the Holy Spirit' by a threefold shaking of hands and laying on of hands. Despite similarities with the Roho movement in western Kenya, the Akurinu movement was formed with little or no contact with western missions or spiritual churches elsewhere. It has consciously attempted to form a radically African type of Christianity, where the patterns of older forms of Christianity play no significant role.[16]

Independent Pentecostal missionaries from Canada arrived in Tanganyika (now Tanzania) in 1913, but two of the three died within three months. Scandinavian missionaries followed them in the 1930s from the Swedish Free Mission and the Finnish Free Mission and created churches, hospitals, orphanages, schools, colleges, a radio station and clinics across the country. The churches resulting from this work are now called the Pentecostal Churches Association in Tanzania, one of the larger classical Pentecostal churches in the country. The Tanzanian AG has grown extensively since its founding in the 1940s to become probably the largest. The PAC (known as the Pentecostal Assemblies of God, Tanzania), PHC and Elim (UK), among many others, are also operating in Tanzania. Some of these churches were started by Kenyans or by Tanzanians from Kenya and Malawi. As is true of Pentecostals worldwide, the Tanzanian Pentecostal denominations have suffered from many schisms, especially since the 1980s.[17]

---

[16] Anderson, *African Reformation*, pp. 158–60.   [17] D. J. Garrard, 'Tanzania', *NIDPCM*, pp. 264–9.

From western Kenya, Pentecostalism spread to Uganda through Ugandans returning from Kenya, but because of the ravages of corrupt and oppressive dictatorships and a protracted civil war, the Pentecostal and Charismatic movements in this country have developed relatively late. Numerous Pentecostal and Charismatic groups have arisen since the overthrow of Milton Obote in 1986 and most of the classical Pentecostal missions in Kenya are now operating there as well as many new ones. An unfortunate characteristic of Pentecostalism in East Africa has been a lack of co-operation between the various, often very similar, Pentecostal missions.

Ethiopia has one of the fastest growing evangelical churches in the world, and the great majority are Pentecostal and Charismatic. The first Pentecostals in Ethiopia and Eritrea were missionaries from the Finnish Free Foreign Mission, who arrived in 1951 and set up clinics, schools and orphanages. Most left the country after the 1974 revolution, but the churches continued and have been under Ethiopian leadership since 1967, known as Sefer Ghenet (Church of Guenet). There are many autonomous Ethiopian Pentecostal and Charismatic churches, and involvement by Swedish and Canadian Pentecostals and by US AG missionaries in recent years has assisted some of these churches in various ways like famine relief, childcare and leadership training. The Lutheran/Evangelical church, since a merger in 1975 called Evangelical Church Mekane Yesu, has a large number of Charismatic members and ministers, and there are Charismatics in the Ethiopian Orthodox Church too.[18]

WEST AFRICAN CHURCHES

West Africa is one of the hot spots of the world as far as Pentecostalism is concerned, having rapidly become one of the most prominent and influential religious movements across this region. Some of the first missionaries from Azusa Street, including Lucy Farrow, were African Americans who went to Liberia in 1907. Their stay was short-lived and little is known about their work among the English-speaking Americo-Liberians or whether it even survived their departure. But the complex West African Pentecostal history really begins with African preachers. In 1913 and 1914 one of the most influential African Christian prophets, the Grebo Liberian William Wade Harris (1865–1929), began preaching in the Ivory Coast (Côte d'Ivoire) and on the west coast of the Gold Coast (Ghana). He preached from the Bible about one true God, healing and the rejection of 'fetishes' and other practices

---

[18] D. J. Garrard, 'Ethiopia', *NIDPCM*, pp. 85–8.

associated with traditional religions. Wearing a simple white robe, a round hat, black bands crossed around his chest and a cross in his hand, these were to be the symbols of his followers. Harris and two women companions would approach a village singing songs accompanied by calabash rattles. People would gather and Harris would preach fervently, inviting them to renounce traditional religion and believe in God. Those who did so were baptized from the water in Harris' gourd dish, and the Bible was placed on their heads. Sometimes people possessed by evil spirits were invited to touch the prophet's staff and were sprinkled with holy water. It is said that Harris performed several miracles displaying the power of God at this time, and is thought to have baptized some 120,000 adult Ivorian converts in a year. He was deported by French colonial authorities in 1914, when village prayer houses set up by his followers were also destroyed, but this was one of the greatest influxes of Africans to Christianity ever seen.

Although Harris directed people to existing mission churches, thousands of his followers found themselves disagreeing with Methodist financial policy, their prohibition of polygamy and the foreign liturgy that was so different from the African hymn singing and dancing practised by Harris. They organized themselves into the Harrist Church which grew rapidly, although increasingly identified with the nationalist struggle and severely persecuted by the French administration. The Harrist Church in the Ivory Coast was only officially registered in 1955, and by 2000 it had an estimated 200,000 adherents, one of the four largest churches in the country and one of four nationally recognized religions (the others being Islam, Catholicism and Protestantism). Other churches in the Ivory Coast were to emerge in the Harrist tradition and Harris' influence was to be felt in neighbouring Ghana. There, the first 'spiritual church' to be formed was the Church of the Twelve Apostles, begun in 1918 by Harris' converts Grace Tani and Kwesi John Nackabah to realize Harris' instruction that twelve apostles should be appointed in each village to look after his flock. This new church followed Harris' emphasis on healing through faith and the use of holy water, administered in healing 'gardens' (communal dwellings). In 1938 the church considered affiliating with the Apostolic Church from Britain, but withdrew when their missionary McKeown insisted that tambourines be substituted for calabash rattles, reportedly seen as an attempt to deprive Africans of the power to ward off evil spirits.

The four main classical Pentecostal denominations in Ghana today are the largest, the Church of Pentecost, the Assemblies of God, the Apostolic Church of Ghana and the Christ Apostolic Church. Three of these have origins in the work of a remarkable Ghanaian, Peter Anim (1890–1984), and his

Northern Irish contemporary James McKeown (1900–89). Anim, regarded as the father of Pentecostalism in Ghana, came into contact with the publication of the Faith Tabernacle church in Philadelphia, USA in about 1917 and he received healing from stomach ailments in 1921. He resigned from the Presbyterian church to became an independent healing preacher who gathered a large following, adopting the name Faith Tabernacle in 1922. Similar developments in Nigeria took place at the same time, when David Odubanjo became the leader of Faith Tabernacle there. Recognition was awarded these African leaders entirely through correspondence and no personal visits were made from Philadelphia to West Africa. In the meantime, Anim's evangelistic activities were creating churches throughout southern Ghana and as far as Togo in the east. When a report of the dismissal of the US leader of Faith Tabernacle reached Anim in 1930 he broke the connection and changed the name of his organization to Apostolic Faith, after the periodical *Apostolic Faith* from Portland, Oregon. Two years later a Pentecostal revival broke out in this church and many were baptized in the Spirit and spoke in tongues. Nigerian leader Odubanjo made contact with the Apostolic Church in the UK and Anim and two leaders travelled to Lagos to meet their representatives in 1932. Anim affiliated with the Apostolic Church in 1935 and negotiated with the Bradford headquarters for missionaries to be sent to Ghana.

In 1937 James and Sophia McKeown arrived as these missionaries. When McKeown contracted malaria soon afterwards, he was taken to hospital for treatment, a position that Anim and his followers found deviating from their understanding of divine healing without the use of medicine. This led to the withdrawal of Anim and many of his members in 1939 to found the Christ Apostolic Church. McKeown himself came into conflict with the Apostolic Church and seceded in 1953 to form the Gold Coast (after independence, Ghana) Apostolic Church. From the beginning, although McKeown was Chairman of the church, he worked with an all-Ghanaian executive council and Ghanaians took the initiatives for the expansion of the church. To all intents and purposes this was an autochthonous Ghanaian church. In 1962 President Kwame Nkrumah intervened in a protracted legal battle over church properties between the two Apostolic churches and ordered McKeown to change the name, when 'Church of Pentecost' (COP) was adopted. In 1971 the COP affiliated with the Elim Pentecostal Church in Britain, a co-operative arrangement that still exists. Elim have assisted in the areas of leadership training, radio ministry and publishing, and in 2003 one British Elim couple was working in Pentecost University College, the ministerial training college of the church. McKeown began to withdraw from his dominant role in the church from the 1960s, when he would spend increasing time in Britain, eventually spending only half the year in Ghana. On his retirement and departure from Ghana in 1982, he was followed as Chairman by Apostle F. S. Safo (1982–87), Prophet M. K. Yeboah (1988–98), and Apostle Michael K. Ntumy, elected in 1998. Another important event occurred in 1969, when the three Anim-derived Apostolic churches and the Assemblies of God formed the Ghana Pentecostal Council. By 1998 150 denominations had joined this organization, a remarkable and unusual feat of Pentecostal and Charismatic ecumenism.[19]

In 1915, a popular Anglican revivalist preacher in the Niger River Delta of Nigeria, Garrick Braide, preached the destruction of fetishes and healing through prayer. His followers became the Christ Army Church, the first 'spiritual church' in Nigeria. Braide himself was regarded as a threat to the British colonial authorities and was imprisoned for seditious behaviour. In Yorubaland in western Nigeria, an Anglican Church leader Joseph Shadare formed a prayer group in 1918 called the Precious Stone Society to provide spiritual support and healing for victims of the influenza epidemic. This group left the Anglican Church in 1922 over the issue of infant baptism and affiliated with Faith Tabernacle, with an emphasis on divine healing and adult baptism by immersion. Contact with the church in the USA was severed in 1925 over the matrimonial affairs of its leader. In the same year, the Eternal Sacred Order of Cherubim and Seraphim Society was founded by another Anglican, Moses Orimolade Tunolashe (who became known as Baba Aladura, a title used by subsequent leaders of this church) and the fifteen-year-old girl Abiodun Akinsowon (later called Captain Abiodun), for whom Orimolade was called upon to pray for healing. Orimolade had begun preaching in about 1915 after partially recovering from a long illness.[20] This new movement emphasized prayer and so its followers were called *Aladura*, ('praying people') a term that distinguished them from other churches at the time. Orimolade took the revival to other parts of Yorubaland, where the largest and most numerous AICs in West Africa are now found.

The greatest expansion of the Aladura movement took place after a revival that began in 1930. A former member of Faith Tabernacle, Joseph Babalola, met Shadare at Ilesha and began preaching. Babalola heard a voice calling him to preach using prayer and 'water of life' (blessed water) which would

---

[19] E. Kingsley Larbi, *Pentecostalism: The Eddies of Ghanaian Christianity* (Accra, Ghana: Centre for Pentecostal and Charismatic Studies, 2001), pp. 99–294.

[20] Harold W. Turner, *History of an African Independent Church (1) The Church of the Lord (Aladura)* (Oxford: Clarendon Press, 1967), pp. 6, 11–12.

Figure 6. First Executive Council with James McKeown, Church of Pentecost, Accra, Ghana, 1963.

Figure 7. James McKeown and Ghanaian President General Acheompong at Church of Pentecost convention, Accra, Ghana, 1978.

heal all sicknesses. The church that Babalola helped establish had associated first with Faith Tabernacle and then with the Apostolic Church after the arrival of British missionaries in 1932. But in 1939 it followed Anim in Ghana and broke with the Apostolic missionaries after they objected to the use of 'water of life'. The Africans in turn objected to the missionaries using medicine and quinine for healing, a practice they saw as a compromise of the doctrine of divine healing.[21] The Christ Apostolic Church (CAC) was constituted in 1941 and is now the largest Aladura church in Nigeria and one of the largest AICs in Africa, with some two million affiliates. This church considers itself a Pentecostal church and follows the Apostolic Church in both polity and theology but with significant modifications. Both in Ghana and Nigeria, after the disagreements with European missionaries, the missionaries remained and formed separate church organizations that still exist, the Apostolic Church being a significant church in both countries. Josiah Ositelu, an Anglican schoolteacher involved in the prophetic exposure of witchcraft, was also associated with Shadare and Babalola during the 1930 revival, founding the Church of the Lord (Aladura) in 1930 after disagreements over his calling on the names of angels and his practices of polygamy and witchcraft exposure.[22] The Aladura movement in Nigeria, although influenced by western Pentecostalism, was essentially an African Pentecostal revival mostly among city people and marked by the rejection of traditional religion – the CAC also rejected polygamy and the use of all medicine. In more recent times, the CAC in both Ghana and Nigeria have modified their strict stance on medicine. By 1950 Aladura churches were at the centre of Yoruba society and are still a significant and virile force in Nigerian Christianity.

AN AFRICAN REFORMATION

I have referred to the growth and development of Pentecostal and Charismatic and 'Spirit' churches in the twentieth century as an 'African Reformation'. Such a fundamental change has indeed taken place in African Christianity that Pentecostalism has become its dominant expression in many countries. This has been further accelerated by the enormous growth of new Pentecostal and Charismatic churches in Africa since the 1970s (see chapter 8). This remarkable growth and the corresponding decline in membership among many older churches gives us pause to consider

---

[21] Peel, *Aladura*, p. 91; Turner, *History*, p. 32; Johnstone and Mandryk, *Operation World*, p. 488.
[22] Turner, *History*, pp. 22–5; Johnstone and Mandryk, *Operation World*, pp. 241, 421.

the reasons. Searching questions about the relevance of the faith and life of older churches in Africa can be posed. If people perceive their teachings and practices as powerless to meet their everyday felt needs, then these churches cannot continue with 'business as usual' in the face of obvious shortcomings. Older churches in Africa are now rethinking their entire strategy and are being changed by the 'Pentecostalization' process taking place. Without such a serious reappraisal, their decline will probably continue and may be terminal.

One of the reasons for the growth of Pentecostal and Charismatic churches may be that they have succeeded where western founded churches have often failed – to provide a contextualized Christianity in Africa. They are essentially of African origin (even when founded by western Pentecostal missionaries) and fulfill African aspirations, with roots in a marginalized and underprivileged society struggling to find dignity and identity in the face of brutal colonialism and oppression. In some parts of Africa, Pentecostalism expanded initially among people who were neglected, misunderstood and deprived of anything but token leadership by their white ecclesiastical 'masters'. But despite these important social and historical factors, fundamentally it is the ability of African Pentecostalism to adapt to and fulfill religious aspirations that continues to be its main strength. An African style of worship and liturgy and a holistic Christianity that offers tangible help in this world as well as in the next together form a uniquely African contextualization of Christianity. This contextual Christianity meets needs more substantially than the often sterile Christianity imported from Europe. If older churches fail to address and remedy these shortcomings, they may continue to minister to a decreasing membership content either to practise Christianity side by side with African traditional religions or to succumb to a secular society and disappear.

7

Pentecostalism in Asia, Australia and the Pacific

Asia, the world's largest continent with the greatest religio-cultural diversity, has a significant Christian population, 9.6 per cent of the total population of Asia in 2000, some 313 million people, according to the *World Christian Encyclopedia*. Observers have spoken of the 'explosive' growth of Pentecostalism in several Asian countries, with an estimated 135 million Pentecostals/Charismatics in Asia comparing favourably with 80 million in North America, 141 million in Latin America, 126 million in Africa and only 38 million in Europe.[1] According to these statisticians, Asia has the second largest number of Pentecostal and Charismatics of any continent and seems to be fast catching up with Latin America. Together with Africa, these three continents have some three quarters of all the Pentecostals and Charismatics in the world. Furthermore, at least a third of the Asian Christian population is Charismatic or Pentecostal, a proportion that is steadily rising. There are now more evangelicals in Asia than in the entire western world. Harvey Cox speaks of 'the rapid spread of the Spirit-oriented forms of Christianity in Asia'.[2] Asian Pentecostal and Charismatic churches, like their counterparts in Africa and Latin America, have a distinctly different character moulded by the particular contexts of various Asian peoples. These contexts must be taken into account when assessing this vibrant part of world Christianity. Among other things, Hwa Yung has shown that Pentecostal phenomena in Asia have existed long before the arrival of western Pentecostalism and the Charismatic movement in Asia must not be interpreted in the light of the familiar theme of three 'waves' of Pentecostalism from the USA.[3]

---

[1] David B. Barrett, George T. Kurian and Todd M. Johnson, *World Christian Encyclopedia* (2nd edition), vol. 1 (New York: Oxford University Press, 2001), pp. 13–15.

[2] Cox, *Fire*, p. 214; Johnstone and Mandryk, *Operation World*, p. 41.

[3] Hwa Yung, 'Pentecostalism and the Asian Church', Allan Anderson and Edmond Tang (eds.), *Asian and Pentecostal: The Charismatic Face of Christianity in Asia* (Oxford: Regnum, 2004).

PENTECOSTALISM IN INDIA AND SRI LANKA

There were an estimated 33 million Pentecostals and Charismatics in India in 2000, only exceeded by Brazil, the USA, China and Nigeria. The majority of these are in South India. The earliest Pentecostal revival in Asia was that associated with the Tamil Anglican evangelist John Christian Aroolappen in Tamilnadu in 1860–61 when many Charismatic gifts were reported, followed by another in Travancore (Kerala) in 1874–75.[4] In the 1905–07 revival that occurred at Pandita Ramabai's Mukti Mission in Pune, young women baptized by the Spirit saw visions, fell into trances and spoke in tongues. Ramabai (1858–1922) understood this revival to be the means by which the Holy Spirit was creating a contextual form of Indian Christianity, writing in 1905:

Let the revival come to Indians so as to suit their nature and feelings, [as] God has made them. He knows their nature, and He will work out His purpose in them in a way which may not conform with the ways of Western people and their lifelong training. Let the English and other Western Missionaries begin to study the Indian nature, I mean the religious inclinations, the emotional side of the Indian mind. Let them not try to conduct revival meetings and devotional exercises altogether in Western ways and conform with Western etiquette. If our Western teachers and foreignised Indian leaders want the work of God to be carried on among us in their own way, they are sure to stop or spoil it.[5]

Although this revival did not result directly in the formation of Pentecostal churches and Ramabai was later to distance her movement from Pentecostalism, the Mukti revival had other far-reaching consequences, as we have seen in its influence on the Chilean revival. Under the ministry of the Garrs from Azusa Street, Pentecostal revival broke out in Kolkata (Calcutta) in 1907, but the Garrs soon left for Hong Kong. Thomas Barratt from Norway was one of the first representatives from western Pentecostalism to preach in India, at a missionary convention in 1908. But the first Indian Pentecostal congregation commenced in Kerala in 1911 at Thuyavur near Adur, led by Paruttupara Ummachan as a result of the work of independent German-American missionary George Berg. Berg, baptized in the Spirit at Azusa Street, arrived in 1908 (although he had been a Brethren missionary in India before that) and he used his contacts in Kerala to spread the

---

[4] Stanley M. Burgess, 'Pentecostalism in India: An Overview', *AJPS* 4:1 (2001), 85; Ivan M. Satyavrata, 'Contextual Perspectives on Pentecostalism as a Global Culture: A South Asian View', Dempster, Klaus and Petersen, *The Globalization of Pentecostalism*, p. 205.

[5] Pandita Ramabai, 'Stray Thoughts on the Revival', *The Bombay Guardian and Banner of Asia*, 7 November, 1905, p. 9.

PANDITA RAMABAI, MANORAMABAI, MISS ABRAMS,
MR. GADRE, AND SOME MEMBERS OF THE STAFF

Figure 8. Pandita Ramabai (centre), Minnie Abrams (front centre) and staff,
Pune, India, 1907.

Pentecostal message there. Another Azusa Street product, Robert Cook (1880–1958), who had met Berg at a convention in the USA in 1912, arrived in Bangalore as an independent Pentecostal missionary in 1913, clashed with Berg, and the latter left India the following year. The earliest Indian Pentecostal leaders Robert Cumine, Paruttupara Ummachan, Umman Mammen and Pandalam Mattai were contacts of Berg. Cook affiliated with the AG, then left in 1929 and eventually formed the Church of God (Full Gospel) in 1936, under the CGC, establishing many Pentecostal congregations in

Figure 9. Mark Buntain and Indian children at the Mission of Mercy, Calcutta, India, 1988.

South India. Both Cook and Berg established orphanages and schools for children. In the 1920s more Indian evangelists and leaders, mainly from Brethren or Holiness background, became Pentecostal. Mary Chapman came from the USA to Madras as the first AG missionary to India in 1915, followed in 1926 by John Burgess, who commenced Bethel Bible College in Kerala, a source for the expansion of the AG in the region. Within a relatively short time a complex network of Pentecostal missions was established all over India. These Pentecostal missionaries and many later ones also established many charitable institutions. The best known today is the work started among the destitute by Canadians Mark and Huldah Buntain in 1953, the Calcutta Mission of Mercy that feeds 22,000 people a day and runs a hospital, a nursing college and six schools.[6] The AG in India formed a regional council for South India in 1929 and has had independent districts with Indian leadership since 1947 (in South India since 1957).

The history of Indian Pentecostalism is a complicated one, with so many complex relationships and historical connections between its main

---

[6] Shamsundar M. Adhav, *Pandita Ramabai* (Madras: Christian Literature Society, 1979), p. 216; Burgess, 'Pentecostalism in India', pp. 90, 93; Michael Bergunder, 'Constructing Indian Pentecostalism: On issues of methodology and representation', Anderson and Tang, ch. 8; A. C. George, 'Pentecostal Beginnings in Travancove, South India', *AJPS* 4:2 (2001), 215–37.

protagonists that it cannot be construed as the history of western missions. K. E. Abraham (1899–1974), formerly a Syrian Orthodox schoolteacher and ardent nationalist, joined the Pentecostal movement in 1923 through the ministry of C. Manasseh and influenced the emergence of Indian leaders thereafter. He worked with Cook until separating from him in 1930. Although there were many Indian preachers, no Indians were ordained until Pastor Paul, leader of the Ceylon Pentecostal Mission, visited Kerala and ordained them, and the two existing Pentecostal denominations were entirely controlled by foreign missionaries. The break with the missionaries revolved around the issue of funding for church buildings, which the missionaries controlled. Abraham emphasized the autonomy of the local church and said that foreign missionaries were 'non-biblical and non-apostolic'. He, together with other Indian leaders K. C. Cherian, P. T. Chacko and P. M. Samuel founded the Indian Pentecostal Church of God, which planted its first congregations in Tamilnadu, Andhra Pradesh and Karnataka; and Abraham started the Hebron Bible School for training Indian pastors. The IPCG and the AG are the two largest Pentecostal denominations in India, with 750,000 affiliates each in 2000, but in Kerala Pentecostal leadership has been dominated by high-caste Syrian Christians. The IPCG suffered the first of many schisms in 1953, when the Sharon Pentecostal Fellowship Church was formed. The IPCG, with the Christian Assemblies of India (433,000) and the Assemblies (Jehovah Shammah) (250,000) are the biggest independent Indian Pentecostal churches. Ramankutty Paul, a Dalit from Kerala, returned to India from Sri Lanka in 1924 to establish another independent and very influential Pentecostal denomination with headquarters in Madras (Chennai), the Ceylon Pentecostal Mission (since 1984 The Pentecostal Mission). This is an exclusivist sect where celibacy is encouraged to increase spiritual power. Most independent Indian Pentecostal denominations like the CPM have strict rules for members including opposition to all forms of jewellery and the ordination of women. There are some 15 million members of Neocharismatic groups, some of the more prominent being the New Life Fellowship founded in 1968 by S. Joseph in Mumbai (Bombay), the Manna/Rock Church (also founded in 1968) of Ernest Komanapalli and the Nagaland Christian Revival Churches (1952).

Indian Pentecostals have also had their share of healing evangelists, the first successful one being Paulaseer Lawrie in the 1960s, who left Pentecostalism in 1967 to become a Hindu guru and avatar. The best known and most influential Charismatic evangelist in South India today is D. G. S. Dhinakaran of Tamilnadu, who remains a member of the Church of South India and whose Jesus Calls Ministry has extensive healing campaigns and many parallels with Oral Roberts' organization in the USA, including a prayer tower and a Christian university. Catholic Charismatics are also strong in India (but have little or no contact with Pentecostals), the leading person today being the healing evangelist from Kerala, Mathew Naikomparambil.[7] Pentecostalism is clearly the fastest growing form of Christianity in what will soon be the most populous nation on earth.

Pentecostalism is relatively small but significant in Sri Lanka, formerly Ceylon. The Garrs made a brief visit there in 1907 and CMS preacher D. E. Dias Wanigasekera became an itinerating preacher of the Pentecostal message. Anna Lewini, a Danish missionary, arrived in Colombo in 1922 and began revival meetings with co-workers J. S. Wickramaratne and J. J. B. de Silva. They founded the Glad Tidings Hall (later Colombo Gospel Tabernacle), the first Pentecostal church in Sri Lanka. AG missionary Walter Clifford arrived in 1924 and took over leadership of the Glad Tidings Hall, leading the AG in Sri Lanka until 1948. The AG of Ceylon became an independent entity in 1947 and has become the third largest Christian denomination in the country.

W. D. Grier came as an independent Pentecostal missionary from 1913–17, after which Alwin de Alwis took charge of his work. The visit of the famous Indian Christian mystic Sadhu Sundar Singh in 1918 with his ministry of praying for the sick made a strong impression on Christians in Sri Lanka, especially on Ramankutty Paul and Alwin de Alwis, who started the Ceylon Pentecostal Mission in 1923, seceding from the Glad Tidings Hall. The CPM practises an ascetic lifestyle in 'Faith Homes', communities of members throughout Sri Lanka that are places for prayer and healing (with the rejection of medicine), where private possessions are forbidden and celibacy of ministers is mandatory. Emphasis is placed on preparing for the return of Christ. Alwin de Alwis remained head of the CPM in Ceylon until 1962 and CPM churches were established in India and Malaysia. In India the church developed under the leadership of 'Pastor Paul'.[8]

PENTECOSTALS IN SOUTH EAST ASIA

Christians form a sizeable minority in South East Asia and Pentecostals are found throughout the region. British PMU missionaries were in

---

[7] Michael Bergunder, '"Ministry of Compassion": D. G. S. Dhinakaran – Christian Healer-Prophet from Tamil Nadu', Hedlund, *Christianity is Indian*, pp. 160–1; Roger Hedlund, 'Indigenous Pentecostalism in India', Anderson and Tang, *Asian and Pentecostal*, ch. 9; Paulson Pullikottil, 'Ramankutty Paul: A Dalit Contribution to Pentecostalism', Anderson and Tang, *Asian and Pentecostal*, ch. 10.

[8] E. Leembruggen-Kallberg, 'Sri Lanka', *NIDPCM*, pp. 248–53.

south-west China from 1910, and from there they conducted outreaches into neighbouring Burma (today, Myanmar) and Thailand from 1921 onwards, where most of their work was among the Lisu, Karen and Rawang minorities in the interior. AG missionaries Leonard and Olive Bolton and Clifford and Lavada Morrison sent Lisu workers into Myanmar in the 1920s and the AG was established there in 1931. Now by far the largest Pentecostal church in Myanmar, the AG has been forced to work without foreign missionaries since 1966 and has developed a strong national character. Today the AG is led by Myo Chit, a Bama (Burmese) pastor of the largest Pentecostal congregation in Yangon.[9]

Pentecostalism in Thailand was influenced by the ministry of Chinese evangelist John Sung in 1938–9. Finnish Pentecostal missionaries Hanna and Verner Raassina arrived there in 1946 and established the Full Gospel Church, and they were followed by other Finnish missionaries. The UPC was established in 1962 by the Thai convert Boonmak Kittisan and Danish missionary Elly Hansen. The Hope of Bangkok was founded by Kriengsak Charunwongsak (1955–) in 1981 and is now known as the Hope of God International, the largest Pentecostal and Charismatic church in the country and the only significant church founded by a Thai. By 1997 this church had 800 congregations across Thailand.[10]

Malaysia and Singapore have vibrant Pentecostal and Charismatic churches, but these are almost entirely among the Chinese and Indian populations. John Sung's charismatic healing evangelism in Malaya and Singapore among the Chinese from 1935–40 had a great impact. The first Pentecostal missionaries in Malaysia were Indians A. K. Titus and V. V. Samuel of the CPM, who arrived in 1930 and established Faith Homes, holding regular conventions and working predominantly among migrant Indians. They registered in 1952 as the Pentecostal Church of Malaya. The AG began work among the Chinese in Malaya in 1934 and among the Indian (Tamil) population in 1968. It was officially registered in 1953. The controversial but dynamic ministry of the former Hong Kong actress Mui Yee resulted in the creation of the New Testament Churches in the 1960s. They met stiff opposition in Malaya but fared better in Singapore, where Elder Goh Ewe Kheng and his Church of Singapore became a respected Charismatic church in the city. The most successful Charismatic churches in recent years have been the English-speaking city congregations, the largest

[9] Chin Khua Khai, 'The Assemblies of God and Pentecostals in Myanmar', Anderson and Tang, *Asian and Pentecostal*, ch. 11.
[10] D. D. Bundy and D. W. Dayton, 'Thailand', *NIDPCM*, pp. 269–70; James Hosack, 'The Arrival of Pentecostals and Charismatics in Thailand', *AJPS* 4:1 (2001), 109–17.

being the Full Gospel Assembly in Kuala Lumpur founded by Koh Eng Kiat in 1979, the City Harvest Church (AG) and the Faith Community Baptist Church in Singapore.[11]

The greatest Pentecostal expansion in South East Asia has occurred in Indonesia, where there are nine to twelve million Pentecostals and Charismatics, 4–5 per cent of the total population in a country that is 80 per cent Muslim. Pentecostalism was introduced to what was the Dutch East Indies by Gerrit Polman's periodical *Spade Regen* and was taken to Bali in 1921 by Dutch American missionaries from Bethel Temple (a Oneness church in Seattle) the Groesbeeks and van Klaverens. They were ordered to leave Bali by the Dutch colonial government and they moved to Java in 1922, where Pentecostal churches began. The Pentecostal Congregations in the Dutch Indies was registered in 1924, to become the Pentecostal Church of Indonesia (PCI) in 1942. There have been some forty major schisms from this church, the largest of which is the Indonesian Bethel Church, a denomination that stresses the autonomy of the local church. The 'Bethany' congregations of over 10,000 in several Javanese cities have developed from the Bethel Church. The AG began with the work of independent missionaries who arrived in Indonesia in 1936–37 from the USA and opened Bible schools after 1945.

The unique 'Indonesian Revival' followed the overthrow of Sukarno's Communist government in 1965 and was concentrated in West Timor. A healing evangelist from Rote island called Johannes Ratuwalu went to West Timor in 1964 and held healing campaigns supported by the Christian Evangelical (Reformed) Church, and several thousand healings were reported. The following year, a team of Bible students from East Java arrived and many conversions were reported. Evangelistic teams created to travel all over the island became a feature of this revival. One of the team leaders was Pak Elias, from the original student team and from West Timor, whose ministry was characterized by healing, miracles, confrontations with sorcerers and exorcisms. Another leader was Melchior (Mel) Tari, whose reports of miracles (*Like a Mighty Wind*, 1973) became a bestseller in the West.[12] Kurt Koch indicates that this was not a Pentecostal revival because speaking in tongues was virtually absent, but even his account abounds with other Pentecostal phenomena. But it was not only in Timor that revival occurred. Over two million Javanese became Christians between 1965 and 1971, the greatest ever turning of Muslims to Christianity. The

[11] Tan Jin Huat, 'Pentecostal and Charismatic Origins in Malaysia and Singapore', Anderson and Tang, *Asian and Pentecostal*, ch. 12.
[12] Mel Tari, *Like a Mighty Wind* (London: Coverdale House, 1973).

Pentecostal churches gained the most members during this revival, especially after Reformed churches discouraged the emphasis on healing and miracles. PCI grew from 100,000 in 1963 to 400,000 five years later. In 2000 the three largest Pentecostal denominations in Indonesia were PCI with 1.4 million affiliates, the Bethel Church with 700,000 and the Pentecostal Church of God with 310,000. Several Pentecostal denominations have (since 1960) joined the ecumenical Indonesian Council of Churches. There has been heavy persecution of Christians in Indonesia, and Islamic militants have burnt down over a hundred Pentecostal church buildings in recent years.[13]

Although the Philippines is predominantly Catholic, Pentecostalism has a high profile there. The first Pentecostal missionary to arrive in the Philippines was Joseph Warnick in 1921, who with a local preacher Teodorico Lastimosa began the Philippine Church of God. The first AG missionary in the Philippines, Benjamin Caudle, arrived in 1926 but soon returned to the USA, to be followed by several Filipino missionaries converted in the USA. The first of these, Cris Garsulao, commenced churches in the southwest in 1928. In 1939 another US missionary, Leland Johnson, set up the AG under the USA headquarters, to become an autonomous district in 1953. Vicente Defante, a Filipino convert of Aimee McPherson, commenced the Foursquare Church in 1931. Pentecostals have grown to such an extent that they are regarded as a challenge to the Catholic Church. The three largest Pentecostal and Charismatic churches are the Jesus is Lord Church founded by Bishop Eddie Villanueva in 1978, the Jesus Miracle Crusade (both these are Filipino founded churches) and the Assemblies of God. There are also more distinctly Filipino movements of a Pentecostal character, such as the Santuala movement among the mountain peoples of Luzon. Large new Filipino Charismatic churches have been established like 'Jesus is Lord', which grew to 300,000 in ten years and now may be the largest Charismatic church in the Philippines with two million affiliates, a television station and an active socio-political programme. Former AG missionary Lester Sumrall started Bethel Temple in Manila in 1953 (now Cathedral of Praise) and Butch Conde founded the Bread of Life Ministries in 1982. The rapid growth of this Filipino independent church is attributed to the personal care of new converts and neighbourhood 'cell groups' presided over by trained leaders. But there are many other churches founded by Filipinos,

---

[13] Kurt Koch, *The Revival in Indonesia* (Baden, Germany: Evangelization Publishers, 1970), pp. 123, 176, 265; Gani Wiyono, 'Pentecostalism in Indonesia', Anderson and Tang, *Asian and Pentecostal*, ch. 13; Mark Robinson, 'The Growth of Indonesian Pentecostalism', Anderson and Tang, *Asian and Pentecostal*, ch. 14; Johnstone and Mandryk, *Operation World*, p. 339.

totalling some 2.2 million affiliates in 2000. But dwarfing all these churches is the Catholic Charismatic movement of Mario ('Brother Mike') Velarde, El Shaddai, with some seven million members. This is a unique and highly influential Filipino movement that commenced in 1982 as a radio station and has managed to bring the message of the power of the Spirit to popular Catholicism. There has been some discussion among Catholic scholars about the reasons for the growth of these movements and reasons given include events in the macro-level of Philippine society. Salazar identifies the management of resources within the Pentecostal churches themselves such as member recruitment and socialization, information dissemination, ample finances and symbolic and ritual elements as being reasons for their growth. In particular, he mentions the celebratory rituals, healing services and other practices that resonate with the local culture. He concludes that these elements together 'help contribute to an experience of community, belongingness, hope, and confidence among the members'.[14]

CHINESE 'PENTECOSTAL' CHURCHES

The phenomenon of independent Christianity in China cannot easily be labelled 'Pentecostal'. We know that western Pentecostal missionaries were active in China from 1907, but there was only a total of five million Christians in mainland China estimated at the time of the exodus of westerners in 1949. Something quite astounding has happened since that time. It is extremely difficult to assess church membership in China, especially in the case of movements unrecognized by the government and estimates vary between twenty million (official figures) and seventy-five million. But there has nevertheless been a remarkable growth of Christianity in China, especially in unregistered independent house churches. One estimate put the number of people in Chinese house churches at between thirty and eighty million in 2000 and the number of Pentecostals and Charismatics at fifty-one million,[15] although they might not (and usually don't) call themselves by these names. If these figures approximate the truth, then China now has the largest number of Pentecostal and Charismatic Christians in

---

[14] Robert C. Salazar (ed.), *New Religious Movements in Asia and the Pacific Islands: Implications for Church and Society* (Manila: De La Salle University, 1994), pp. 190–205; Johnstone and Mandryk, *Operation World*, p. 521; Jeong Jae Yong, 'Filipino Pentecostal Spirituality: An Investigation into Filipino Indigenous Spirituality and Pentecostalism in the Philippines', ThD thesis, University of Birmingham, 2001, pp. 51, 66, 106; Joseph Suico, 'Pentecostalism in the Philippines', Anderson and Tang, *Asian and Pentecostal*, ch. 15; Lode Wostyn, 'Catholic Charismatics in the Philippines', Anderson and Tang, *Asian and Pentecostal*, ch. 16.

[15] Johnstone and Mandryk, *Operation World*, pp. 161, 163.

Asia and perhaps in the world. The differences between these independent churches and forms of Pentecostalism found in the West are considerable, but there are many similarities to the Spirit churches of Africa. Chinese churches have developed in isolation from the rest of Christianity for at least fifty years, but have developed a spirituality that can probably be described as Pentecostal.

China has experienced extensive revivals this century, in particular the Manchurian revival of 1908 and the Shandong Revival of 1930–32. The latter was more specifically Pentecostal, when Baptists and Presbyterians received Spirit baptism with manifestations of people being hurled to the ground, 'holy laughter', all-night prayer meetings and healings. As they were excluded from Baptist and Presbyterian churches, Chinese revival leaders formed a loose association called the Spiritual Gifts Society. The Chinese independent churches grew rapidly at a time when severe opposition faced them. Two of these, the True Jesus Church and the Jesus Family may be considered Pentecostal and together with the evangelical Little Flock/ Local Church/Christian Assembly churches, are referred to in China as 'Old Three-Self' churches. They were in conflict with the government-recognized union of churches called the Three-Self Patriotic Movement (TSPM) for half a century. This conflict resulted in their being banned during the 1950s as promoters of 'American imperialism, feudalism and capitalism', the 'unlawful activities' of faith healing and exorcism, and the 'immoralities' of 'spiritual dance'. All church activities in China, including those of the TSPM, were banned in 1966 but recommenced at the end of the 1970s, after which there appears to have been rapid growth. Although the Chinese churches that re-emerged were not able to use their former names, Daniel Bays points out, they 'revealed some striking continuities with the earlier period of revivalism'. The house church movements are widely diverse but are characterized by being 'usually vibrant in faith, evangelistic in outreaching, fundamentalist in doctrine, informal in liturgy, spontaneous in development, and flexible in structure'. Bays asks whether this Chinese type of revivalism 'is a handy and effective means for indigenous Christian leaders to break free of domination by [foreign] missions'.[16]

Paul Wei founded the International Assembly of the True Jesus Church (TJC) in 1917 in Beijing, at first called the 'Restored True Jesus Church of

---

[16] Daniel H. Bays, 'Christian Revival in China, 1900–1937', Blumhofer and Balmer, *Modern Christian Revivals*, pp. 162, 173–5; *Bridge: Church Life in China Today* (ed. Deng Zhaoming), (Hong Kong: Christian Study Centre on Chinese Religion and Culture, 1983–93), 54: p. 7; 62: pp. 11, 13; Gotthard Oblau, 'Pentecostal by Default? Contemporary Christianity in China', Anderson and Tang, *Asian and Pentecostal*, ch. 18.

All Nations'. After Wei died in 1919, Zhang Lingsheng, who had received Spirit baptism through an Apostolic Faith missionary in Shanghai in 1909, succeeded him. It appears that Zhang had met US Pentecostal missionaries who had convinced him of the Oneness doctrine. The TJC was a radically anti-foreign independent church that owed much of its early growth to the efforts of three preachers led by Barnabas Zhang, who travelled the length and breadth of China on foot, reporting many signs and miracles, establishing churches and baptizing many thousands. By 1929, the TJC was found throughout China, Taiwan, Singapore, Malaysia and Hong Kong, its main attractions being deliverance from demons and opium addiction and the healing of the sick. By 1949 there were over 700 churches with over 100,000 members. Government opposition to the TJC increased and in 1958 it was banned, only able to recommence openly in 1980. In Taiwan it has been one of the fastest growing churches, with over 28,000 members by 1968. The increase in emigration of Chinese to Europe and North America resulted in the formation of the TJC in the West. During the Cultural Revolution, the church in mainland China, forced underground, grew rapidly. By 2001, an estimated 10 per cent of Protestants in China – over 200,000 in Jiangsu province alone – were members of the TJC, and in some areas almost whole villages were converted to this church. Depending on how many Protestants there are in China, the figure for TJC members could be at least three million. The church has also suffered from many schisms, including former leaders like Barnabas Zhang (who was excommunicated in 1931). A Oneness Pentecostal church reported to be rigidly exclusivist, it considers itself the only 'true' church. Members observe the Sabbath and the Ten Commandments, both adults and children are baptized by immersion face downwards in running water in the name of Jesus as 'important for salvation', after which a sacrament of foot washing is held. This movement practises common Pentecostal phenomena of speaking in tongues, trembling, singing, leaping and dancing in the Spirit. The international leadership of the church is presently administered from Taiwan (where it is one of the largest churches), but political tension between Taiwan and the mainland means that the mainland church remains isolated. The 1992 church statistics reported churches throughout Asia and as far as West Africa and South America. Outside Asia, however, the TJC remains a wholly Chinese church.[17]

---

[17] *Bridge* 41: p. 8; 62: pp. 5, 9–12; 63: pp. 3, 5–7, 9–11, 14; Bays, 'Christian Revival', p. 170; French, *Our God is One*, pp. 149–50; Deng Zhaoming, 'Indigenous Chinese Pentecostal Denominations', Anderson and Tang, *Asian and Pentecostal*, ch. 19.

The second prominent, although smaller Chinese Pentecostal church, is the Jesus Family, founded by Jing Dianying at Mazhuang, Shandong in 1927. A communitarian group forbidding private ownership, members live simply, work hard and contribute to the community after the pattern of the early church. Jing and others established a Christian savings society in 1921, a co-operative store attempting to meet the needs of the socially marginalized, followed by a silk reeling co-operative in 1926. After Jing's contact with a Pentecostal community, the Jesus Family was formed and steadily increased in numbers. Those who joined the community had to renounce the world and their allegiance to natural families, committing themselves totally to the community. Jing sent out believers to set up other Family homes throughout China and by 1949 there were 127 communities with over 10,000 members. The range of economic activities in these houses increased to make them self-supporting. The original home in Mazhuang was the largest with over 500 members, 100 houses and at least 10 working units. Although the Family supported the Communist revolution in keeping with its own egalitarian principles, in 1952 Jing was arrested on several charges including imperialism and anti-Communism, and the Family was officially dissolved and severely repressed. In spite of this, the movement continued incognito and in 1977, meetings resumed in Mazhuang. The old meeting place was restored by 1984 and a two-storey hostel commenced in 1988. By 1992, there were an estimated 23 families constituting 100 people in the Mazhuang community. The largest Family group today is in Feng Jia Wang She, where members run what was claimed to be the only Christian hospital in China. Most Christian groups in central Shandong are of Family background, and their influence remains in other provinces. Apart from the strong sense of community, other characteristic Family beliefs that remain are early morning emotional prayer meetings with loud crying, simultaneous prayer and manifestations of the Spirit like speaking in tongues, trances, revelations through dreams, visions and other means, hymn singing (Jing wrote many hymns) and sharing testimonies. Although these phenomena characterize Pentecostal movements all over the world, in the Family these meetings last for at least three hours and the regimented work activities revolve around the daily meetings. The Family has suffered further repression since 1992, with several key leaders imprisoned and buildings demolished.

The third 'Old Three-Self' church is known widely in China variously as the Christian Assembly and the Little Flock, perhaps the largest of the Chinese autochthonous churches and founded in 1928 by Ni Doushen (1903–72), better known in the West as 'Watchman Nee'. Although this movement has several Pentecostal characteristics such as prayer for healing the sick, it has its roots in the Brethren and Holiness movements and is not a 'Pentecostal' church. Ni was imprisoned for twenty years in Shanghai under conditions of extreme hardship until his release just before his death in 1972. He has had a tremendous influence on global Pentecostalism, particularly through his popular devotional books that have made him one of the best-known Chinese Christian leaders of all time. One of the main offshoots from Ni's movement was the Local Church of Li Changsou ('Witness Lee'), formed after Li fled to Taiwan with a group of followers and took over the Assembly Halls there, moving again to the USA in 1962. When he introduced the loud, public confession of sins and 'calling on the name of the Lord' to release the Spirit, his followers became known as 'Yellers' or 'Shouters', and their services became noisy and emotional. They developed other unorthodox doctrines and considered themselves the only true church. They quickly spread in China, but in 1983 they were banned and leaders imprisoned. Although there are several churches that can rightly be called 'Pentecostal', grassroots Christianity in China has many varieties and it would be misleading to describe them all as 'Pentecostal' or 'Charismatic' before more is known about them. Nevertheless, most observers consider them to have 'Pentecostal' features, and that is why they are an important part of this study.[18]

KOREAN PENTECOSTALISM

South Korea is a pluralistic society greatly influenced by religious and cultural values from the USA. The growth of Pentecostalism there has been singularly dramatic, not only because of the enormous classical Pentecostal congregations, but also in the 'Pentecostalization' of Korean Protestantism through which most Protestants are affected by a Charismatic emphasis. Protestantism was only introduced to Korea in 1884, but by 2000 it formed about a third of the population with 55,000 congregations in 151 different denominations. Korean Protestantism has had a history of revivalism, the most notable being the Wonsan revival of 1903 and the 'Korean Pentecost' that commenced at a meeting of Methodist and Presbyterian missionaries at Pyongyang in 1907. In 1906–10, 80,000 Koreans became Christians. Preachers whose ministry was accompanied by miracles and healings – especially

---

[18] *Bridge* 34: p. 17; 54: pp. 8, 11–14; Deng, 'Indigenous Chinese'; Edmond Tang, '"Yellers" and Healers: Pentecostalism and the Study of Grassroots Christianity in China', Anderson and Tang, *Asian and Pentecostal*, ch. 20.

Presbyterian pastors Kil Sun Joo and Kim Ik Du (a healing revivalist) and Methodist mystic Yi Yong Do – continued the revival until the 1930s. Although prayer on mountains was a feature of Yi Yong Do's ministry, the present-day 'prayer mountain movement' probably started with Methodist Elder Ra Woon Mong in 1940. Ra's Yongmun Prayer Mountain and the camp meetings and schools he established there had a great influence on the Korean church and were patterns for many to follow. The revival movement was also known as the 'Holy Spirit movement' and was clearly a 'Charismatic' movement that permeated all Protestant churches, although the Presbyterians and the Methodists declared both Yi Yong Do and Ra were heretics because of their unorthodox views.[19]

Classical Pentecostalism came to Korea in 1930 when Mary Rumsey, a former Methodist baptized in the Spirit at Azusa Street and missionary in Japan since 1927, arrived to establish the first Pentecostal church in 1932 in Seoul with Heong Huh, a former worker in the Salvation Army. Growth was at first slow and in 1953 eight churches with some five hundred members were constituted as the Korean Assemblies of God (KAG) under the chairmanship of Arthur Chesnut, first AG missionary to Korea, who had arrived in 1951. In 1957 Heong Huh became the first Korean Chairman. The most remarkable growth of a single congregation ever recorded took place under the ministry of David (formerly Paul) Yonggi Cho (1936–) and his future mother-in-law Jashil Choi (1915–89), who began a small tent church in a slum area of Seoul in 1958 with five members. By 1962 this congregation had grown to 800 and in 1964 Cho built a sanctuary to seat 2,000 people. He bought property in Yoido in 1969 and dedicated a new 10,000-seat auditorium there in 1973. This Full Gospel Central Church as it was then known, was now receiving international attention.

By 1982 the KAG was the third largest Protestant group with over half a million, half of whom were in Cho's movement. In 1980 the highly organized nation-wide evangelistic campaign 'Here's Life, Korea' in which almost a million received training in evangelism further boosted Korean Pentecostal membership. Protestant congregations in Seoul doubled in two years and most were of a Pentecostal nature. In 1984 the name of Cho's

---

[19] Martin, *Tongues of Fire*, pp. 135, 146; Cox, *Fire*, p. 220; Johnstone and Mandryk, *Operation World*, p. 387; Jeong Chong Hee, 'The Formation and Development of Korean Pentecostalism from the Viewpoint of a Dynamic Contextual Theology' (ThD thesis, University of Birmingham, 2001), pp. 136, 203–8, 218; Lee Jae Bum, 'Pentecostal Type Distinctives and Korean Protestant Church Growth' (PhD thesis, Fuller Theological Seminary, 1986), pp. 181–6; Lee Young Hoon, 'The Korean Holy Spirit Movement in Relation to Pentecostalism', Anderson and Tang, *Asian and Pentecostal*, ch. 22.

Figure 10. Tent where Yonggi Cho started his church, Taejo-dong, Seoul, Korea, c. 1959.

church was changed to the Yoido Full Gospel Church (YFGC) and it joined the Assemblies of God in the USA after a disagreement with the KAG. Cho then founded a denomination called Jesus Assemblies of God, but rejoined the KAG in 1991. Cho's younger brother Yongmok Cho, who pastors the second largest congregation in Korea, remained head of Jesus Assemblies of God, one of four AG denominations and the second largest with 300,000 affiliates. Some efforts have been made to unite the AG divisions. Yonggi Cho became chairman of the World Pentecostal Assemblies of God in 1992 and YFGC planted churches all over Korea. Amplifying the fourfold 'full gospel' of the early Pentecostals, Cho teaches that the 'five-fold message of the Gospel' includes (1) renewal, (2) the fullness of the Spirit, (3) healing, (4) blessing and (5) the Second Coming. In addition, the 'three-fold blessings of salvation' include 'soul prosperity', 'prosperity in all things' and 'a healthy life'. By 1993 the YFGC reported 700,000 members under 700 pastors and was the largest Christian congregation in the world. By 2000 the Full Gospel (AG) churches with some 1.1 million affiliates, was by far the largest Pentecostal denomination in Korea. Several other US American Pentecostal denominations have established themselves, including the CGC in 1963

Figure 11.   David Yonggi Cho, Seoul, Korea, 2002.

and the ICFG in 1969. When the KAG joined the ecumenical Korean National Council of Churches in 1999, it was the first time any AG church had done so, and this in the face of disapproval by the AG, USA.[20] Korean Pentecostalism certainly represents a truly remarkable form of Christianity.

[20] Jeong Chong Hee, 'Korean Pentecostalism', pp. 161–95; Johnstone and Mandryk, *Operation World*, p. 387.

JAPANESE PENTECOSTALISM

Compared with neighbouring South Korea, Pentecostalism in Japan is rather small, but it is the one segment of Christianity that is actively growing. It did not have a good start, however. Martin L. Ryan and a party of fourteen USA 'Apostolic Light' missionaries arrived in Yokohama in 1907, to be followed by Estella Bernauer and Yoshio Tanimoto in 1910 – the latter the first Japanese Pentecostal, returning from study in the USA. Many other independent missionaries arrived thereafter from several western countries, some of these missionaries being Oneness Pentecostals. Most were ill prepared, could not speak Japanese and lacked cultural sensitivity and financial resources, if not zeal. Exceptions were British missionaries William and Mary Taylor, who were with the PMU from 1911, then with the AG, and finally with the Japan Apostolic Church in the 1950s. Their 'Door of Hope' ministry in Kobe worked with destitute women and children. Their Japanese female assistant Nikki may have been the first Japanese person to receive Spirit baptism in Japan. The first Japanese pastor was Ichitaro Takigawa, ordained in 1915. By 1919, a revival started under British businessman turned Oneness missionary Leonard Coote in Yokohama. The Pentecostal movement began to take root until devastated by the 1923 earthquake and the Second World War. Coote, who joined the PAW in 1920, was probably the most influential Pentecostal missionary in Japan at least until the 1950s. He established Ikoma Bible School in 1929, a means of training many Japanese pastors. The Japan Apostolic Church emerged from this school in 1933. The Japan Assemblies of God (earlier called the Japan Bible Church) evolved from the work of the Jeurgensen family (comprising six missionaries), who arrived in 1913 and formally constituted the church in 1920. Kiyoma Yumiyama, the first Japanese AG pastor, commenced the Holy Spirit Bible Institute in 1931 and became superintendent of the Japan AG when it was reconstituted in 1949 after the devastation of war. The Japan AG is now the largest of the classical Pentecostal churches. It has been strengthened by a determined outreach from Korea, especially from Yonggi Cho's YFGC, which since 1978 has established a large congregation in Tokyo and in other cities, although with a majority of Korean members.

There are several independent Japanese Pentecostal churches, some of which have combined elements of Christianity, Japanese folk religion and Judaism. The Spirit of Jesus Church (SJC) was founded in 1941 by Jun Marai, head of the Japan Bible Church during the war. He met the True Jesus Church in Taiwan and was inspired by them to found a Oneness Sabbatarian church after their pattern. The SJC experienced rapid growth after the war and today is probably the largest Pentecostal denomination in Japan. Ikuru Teshima commenced the Original Gospel movement, also known as the Makuya (Tabernacle) movement in 1948, which split from the Japanese Nonchurch movement in 1953 after its members spoke in tongues. This is also a large denomination by Japanese Christian standards, has had no contact with western Pentecostalism, is strongly nationalistic, keeps Old Testament laws including the Sabbath and reputedly incorporates Japanese religious practices like walking on coals and water cleansing. The Holy Ekklesia of Jesus is the third largest of the Japanese-founded churches, created by Tajeki Otsuki in 1946 and emphasizing healing by anointing oil, holy water and handkerchiefs. These independent churches are an important part of Japanese Pentecostalism.[21]

The growth of Pentecostalism in the southern and eastern regions of Asia in its many varieties has been a remarkable development in the history of Christianity in this vast continent. From small, marginalized sects stemming from evangelical missions, Pentecostalism has become one of the most significant expressions of Asian Christianity that has permeated every denomination and created new ones that are distinctively Asian. The twenty-first century may see Asian Pentecostalism becoming a world leader in influence and extent.

PENTECOSTALS IN AUSTRALIA AND THE PACIFIC

Turning to the 'down under' side of the equator, Pentecostalism in Australia and New Zealand experienced similar underlying currents as those in other western countries. Keswick and Holiness teachings, revivals in other parts of the world and the healing movement of Dowie were all important influences. The first Pentecostal congregation in Australia, the Good News Hall, was founded by Jeannie ('Mother') Lancaster in 1909, and evangelists Smith Wigglesworth and Aimee Semple McPherson visited for evangelistic meetings in 1921. Pentecostal denominations were formed in 1926 when South African evangelist Frederick van Eyk established the Apostolic Faith Mission as an association of churches that included Lancaster's Good News Hall. In the same year the Pentecostal Church of Australia was formed through the evangelistic efforts of the US American A. C. Valdez, Sr. together with Charles Greenwood in Melbourne. These two groups united in 1937 to

---

[21] Paul Tsuchido Shew, 'Pentecostals in Japan', Anderson and Tang, *Asian and Pentecostal*, ch. 21; Masakazu Suzuki, 'A New Look at the Pre-war History of the Japan Assemblies of God', *AJPS* 4:2 (2001), 239–67; Makito Nagasawa, 'Makuya Pentecostalism: A Survey', *AJPS* 3:2 (2000), 203–18; Johnstone and Mandryk, *Operation World*, p. 371.

create the AG in Australia, the largest Pentecostal denomination in Australia today. Leo Harris, briefly an itinerant minister in the AG, left in 1944 when he embraced British Israelism to form National Revival Crusade together with some New Zealand churches, to become the Christian Revival Crusade in 1963, another large Australian denomination. In 1974 the Christian Outreach Centres began in Brisbane, grew rapidly and became the second largest Pentecostal denomination in Australia. There are numerous other Pentecostal and Charismatic groupings in Australia, constituting some 10 per cent of the country's population altogether. From the Hills Christian Life Centre in Sydney led by Brian Houston (an AG church) come the Hillsongs, a musical group known since the 1990s for composing some of the most popular worship songs used in Pentecostal and Charismatic churches throughout the world.[22]

Australian Pentecostalism influenced Aotearoa New Zealand (NZ). Smith Wigglesworth visited NZ in 1922 and again in 1923–24 to have the first large-scale Pentecostal meetings in the country. A. C. Valdez, Sr. followed in 1924 and set up the Pentecostal Church of New Zealand after the Australian model. Several schisms ensued, some setting up the AG in 1926 and others joining the Apostolic Church when it came to NZ in 1932. Another group formed in 1939 developed an interest in British Israelism and joined Leo Harris' Christian Revival Crusade in 1941. Another group joined the Latter Rain movement and now call themselves the New Life Churches of NZ. Finally, the Pentecostal Church disbanded in 1952 and the remainder of its churches became the Elim Church of NZ linked to Elim in the UK. As in the rest of the western world, the greatest expansion of Pentecostalism in NZ occurred after 1960 and the largest Pentecostal churches in NZ today are the AG, the Apostolic Church, New Life and Elim, together forming a significant part of NZ Christianity.[23]

The Pacific Islands cover a vast area with many different cultures and languages. In almost all of these island nations Pentecostal and Charismatic Christianity has come and grown rapidly, especially since the 1970s. The AG is the biggest Pentecostal denomination in the region, but it competes with several other movements. AG missionaries went to Fiji and American Samoa in 1926 from the USA and started the first church in Fiji in 1929. Fijian AG missionaries took the work to Tonga in 1966 and to the Solomon Islands in 1971. It is now the third largest denomination in Fiji

---

[22] M. Hutchinson, 'Australia', *NIDPCM*, pp. 26–9; Johnstone and Mandryk, *Operation World*, pp. 83–4.
[23] B. Knowles, 'New Zealand', *NIDPCM*, pp. 187–91; Johnstone and Mandryk, *Operation World*, p. 480.

with over 50,000 affiliates. A breakaway from the AG took place in 1988, when a Fijian independent church called the Apostles Gospel Outreach Fellowship International was formed. Papua New Guinea has over twenty Pentecostal and Charismatic organizations, with the result that over 12 per cent of the country's population (over half a million) was Pentecostal and Charismatic in 2000. In Tonga, the largest Pentecostal and Charismatic movement is the Tokaikolo Christian Fellowship, founded by Senitulu Koloi in 1978 after he seceded from the Free Wesleyan Church. In Samoa, the First Samoan Full Gospel Church broke away from the AG. Australian Pentecostal and Charismatic churches like Christian Outreach Centres and Christian Revival Crusade have established themselves in the Pacific, the Apostolic Church has come from New Zealand and CGC, UPC and ICFG missionaries have come from the USA.[24] Pentecostalism is now an important part of the Pacific region's Christianity.

---

[24] M. Ernst, 'Pacific Islands (Survey)', 'Fiji', 'Papua New Guinea', 'Samoa', 'Tonga', *NIDPCM*, pp. 99–102, 194–7, 221, 271–2; Johnstone and Mandryk, *Operation World*, pp. 250, 509–10, 627.

8

The Charismatic Movement and the
New Pentecostals

There is a certain ambiguity between the words 'Pentecostal' and 'Charismatic' that will already be apparent to the reader of this book. It is now generally accepted that the term 'Charismatic Movement' in its original usage referred to the practice of spiritual gifts and the baptism in the Spirit in the older, 'historic' or 'mainline' churches since the 1960s. With the development of 'nondenominational' Charismatic churches and organizations a decade or two later, the term was broadened to refer to all those movements outside denominational or 'classical' Pentecostalism where spiritual gifts are exercised. It is often impossible now to distinguish between 'Pentecostals' and 'Charismatics', and there are often as many theological and liturgical differences between classical Pentecostals themselves as there are between them and Charismatic churches. Terms like 'neopentecostals' and 'neocharismatics' have been used to refer to these later churches, but here we will simply call them 'New Pentecostals' because of their comparatively recent origins in the last quarter of the twentieth century.

Most observers consider that the Charismatic Movement, the practice of Pentecostal phenomena or of spiritual gifts in the 'mainline' Protestant churches, began in the Episcopalian Church in the USA in 1960, and in the Roman Catholic Church in the same country in 1967. The attention of the western world focused on events surrounding the resignation of Dennis Bennett from being rector of his church in California, often regarded as the commencement of the Charismatic movement in the western world. But this event, for all its significance, was the culmination rather than the commencement of a movement that had already been around for decades in the western world and in some cases much longer than that. We must remember that the commencement of Pentecostalism in Europe at the beginning of the twentieth century (unlike in North America) was in fact a 'Charismatic' and ecumenical movement in the 'mainline' churches. Many of the early leaders like T. B. Barratt, Alexander Boddy, Jonathan Paul and Louis Dallière never intended to leave their churches (and some never did leave) but to continue with their newfound Pentecostal experience to renew and revitalize churches that had grown somewhat old and tired. The same was true of the revivals in India in 1905–7, the 'Korean Pentecost' from 1907 in the Presbyterian and Methodist churches, and of Willis Hoover and the Pentecostal revival among the Methodists in Chile in 1909. Spiritual gifts (including tongues) had been experienced in 'mainline' churches in India and Korea in 1905–7, in the Anglican church in England from 1907–25, in German Lutheran and Reformed churches from 1907 to at least 1914, in the French Reformed Church from the 1930s onwards and in the Anglican African healing movement in South Africa, *Iviyo*, in the 1940s, to give but a few examples.

There were other significant influences prior to 1960 that helped change the attitude of many in the older churches to the Pentecostal experience, especially in North America. The acceptance of the white classical Pentecostal denominations into the NAE in 1943 signalled the beginning of the thawing of relationships between Pentecostals and evangelical churches, although it also led to the 'evangelicalization' of these Pentecostal denominations. Another influence was the role of the independent healing evangelists who were not affiliated to any classical Pentecostal denomination or if they were, operated independently of them. Many Christians outside these denominations were exposed to Pentecostal experience as a result of the ministry of William Branham, Oral Roberts, T. L. Osborne and other healing evangelists in the late 1940s and 1950s. Roberts initiated a weekly national television programme in 1955 that brought his healing campaigns with their Pentecostal subculture into homes across the nation. His monthly glossy magazine *Abundant Life* had a circulation of over a million and he soon became the best-known Pentecostal in the world.[1]

In 1951 the Full Gospel Business Men's Fellowship International (FGBMFI) was organized by Los Angeles millionaire, Armenian Pentecostal and California dairy farmer Demos Shakarian (1913–93), who became its president. This organization, initially of Pentecostal businessmen, received the backing of Oral Roberts, who spoke at its first meeting and often thereafter. The FGBMFI emphasized bringing the Pentecostal experience to laymen and grew quickly. It did not admit either women or church ministers into membership and was unashamedly capitalistic in ethos. Soon it

[1] Hollenweger, *The Pentecostals*, pp. 6–7; P. G. Chappell, 'Roberts, Granville Oral', *NIDPCM*, pp. 1024–5.

attracted men from 'mainline' churches as well as Pentecostals, encouraging its members to be active in and loyal to their own churches. The FGBMFI was an instrument to bring Charismatic experience to these churches and it introduced the Pentecostal healing evangelists to them, especially Oral Roberts. Its annual conventions held since 1953 featured all the leading independent healing evangelists and drew thousands. Its chapter meetings were held in plush hotel ballrooms and restaurants, a marked departure from the Pentecostal meetings of the past in tents and storefront buildings. The FGBMFI also helped finance the ultramodern Oral Roberts University in Tulsa, Oklahoma in 1965 and sowed the seeds for the 'prosperity gospel' that emerged in the 1970s, featuring some of the early 'faith preachers' like Kenneth Hagin, Sr. and Kenneth Copeland in its conventions. By 1972 the FGBMFI had about 300,000 members in the USA and continued to grow steadily, spreading over the world to more than a hundred nations. It had an influential monthly magazine *Voice* that publicized the Charismatic experiences of people from 'mainline' churches and a weekly TV programme called *Good News* hosted by Shakarian. Shakarian's place as president of the organization was taken over by his son Richard in 1988.[2]

Another important figure was South African David du Plessis (1905–87), nicknamed 'Mr Pentecost', who had, since 1951, travelled around the world as an unofficial spokesperson for Pentecostalism in ecumenical circles. Du Plessis received a prophecy from visiting English evangelist Smith Wigglesworth in 1936 that he would take the Pentecostal experience around the world and that there would be a Pentecostal revival in 'mainline' denominations. Du Plessis was general secretary of the AFM in South Africa from 1936 until 1947, when he moved to Switzerland to help organize the first Pentecostal World Conference. In 1948 he moved to the USA and after some time with the CGC he affiliated with the AG in 1955. His friendship with Princeton president and International Missionary Council president John McKay brought him into the ecumenical movement. In 1952 he addressed the IMC meeting in Willingen, Germany and in 1954 the WCC assembly at Evaston, Illinois, after which he attended every WCC assembly until 1983. He was warmly received in organizations and institutions like the WCC and in congregations and seminaries of all denominations. His work brought many within mainline churches to the Pentecostal experience. Because of their opposition to his ecumenical contacts and du Plessis' refusal to give them up, the AG (whose Chairman Thomas Zimmerman was president of the NAE at the time) withdrew du Plessis's credentials in 1962 and they

[2] J. R. Ziegler, 'Full Gospel Business Men's Fellowship International', *NIDPCM*, pp. 653–4.

were only reinstated in 1980. Du Plessis was involved in organizing the Pentecostal-Catholic dialogue that began in 1972 and became an effective bridge between Pentecostalism, the ecumenical movement and the Charismatic Movement in both its Protestant and Catholic forms.[3]

Several ministers received Spirit baptism in the 'mainline' churches in the 1940s and 1950s and promoted spiritual renewal thereafter, including Lutheran pastor Harald Bredesen (1918–) in 1946, Methodist minister Tommy Tyson in 1952, Disciples of Christ minister Don Basham in 1953, Episcopalian vicar's wife and healing minister Agnes Sanford (1897–1982) in 1953–54, and Mennonite pastor Gerald Derstine in 1954. Richard Winkler, rector of Trinity Episcopal Church in Wheaton, Illinois started the first Charismatic prayer meeting among Episcopalians in 1956 following his Spirit baptism, and he was featured in *Life* magazine for his ministry of exorcism. Presbyterian minister James Brown received Spirit baptism in 1956 and began a similar meeting in his church in Parkesburg, Pennsylvania; Bredesen began a Charismatic prayer meeting in his church in New York in 1957; and Agnes Sanford spoke privately to many ministers about the baptism in the Spirit and was a major promoter of the Charismatic renewal in the 1950s.

But none of these meetings received the publicity that the 1960 events did. California does seem to hold special significance for North American Pentecostalism for more than one generation. Episcopalian rector in Van Nuys (suburban Los Angeles), Dennis Bennett (1917–91) and his colleague Frank Maguire, vicar in Monterey Park, received Spirit baptism in November 1959 together with many of their church members. But they did not make it public until Bennett testified in a Sunday sermon in April 1960 at his St Mark's Episcopal Church. The testimony caused controversy and he was asked to resign, which he did formally in a pastoral letter explaining the compatibility of his Charismatic experience with Episcopalian teaching. The Bishop of Los Angeles wrote to the parish with a ban on speaking in tongues. One of the Charismatic members, Jean Stone contacted the press and Bennett's story was reported in *Time* and *Newsweek*. Other Charismatics were encouraged to become more public in their testimony. The 'Charismatic renewal' (a term coined by Stone and Bredesen) or 'Neo-Pentecostalism' was now out of the closet. Bennett was contacted by a sympathetic bishop in Washington State and appointed rector of a small, struggling Episcopal church, St Luke's, Seattle, where he was able to share his experience with a congregation willing to listen. The church grew rapidly until it was the largest in the diocese and a place to which

---

[3] R. P. Spittler, 'Du Plessis, David Johannes', *NIDPCM*, pp. 589–93.

people came to receive Spirit baptism – at one stage Bennett was ministering to 2,000 people a week. Eventually, Bennett's testimony was published as *Nine O'Clock in the Morning* (1970) and became a bestseller. He became a national figure and through him other ministers became involved in the Charismatic movement, including Episcopalians, Methodists, Reformed, Baptists, Lutherans and Presbyterians. Jean Stone began the quarterly magazine *Trinity* in 1961, which after the FGBMFI's *Voice* was the main publication promoting Charismatic renewal until it ceased publication in 1966.

The Charismatic movement spread during the 1960s throughout the USA and Canada. Two prominent early leaders were Bredesen and Lutheran pastor Larry Christenson (1928–) from San Pedro, California, both of whom had received Spirit baptism through attending classical Pentecostal meetings. Bredesen brought the Charismatic experience to students from several denominations at Yale University in October 1962, an event which received international publicity through a report in *Time*. He was one of the most prominent people representing the Charismatic movement in the media. Christenson, who related the compatibility of his Spirit baptism with the Lutheran tradition, visited Britain and Germany in 1963. He was instrumental in the start of the Charismatic movement in Britain and reported the presence of Lutherans in Germany who had spoken in tongues for sixty years. The Episcopalian bishop of Montana was sympathetic to the Charismatics and the movement flourished in that diocese. But Charismatics were not universally welcomed in their churches. The Episcopalian Bishop of California James Pike and the Methodist bishop Gerald Kennedy positioned themselves against them. Pike forbade speaking in tongues in his diocese in 1963, warning of a 'heresy in embryo' that was 'dangerous to the peace and unity of the church'. The conservative denominations, the Southern Baptist Convention, the Church of the Nazarene and the Lutheran Church, Missouri Synod expelled Charismatic ministers and congregations. Despite official disapproval, the Charismatic renewal continued unabated among the Southern Baptists. But such resistance often caused Charismatics to leave their churches, resulting in divided churches and hurt people, but also precipitating the rise of new independent Charismatic churches.[4]

EXPANSION

In spite of the opposition, Charismatic experiences in the older churches were encouraged by news reports of Charismatic happenings and by

---

[4] Dennis Bennett, *Nine O'Clock in the Morning* (Plainfield, NJ: Bridge Publishing, 1970); P. D. Hocken, 'Charismatic Movement', *NIDPCM*, pp. 477–519; Synan, *Holiness-Pentecostal*, pp. 226–33.

hundreds of popular publications – the two most influential of which were probably David Wilkerson's *The Cross and the Switchblade* (1963) and journalist John Sherrill's *They Speak with other Tongues* (1964).[5] Sherrill's book was a pioneering one that suggested that Middle America with its stately churches and comfortable lifestyles could embrace the Pentecostal experience – it was not reserved for people on the 'other side of the tracks'. This book was one of the most important in the growth of the Charismatic movement. John and Elizabeth Sherrill also collaborated with Wilkerson in the writing of his equally significant book. Wilkerson (1931–) was a rural AG pastor who started Teen Challenge in Brooklyn, New York in 1958, a remarkably successful rehabilitation centre for drug addicts that established other such centres throughout the nation and in several other countries. He said that the astonishing success rate in providing deliverance for addicts was due to the experience of Spirit baptism that he urged all his converts to have. The *Reader's Digest* carried Wilkerson's story around the world and his book was eventually made into a film starring the former pop singer Pat Boone, himself a Charismatic. Wilkerson established World Challenge in 1972, an organization to co-ordinate his expanding ministry and in 1987 he resigned from the AG and joined up with his brother Don to found Times Square Church in New York. Many well-known personalities, by being part of the Charismatic movement, made it more socially acceptable – singers Pat Boone and Johnny Cash and General Ralph Haines were some examples. Boone baptized many people in his swimming pool in 1971 after his Charismatic experience.

The 'Jesus People' movement was a Charismatic revival movement that began on the Pacific Coast in 1967 among young people, in which thousands of former hippies became Christians through ministries in Christian coffee-houses offering deliverance from drug addiction. Some of the best-known of these were The Living Room founded by Ted Wise in San Francisco, The Ark started by Linda Meissner in Seattle, and His Place run by Arthur Blessitt in Los Angeles. Converts often lived in Christian communes in rural areas and kept aspects of their hippie subculture. One of the leading centres of this movement was the Calvary Chapel led by Chuck Smith, which in a few years grew to 25,000 mainly young people attending its Sunday services. By the early 1970s an estimated 300,000 young people were in the Jesus People movement.[6]

---

[5] David Wilkerson, *The Cross and the Switchblade* (New York: Random House, 1963); John L. Sherrill, *They Speak with Other Tongues* (New York: McGraw-Hill, 1964).
[6] Synan, *Holiness-Pentecostal*, pp. 255–6; Riss, *A Survey*, pp. 148–52.

The Charismatic movement was further publicized by television broadcasts – particularly those of Oral Roberts and Pat Robertson (1930–), a southern Baptist minister who resigned in 1987 and unsuccessfully contended for the Republican presidential nomination. Roberts left the Pentecostal Holiness Church to join the United Methodist Church in 1968 to more firmly anchor himself within the Charismatic movement. He became a local preacher there and the Graduate School of Theology at Oral Roberts University (headed by a Methodist theologian) became a recognized seminary for training Methodist ministers in 1982. Roberts' son Richard became head of his massive organization and university in 1993. There were many TV evangelists in the USA, including Jimmy Swaggart (1935–) and Jim Bakker (1940–), whose sensational falls in 1987–88 were a source of embarrassment for the Pentecostal movement. Bakker was an ordained AG pastor whose empire included a television network (PTL Network) and a Christian entertainment complex. He resigned from PTL and as an AG minister in 1987 because of allegations of a 1980 sexual encounter and mounting suspicion of financial irregularities. Swaggart led the opposition, declaring him a 'cancer'. Bakker was finally convicted of fraud and sentenced to 45 years in prison in 1989, reduced on appeal in 1991; he was released on parole in 1994 after which he made a full confession and renounced his belief in the 'prosperity gospel'. Swaggart too was an AG minister, a world-renowned evangelist and singer who presided over a multi-million dollar organization. After his refusal to accept the discipline of the AG leadership for sexual misconduct his ministerial credentials in the AG were withdrawn. At about the same time, Oral Roberts was seriously criticized for his fund-raising techniques for his ailing medical school. These various revelations did much to damage the reputation of Pentecostals and Charismatics and the secular media had a field day. But Robertson's Christian Broadcasting Network (CBN, commenced in 1959) and Paul Crouch's Trinity Broadcasting Network (TBN, started in 1973) have managed to avoid controversy and have continued from strength to strength. Robertson founded CBN University (now Regent University) in Virginia Beach in 1977 and he still directs a multi-media operation there. Crouch's TBN broadcasts around the world and he directs his organization from Phoenix, Arizona.[7]

In 1967 the Charismatic movement made a spectacular new entrance into the Catholic Church, long regarded by Pentecostals as beyond the

---

[7] Synan, *Holiness-Pentecostal*, pp. 289–90; S. M. Burgess, 'Bakker, James Orsen ('Jim'). *NIDPCM*, pp. 352–5; D. Hedges, 'Swaggart, Jimmy Lee', *NIDPCM*, p. 1111.

pale of Christian acceptability. At the Second Vatican Council Pope John XXIII had prayed that the Council might be a 'new Pentecost' for the church and Catholic Charismatics now see themselves as a fulfilment of that prayer. The movement began when two lay theology faculty members at Duquesne University in Pittsburgh, Ralph Kiefer and Bill Storey, who had read *The Cross and the Switchblade* and *They Speak With Other Tongues* received Spirit baptism and passed it on to about thirty students at a retreat, who then formed the first Catholic Charismatic prayer group. It spread from there to faculty and students at the University of Notre Dame, South Bend, Indiana and Michigan State University. It grew rapidly to include 300,000 people by 1976, spreading internationally into Latin America, Europe and Asia. Early leaders at Notre Dame were Ralph Martin (1942–) and Stephen Clark (1940–), who joined a campus ministry at the University of Michigan in Ann Arbor where they formed a Charismatic community. An annual conference was held at Notre Dame, increasing in size every year to 30,000 at its peak in 1974. A magazine from the movement called *New Covenant* had 60,000 subscribers in over a hundred countries and the Catholic Charismatics soon spread worldwide. From 1973 Cardinal Léon-Joseph Suenens (1904–96), primate of Belgium and one of the four moderators of the Second Vatican Council, was the acknowledged leader of Catholic Charismatics and advisor to the pope on Charismatic issues. At first the movement was called 'Catholic Pentecostal', but after 1974 was known as the 'Catholic Charismatic' movement. Important centres of the movement in the USA were the People of Praise Community in Notre Dame led by Kevin Ranaghan (1940–), one of the original Notre Dame Charismatics; a Charismatic monastery at Pecos, New Mexico and the thriving Word of God Community in Ann Arbor under the leadership of Martin and Clark.

An important feature of the movement in the early 1970s was the theological reflection made in publications by Catholic scholars, placing the movement firmly within Catholic tradition. These included the Benedictine scholar Kilian McDonnell, Edward O'Connor, and the more popular writings of Kevin and Dorothy Ranaghan.[8] Kevin Ranaghan was executive director of the Catholic Charismatic Renewal's National Service Committee from its inception in 1970 until 1985. The formal structures given to the Catholic Charismatic movement provided an effective leadership, communication between the different communities and prayer groups and

[8] Kevin and Dorothy Ranaghan, *Catholic Pentecostals* (New York: Paulist Press, 1969); Kilian McDonnell, *Catholic Pentecostalism* (Pecos, NM: Dove Publications, 1970); Edward O'Connor, *The Pentecostal Movement in the Catholic Church* (Notre Dame, IN: Ave Maria Press, 1971).

literature to guide participants in the renewal. As a result the movement was able to expand rapidly. In 1975 Pope Paul VI addressed a weekend Congress of 10,000 Catholic Charismatics in Rome, in which he encouraged the 'spiritual renewal' and the young people who would 'shout out to the world the greatness of Pentecost'. On this occasion Cardinal Suenens conducted the first Charismatic mass at St Peter's Square. This was a climax for a movement whose doors had been opened by Pope John XXIII and the Second Vatican Council ten years earlier. By 2000 there were an estimated 120 million Catholic Charismatics, some 11 per cent of all Catholics worldwide and almost twice the number of all the classical Pentecostals combined.[9] This was a remarkable achievement for a movement only thirty years old, and it probably stemmed the tide of the exodus from the Catholic Church into classical Pentecostalism in most continents – the notable exception being Latin America.

During the 1970s a number of official, fairly positive reports on the Charismatic renewal were commissioned by major Protestant denominations, beginning with that of the United Presbyterians in 1970 and ending with one by the WCC in 1980. These various reports, while sometimes critical, were generally supportive of the continuation of spiritual gifts and encouraged their members to remain in the church. Protestant denominations began to follow the Catholic lead in organizing their own annual national Charismatic conferences. The Episcopalians, led by Dennis Bennett and the Lutherans, led by Larry Christenson until 1995, were the strongest and most organized. The former created the Episcopal Renewal Fellowship in 1973, renamed Episcopal Renewal Ministries in 1980; the Lutherans formed the Lutheran Charismatic Renewal Services in 1974.

As the Charismatic Movement expanded in the USA and Canada to include some 10 per cent of all 'mainline' church members, so it spread worldwide. In West Germany, Lutheran pastor Arnold Bittlinger (1928–) became a leader in the Charismatic movement there after his experience of the Spirit in 1962, and he arranged the conference with Larry Christenson the following year. He promoted the renewal in West Germany and in ecumenical circles and was involved in the first five-year dialogue between Catholics and Pentecostals (1972–77) (see chapter 12). Bittlinger was also part of a Charismatic ecumenical community set up at Schloss Craheim in 1968, for ten years the centre of the renewal in West Germany. The first

[9] Synan, *Holiness-Pentecostal*, pp. 246–52; T. P. Thigpen, 'Catholic Charismatic Renewal', *NIDPCM*, pp. 460–7; D. B. Barrett and T. M. Johnson, 'Global Statistics', *NIDCPM*, p. 286.

continental European Charismatic Leaders' Conference was held there in 1972 with sixteen countries represented and from then on held every two years until 1988. A 'Pentecost over Europe' celebration was held at Strasbourg in 1982 with 20,000 participants mainly from France, West Germany and Switzerland, but having a similar effect in Europe to the Kansas City conference in the USA described below. The European Charismatic Consultation replaced earlier committees and had its first conference in Disentis, Switzerland in 1989.

The Charismatic movement in France began in the 1930s, and Louis Dallière's Union de Prière was formed as a Charismatic group within the Reformed Church after the Second World War. Baptist pastor Jules Thobois received Spirit baptism in 1947 and the Baptist Federation officially allowed Charismatic practices in Baptist churches from 1952. After 1968 Protestant pastors received Spirit baptism through the ministries of Clément le Cossec and former Pentecostal turned Reformed pastor Thomas Roberts (see chapter 5). The Catholic Charismatic movement in France spread rapidly from 1972–75, especially through the translation into French of Ranaghan's *Catholic Pentecostals*. There are currently half a million Catholic Charismatics in France, more than anywhere else in Europe. Nevertheless, the Catholic Charismatic movement spread in Europe to include significant prayer groups and communities in Belgium, Italy, Spain, Portugal, Hungary, Czechoslovakia and Poland. The Protestant renewal has spread to the Netherlands, the Scandinavian countries (especially Finland), East Germany and Switzerland.

In Britain, the Pentecostal movement had begun in an Anglican church and Anglicans were the first to welcome the Charismatic movement there too. The initial home for the movement was All Souls Church in London, where the well-known evangelical John Stott was rector – although he himself was clearly not Charismatic and was soon to distance himself from it and the activities of his curate, Michael Harper (1931–). Frank McGuire had been in touch with Stott and Harper and had shared with them his experience in California. Harper received Spirit baptism in 1962 and in 1965 wrote the influential book *As at the Beginning*. The first Anglican parish to become Charismatic was St Mark's, Gillingham, Kent in 1963 under John Collins, a former assistant at All Souls, and where David Watson (1933–84) was curate until his appointment as vicar to St Cuthbert's, York, another centre of the renewal. Early British Charismatic leaders were Anglicans David Watson, John Perry (vicar at St Andrew's, Chorleywood) and Michael Harper; and Baptist pastors David Pawson (Gold Hill and later Guildford) and Barney

Coombs (East Acton and Basingstoke). Harper arranged a meeting of ministers for Larry Christenson's brief visit to London in 1963 and later that year for David du Plessis. Jean Stone and Dennis Bennett visited the UK in 1964 and 1965 respectively, and in all these special meetings more and more people were brought into the renewal. In 1964 Harper organized the first Charismatic conference at an Anglican retreat centre at Stoke Poges where the main speaker was the Scottish former Brethren, Campbell McAlpine. From 1964 to 1975 Harper was founder and full-time director of the Fountain Trust, the leading organization in Britain promoting the Charismatic renewal, solidly ecumenical in vision and embracing all denominations. Harper also organized a major international and ecumenical conference in 1971 in Guildford, including over forty Lutheran and thirty Catholic delegates. Further national conferences were held in Nottingham (1973) and Westminster (1975) giving the movement in Britain a greater sense of identity and cohesion.

Tom Smail (1928–), a Presbyterian minister, became director of the Fountain Trust in 1975 and edited a theological journal, *Theological Renewal* – but the closure of the Trust and its journal in 1980 signalled the end of the Charismatic renewal for some. Smail became an Anglican priest and vice-principal of a theological college. Harper left the Anglican church over women's ordination and became an Antiochian Orthodox priest in 1995 (eventually becoming a bishop), thereby diverting his energies elsewhere. The focus of the Charismatic movement in the UK now shifted from an ecumenical movement to denominational groupings: the Anglican Renewal Ministries formed in 1981, the Dunamis Renewal Fellowship started in 1983 by Methodist Charismatics, who published the periodical *Dunamis*, and Mainstream, founded in 1978 among the Baptists, an attempt to hold together the Charismatic and evangelical strands of the Baptist Union after some prominent Charismatics had become independent.

The first Catholic Charismatics in Britain were those influenced by the Dominican Simon Tugwell in the late 1960s. But the Catholic Charismatic movement was only organized later with a National Service Committee of Catholic Charismatic Renewal and a magazine *Goodnews*. Peter Hocken (1932–) has been an influential British Catholic Charismatic priest since his Pentecostal experience in 1971. He moved to the Mother of God Community in Gaithersburg, Maryland in 1976, authored several books and served as executive secretary of the Society for Pentecostal Studies from 1989 until 1996. Charles Whitehead, an influential Catholic businessman, has headed the National Service Committee since 1986, and since 1990 has also been president of the International Catholic Charismatic Renewal Services in Rome.[10]

In South Africa the head of the Anglican Church (Church of the Province of South Africa), the Archbishop of Cape Town from 1974–81, Bill Burnett (1917–94) was the highest profile Charismatic, baptized in the Spirit in 1972 while Bishop of Grahamstown. The Charismatic movement spread quickly in South Africa in the 1970s, especially among Anglicans and Baptists. But Bishop Alpheus Zulu of Zululand led an African Anglican Charismatic movement, *Iviyo*, from the 1940s. The Charismatic independents in Latin America have been most influential in other countries, especially those from Argentina and Brazil. The Catholic Charismatics were an estimated two million in twenty-one Latin American countries in 1987. They are especially strong in India (perhaps five million) and in the Philippines (perhaps eleven million). In Kerala, India, Father Michael Naikomparambil leads weekly healing and evangelism meetings that draw crowds of 15,000 and he hosts occasional conferences of 200,000. The Catholic Charismatic movement of El Shaddai in the Philippines led by layman Mike Velarde is the largest of all these national Charismatic movements with seven million members.[11]

THE RISE OF INDEPENDENT PENTECOSTALISM

The Charismatic movement in North America reached its peak in the 1977 Kansas City Charismatic Conference, hailed by its chairman Kevin Ranaghan as the most ecumenical large gathering in 800 years of church history. It was an unprecedented conference uniting some 50,000 Catholics, Anglicans, Protestants and classical Pentecostals that was never to be repeated on such a scale. By 1990 there were an estimated 33 million Pentecostal and Charismatics in the USA, 13 per cent of the total population and by 2000 an estimated 72 million, more than double the number. As the Charismatic movement in the older churches began to decline in the late 1970s, a new 'nondenominational' Pentecostal and Charismatic movement with much weaker links with older churches began to emerge, emphasizing house groups and 'radical' discipleship, and also known as the 'restoration' movement. A popular teacher on radical discipleship was the Argentine Juan Carlos Ortiz, whose book *Disciple* (1975) was an international bestseller.

[10] Douglas McBain, *Fire over the Waters: Renewal among Baptists and others from the 1960s to the 1990s* (London: Darton, Longman and Todd, 1997), pp. 31–9, 52, 72–4; Michael Harper, *As at the Beginning* (London: Hodder and Stoughton, 1965).

[11] Entries: 'India', 'Philippines', 'South Africa', 'Burnett, Bill', *NIDPCM*, pp. 118, 201, 230–1, 450–1.

The terms 'Pentecostal' and 'Charismatic' began to be used interchangeably and the term 'neopentecostal' was applied to the 'nondenominational' churches, later also referred to as 'neocharismatic'. The independent ministries of Oral Roberts, FGBMFI, CBN and TBN had foreshadowed these new churches. Associations of independent churches were formed, one of the first and largest being the National Leadership Conference, formed in 1979. These networks of independent churches were soon the fastest growing segment in the Pentecostal and Charismatic movement in the English-speaking world, spreading to become hundreds of independent global networks.

In the USA, the 'Fort Lauderdale Five' of Charles Simpson (Southern Baptist background), Derek Prince (British Pentecostal), Ern Baxter (Canadian Pentecostal), Bob Mumford (AG) and Don Basham (Disciples of Christ) came together in 1970 to lead a movement known as the 'shepherding' or 'discipleship' movement because of its strong and highly controversial emphasis on submission to 'shepherds' or church leaders. Large numbers of independent Charismatic pastors were associated with this group. This movement was subject to serious criticism and it created a rift in the Charismatic movement from which it never really recovered. In 1975 Pat Robertson came out publicly against the movement on CBN, and Demos Shakarian of FGBMFI and Charismatic healing evangelist Kathryn Kuhlman soon joined him in denouncing it. Critics accused the 'Fort Lauderdale Five' of heresy, of creating a Charismatic denomination and of exploiting 'disciples' who were totally dependent on their shepherds, to whom they had to submit every area of their lives, including the most intimate. The Kansas City Conference in 1977 divided into smaller interest groups representing its various constituencies. The 'shepherding' track drew the largest crowds (12,000) after the Catholic Charismatics, but the controversy was so heated that the so-called 'nondenominational' Charismatics had to have two separate tracks, as neither would fellowship with the other. But the shepherding movement had some 100,000 associated members in North America at its zenith. Its publishing arm Christian Growth Ministries (Integrity Communications from 1978) produced the highly influential *New Wine* magazine that ceased production in 1986, the date of the demise of the shepherding movement. Its leaders moved to Mobile, Alabama after 1978 and were in great demand as conference speakers across the nation and internationally, especially Mumford. The association between the remaining four (Prince had left in 1983) was dissolved in 1986 and the shepherding movement effectively ended. Only Simpson remained in Mobile to form the Fellowship of Covenant Ministers and Conferences in 1987 and continue the association of churches in the shepherding movement, with 350 members.[12]

The British 'restoration' movement was a parallel movement to the shepherding movement and arose in the late 1950s with Arthur Wallis and Dennis Lillie its first leaders. Many of the leaders were former Brethren who had been expelled because of their Pentecostal experience and taught a 'restoration' of the 'five-fold ministry' of apostles, prophets, evangelists, pastors and teachers. Known at first as the 'house church movement', the restoration movement was to become the fastest growing church group in the country, now vaguely called 'New Churches'. By 1982 there may have been 100,000 house groups in Britain. Major new church networks emerged like that of Terry Virgo, founder of New Frontiers, Bryn Jones of Covenant Ministries International, Barney Coombs of Salt and Light Ministries, Gerald Coates of Pioneer People, Tony Morton of Cornerstone Ministries and Roger Forster of Ichthus Christian Fellowship. New Frontiers is now the largest of these networks, nurtured during the 1990s by the annual Stoneleigh Bible Weeks near Coventry. Jones, one of the original group with Wallis, more closely identified with the shepherding movement in the USA than the other leaders did, and his anti-denominational stance somewhat isolated his movement from the others, who now co-operate with the Evangelical Alliance. Coates and Virgo have identified with the 'Toronto Blessing'. Together with the Vineyard Association, which started in Britain in 1987, these church networks are now taking the appearance of new denominations. In 2000, over 400,000 people were affiliated to the New Churches, making it the largest of the Pentecostal and Charismatic groupings in the UK.

Very different from the shepherding and restoration movements and in more continuity with Pentecostal healing evangelists is the 'Word of Faith' movement of the USA's Bible Belt. Known also as 'positive confession' and the 'faith message', and by its detractors as the 'prosperity gospel' and the 'health and wealth' movement, it is widely regarded to have originated in early Pentecostalism and to have been particularly influenced by Baptist pastor E. W. Kenyon (1867–1948). Kenyon taught the 'positive confession of the Word of God' and a 'law of faith' working by predetermined divine principles. The development of the movement was stimulated by the teachings of Pentecostal healing evangelists like William Branham and especially Oral Roberts, the FGBMFI, contemporary popular televangelists and the

---

[12] S. D. Moore, 'Shepherding Movement', *NIDPCM*, pp. 1060–2; Synan, *Holiness-Pentecostal*, pp. 260–6; Hocken, 'Charismatic Movement', *NIDPCM*, pp. 484–8.

Charismatic movement. It is now a prominent teaching in many Pentecostal and Charismatic churches all over the world. Its leading North American exponents have been Kenneth Hagin of Tulsa, Oklahoma (widely regarded as 'father of the Faith Movement'), Kenneth Copeland of Fort Worth, Texas and African American Frederick Price of Crenshaw Christian Centre, Los Angeles, among many others. Hagin, an AG pastor from 1939–49, moved to Tulsa in 1966 and commenced the Rhema Bible Training Centre in 1974, where he taught his faith gospel of health, wealth and success and sold more than 33 million copies of his booklets. More than 16,500 students had graduated from Rhema by 2000, and Hagin's ministry is now run by his son, Kenneth Hagin, Jr. Kenneth and Gloria Copeland have taken over the mantle of leadership of this movement. They have spread their more radical version of the 'faith message' all around the world with their *Voice of Victory* television and radio ministry, run by the Kenneth Copeland Evangelistic Association founded in 1968.

Many Pentecostal and Charismatic preachers in other parts of the world have propounded a modified form of this teaching to suit their own contexts. Leading global exponents include David Yonggi Cho of Korea, Nigerians Benson Idahosa and David Oyedepo, Ghanaians Nicholas Duncan-Williams and Mensa Otabil, Ulf Ekman of Sweden, Edir Macedo of Brazil, Hector Gimenez of Argentina and South African Ray McCauley, to name some of the more prominent. It would be misleading to suggest, however, that the 'faith message' is the only emphasis of these leaders, as for most of them it is but one aspect of a comprehensive ministry. Many Pentecostals and Charismatics have rejected this movement and distanced themselves from it, including the AG in a position paper, John Wimber, David Wilkerson and Jimmy Swaggart.[13]

In the 1980s the 'Third Wave' in Evangelicalism was a term coined by Fuller Theological Seminary's Peter Wagner, following the two 'waves' of the Classical Pentecostal movement and the Charismatic movement. Wagner identified the 'Third Wave' particularly with John Wimber (1934–97), who taught the popular 'Signs and Wonders' course with Wagner at Fuller and whose Vineyard Christian Fellowship in Anaheim, California (commenced in 1977) spearheaded a new emphasis on renewal in the established churches throughout the English-speaking world. Most Charismatics did not stress the 'initial evidence' doctrine of tongues, but they still promoted a crisis experience subsequent to baptism or conversion. The

---

[13] Allan Anderson, 'The Word of Faith Movement', Chris H. Partridge (ed.), *Encyclopedia of New Religions* (London: Lion Publishing, 2003), pp. 90–4; Andrew Perriman (ed.), *Faith, Health and Prosperity: A Report on 'Word of Faith' and 'Positive Confession' Theologies* (Carlisle, UK: Paternoster, 2003).

Third Wave movement moved completely away from this idea of a 'second blessing' experience of the Spirit to Spirit baptism occurring at conversion and an emphasis on the gifts of the Spirit in evangelism and as part of Christian life, a concept that many evangelicals found more acceptable. A network of 500 Vineyard churches in the USA had emerged by 1998. Wimber's influence on the Charismatic renewal in Britain was enormous. His first visit to Britain in 1982 and his laid-back ministry of 'power evangelism' was widely accepted by older churches, especially evangelical Anglicans. The churches of Holy Trinity, Brompton (HTB, under Sandy Millar) and St Andrew's, Chorleywood (Bishop David Pytches) became centres of the new renewal from the mid 1980s onwards. The rapidly expanding and interdenominational Alpha evangelism programme, under Millar's associate Nicky Gumble at HTB, has opened up many non-Charismatic churches to the area of spiritual gifts. By 1998 5,000 British churches were using Alpha materials.

The 1990s has also been the era of the 'cell church'. Based on the pioneering work of David Yonggi Cho in Seoul, Korea, that of Lawrence Kwang in Singapore and the writings of Ralph Neighbour, Jr., the 'cell church' strategy is widely used in the Pentecostal and Charismatic movement. It is particularly effective in maintaining cohesion in 'megachurches' with its emphasis on the home cell group as the focus of pastoral care, discipleship and evangelism.[14]

THE NEW AFRICAN PENTECOSTALS

Since the 1980s, large independent Pentecostal and Charismatic congregations have sprung up all over the world, particularly in Africa, Latin America and North America. These new churches often form loose associations for co-operation and networking, sometimes internationally. By 1988, there were an estimated 100,000 'White-led independent Charismatic churches', most of which were in North America.[15] In many parts of Africa the Pentecostal and Charismatic churches are the fastest growing section of Christianity, appealing especially to younger, educated urban people. Some of the newer churches have been criticized for propagating a 'prosperity gospel' that seems to reproduce the worst forms of North American capitalism in Christian guise. But there is a danger of generalizing

---

[14] David Yonggi Cho, *Successful Home Cell Groups* (Seoul: Seoul Logos Co., 1997); Ralph W. Neighbour, Jr., *Where Do We Go From Here? A Guidebook for the Cell Group Church* (Houston, TX: Touch Publications, 1990).

[15] Synan, *Holiness-Pentecostal*, pp. 275–8.

in making this assessment, especially when such generalizations fail to appreciate the selective reconstructions and creative innovations made by these new Pentecostals in adapting to radically different contexts from those of the 'prosperity preachers' of the USA.[16]

West Africa, and in particular Nigeria and Ghana, has been the scene of an explosion of a new form of Pentecostalism since the mid 1970s, to such an extent that it may become the future shape of African Christianity, which turns increasingly Charismatic.[17] From West Africa this new Pentecostalism has spread rapidly throughout Africa's cities from Monrovia to Mombassa and from Addis Ababa to Cape Town. New Pentecostal and Charismatic churches are fast becoming a major expression of Christianity in Africa, especially in the cities. They began to emerge all over Africa, with a tendency to have a younger and more educated membership than that of classical Pentecostalism. Their services are usually emotional, enthusiastic and loud, especially as most make use of electronic musical instruments. Some of these churches propagate the 'prosperity gospel', but identifying them with this form of US Pentecostalism does not appreciate the reconstruction and innovations made by these movements in adapting to a radically different context. The new Pentecostals are increasing in popularity with educated and young professional people who continue to give financial support and feel that their needs are met there. Methods employed by these churches, like those of other Pentecostals, include door-to-door evangelism, 'cottage meetings' held in homes of inquirers, preaching in trains, buses, on street corners and at places of public concourse, and in 'tent crusades', both large and small, held all over the continent. Access to modern communications has resulted in the popularizing of some western 'televangelists', several of whom make regular visits to Africa and broadcast their own programmes there. The strategies employed by these evangelists are subject to criticism, but this new form of Christianity has nevertheless appealed especially to the urbanized and more westernized new generation of Africans. Many new Pentecostal and Charismatic churches arose in the context of interdenominational and evangelical campus and school Christian organizations like Scripture Union.

The growth of these churches has been most dramatic in Nigeria and Ghana where Christianity has permeated every facet of society and is evident to any visitor. Small businesses in West African cities proclaim its

---

[16] Paul Gifford, *African Christianity: Its Public Role* (London: Hurst, 1998), pp. 334–9; Coleman, *Globalisation*, pp. 31–6.
[17] Allan Anderson, 'The Newer Pentecostal and Charismatic Churches: The Shape of Future Christianity in Africa?', *Pneuma* 24:2 (2002), 167–84; Anderson, *African Reformation*, pp. 167–90.

influence: 'In the Name of Jesus Enterprises', 'To God be the Glory Computers', 'Hands of God Beauty Salon', 'El Shaddai Fast Foods', and 'My God is Able Cold Store' are just a few of the hundreds of names I saw on recent visits to Ghana and Nigeria. Christian slogans are written all over cars, vans and public vehicles. One of the most remarkable new churches in Nigeria is the Deeper Life Bible Church, with churches all over West Africa and over half a million members in Nigeria only ten years after its founding by William Folorunso Kumuyi, a former education lecturer at the University of Lagos. Deeper Life began as a weekly Bible study group in 1973 and spread to other parts of Nigeria. When the first Sunday services were held in 1982, regarded as the foundation date, a new church was formed, which now has some 800,000 affiliates. The Church of God Mission International of Archbishop Benson Idahosa, who died in 1998, with a 'Miracle Centre' headquarters in Benin City is another prominent Nigerian example. Idahosa's wife Margaret (now Bishop) heads the movement, which also runs the All Nations for Christ Bible Institute, probably the most popular Bible school in West Africa, and thousands flock to Benin City every week. Idahosa had formal ties with other new Pentecostal and Charismatic groups throughout Africa, especially in Ghana, where he held his first crusade in Accra in 1978. In September 1999, a 50,000 capacity church sanctuary was dedicated for the Living World Outreach ('Winners Chapel') of David Oyedepo, one of the largest church buildings in the world. This organization commenced in 1989 and has spread to other parts of Africa, most notably to Kenya.[18]

New Pentecostals and Charismatics are also prominent in Ghana. Bishop Nicholas Duncan-Williams, leader of the largest and earliest new church founded in 1980, Christian Action Faith Ministries, was a protégé of Idahosa, trained in his Bible school and formerly member of the Church of Pentecost. Another rapidly growing church is the International Central Gospel Church founded in 1984 by Mensa Otabil, who has recently opened a Christian university college. During the 1980s, rapidly growing independent churches began to emerge in Kenya and Uganda, where they were sometimes seen as a threat by the older churches from which they often gained members. These churches preached the need for a personal experience of God in Christ through being 'born again'. One of the largest denominations in Zimbabwe today is the Zimbabwe Assemblies of God Africa (ZAOGA) under its leader Archbishop Ezekiel Guti, a church that separated from the South African AG in 1967 and had an estimated 1.6 million

[18] Anderson, *African Reformation*, pp. 172–5; Johnstone and Mandryk, *Operation World*, pp. 421, 488.

affiliates by 2000. Guti was trained in a Pentecostal Bible college in the USA in 1971.

The classical Pentecostals and the Spirit churches undoubtedly have played a part in the emergence of these new groups in Africa. The new Pentecostalism is a demonstration of a form of Christianity that appeals to a new generation of Africans. Their more prominent preachers promote internationalism and place high value on making overseas trips and hosting international conventions. Like Pentecostals and Charismatics everywhere, these new churches have a sense of identity as a separated community whose primary purpose is to promote their cause to those outside. The emergence of these churches throughout the world indicates that there are unresolved questions facing the church, such as the role of 'success' and 'prosperity' in God's economy, enjoying God *and* his gifts, including healing and material provision, and the holistic dimension of 'salvation'. The 'here-and-now' problems being addressed by the new Pentecostal and Charismatic churches are problems that still challenge the church as a whole.[19]

TORONTO AND PENSACOLA

In the mid 1990s two sensational and controversial new Charismatic revival movements appeared in North America. In January 1994 a phenomenon to be known as the 'Toronto Blessing' emerged in the Toronto Airport Vineyard church in Canada, pastored by John Arnott. Arnott had been a follower and admirer of Kathryn Kuhlman, Benny Hinn and John Wimber, and had witnessed unusual manifestations, 'signs and wonders' at their meetings. In November 1993 he visited Claudio Freidzon of the AG in Argentina, where a revival had been taking place for some years and where unusual manifestations, including 'holy laughter' and 'falling under the power' (also called 'slain in the Spirit'), were common. These manifestations were to become trademarks of the Toronto movement but were not new, as such manifestations had been reported in many Pentecostal meetings over the past century. One example of this comes from the 1909 Chilean revival, whose leader Willis Hoover reported that he was filled with 'a laughter so strong and uncontrollable that he had to sit and give free reign to it, unable to suppress it'. Maria Woodworth-Etter reported it once in her meetings too, where the most common manifestation was people falling down prostrate 'under the power', sometimes with 'leaping and dancing'. She defended 'dancing in the Spirit' and manifestations of people playing

---

[19] Anderson, *African Reformation*, pp. 175–86; Johnstone and Mandryk, *Operation World*, p. 689.

'heavenly' instruments 'in the Spirit' in her meetings were also frequently reported.[20] The 'revival' in Toronto was initiated by South African preacher Rodney Howard-Browne (reared in the prosperity teachings of Hagin at Ray McCauley's Rhema Bible Church in Johannesburg) and Randy Clark, pastor of the Vineyard Church in St Louis, and it was characterized by unusual manifestations, especially 'holy laughter'. Howard-Browne had been in the USA since 1987 and had a reputation for meetings where 'holy laughter' broke out as early as 1992. In one of Howard-Browne's meetings in Kenneth Hagin's Rhema Bible Church in Tulsa in 1993, Clark experienced the phenomenon personally. He was invited to speak in the Toronto Vineyard, where an outbreak of the 'holy laughter' created pandemonium and was followed later by even stranger animal noises made by people falling 'under the power'. These phenomena attracted worldwide attention and thousands visited Toronto to see and experience the 'revival' for themselves. It was estimated that some 600,000 people had visited the Toronto church by the end of 1995. The phenomena spread to other places in the western world, especially as ministers who had visited Toronto went back with the 'refreshing' to their own churches.

John Wimber and the Association of Vineyard Churches Board were not completely happy with these new developments. They attempted to moderate the 'Toronto Blessing' in September 1994, especially warning against exotic and non-biblical manifestations. The warnings apparently went unheeded and in December 1995 Wimber visited the Toronto church and dissociated himself and his movement from it, which he said was pursuing practices that were not fully consonant with the Vineyard ethos, and that it was changing their definition of renewal. The Toronto church was expelled from the Vineyard Association and became known thereafter as the Toronto Airport Christian Fellowship. The new church almost immediately restructured itself and formed the International Renewal Network, another global association of churches and ministers with similar views. The ebb and flow of visitors to Toronto has decreased and there are signs that the 'Toronto Blessing' is for most involved in it a pleasing but distant memory. Participants in this revival spoke of a new revelation of God the Father's love and of inner healing as a result of what they perceived as a refreshing experience.

One of the most prominent centres promoting the Toronto Blessing in the USA was the Metro Christian Fellowship of Mike Bickle in Kansas City,

---

[20] Hoover, *History*, p. 19; Woodworth-Etter, *Signs and Wonders*, pp. 135, 257; Maria Woodworth-Etter, *The Holy Spirit* (New Kensington, PA: Whitaker House, 1998), pp. 247–8.

from where the 'Kansas City prophets' (the most notable being Paul Cain) operated. Holy Trinity Church, Brompton (HTB) in London under its vicar Sandy Millar and St Andrew's, Chorleywood became leading Anglican centres of this phenomenon in Britain and Sunderland Christian Centre (AGBI) led by Ken and Lois Gott became the main Pentecostal centre. The New Frontiers and Pioneers churches were also practising the Toronto phenomena, among others. After the split between Vineyard and Toronto, many of the British churches continued to support Toronto, with the exception of HTB and the British Vineyard churches, who each gave statements of support for Wimber's position. The Alpha evangelism course of HTB became a more important feature of Charismatic churches in the UK after this.

On Father's Day, June 1995 a second major revival began in an AG church in Brownsville, Pensacola, Florida known variously as the 'Pensacola Outpouring' and the 'Brownsville Revival'. This has also attracted international interest, in which the emphasis seems to have been upon 'old fashioned' repentance. Evangelist Steve Hill (who had himself received the Toronto Blessing at HTB) and the pastor of the Brownsville AG church, John Kilpatrick led this revival. By 1997 this more classical Pentecostal revival, referred to by some of its leaders as a 'last days awakening', claimed over one and a half million visitors from all over the world, some 5,000 people at nightly services and 100,000 converts. Services typically lasted four or five hours, five times a week for five years. The revival has also been accompanied by strange manifestations like twitching and jerking and noisy meetings reminiscent of the classical Pentecostal subculture in the USA, but the focus has been on repentance and forgiveness. Steve Hill preached at almost all the services until 2000 when he moved to Dallas, Texas to begin an itinerant ministry. Both Toronto and Pensacola have become places for pilgrimage for several new 'revival' movements springing up in various parts of the western world. But both movements have also experienced rejection and have resulted in division. There have been sharp criticisms of Toronto and Pensacola, especially from evangelicals, one author referring to them as 'counterfeit revival'.

It may be too early to tell whether these new revival movements will have any lasting effect comparable to other great revivals of history.[21] The history of the Charismatic and 'Third Wave' movements sketched here illustrates a Weberian principle operating throughout Pentecostalism: these revitalizing

[21] M. M. Poloma, 'Toronto Blessing', *NIDPCM*, pp. 1149–52; W. H. Barnes, 'Brownsville Revival', *NIDPCM*, pp. 445–7; David Hilborn (ed.), '*Toronto' in Perspective: Papers on the New Charismatic Wave of the Mid 1990s.* Carlisle, UK: Paternoster/Acute, 2001.

movements of reform and change eventually lose their momentum and are superseded by more innovative movements. Many of the latter are led by people from the older movements but they often also bring new people into the Pentecostal experience. Many institutionalize and become thriving denominations in their own right; others rise and fall and disappear. The new movements in turn influence the older ones, and their potential for reform and renewal is thereby enhanced. A Charismatic Baptist leader I once worked with used the slogan, 'Constant change is here to stay'. Nowhere is this more evident than in the new Pentecostalism, where it is unlikely that this process of renewal, institutionalization and further change will slow down.

9

The writing of Pentecostal history

THE CONTEXT OF PENTECOSTAL HISTORIOGRAPHY

Historians of Pentecostalism have often reflected a bias interpreting history from a predominantly white American perspective, neglecting (if not completely ignoring) the vital and often more significant work of Asian, African, African American and Latino/a Pentecostal pioneers.[1] Some of their histories add the biases of denomination and race and most of the earlier ones tended to be hagiographies. In order to understand the importance of and need for rewriting Pentecostal history, we must first critically examine the presuppositions of existing histories. Some of the first academic histories were written by outsiders: Lutheran theologian Nils Bloch Hoell (whose work first appeared in Norwegian in 1956), British sociologist Malcolm Calley on African Caribbean Pentecostals in Britain (1965), Swiss sociologist Christian Lalive d'Epinay on Chilean movements (1969), a global study by Swiss theologian Walter Hollenweger (1965, 1972), and several North Americans, including the seminal study by social historian Robert Mapes Anderson (1979). To these can be added the more recent and widely acclaimed study of theological roots by historian Donald Dayton (1987) and those of Harvard theologian and one-time secularization theorist Harvey Cox (1995), church historian William Faupel (1996) and Grant Wacker, historian of religion (2001). Hollenweger, Faupel and Wacker, all former Pentecostals, have written sympathetic studies; and Dayton and Cox have a largely positive appraisal, even if the latter's phenomenological conclusions are looked at somewhat warily by classical Pentecostals. From within North American Pentecostalism has come a string of noteworthy histories, from the earliest ones by Frank Bartleman, chronicler of the Asuza Street Revival (1925) and Stanley Frodsham, an early Assemblies of God historian (1946),

---

[1] This chapter is a revised and abridged version of my 'Revising Pentecostal History in Global Perspective', Anderson and Tang, *Asian and Pentecostal*, ch. 7.

to include the more recent works by Blumhofer, McGee, Conn and Synan, among many others.[2]

This list of historians of Pentecostalism is by no means exhaustive. The earlier histories tended to see Pentecostalism as emerging in the USA 'suddenly from heaven' and took what has been described as a 'providential' view of history, tending to discount or ignore 'natural' causes for the rise of the movement.[3] In a provocative article, historian Joe Creech suggests that Bartleman's account in particular created the 'central myth of origin' of Azusa Street that has persisted to the present and that this 'myth' was based on theological and historical paradigms that overlooked other points of origin.[4] Bearing in mind that some studies are intentionally North American in focus and at the risk of oversimplification we suggest that most histories declare or imply that Pentecostalism, fanning out from the western world and in particular from the USA, grew and expanded in Asia, Africa, the Pacific and Latin America because of the work of a number of white 'missionaries' who carried the 'full gospel' to the ends of the earth.

In these histories, the various presuppositions of the writers are often transparent, some of which are now easily dismissed. Bloch-Hoell's study abounds with innuendos showing that he thought that all Pentecostals were psychologically unstable and neurotic. This deprivation theory is repeated in a more subtle form by Lalive d'Epinay and Anderson, who saw Pentecostalism as a refuge for the socially marginalized and underprivileged poor, the 'vision of the disinherited' as Anderson put it, where 'ecstatic religious experience' was 'a surrogate for success in the social struggle'. In contrast, Wacker's most recent contribution sees early North American Pentecostals as representing the entire spectrum of society, including the wealthy middle class.[5] At least as far as the origins of Pentecostalism are concerned, the heroes and heroines are westerners regarded as the main role players responsible for the global expansion of Pentecostalism. The commencement of the movement is always situated in the USA, whether in Cherokee County, North Carolina in the 1890s (according to some Church of God historians), Charles Parham's movement in Topeka, Kansas in 1901 (where many historians start) or the Azusa Street revival led by William Seymour

---

[2] The references to all these histories are in the Bibliography.
[3] Augustus Cerillo, 'The Beginnings of American Pentecostalism: A Historiographical Overview', Blumhofer, Spittler and Wacker, *Pentecostal Currents*, p. 229.
[4] Joe Creech, 'Visions of Glory: The Place of the Azusa Street Revival in Pentecostal History', *Church History* 65 (1996), 406, 408.
[5] Bloch-Hoell, *Pentecostal Movement*, pp. 21, 32; Anderson, *Vision*, p. 152; Wacker, *Heaven Below*, p. 216.

in Los Angeles, 1906 (which most agree was the driving force behind the rapid spread of the movement).

Although the exact place of origin is disputed, the primacy of Azusa Street as the heart or 'cradle' of Pentecostalism was reaffirmed in the 1970s, largely through the influence of Walter Hollenweger and his researchers at Birmingham. Writers began to assert the important role of this predominantly African American church as the generator of Pentecostal churches all over the world. Wacker pointed out that the early histories of the movement suffered from what he called a 'ritualization of Pentecostal history' that included a 'white racial bias' that ignored the central influence of black culture on Pentecostal worship and theology, and in his view, the 'more serious distortion' of a 'persistent gender bias' in which the leading role of women was overlooked.[6] These race and gender distortions are indeed serious problems to overcome, but there may be even graver issues that face Pentecostal historiography. All these interpretations, some of which indeed attempted to correct errors of the past, nevertheless ignored, overlooked or minimized the vital role of thousands of national workers in the early Pentecostal movement, particularly in Asia and Africa. This is partly because in early Pentecostal periodicals carrying reports of missionaries, if national workers are mentioned at all it is usually as anonymous 'native workers' or at best they are mentioned by a single name, often misspelled.

This serious omission arises from the environment in which Pentecostal missionaries carried out their work, to which writers of its history often do not give enough consideration. We cannot separate the spiritual experiences of Pentecostals and Charismatics throughout the world from the wider context of political and social power. The beginning of the twentieth century was the heyday of colonialism, when western nations governed and exploited the majority of people on earth. This rampant colonialization was often transferred into the ecclesiastical realm and was reflected in the attitudes of missionaries, who so often moved in the shadows of colonizers. In the late nineteenth century there was an almost universal belief in the superiority of western culture and civilization. This was the ideology that fired colonialists and missionaries alike, and the belief lingered long into the twentieth century. This affected Pentecostal missionaries too, who were impassioned with ideas of 'global spiritual conquest', an expansionist conviction influenced by premillennial eschatological expectations

---

[6] Grant Wacker, 'Are the Golden Oldies Still Worth Playing? Reflections on History Writing Among Early Pentecostals', *Pneuma* 8:2 (1986), 95.

that the nations of the world had to be 'possessed' for Christ before his imminent coming to rule the earth. This was a long tradition rooted in the nineteenth century Evangelical Awakenings. Undoubtedly, the 'manifest destiny' of the USA influenced Pentecostal missions used to thinking in expansionist terms. Coupled with a belief in the superiority of forms of Christianity 'made-in-America' is a conviction in the superiority of the political and social system found in the USA. This neo-imperialism has been that which has often alienated US missionaries from local national leaders and certainly the perceived hegemony bolstered by US economic and military muscle has not helped the negative image.

In recent years, the southward swing of the Christian centre of gravity that has made Pentecostalism more African and Asian than western heightens the urgency of this debate. Most Pentecostals and Charismatics now live in Asia, Africa and Latin America. India, South Korea, Brazil and Nigeria have become the leading Protestant missionary-sending nations. At the beginning of the twenty-first century, the largest congregations in London, England and in Kiev, Ukraine, each with several thousand members, are led by African Pentecostal pastors. In Africa itself, very large numbers of Christians who are of a Pentecostal and Charismatic orientation can only be understood within that context. In Asia, where probably the largest number of evangelical Christians in any continent of the world live, most are of a Pentecostal and Charismatic type; and Latin America has the largest number of Pentecostals in any continent. Barrett and Johnson's annual statistics give dramatic evidence of how rapidly the western share of world Christianity has decreased. In 1900, 77 per cent of the world's Christian population was in Europe and North America, but by 2000, only 37 per cent of the two billion Christians in the world were from these two continents, projected to fall to 29 per cent by 2025. Furthermore, 26 per cent of the world's Christians are now 'Pentecostal/ Charismatics', a figure expected to rise to 31 per cent by 2025. The 'southward swing' is more evident in Pentecostalism than in most other forms of Christianity. Much of the dramatic church growth in Asia, Africa and Latin America has taken place in Pentecostal and Charismatic and independent Pentecostal-like churches, and perhaps three-quarters of Pentecostalism today is found in these continents. Classical Pentecostal churches with roots in the USA and Canada have probably less than a tenth of their world associate membership in these countries, with at least 80 per cent in the Majority World.[7]

7 David B. Barrett and Todd M. Johnson, 'Annual Statistical Table on Global Mission: 2001', *International Bulletin of Missionary Research* 25:1 (2001), 25; Wilson, *Strategy of the Spirit*, pp. 3, 107, 183.

We obviously need to know who and what is responsible for this explosion of Charismatic Christianity. There are glaring gaps in our knowledge. We would be forgiven for asking where all the national heroines and heroes of Pentecostal history have gone. The historians and chroniclers of the past have sent thousands of Pentecostal labourers to unnamed graves. The historical processes leading to the fundamental changes in global Pentecostal demographics must be charted accurately. Hopefully, however, it is not too late to correct past distortions, but in much of the writing of Pentecostal history until the present day the 'objects' of western missionary efforts, now the great majority of Pentecostals in the world, remain marginalized. This situation has begun to improve with the welcome appearance in the past two decades of academic theses and books that relate to the history of Pentecostalism outside the western world, some of which have been referred to in this book. Michael Bergunder's seminal work on South Indian Pentecostalism is a case in point. Bergunder deals with the issues of historical methodology in a recent very interesting paper, where he writes of the uneasiness some scholars have with an 'American-centred history' of Pentecostalism, as this does not seem to do justice to its multifaceted and global nature. He argues for a way out of this dilemma by focusing on the global network of evangelical and Holiness missionaries and their expectations of 'missionary tongues' in an end-time revival as a root cause for the emergence of Pentecostalism, which was global from its beginnings.[8] But the great gaps in our information remain, and we have only filled in a few of them here. Pentecostal anthropologist Ronald Bueno reminds us that we need to 'rehistoricize' Pentecostal experiences and identities by considering the contribution of the 'local', the 'Pentecostalisms', if we are really to understand the 'global', Pentecostalism.[9] 'Pentecostalism' that is made in the USA is only one part of the total picture of many forms of 'Pentecostalisms', and the hidden treasures of these local histories need to be discovered.

AZUSA STREET 'JERUSALEM'?

Bartleman spoke of Azusa Street as the 'American Jerusalem'. But the made-in-the-USA assumption is a great disservice to worldwide Pentecostalism, reflected in the ongoing debate about Pentecostal origins. Cerillo says that

---

[8] Bergunder, 'Constructing Indian Pentecostalism', Anderson and Tang, *Asian and Pentecostal*, ch. 8.
[9] Ronald N. Bueno, 'Listening to the Margins: Re-historicizing Pentecostal Experiences and Identities', Dempster, Klaus and Petersen, *The Globalization of Pentecostalism*, p. 269.

one theory of the complex origins of Pentecostalism cannot be emphasized to the exclusion of others.[10] The most popular theory in the more recent written histories seems to be one that places the Azusa Street revival at the centre of Pentecostalism, the 'Jerusalem' from which the Pentecostal gospel reached the 'ends of the earth'. The first two decades of the Pentecostal movement were marked by feverish and often sacrificial missionary activities. By 1910, only four years after the commencement of the Azusa Street revival, it was reported that Pentecostal missionaries from Europe and North America were in over fifty nations of the world. From its beginning, Pentecostalism in the western world was characterized by an emphasis on evangelistic outreach and all Pentecostal missionary strategy placed evangelism at the top of its priorities, linked as it was to a particular premillennial eschatology. The Pentecostal revival resulted in a category of ordinary but 'called' people named 'missionaries' spreading out to every corner of the globe within a remarkably short space of time. Harvey Cox suggests that the rapid spread of the movement was because of its heady and spontaneous spirituality. It touched people emotionally and its emphasis on experience was spread through testimony and personal contact. Faupel chronicles the sending out of workers from Azusa Street's Apostolic Faith Mission, the role of this congregation as a magnet to which Christian leaders were drawn, the creation of new Pentecostal centres and the spread to the nations of the world. In these various early expanding activities, a lack of central organization resulted in what Faupel describes as 'creative chaos'.[11]

Despite the significance of the Azusa Street revival as an African American centre of Pentecostalism that profoundly affected its nature, when this is assumed to be the 'Jerusalem' from which the 'full gospel' reaches out to the nations of earth, the truth is distorted and smacks of cultural imperialism. We have seen in the previous chapters that there were several centres of Pentecostalism from which great expansion took place, even in North America. There were many 'Jerusalems': Pyongyang, Korea; Pune, India; Wakkerstroom, South Africa; Lagos, Nigeria; Valparaiso, Chile; Belem, Brazil; Oslo, Norway; and Sunderland, England – among other centres. Pentecostalism has many varieties very different from the North American 'classical Pentecostal' kind. My understanding of 'Pentecostalism' throughout this study includes 'Charismatic' Christianity and those movements where the practice of gifts of the Spirit is encouraged, which may include or

[10] Bartleman, *Azusa Street*, p. 63; Augustus Cerillo, Jr, 'Interpretative Approaches to the History of American Pentecostal Origins', *Pneuma* 19:1 (1997), 29–49.
[11] Faupel, *Everlasting Gospel*, pp. 212–22; Cox, *Fire*, p. 71.

exclude speaking in tongues. As Everett Wilson has observed, Pentecostalism has had many beginnings, and there are many 'Pentecostalisms'.[12] The Azusa Street revival was certainly significant in reminding North American Pentecostals of their non-racial and ecumenical origins and ethos, an interracial fellowship that was unique and has given inspiration to many. It has motivated Black South African Pentecostals, for many decades denied basic human dignities by their white counterparts in the same Pentecostal denominations, some of which were founded by Azusa Street missionaries.[13] The stimulus of the movement from a predominantly black church led by Seymour, undoubtedly rooted in the slave culture of the nineteenth century, is certainly significant. Many of the early manifestations of Pentecostalism were a reflection of the African religious culture from which the slaves had been forcefully abducted. Seymour was deeply affected by this spirituality, a holistic spirituality that made the Pentecostal and Charismatic message so suitable to cultures all over the world, where experience of divine intervention was more important than the creeds, controversies and doctrinal arguments that soon racked the North American movement.

Although Pentecostal missiologist Pomerville continued the earlier 'providential' view of Pentecostal history, he declared that Pentecostalism had originated in a series of roughly spontaneous and universal beginnings in different parts of the world, and that no attempt should be made to restrict its commencement to one geographical location such as Los Angeles.[14] This represented a new approach to the problem of origins, but Pomerville's insistence on spontaneity meant that he tended to ignore the complexity of historical and social factors that linked the different 'outpourings' to each other. Without minimizing the importance of Azusa Street, we must give due recognition to places in the world where Pentecostal revival broke out independently of this event and in some cases even predated it. One example is the 'Korean Pentecost', which began among missionaries in Pyongyang in 1903 and soon spread to thousands of Korean people. This revival seemed to have been unaffected by the nineteenth century Evangelical Awakenings; it predated the 1904 Welsh Revival and it quickly took on a Korean character all of its own. The Korean revival affected revivals

---

[12] Everett A. Wilson, 'They Crossed the Red Sea, Didn't They? Critical History and Pentecostal Beginnings', Dempster, Klaus and Petersen, *Globalization of Pentecostalism*, p. 107.

[13] Allan Anderson, 'Dangerous Memories for South African Pentecostals', Anderson and Hollenweger, *Pentecostals after a Century*, p. 105; Anderson, *Zion and Pentecost*, pp. 58, 85.

[14] Paul Pomerville, *The Third Force in Missions* (Peabody, MA: Hendrickson, 1985), p. 52.

in China like the Manchurian Revival of 1908,[15] and irrevocably changed the face of East Asian Christianity. Korean Pentecostals are unanimous in acknowledging the contribution of the earlier revival to their own movement. The revival greatly influenced the present dominance of the Charismatic movement in the Presbyterian and Methodist churches there, many of whose characteristic practices have been absorbed by the classical Pentecostal churches (like Yonggi Cho's YFGC) that came over two decades later. Furthermore, although strictly speaking this is not a classical Pentecostal revival and in spite of North American Protestant missionary participation in its beginning, early Korean revival leaders in the Presbyterian and Methodist churches were much more 'Pentecostal' than the missionaries might have wanted them to be, and their characteristic revival practices persist in Protestant and Pentecostal churches in Korea today.

In the case of China, Daniel Bays has shown that the influence of Pentecostalism has accelerated the development of 'indigenous churches', particularly because Pentecostals were closer to the 'traditional folk religiosity' with its 'lively sense of the supernatural' than other churches were. Most of the grassroots Chinese churches are Pentecostal 'in explicit identity or in orientation'. Bays says that Pentecostalism in China, 'especially its egalitarian style and its provision of direct revelation to all', also facilitated the development of churches independent of foreign missions.[16] This was equally true of Pentecostalism in Africa and Latin America – something the early Pentecostal missionaries from the West could not have anticipated and probably would not have encouraged.

Similarly in India, the 1905–7 revival at Pandita Ramabai's Mukti Mission in Poona, in which young women baptized by the Spirit had seen visions, fallen into trances and spoken in tongues, began before the Azusa Street revival, although tongues first occurred there only in December 1906. This revival was understood by Ramabai herself to be the means by which the Holy Spirit was creating an Indian Christianity. *The Apostolic Faith*, the periodical from Azusa Street, greeted news of this revival in its November 1906 issue with 'Hallelujah! God is sending the Pentecost to India. He is no respecter of persons'. There is no mention of missionaries or of Ramabai's mission, but it suggests that there, 'natives . . . simply taught of God' were responsible for the outpouring of the Spirit and that the gifts of the

---

[15] Daniel H. Bays, 'Christian Revival in China, 1900–1937', Blumhofer and Balmer, *Modern Christian Revivals*, p. 163.

[16] Daniel Bays, 'The Protestant Missionary Establishment and the Pentecostal Movement', Blumhofer, Spittler and Wacker, *Pentecostal Currents*, p. 63.

Spirit were given to 'simple, unlearned members of the body of Christ'. Of course, the Indian people are not named, not even the internationally famous Pandita Ramabai! Nevertheless, Pentecostal missionaries worked with the Mukti Mission for many years and Ramabai received support from the fledgling Pentecostal movement in Britain, where she was mentioned in the Pentecostal periodical from Boddy's church in Sunderland, *Confidence*. However, the first Pentecostal outpouring in India took place much earlier than Mukti, in Tamil Nadu in 1860–65 under the Tamil evangelist John Aroolappen and in Travancore in 1873–81. As McGee points out, Pentecostalism had already established itself in India 'before word of Azusa reached the subcontinent'.[17] Although the Tamil Nadu and Mukti revivals themselves may not have resulted directly in the formation of Pentecostal denominations, the Mukti revival in particular had other far-reaching consequences that penetrated parts of the world untouched by Azusa Street.

Perhaps the most important of these consequences crossed the oceans to South America. We have seen how in 1907, US American Methodist revivalist Willis Hoover heard of the Mukti revival through a pamphlet by his wife's former classmate Minnie Abrams. Later, he enquired about the Pentecostal revivals in other places, especially those in Venezuela, Norway and India among his fellow Methodists. The revival in Hoover's church in 1909 resulted in his expulsion from the Methodist Church in 1910 and the formation of the Methodist Pentecostal Church, to become the largest non-Catholic denomination in Chile. The vast majority of Chilean Pentecostals are quite different from classical Pentecostals in North America and trace their origins to the Valparaiso events.[18] In 1909 Luigi Francescon took the Pentecostal message to Italian communities in Argentina and Brazil; and in 1911 Gunnar Vingren and Daniel Berg began what became the AG in Brazil three years before it was constituted in the USA. This is now the largest Protestant denomination in Latin America and the largest AG in any nation, quite independent of its USA counterpart. The first missionaries to Brazil were connected with William Durham's church in Chicago, but were separate from the US movement and looked to Sweden for their main support. However, although these western missionaries are usually given the credit for the foundation of these large denominations, their rapid growth was mainly due to the efforts of the mostly now unknown national workers.

---

[17] McGee, '"Latter Rain" Falling', 648–65; Adhav, *Pandita Ramabai*, p. 216; *Apostolic Faith* 3 (1906), p. 1; *Confidence* 1:6 (1908), p. 10.

[18] Hoover, *History*, pp. 9, 164; Juan Sepúlveda, 'Indigenous Pentecostalism and the Chilean Experience', Anderson and Hollenweger, *Pentecostals after a Century*, pp. 111–15.

Petersen has shown that in Central America, strong Pentecostal churches emerged 'with little external assistance or foreign control'.[19]

All over the world untold thousands of revivalists without western connections were responsible for the spread of the Pentecostal gospel. In the Ivory Coast and the Gold Coast (now Ghana), the Liberian Grebo, William Wade Harris spearheaded a revival in 1914 quite distinct from the western Pentecostal movement but with many Pentecostal phenomena including healing and speaking in tongues. This revival resulted in 120,000 conversions in a year, the largest influx of Africans to Christianity the continent had ever seen. We may never know whether Harris had any encounter with African American missionaries from Azusa Street working in Liberia (a tantalizing conjecture), but there were certainly no connections thereafter. Chinese evangelists crisscrossed that vast nation and beyond with a Pentecostal message similar to but distinct from its western counterpart, resulting in many thousands of conversions to Christianity. A Chinese preacher, Mok Lai Chi, was responsible for the early spread of Pentecostalism in Hong Kong and started a Pentecostal newspaper there in 1908.[20] These various Pentecostal revivals were not primarily movements from the western world to 'foreign lands', but more significantly movements within these continents themselves.

We have taken for granted an obscure history of Pentecostalism for so long that the multitudes of nameless people responsible for its grassroots expansion have passed into history unremembered and their memory is now very difficult to retrieve. Despite the undeniably courageous work of the early Pentecostal missionaries from the West, the more important contribution of African, Asian, Latin American and Pacific evangelists and pastors must be properly recognized. A hankering after a 'conquest of the heathen' that has tended to dominate Pentecostal missions from the West creates more problems than it attempts to solve, particularly in those parts of the world where Christianity has been linked to colonial expansionism. Most of Pentecostalism's rapid expansion in the twentieth century was not mainly the result of the labours of missionaries from North America and Western Europe to Africa, Asia and Latin America. It was rather the result of the spontaneous contextualization of the Pentecostal message by thousands of preachers who traversed these continents with a new message of the power of the Spirit, healing the sick and casting out demons. This may

---

[19] Douglas Petersen, 'The Formation of Popular, National, Autonomous Pentecostal churches in Central America', *Pneuma* 16:1 (1994), 23.

[20] Bays, 'Protestant Missionary Establishment', p. 54.

be one of the most important reconstructions necessary in the rewriting of Pentecostal history.

One of the reasons for the distorted picture we have of Pentecostal history is the problem of documentary sources. Our writing of early Pentecostal history outside the western world depends almost entirely on letters, reports and periodicals of western Pentecostals and their missionaries. These documents were usually loaded for western consumption in order to bolster financial and prayer support in North America and Europe; and so the reports mostly talked about the activities of the missionaries themselves and not their so-called 'native workers'. History cannot be understood from written sources alone, especially when these sources are the only written documents from this period and almost exclusively reflect the 'official' positions of power and privilege of their authors. We have to read 'in between the lines' of the documents, minutes and newsletters to discover the hints of a wider world than that which they described. This is certainly a hazardous exercise, for the possibilities of misinterpretation become greater with incomplete information, especially in the case of those who have already died and whose voices have been 'lost'. The importance of retrieving oral traditions is underlined here, for we must record for posterity the stories of those still living who remember the past. In several parts of the world, the early histories of Pentecostalism are still within living memories and these must be recounted before it is too late. Of course, the further back in time we go, the more difficult it is to recover the histories 'from below', as the sources become scarcer.

Some of the reading between the lines that is done might cast early Pentecostal missionaries in a less favourable light. There can be little doubt that many of the secessions that took place early on in western Pentecostal mission efforts in Africa, China, India and elsewhere were at least partly the result of cultural and social insensitivities on the part of the missionaries. Early Pentecostal missionaries frequently referred in their newsletters to the 'objects' of their mission as 'the heathen', and were slow to recognize national leadership when it arose with creative alternatives to western forms of Pentecostalism.[21] Missionary paternalism, even if it was

---

[21] Allan Anderson, 'Signs and Blunders: Pentecostal Mission Issues at 'Home and Abroad' in the Twentieth Century', *Journal of Asian Mission* 2:2 (2000), 193–210; *Confidence*, 1:2 (May 1908), p. 19; 2:5 (May 1909), p. 110.

'benevolent' paternalism, was widely practised. In country after country, white Pentecostals followed the example of other expatriate missionaries and kept control of churches and their national founders, and especially of the finances they raised in western Europe and North America. Most wrote home as if they were mainly (if not solely) responsible for the progress of the Pentecostal work there. The truth was often that the churches grew in spite of (and not because of) these missionaries, who were actually denying their converts gifts of leadership.

To give an example from South Africa, in the formation of the AFM, African pastors were left out of executive leadership and given only nominal and local leadership opportunities, and racial segregation had become the accepted practice of the church. Although African pastors and evangelists were largely responsible for the growth of the Pentecostal movement in South Africa, they were written out of its history – with the exception of Nicholas Bhengu, whose enormous contribution to the development of the South African AG was impossible to ignore. The schisms that occurred within the AFM from 1910 onwards resulted in hundreds of other denominations, including the creation of the largest church in South Africa today, the Zion Christian Church, whose founder Lekganyane was a preacher in the AFM and a fellow worker with John G. Lake. Because these early African Pentecostals were seen as the 'opposition' to the work of white Pentecostals, they were often accused of 'misconduct' and thought of as unable to lead churches. One could argue that their work was more effective and relevant to their context and they developed in quite different directions from that of the churches from which they seceded. These African Pentecostal churches, although perhaps not 'classical Pentecostals' in the usual sense of the word, practise characteristic Pentecostal spiritual gifts (especially healing, prophecy and speaking in tongues), and now represent almost half of the African population of southern Africa.[22]

There are also examples from later Pentecostal history. In Nigeria Pentecostal evangelist Babalola and his colleagues founded the CAC in 1941 after British Pentecostal missionaries objected to Africans sprinkling the 'water of life' (water that had been prayed for) in healing rituals. The African leaders in turn found the missionaries' use of quinine to prevent malaria inconsistent with their proclamation of divine healing. We can only wonder whether water or quinine had the upper hand in the exercise of faith in this instance! At about the same time in Ghana, British Apostolic

---

[22] Anderson, *Zion and Pentecost*, pp. 13, 41, 60–70, 89–93.

missionaries found a large African church wanting to work with them, but the Europeans insisted that they substitute their calabash rattles used in worship (part of a well established African Christian tradition) for tambourines. The missionaries reported that the Africans had thought that the missionaries wanted to deprive them of their power to ward off evil spirits. The same missionaries later fell out with the Africans over the use of quinine. Many of these and similar struggles were evidence of cultural misunderstandings and insensitivity that could have been avoided. African Pentecostal churches in Nigeria and Ghana today far outnumber those founded by European missionaries.

We do not always have to read between the lines, however. Sometimes western Pentecostal missionaries were patronizing and impolite about the people they were 'serving' and their racism was blatant. One missionary woman writing from Mbabane, Swaziland in 1911, spoke of the work among 'the native boys', quickly explaining that 'all [African males] are called 'boys' – from infancy to grey hairs'. The use of 'boys' to refer to grown African men was a common practice among Pentecostal missionaries. Another Pentecostal missionary in the Congo used a whip to 'discipline' his African luggage bearers and boasted of the effectiveness of this 'thrashing'.[23] A British PMU missionary in Tibet, Frank Trevitt, reported that they had 'only wild Tibetans about us continually', and spoke of Tibet as 'this dark, priest-ridden country'.[24]

Nevertheless, the exploits of western missionaries were certainly impressive and we cannot assume that all were racist bigots. We can only greatly admire their sacrificial efforts and (in most cases) their selfless dedication, as many even laid down their lives through the ravages of tropical disease and a few were killed by hostile opponents. They were often very successful in adapting to extremely difficult circumstances; and many showed a servant heart and genuinely loved the people they worked with. They achieved much against what sometimes seemed overwhelming odds. But many of these missionaries supposedly responsible for the spread of the Pentecostal gospel throughout the world were by no means exemplary. For them, 'mission' was understood as 'foreign mission' (mostly cross-cultural, from 'white' to 'other' peoples) and they were mostly untrained and inexperienced. Their only qualification was the baptism in the Spirit and a divine call, their motivation was to evangelize the world before the imminent coming of Christ and so evangelism was more important than education or

[23] *Confidence* 4:1 (January 1911), pp. 16, 18; 8:5 (May 1915), p. 98; 127 (October–December 1921), p. 61; *Things New and Old* 3:1 (April 1923), p. 7.
[24] *Flames of Fire* 9 (January 1913), p. 5; *Confidence* 6:3 (March 1913), p. 62.

'civilization'. Pentecostal workers from the western world usually saw their mission in terms of having come from a civilized, Christian 'home' to a Satanic and pagan 'foreign land', where sometimes their own personal difficulties, prejudices (and possible failures) in adapting to a radically different culture, living conditions and religion were projected in their newsletters home. In 1911, one English missionary expressed this fear as she wrote home from western China:

Please pray for us and the people here, who are living and dying in Satan's kingdom. His reign here is no uncertain one, but a terrible, fearful, crushing rule, driving the people to wickedness and sin such as is not dreamt of in England. It is a force which can be felt everywhere, an awful living presence.[25]

They went out, like many other Christian missionaries before them, with a fundamental conviction that the western world was a 'Christian' realm, that they were sent as 'light' to 'darkness' and that the ancient cultures and religions of the nations to which they were sent were 'heathen', 'pagan' and 'demonic', to be 'conquered' for Christ. Western culture was 'Christian' culture and all other cultures were dark problems to be solved by the light of the gospel, replacing the old 'paganism' with the new 'Christianity'. Missionaries went out with the conviction that their 'future labours' would be among 'the poor heathen in darkness'.[26]

Religious intolerance and bigoted ignorance were common features of some of their reports, illustrated by their attitude to other religions. British PMU missionary in India in 1914, Grace Elkington, lamented: 'Oh, what a dark, sad land this seems to be, and the longer one lives in it, the more one feels the darkness all around'. Almost four years later, she wrote of Hindu temples as 'the works of the devil', and that 'a favourite god of the Hindus' was 'supposed to be an incarnation of the second person of the Hindu Trinity'. Another missionary discussed Hinduism, quoting Paul: 'they sacrifice to devils, and not to God' and said that 'The Devil' was 'at the bottom of all their worship'. At a missionary convention in London in 1924, Walter Clifford, on furlough from India, described Hinduism as 'a religion of fear, not a religion of love' and that many of the Indian holy men were 'demon possessed', because 'you can see the devil shining out of their eyes. They have given themselves over to him'.[27] Young PMU worker Frank Trevitt (who died in China in 1916) sent back this report from 'dark

[25] *Confidence* 4:9 (September 1911), p. 214.
[26] *Flames of Fire* 35 (February 1916), p. 4; 49 (May 1917), p. 40.
[27] *Confidence* 7:12 (December 1914), p. 238; 10:1 (January–February 1917), p. 11; 11:3 (July–September 1918), p. 57; *The Pentecostal Witness* 1 (July 1924), p. 4; *Redemption Tidings* 1:2 (October 1924), p. 17.

China', obviously identifying a treasured Chinese national symbol with the devil:

This is heathendom truly, without light or love, not even as much as a dumb beast would have. Well, we have seen much of this spirit, which truly is the 'Dragon's' spirit, which is as you know, China's ensign . . . Oh, how one's heart longs and sighs for the coming of Christ's glorious Ensign, to be placed where the Dragon holds such sway.[28]

Later on, Trevitt referred to Tibetan Lama priests as Satan's 'wicked messengers' and that 'Satan through them hates Christ in us'. John Beruldsen reported on a visit to a Mongolian 'Lama Temple' in Beijing and describes a priest worshipping 'a large idol from 90 to 100 English feet high'. He comments, 'One could almost smell and feel the atmosphere of hell in these places. Poor benighted people! The power of God could save them from it all, if only they knew it'. Fanny Jenner, observing religious rituals in Yunnan, China wrote, 'the heathen spent one whole day in worshipping the graves of relatives – burning incense and weeping and wailing. Oh the mockery of it all. How Satan blinds their minds!' Elizabeth Biggs reports from Likiang on a visit to a Tibetan Buddhist lamasery that 'the seat of Satan might be a good name for such a place', because 'the demonic power was keenly felt, and the wicked faces of these lamas haunted us for many days after'.[29] One can surmise that their converts and the 'native workers' who had spent their lives in these ancient religions would have had a more nuanced and better informed view of their old beliefs and therefore would have been more able to communicate effectively in this religious worldview.

Racism was frequently in missionary reports. *Confidence* published a conference address in 1915 by a missionary from Africa, Miss Doeking, 'Leopard's Spots or God's masterpiece, which?', referring to African people as follows:

The savage is God's opportunity, the masterpiece of our common creator, who delights in tackling impossibilities . . . unless the superior races are ready to humble themselves, we may yet witness such an awakening of the despised races as will put to shame the pride of their superiors.[30]

The so-called 'superior races' of Europe were at that very time engaged in such a horrible and dehumanizing war that the rest of the world could be

---

[28] *Confidence* 4:8 (August 1911), p. 191.
[29] *Confidence* 5:9 (May 1912), p. 215; 5:12 (December 1912), p. 286; 6:4 (April 1913), p. 84; 8:6 (June 1915), pp. 118–19; *Flames of Fire* 48 (April 1917), p. 29.
[30] *Confidence* 8:8 (August 1915), p. 154.

forgiven for wondering who were actually the 'savages'. The incriminations went on. In South Africa, the AFM had by 1917 separated the 'white' churches from the others and declared, 'we do not teach or encourage social equality between Whites and Natives'.[31] An English worker in India described her visit to a 'low caste village' with a 'little organ' singing hymns, and commented, 'They are so dull and ignorant and have to be taught like children in the K. G. classes', but added patronizingly, 'They followed intelligently, as was shown by their remarks'. Her companion missionary obviously felt the same way, speaking of 'these village women of India', and 'how dull they are, and how slow to grasp anything new'.[32]

In the light of these and many other reports, it is no wonder that missionaries saw themselves as the prime movers in the Pentecostal revival. The people they were working with were too 'far gone' to be able to exercise really effective leadership in the churches that were springing up. There were exceptions to this bigotry, however. PMU chairman Cecil Polhill urged his missionaries to pursue indigenization, in an interesting article published in the organization's periodical, *Flames of Fire* in 1917. With remarkable insight for this period, nurtured by his many years of association with the China Inland Mission, he asserted:

Is not that day far nearer in not a few of our fields of work in Asia and Africa than we as yet commonly recognize? The Christians are reckoned by their thousands and tens of thousands. In nature and temperament they are far better qualified than we to present the message to their fellow countrymen. Intellectually they are often fully our equals. Spiritually the power that works in us is also the power that works in them.[33]

There are signs that PMU missionaries took his advice seriously, but that not all Pentecostal missionaries were convinced of the virtues of national leadership. A PMU worker in India, Minnie Thomas, replied to Polhill's urging that 'for India at least, it is quite a new thought that the churches should be in the hands of Indian Pastors and Elders', and she added wistfully, 'but I am sure it is the *Lord's* plan'. In spite of these and other hesitations, autochthonous leadership was to become one of the strongest features of Pentecostalism throughout the world.[34] Four years earlier in 1913, Dutch Pentecostal missionary Arie Kok of the PMU from the western Yunnan

---

[31] Anderson, *Zion and Pentecost*, p. 86.
[32] *Flames of Fire* 27 (May 1915), p. 3; 33 (November–December 1915), p. 9.
[33] *Flames of Fire* 49 (May 1917), p. 38.
[34] *Flames of Fire* 48 (April 1917), p. 31; *Things New and Old* 1:6 (January 1922), p. 45; 2:4 (October 1922), p. 7.

province in China had begun to rely more on national helpers for the progress of the work, and writes:

I feel that if the natives themselves do not carry the good news to their own people, the task will be impossible for us foreigners . . . The Lord is teaching us more and more that the natives are the best evangelists to their own people. So we are praying and believing for a band of native witnesses, filled with the love and the Spirit of God, who are to carry the glad tidings to their own villages.[35]

By this time missionaries in China were turning their attention to learning to be more sensitive to the cultures and languages of the people, and the churches were quickly turning Chinese in orientation. The missionaries may not have foreseen or planned this result, but it was one that was to be of vital importance for the future. The evacuation of most western missionaries from China in 1949 meant that a strong Chinese church could continue to gain strength without them. Other missions like Burton's Congo Evangelistic Mission rejected the use of interpreters and thus forced their workers to learn languages, for as James Salter rightly observed, 'To learn the language is the way to the hearts of the people'. But the paternalism of Burton's policy was clearly stated in 1925 and was characteristic of most western Pentecostal missions at the time: 'The great needs are Spirit-filled native evangelists, and a few white workers to superintend and help them'. Forty-five years after Burton had begun this mission in 1915, it was still directed by an all white Field Executive Council and had sixty-five missionaries working in fourteen mission compounds. When all the missionaries were forced to leave the Congo in 1960 during the civil war, the churches they left behind began to multiply much more rapidly than before, and ten years later had more than doubled in number.[36] In all these cases we know the names of the missionaries, but those of the national leaders of the churches are harder to come by.

Historians speak of a 'new history' written in deliberate reaction against traditional history and its paradigms. The 'new history' is concerned with the whole of human activity, 'history from below' rather than 'history from above', history taken from the perspective of the poor and powerless rather than from that of the rich and powerful. In the writing of Pentecostal history, there needs to be 'affirmative action' to redress the balance, where the contribution of national workers, pastors and evangelists is emphasized. We need to plumb the depths of oral histories and bring to light that which

[35] *Confidence* 6:10 (October 1913), pp. 206–7.
[36] *Things New and Old* 3:3 (August 1923), p. 1; *Redemption Tidings* 1:4 (January 1925), p. 12; Harold Womersley, *Wm. F. P. Burton: Congo Pioneer* (Eastbourne, UK: Victory Press, 1973), pp. 77, 113.

has been concealed for so long. Consequently, the work of the western missionaries, who came from countries of power and wrote newsletters for their own specific purposes, is put into correct perspective. We cannot continue to ignore the failings of these missionaries and give an exaggerated importance to people whose role was usually catalytic and not central. Asia, Africa and Latin America have their own Christian heroes, who are not just the western missionaries that went there! The voices of these national pioneers should be heard in the writing of our histories. In the western world, information on western missionaries to Africa, Asia, the Pacific and Latin America is completely disproportionate to their role and contribution, mainly because of the scarcity of written information on national leaders. A serious and extensive rewriting of global Pentecostal history needs to be done in which the enormous contributions of these pioneers is properly recognized, so that US American classical Pentecostals in particular shed their often-heard assumption that Pentecostalism is a made-in-the-USA product that has been exported to the world.

The Pentecostal experience of the power of the Spirit was the reason for an unprecedented flexibility on the part of its emissaries to the various cultures into which they took the Pentecostal message. But we must rectify the historiographical imperialism and ethnocentrism of the past. The revising of the history of Pentecostalism in the twenty-first century must be undertaken, not by emphasizing the missionary 'heroes' of the powerful and wealthy nations of the world, but by giving a voice to the people living in the world's most marginalized parts. We must listen to the 'margins' by allowing the hitherto voiceless and often nameless ones to speak, and by recognizing the contribution of those unsung Pentecostal labourers of the past who have been overlooked in our histories and hagiographies. Then together we will come to an honest appraisal of our histories and be better able to suggest solutions to the problems of division, parochialism, racism and ethnocentrism that still plague Pentecostalism today.

PART TWO

Pentecostal and Charismatic theology in context

A theology of the Spirit

The news has spread far and wide that Los Angeles is being visited with a 'rushing mighty wind from heaven' . . . No instruments of music are used, none are needed. No choir – but bands of angels have been heard by some in the spirit and there is a heavenly singing that is inspired by the Holy Ghost. No collections are taken. No bills have been posted to advertise the meetings. No church or organization is back of it. All who are in touch with God realize as soon as they enter the meetings that the Holy Ghost is the leader.[1]

THE BAPTISM IN THE SPIRIT

Frank Bartleman, eye-witness of the Azusa Street revival concurred, 'The meetings were controlled by the Spirit', he declared.[2] By the early Pentecostals at Azusa Street so proclaiming that the 'Holy Ghost is the leader', they saw all the manifestations occurring in their meetings as the sovereign work of the Holy Spirit and the manifestation of God's power, the revival promised in the Scriptures to come in the 'last days'. If there is one central and distinctive theme in Pentecostal and Charismatic theology, then it is the work of the Holy Spirit. The history sketched in this book has shown that all the various expressions of Pentecostalism have one common experience, that is a personal encounter with the Spirit of God enabling and empowering people for service. Pentecostals often declare that 'signs and wonders' accompany this encounter, certain evidence of 'God with us'. Through their experience of the Spirit, Pentecostals and Charismatics make the immanence of God tangible. Former Anglican Bishop of Winchester, John V. Taylor, put it:

The whole weight of New Testament evidence endorses the central affirmation of the Pentecostalists that the gift of the Holy Spirit transforms and intensifies the quality of human life, and that this is a fact of experience in the lives of Christians.

---

[1] *The Apostolic Faith* 1:3 (Los Angeles, November 1906), p. 1.   [2] Bartleman, *Azusa Street*, p. 59.

The longing of thousands of Christians to recover what they feel instinctively their faith promises them is what underlies the whole movement.[3]

Although different Pentecostals and Charismatics do not always agree on the precise formulation of their theology of the Spirit, the emphasis on divine encounter and the resulting transformation of life is always there. This is what likens Pentecostals and Charismatics to the mystical traditions, perhaps more than any other contemporary form of Christianity. This testimony from Azusa Street in 1906 of Glenn Cook, one of the revival leaders under Seymour, is typical of hundreds at that time and thousands since:

I had been seeking about five weeks, and on a Saturday morning I awoke and stretched my arms toward heaven and asked God to fill me with the Holy Ghost. My arms began to tremble, and soon I was shaken violently by a great power, and it seemed as though a large pipe was fitted over my neck, my head apparently being off. I was now filled with the Holy Ghost. I cannot describe the power I felt. The nearest description that could be given would be the action of a pump under terrific pressure, filling me with oil. I could feel the filling in my toes and all parts of my body which seemed to me to swell until I thought I would burst. . . .

It was now time for me to arise and go to work, so I got up without speaking in tongues. I believe I would have spoken in tongues then, if I had remained in the hands of the Lord long enough. About thirty hours afterwards, while sitting in the meeting on Azusa Street, I felt my throat and tongue begin to move, without any effort on my part. Soon I began to stutter and then out came a distinct language which I could hardly restrain. I talked and laughed with joy far into the night. Praise His name for such a wonderful experience of power and love and joy.[4]

Most of these testimonies spoke of a longing for the experience, followed by extreme physical sensations and feelings of elation, and culminating in a release usually involving speaking in tongues, either at the same time as the 'baptism' or soon afterwards. T. B. Barratt, Methodist pioneer of Pentecostalism in Europe, had already received the baptism a month earlier and was now seeking the 'full Bible evidence' of the gift of tongues. His testimony from a meeting in New York illustrates this process and is just as dramatic:

It was at a meeting in a little hall. The power was very great. We could not close and I determined to stay, God helping, till the victory was won. What a scene we had. Some were seeking sanctification and others the baptism with fire, and I the gift of tongues or any other the Lord saw fit to send me.

---

[3] John V. Taylor, *The Go-Between God: The Holy Spirit and the Christian Mission* (London: SCM, 1972), p. 199.
[4] G. A. Cook, *The Apostolic Faith* 1:3 (November 1906), p. 2.

Sister Maud Williams who got the blessing in Ontario, Canada and has the gift of tongues, laid her hands on my head and after that I had no more strength in me, although I am physically very strong now. I lay on the floor by the platform in a reclining position. At about half past twelve I asked a brother there and Sister Leatherman to lay their hands on my head again. And just then she says she saw a crown of fire and cloven tongues over my head. The brother saw a supernatural light.

Immediately I was filled with light and such a power that I began to shout as loud as I could in a foreign language. Between that and four o'clock in the morning, I must have spoken seven or eight languages, to judge from the various sounds and forms of speech used. I stood erect at times preaching in one foreign tongue after another, and I know from the strength of my voice that 10,000 might easily have heard all I said. Nine persons remained till three o'clock and are witnesses of the whole scene. The most wonderful moment though was when I burst into a beautiful baritone solo, using one of the most pure and delightful languages I have ever heard. The tune and words were entirely new to me, and the rhythm and cadence of the verses and chorus seemed to be perfect. . . .

That night will never be forgotten by any who were there. Now and then after a slight pause, the words would rush forth like a cataract. At times I had seasons of prayer in the Spirit when all New York, the United States, Norway, all Scandinavia and Europe, my loved ones and friends lay like an intense burden on my soul. Oh what power was given in prayer. My whole being was at times as if it were on fire inside, and then I would quiet down into sweet songs in a foreign language. Oh what praises to God arose from my soul for His mercy. I felt strong as a lion and know now where David and Sampson got their strength from. Today I have been speaking and singing in tongues wherever I have been. Glory to God. Go on praying.[5]

The first Pentecostals spoke universally of this central experience they called 'baptism in the Spirit' or 'filling with the Spirit' and many believed that this baptism was normally accompanied by speaking in tongues. Barratt's experience included singing in tongues, a phenomenon that still occurs regularly in Pentecostal and Charismatic meetings during 'praise and worship' times. Early nineteenth century Scottish Presbyterian pastor and revivalist Edward Irving was one of the first to describe speaking in tongues as the 'introductory and continuing evidence of supernatural empowerment' that was intended for every Christian believer.[6] The first and subsequent issues of the Azusa Street newspaper *The Apostolic Faith* declared the official position, 'The Baptism with the Holy Ghost is a gift of power upon the sanctified life; so when we get it we have the same

---

[5] T. B. Barrett, *The Apostolic Faith* 1:4 (December 1906), p. 3.
[6] G. R. McGee, 'Initial Evidence', *NIDPCM*, p. 785.

evidence as the Disciples received on the Day of Pentecost (Acts 2:3,4), in speaking in new tongues'.[7] The 'third blessing' of Spirit baptism accompanied by tongues speaking was the doctrine that distinguished these early Holiness Pentecostals from other radical Holiness people. Undoubtedly, speaking in tongues was the most distinctive and central preoccupation of early Pentecostal experience.[8]

William Seymour and most early Pentecostals, following Charles Parham, believed that in speaking in tongues they had been given a gift of foreign languages (*xenolalia*) with which to preach the gospel to the ends of the earth in the 'last days'. Declared *The Apostolic Faith*, 'The baptism with the Holy Ghost makes you a witness unto the uttermost parts of the earth. It gives you power to speak in the languages of the nations'.[9] Several issues of this newspaper claimed that actual foreign languages had been given to recipients of Spirit baptism at Azusa Street, by which their mission fields were identified. The belief in the restoration of tongues for missionary evangelism had been around in the Holiness and evangelical movements for at least two decades before the beginning of Pentecostalism, but this was seen as the fulfilment of that expectation. Many Pentecostal missionaries were later disillusioned when their hearers did not understand their tongues, but most adjusted their theology to a belief in 'unknown' tongues, *glossolalia* instead of *xenolalia*. Cecil Polhill of the PMU wrote in 1909 of the 'Hall-Mark' of the Pentecostal baptism and what he called the 'Missionary Test':

In spite of what seemed to be a disappointment when they found they could not preach in the language of the people, and in spite of mistakes made chiefly through their zeal, God has blessed, and now more than ever the Pentecostal movement is truly a Missionary Movement.[10]

Parham, however, remained convinced of *xenolalia* all his life and decried the majority of Pentecostals who had abandoned this belief for *glossolalia*. Today most Pentecostals and Charismatics believe in the gift of speaking in unknown tongues for personal edification, although recent studies have shown that many Pentecostals do not practise tongues speaking on a regular basis, if at all.

Classical Pentecostals are usually taught to believe in the two distinct doctrines of 'consequence' or 'initial evidence' (that speaking in tongues is

---

[7] *The Apostolic Faith* 1:1 (September 1906), p. 2.   [8] Wacker, *Heaven Below*, p. 42.
[9] *The Apostolic Faith* 1:4 (December 1906), p. 1.
[10] *Confidence* 2:8 (Sunderland, UK, August 1909), p. 181.

the consequence, or primary evidence of Spirit baptism), and 'subsequence' (that Spirit baptism is a definite and subsequent experience to conversion). We have seen that the doctrine of 'consequence' or 'initial evidence' was probably first formulated in 1901 by Charles Parham, who made the theological link between tongues speaking and Spirit baptism. The doctrine was emphasized by the Azusa Street mission and has been a characteristic of North American Pentecostalism ever since, permeating all the early publications from the movement and continuing to be a fundamental belief of most classical Pentecostal denominations in the western world. We have also seen that the doctrine of 'subsequence' had earlier origins in the nineteenth century Holiness movement. The Holiness interpretation of the teachings of John Wesley was such that he was thought to have taught a 'second work of grace' subsequent to conversion that came to be called 'perfect love' or 'sanctification'. 'Finished Work' Pentecostals came to identify this second and subsequent work of grace as the baptism in the Spirit, although the Holiness Pentecostals added Spirit baptism to the two works of grace and spoke of it as a third work of grace.

Pentecostals usually support the doctrines of 'consequence' and 'subsequence' by referring to the book of Acts, especially the Day of Pentecost experience (Acts 2:4), the experience of the Samaritans (Acts 8:4–19), Cornelius (Acts 10:44–8) and the disciples at Ephesus (Acts 19:1–7) as 'normative models for all Christians'. These passages, it is said, indicate that there is an experience of receiving the Spirit some time after conversion and that in each case, expressly or by implication, those who received the Spirit spoke in tongues. Pentecostals point further to the experience of Paul, who wished that all the Corinthian believers spoke in tongues but thanked God that he spoke in tongues 'more than you all' (1 Corinthians 14:5,18). Classical Pentecostals have got around the implied statement of Paul that not all speak in tongues (1 Corinthians 12:30) by distinguishing between tongues as a 'sign' (as evidence of Spirit baptism) and tongues as a 'gift' (not for all believers to use in church meetings). On the basis of these Scriptures, Pentecostals claim that the normative pattern of Spirit baptism is the 'initial evidence' of speaking in tongues. The statement of faith of the Pentecostal and Charismatic Churches of North America affirms this: 'We believe that the full gospel includes holiness of heart and life, healing for the body, and baptism in the Holy Spirit with the evidence of speaking in other tongues as the Spirit gives the utterance'.[11] Some Charismatics, especially those from

---

[11] Cited in J. R. Williams, 'Baptism in the Holy Spirit', *NIDPCM*, pp. 354–5; Robert P. Menzies, *Empowered for Witness: The Spirit in Luke-Acts* (Sheffield: Sheffield Academic Press, 1994), p. 233; Lederle, *Treasures Old and New*, pp. 27–8.

the early years of the movement, have followed this teaching, like Rodman Williams, a Presbyterian scholar, who says that speaking in tongues is the 'primary activity consequent to the reception of the Holy Spirit'. Lederle calls these Charismatics 'neo-Pentecostals' because their theology of subsequence does not differ substantially from that of classical Pentecostals and in many independent Charismatic churches it is identical.[12] Some Oneness Pentecostals see the baptism in the Spirit with the evidence of tongues as part (with baptism in Jesus' Name) of the salvation process; they have collapsed the three experiences into one. With most Pentecostals, however, the belief is that Spirit baptism is a distinct and separate experience that follows salvation; and it follows that for them, some Christians can be 'saved' but not yet filled with the Spirit.

THE DEBATES ON SPIRIT BAPTISM

The doctrines of 'consequence' and 'subsequence' have been hotly debated. At first the debate was rather one-sided, with mainly conservative evangelical scholars making polemical arguments against the Pentecostal position without Pentecostals having the opportunity to reply. Harsh critics accused Pentecostals of heresy and of being inspired by Satan. The debates have become more sophisticated in recent years as Pentecostals have begun to be trained in the skills of academic theology. James Dunn, in his first book *Baptism in the Holy Spirit*, was one of the most influential evangelical scholars to enter into serious debate with Pentecostals on the subject of subsequence and he has more recently responded to Pentecostal criticisms of his book. His main argument is that the gift of the Spirit (or Spirit baptism) is primarily an experience linked to conversion and is not a distinctively subsequent experience that Christians should be encouraged to seek. In other words, in his view Spirit baptism is synonymous with conversion. He says that to 'become a Christian, in short, is to receive the Spirit of Christ, the Holy Spirit. What the Pentecostal attempts to separate into two works of God is one single divine act'.[13] Several Pentecostal and Charismatic scholars have written long treatises in defence of the doctrine of subsequence in reply, the substance of which was that while they agreed

---

[12] J. Rodman Williams, *Renewal Theology (2): Salvation, the Holy Spirit, and Christian Living* (Grand Rapids, MI: Zondervan, 1990), p. 211; Lederle, *Treasures Old and New*, pp. 45–7.
[13] J. D. G. Dunn, *Baptism in the Holy Spirit: A Re-examination of the New Testament Teaching on the Gift of the Spirit in Relation to Pentecostalism Today* (London: SCM, 1970), p. 96; Dunn, 'Baptism in the Spirit: A Response to Pentecostal Scholarship on Luke-Acts', *Journal of Pentecostal Theology* 3 (1993), 3–27.

with Dunn's contention that Paul's theology of the Spirit is primarily sote-riological and initiatory (emphasizing the role of the Spirit in conversion), the theology of Luke is predominantly charismatic and prophetic, empha-sizing empowering for mission. Dunn is therefore reading Pauline theology into the Lukan accounts, they maintain.[14] Canadian evangelical theologian Clark Pinnock has also entered this debate with a more sympathetic view of the classical Pentecostal position, but one with which the 'Third Wave' movement would feel more comfortable. Pinnock says that conversion is a 'Spirit event', and that water and Spirit baptism are associated occasions 'when the Spirit comes'. In his view, water baptism symbolizes Spirit bap-tism. From the perspective of Acts, he says that baptism 'ought to be an occasion of charismatic experiences', but the fact that this is neglected in many churches is 'the major cause of a thirst for a second blessing or Spirit baptism today'. He says that the second blessing doctrine is the reaction to bad teaching and practice in the church, because 'if the power dimension is overlooked (as it often is), the deficit will have to be made up later' and from this perspective, 'there is always subsequence, always more'. In a sim-ilar vein John V. Taylor writes of the importance of a shared experience of the Spirit for every Christian, and that 'it is better to call it incorrectly a second blessing and lay hold of the reality of new life in Christ than to let the soundness of our doctrine rob us of its substance'.[15]

The doctrine of 'consequence', another cornerstone of classical Pente-costal theology, has also been challenged. As far back as the year the Azusa Street revival began (1906), Minnie Abrams of Pandita Ramabai's Mukti Mission in India wrote that speaking in tongues would 'usually' but 'not nec-essarily' follow Spirit baptism. After his falling-out with Parham, William Seymour also questioned the 'initial evidence' doctrine, as did some of the early European Pentecostal leaders, and so did Willis Hoover and the Chilean Pentecostal movement. In 1918, healing evangelist and early AG executive member F. F. Bosworth resigned from the denomination over the issue, saying that the gift of tongues was one of many possible evidences of Spirit baptism.[16] One of the first classical Pentecostals in more recent years to challenge the assumptions of 'initial evidence' was Gordon Fee (1936–), a well-known New Testament scholar and minister in the AG. He suggested that although Pentecostals could describe speaking in tongues as

---

[14] See Ervin (1984); Stronstad (1984); Shelton (1991); Menzies (1994) in Bibliography.

[15] Clark H. Pinnock, *Flame of Love: A Theology of the Holy Spirit* (Downers Grove, IL: InterVarsity Press, 1996), pp. 167, 169; Taylor, *Go-Between God*, p. 202.

[16] G. B. McGee, 'Initial Evidence', *NIDPCM*, pp. 784–91.

'repeatable' they could not claim it was 'normative'.[17] AG New Testament scholar Robert Menzies defends the issue of 'evidential tongues', saying that Pentecostals have been able to offer clear theological support for this position:

> The Pentecostal doctrine of evidential tongues is an appropriate inference drawn from the prophetic character of Luke's pneumatology (and more specifically the Pentecostal gift) and Paul's affirmation of the edifying and potentially universal character of the private manifestation of tongues. . . . Therefore, when one receives the Pentecostal gift, one should *expect* to manifest tongues, and this manifestation of tongues is a uniquely demonstrative sign (evidence) that one has received the gift.[18]

Vinson Synan says that 'tongues as initial evidence became the distinctive doctrine of the Pentecostal churches' but warns of those Pentecostals who had lost their resolve on the 'initial evidence' position, in particular those who were teachers and students in evangelical seminaries. He cites the attraction of Fee's position that tongues are normal but not normative and the well-known ICFG pastor Jack Hayford's argument that tongues should not be seen as 'proof' of Spirit baptism (which cannot be categorically proven) but as a 'provision' and 'privilege' open for all Christians. Synan argues that 'initial evidence' is vindicated by comparing the growth of those churches that maintained this doctrine (AG, COGIC) with those churches that were opposed to the doctrine and out of which the former emerged (Christian and Missionary Alliance, Church of Christ [Holiness]). He says that it is 'unthinkable that the Pentecostal movement could have developed as it did without the initial evidence position'.[19] Of course, there are many other reasons for the growth of churches; and the Southern Baptists, who are much bigger than the Pentecostal denominations, are opposed to 'initial evidence'. There are also Pentecostal denominations that have not grown significantly while holding to 'initial evidence'. Menzies and Synan have aligned themselves squarely with the Classical Pentecostals they represent. The AG in the USA reaffirmed their belief in classical Pentecostal pneumatology in their General Council in 1991, declaring that Spirit baptism is an experience 'distinct from and subsequent to conversion', and that speaking in tongues is the 'initial physical evidence' of this.[20] In the

---

[17] Gordon D. Fee, *Gospel and Spirit: Issues in New Testament Hermeneutics* (Peabody, MA: Hendrickson, 1991), p. 98.

[18] Menzies, *Empowered for Witness*, pp. 246, 254–5.

[19] Vinson Synan, 'The Role of Tongues as Initial Evidence', Mark W. Wilson (ed.), *Spirit and Renewal: Essays in Honor of J. Rodman Williams* (Sheffield, UK: Sheffield Academic Press, 1994), pp. 69, 75, 79–82.

[20] Menzies, *Empowered for Witness*, p. 230.

same year, Gordon Fee published his controversial book *Gospel and Spirit*, in which he argued that the doctrine of subsequence is not clearly taught in the New Testament and should not be seen as normative. He stated that the Pentecostal experience of the Spirit was a valid one, but his critique of Pentecostal theology created a strong reaction, perhaps particularly because Fee was coming from within classical Pentecostalism as one of its best-known scholars. Menzies, for example, charged that Fee's analysis meant that Pentecostals had nothing new to offer the broader Christian world theologically, it challenged Pentecostal understanding of Spirit baptism at its deepest level and it undercut crucial aspects of Pentecostal theology.[21] Some felt that this was a stab at the heart of Pentecostal theology.

Some Pentecostals and Charismatics, while acknowledging a distinct experience of Spirit baptism, think that tongues may follow this experience but are not essential evidence of the baptism. Others see Spirit baptism as an initiatory experience that is part of (or the final stage of) the conversion process and that gifts of the Spirit (including tongues) are given to all believers. Still others, especially Catholic Charismatics, see Spirit baptism in sacramental terms, as a release of the Spirit already given in baptism. This view seeks to be more accommodating to the theological positions of the older church traditions. There were other sources of opposition to a dogmatic stance on subsequence and consequence, including Fuller Seminary's Peter Wagner and the 'Third Wave' movement associated with John Wimber and his Vineyard Association, who said that 'signs and wonders' (including tongues) were to be sought as evidence of the Spirit's indwelling at conversion.[22] Pinnock, like Fee, said that tongues should be seen as 'normal rather than normative' and that speaking in tongues is a 'noble and edifying gift'. John V. Taylor pointed out that by prescribing the evidence of a subsequent and individualistic experience of Spirit baptism, Pentecostals had 'fallen as much as the Catholics and Protestants for the temptation to systematize the movement of God's free Spirit, specifying the conditions of his coming and the signs that prove it'.[23] This is a charge that most Pentecostal theologians must still come to terms with.

THE ESSENCE OF PENTECOSTAL THEOLOGY

Because of these different positions on what has been declared the central point of classical Pentecostal theology, it seems that Pentecostal theology

---

[21] Ibid., p. 235; Fee, *Gospel and Spirit*, p. 98.
[22] Lederle, *Treasures Old and New*, pp. 44–5, 104–5; Synan, 'Role of Tongues', p. 78.
[23] Pinnock, *Flame of Love*, p. 172; Taylor, *Go-Between God*, p. 200.

needs to be evaluated from a different perspective. Steven Land with his analysis of 'Pentecostal spirituality' offers a way out of the impasse. He points out that Pentecostalism cannot and should not simply be identified with a rationalistic evangelicalism. The starting point for Pentecostal theology is its distinctive spirituality: 'the Holy Spirit who is "God with us"'. The central Pentecostal concern is 'to emphasise the lived reality of the faith, the life and service of the people of God who are organically constituted as the body of Christ by the indwelling of the Holy Spirit'. At the heart of this spirituality is prayer, through which people respond to God's revelation. Pentecostal spirituality has its origins in many different sources, but Land (from his own Holiness Pentecostal background) sees the Wesleyan and African American sources as the most important spiritualities affecting Pentecostalism's founders. These sources together gave rise to the movement of 'participation in the Spirit'.[24] Some years before, Walter Hollenweger made a similar analysis. He said that early Pentecostals overcame dogmatic differences by forging an ecumenical bond whose basis was 'the presence of the living God, the reality of the Holy Spirit, which people looked forward to receiving in conversion, sanctification, the baptism of the Spirit and the gifts of the Spirit'. These Pentecostals did not try to work out theological problems because the only 'single legitimate aim before the second coming of Jesus on the clouds of heaven' was 'to sanctify and unite the children of God and to evangelize the world within a single generation'.[25] In spite of the inevitable dissipating of this early Pentecostal vision through institutionalization, for most Pentecostals and Charismatics today this experience of the imminence of God through prayer, worship and gifts of the Spirit enabling believers to evangelize is still their main characteristic. The fullness of the Spirit is always encountered in the abiding presence of God through prayer and worship.

The experience of the fullness of the Spirit is the essence of Pentecostal and Charismatic theology, especially where there is no need to harmonize this theology with conservative evangelical theology. There are several ways in which this Pentecostal and Charismatic pneumatology can be evaluated. One area concerns the holistic worldview of most societies, where all existing things are seen as a present material-spiritual or holistic unity and in this worldview the 'spirit' (or in a Christian context, the 'Spirit') pervades everything. In Pentecostal and Charismatic churches in Africa, Asia, the Pacific and Latin America, the all-encompassing Spirit is involved in every

---

[24] Steven J. Land, *Pentecostal Spirituality: A Passion for the Kingdom* (Sheffield, UK: Sheffield Academic Press, 1993), pp. 29, 32–3, 35, 37, 52.
[25] Hollenweger, *The Pentecostals*, pp. 505–6.

aspect of both individual and community life. This is particularly evident in the person of the prophetic or charismatic leader, who is pre-eminently a man or woman of the Spirit. Theology is acted out rather than philosophized in the rituals, liturgies and daily experiences of these Pentecostals. Pneumatology therefore becomes the most prominent part of an enacted theology in these churches. Gary Badcock says that the role of the Spirit in African Christianity is closely related to the 'theme of wholeness, in terms of the perception and realization of the vitalist principle that ultimately binds the whole of society and world together, in the normal expectation of healing and visions, in the simple celebration of life'.[26] Pentecostal and Charismatic pneumatology is a dynamic and contextualized manifestation of biblical revelation. In the worldview of most people, action and expression are as important as reflection and religion is especially something that you *do*. The tendency to oppose or discount the emotional in Christian worship made some western forms of Christianity unattractive, but the emphasis on the Spirit in Pentecostalism gave Christianity new vibrancy and relevance. The biblical concept of the Spirit made 'divine involvement' (God intervening in human affairs) possible for Christians in tangible ways. Many have possibly misunderstood the seemingly strange and unnerving manifestations in Pentecostalism (especially in the Third World), but many have also missed the essential, dynamic nature of 'spiritual' Christianity as portrayed in the Bible and have crowded it out with rationalistic theologizing. The Holy Spirit is the one to whom credit is given for everything that takes place in many Pentecostal and Charismatic churches. The Spirit causes people to 'receive' the Spirit, to prophesy, speak in tongues, heal, exorcize demons, have visions and dreams, live 'holy' lives – and generally the Spirit directs the life and worship of these churches, the 'leader' of all its activities.

I have illustrated this emphasis in my research in African Pentecostalism. Pneumatological 'manifestations' in African churches from the perspective of the participants in these churches are seen as manifestations of the presence of the Holy Spirit. The fact that no less 'unusual' manifestations of the Spirit were experienced in biblical times means that these manifestations must be accepted as genuine responses to the working of the Spirit among ordinary people. Sometimes there may be play-acting and manipulation through spurious manifestations of the Spirit – but Christianity throughout the world has false prophets and people who use religious sanctions to

---

[26] Gary D. Badcock, *Light of Truth and Fire of Love: A Theology of the Holy Spirit* (Grand Rapids, MI: Eerdmans, 1997), p. 140.

enforce their will. And yet as I have elsewhere observed, a criticism often justifiably levelled at Pentecostals is that sometimes a theology of success and power is expounded at the expense of a theology of the cross. When the Spirit is seen as a quick-fix solution to human distress and want, there is a tendency to disparage the role of suffering in the lives of those Christian believers whose needs seem to remain unanswered. There are not always instant solutions to life's problems; and spirituality should not be measured in terms of success. People are not only convinced by the triumphs of Christianity but also by its perseverance in trials. The Spirit is also a gentle dove, a Spirit of humility, patience and meekness, of love, joy and peace. Overemphasizing the power of the Spirit often leads to bitter disappointment and disillusionment when that power is not evidently and immediately manifested. Pentecostal pneumatology must not only provide power when there is a lack of it, but must also be able to sustain people through life's tragedies and failures, especially when there is no visible outward success.[27]

CONTEXTUAL PNEUMATOLOGY

Pentecostal churches in the Majority World have made a real and vital contribution to a dynamic and contextual pneumatology. The difficulty with some western approaches to theology is a dualistic rationalizing that does not adequately understand a holistic worldview uniting physical and spiritual, and personal and social, for there is a presumed interpenetrating of both. The so-called 'contextual theologies' are often articulated within the parameters of western theology. The theological vacuum created as a result has often been filled by the grassroots theology of Third World Pentecostals, a theology from the underside and a peoples' theology. The Pentecostal churches have made possible a dialogue between autochthonous worldviews, religions and Christianity at an existential level. This has largely been more effective than so-called 'indigenous theologies' that have often tended to be justifications for the continuation of pre-Christian religions. Both the Bible and human experience in most of the world often transcend and defy explanations and rationalizations. John Wimber described the modern western worldview as dominated by secularism. It assumes that life goes on 'in a universe closed off from divine intervention, in which truth is arrived at through empirical means and rational thought'. He says that materialism 'warps our thinking, softening convictions about the

---

[27] Anderson, *Moya*, pp. 41–6, 104–20; Anderson, *Zion and Pentecost*, pp. 239, 244–55.

supernatural world', and that westerners live as if 'material cause-and-effect explains all of what happens to us'. Rationalism becomes the 'chief guide in all matters of life' and anything that cannot be explained 'scientifically' is denied.[28] Because of this, direct experience of the spirit world and the so-called 'supernatural' is often missing from western theology. As God is only concerned with 'spiritual' and 'sacred' matters, people can look after all 'secular' needs by their increasing knowledge. There is a real danger that Christianity, if not disentangled from this rationalistic theology, will become largely irrelevant for most of the world. As Badcock observes, 'the tendency of the Western institutional churches toward a more rationally definable ecclesial life ordered through ministerial office, the Word, and the sacraments tends to be regarded as culturally alien and religiously undesirable' in many other contexts.[29]

Africa is illustrative of this tension, where many people regarded western missionaries with their logical presentations of 'theology' as out of touch with the real, holistic world that Africans experienced. Their deepest felt needs were not addressed and their questions remained unanswered. Because the real implications of the questions arising from the African worldview were not fully grasped by much of the theology taught in Africa, the full significance of the Christian answer was also overlooked. In contrast, Pentecostal and Spirit churches were motivated by a desire to meet the physical, emotional and spiritual needs of Africa, offering solutions to life's problems and ways to cope in a threatening and hostile world. Their pastors, prophets, bishops and evangelists proclaimed that the same God who saves the 'soul' also heals the body and is a 'good God' interested in providing answers to human fears and insecurities, accepting people as having genuine problems and trying conscientiously to find solutions to them. The God who forgives sin is also concerned about poverty, sickness, barrenness, oppression by evil spirits and liberation from all forms of human affliction and bondage. This message makes Pentecostalism attractive to people in these contexts. The insight shared by Africa and other Majority World societies that life is a totality, that there can be no ultimate separation between sacred and secular, and that religion must be brought to bear on all human problems is their great contribution to the West. It is a belief and faith that the West now desperately needs in the face of the devastation brought by secularization.[30]

[28] John Wimber, *Power Evangelism: Signs and Wonders Today* (London: Hodder and Stoughton, 1985), pp. 77–8.
[29] Badcock, *Light of Truth*, p. 137.   [30] Anderson, *Moya*, pp. 100–4.

In most religions of the world, almost everything is invested with religious meaning and there is no clear-cut division between 'spiritual' and 'secular'. This spirituality is often pragmatic, practical and this-worldly rather than esoteric and reflective, as one finds in some western and other-worldly forms of Christian spirituality. We will define 'spirituality' here as that pertaining to and describing the spiritual or religious life of people and all that is affected by it or all that it affects. The operative word in this definition is *experience*. Spirituality can be described as people's awareness and lived experience of God. Examples of this understanding are found in the so-called 'mystical' religious traditions – and this includes Pentecostalism, in particular with its accompanying phenomena of 'ecstasy' in the Spirit. In recent years, partly through the influence of post-modern thought, there has been a much greater acknowledgement of the importance of the role of experience in defining reality, and theology now recognizes that 'experience is an authentic source of divine revelation'.[31]

Harvey Cox, one of the foremost observers of modern religions, speaks of 'the reshaping of religion in the twenty-first century' and 'the unanticipated reappearance of primal spirituality in our time'. But this he sees especially in the context of the rapid growth of Pentecostalism throughout the world. Cox describes the remarkable rise of Pentecostalism as a resurgence of what he calls 'primal spirituality' with three dimensions: (1) *primal speech*, found in glossolalia, 'another voice, a language of the heart'; (2) *primal piety*, found in the resurgence of 'trance, vision, healing, dreams, dance, and other archetypal religious expressions'; and (3) *primal hope*, which he describes as 'pentecostalism's millennial outlook . . . that a radical new age is about to dawn'. Cox describes speaking in tongues and says that this responds to 'an ecstasy deficit' in our contemporary world and is 'an ecstatic experience, one in which the cognitive grids and perceptual barriers that normally prevent people from opening themselves to deeper insights and exultant feelings, are suspended'. He suggests that this is a type of 'primary speech' by which people can 'safely become as little children, at least temporarily'. It is also 'breaking through the limitations of human language' and the means by which humans can speak to God. Pentecostalism is thus 'closer to the most sublime forms of mysticism than are the more respectable denominations that sometimes look down on it'. Tongues as a form of

---

[31] Philip Sheldrake, *Spirituality as History* (London: SPCK, 1995), p. 41.

'ecstatic utterance' are for Cox another example of what links the religions together.[32]

Different spiritualities sometimes involve an interface between western and autochthonous worldviews and in the case of Pentecostal movements, between 'historical' and 'Pentecostal' Christianity. African Pentecostal spirituality as described in my own publications consists of a free and spontaneous Christian liturgy that does not betray its essentially Christian character, although to a large extent liberated from the foreignness of western forms of Christianity. A major reason for the attraction of Pentecostal churches for people oriented to popular religiosity was a sympathetic or at least a serious approach by Pentecostal preachers to African life and culture, fears and uncertainties, and to the worldview of spirits, magic and witchcraft. The Pentecostal and Spirit churches, with their firm commitment to a cohesive community and their offer of full participation to all, provided substantially for universal human needs. The relationship between the popular spiritualities and the new Christian spirituality introduced by Pentecostal and Charismatic movements has seldom been studied. Inadequate theories by sociologists, missiologists and other scholars have sometimes failed to recognize the obvious, that Pentecostalism is essentially a religious (or 'spiritual') movement with spiritual reasons for its burgeoning strength. A study of the spiritualities motivating Pentecostalism and its relationship with other spiritualities, therefore is extremely valuable. Chinese American Pentecostal theologian Amos Yong writes of the importance of (1) a holistic understanding of human religiosity and that the Pentecostal and Charismatic experience 'demands interpretation of the experiential dimension of spirituality over and against an emphasis on textuality in religious life'. Pentecostal spiritualities reflect the conviction that Pentecostals experience God through the Spirit and are expressed in liturgies that are primarily oral, narrative and participatory. It is also (2) a pneumatocentric spirituality, where the Spirit invades all human life.[33] The popularity of Pentecostal and Charismatic forms of Christianity in the developing world can also in part be attributed to a particularly *contextual* spirituality. Pentecostalism purports to provide for much more than the 'spiritual' problems of life. The important role given to divine healing and exorcism, the particular emphasis on the power of the Spirit, but also the comprehensive community projects and significant involvement in political and civic

[32] Cox, *Fire*, pp. 81–8, 91–2, 96.
[33] Amos Yong, *Discerning the Spirit(s): A Pentecostal/Charismatic Contribution to Christian Theology of Religions* (Sheffield, UK: Sheffield Academic Press, 2000), pp. 134, 162, 319.

organizations and trade unions, represent a new and vigorous spirituality offering help to human problems. This spirituality is a holistic approach to Christianity that appeals more adequately to popular worldviews than older Christian traditions had done, and in some respects was also more satisfying than 'traditional' religions had been. Furthermore, throughout Africa, Asia, the Pacific and Latin America, Pentecostalism has been more meaningful precisely because it has continued some pre-Christian religious expressions and ritual symbols and invested them with new meanings.

In the Preface to his fascinating book *Fire from Heaven*, Cox speaks of his thinking in the 1960s that there was need of a theology for a post-religious age 'that many sociologists had confidently assured us was coming', and this theology he expressed in *The Secular City*. He has since discovered that 'it is secularity, not spirituality, that may be headed for extinction'. He admits that his earlier view might have been wrong and that instead of the 'death of God' and the decline of religion something quite different had taken place. There is now what he calls a 'religious renaissance' throughout the world, touching every sort of religious expression, a period of renewed religious vitality. He says that during the 1960s, most western scholars missed the fact that not only were people disillusioned with traditional religions, but also disappointed by 'the bright promises of science and progress'. Cox remarks that the 'kernel of truth' in the 'overblown claims' of the 'death of God' theologians was that 'the abstract deity of western theologies and philosophical systems had come to the end of its run'.[34] The dramatic growth of Pentecostalism for Cox seemed to bear out what he had said long ago and not to contradict it:

The volcanic eruption of a Christian movement that relies on the direct experience of the Divine Spirit rather than on archaic creeds and stately rituals seems to corroborate their diagnosis while it completely undercuts their prescription.[35]

In a penetrating article, Amos Yong pleads for a Pentecostal theology of religions, something that has been neglected by Pentecostal theologians. He points out that Pentecostals in the Third World, especially those who are part of Christian minorities, are in constant interaction with other religions. He says that the experiences of the Spirit common to Pentecostals and Charismatics demonstrate 'indubitable similarities across the religious traditions of the world'. This opens up the way for a constructive Pentecostal

---

[34] Cox, *Fire*, pp. xvi, 83, 104.
[35] Harvey Cox, 'Foreword', Allan Anderson and Walter J. Hollenweger (eds.) *Pentecostals After a Century: Global Perspectives on a Movement in Transition* (Sheffield, UK: Sheffield Academic Press, 1999), p. 7.

theology of religions that explores 'how the Spirit is present and active in other religious traditions'.[36] Yong's article demonstrates that Pentecostal spirituality is a useful starting point for understanding other religions.

The great attraction of Pentecostal spirituality is that it claims to provide answers to existential problems throughout the world. In their encounter with other religions, Pentecostals and Charismatics have themselves been challenged and enriched in the content of their proclamation, which without the encounter would have been impoverished and foreign. Pentecostal and Charismatic churches offer realistic solutions for these problems through the indwelling Spirit, they accept them as genuine problems, conscientiously attempt to provide explanations for them and expect something to happen to resolve the problems through faith in God. In addition, pre-Christian beliefs and practices have been transformed in many inculturated Pentecostal churches so that Christianity is presented as an attractive and spiritual alternative.

Contextualization not only takes into account cultural values, but also tries to make the gospel relevant to the current situation of social change and new economic and political contexts. It may be argued that some Pentecostal and Charismatic movements have attempted to do just this and that their success has had a profound effect on older churches. Until recently, Pentecostals did not talk about their 'spirituality' as it was not part of their religious vocabulary. But 'Pentecostal spirituality' has become recognized as a distinctive form of Christian spirituality that can be described through its various activities and rites.[37] It may be significant that the first publication in the *Journal of Pentecostal Theology Supplement Series* was entitled *Pentecostal Spirituality: A Passion for the Kingdom*, which Steven Land describes as:

The dimension of praise, worship, adoration and prayer to God . . . [and] the abiding, decisive, directing motives and dispositions which characterize Pentecostals . . . this depth of conviction and passion . . . is a steadfast longing for the Lord and the salvation of the lost . . . . a continuous, joyous exclamation of the inbreaking presence and soon to be consummated kingdom of God.[38]

This 'passion for the kingdom' is the way Land describes 'Pentecostal spirituality', centred in the Pentecostal experience of the 'lived reality by the eschatological, missionary community, expressed by prayer and integrated by "apocalyptic affections"'.[39] A more recent title in the *JPTS* series is

---

[36] Amos Yong, '"Not Knowing Where the Wind Blows . . .": On Envisioning a Pentecostal-Charismatic Theology of Religions', *Journal of Pentecostal Theology* 14 (1999), 85–6, 99–100.

[37] Daniel E. Albrecht, *Rites in the Spirit: A Ritual Approach to Pentecostal/Charismatic Spirituality* (Sheffield, UK: Sheffield Academic Press, 1999), pp. 9, 14.

[38] Land, *Pentecostal Spirituality*, pp. 22–3.   [39] Ibid., pp. 218–19.

Daniel Albrecht's *Rites in the Spirit*, which has the subtitle *A Ritual Approach to Pentecostal/Charismatic Spirituality*. He approaches the subject through the lens of rituals observed in three Californian Pentecostal and Charismatic churches. Although his descriptions of spirituality might not be appropriate for many other parts of the world, his methodology is relevant, for Pentecostal and Charismatic spirituality is best expressed in the actions of Pentecostal and Charismatic people at worship, ceremony and prayer. Comparing Pentecostals and Charismatics in the USA, Albrecht finds 'a fundamental common belief in the imminent activity of God's Spirit', and that the 'fundamental goal of the Pentecostal service' is 'experiencing or encountering God'. For him, this is the essence of Pentecostal and Charismatic spirituality.[40] Whatever else they might show, these studies indicate that Pentecostal spiritualities are centred on the experience of the Spirit that pervades the whole person, makes Jesus Christ more real and relevant to daily life and inspires testimony, praise, unknown tongues, prophecies, healings, dancing, clapping, joyful singing, and many other expressions that characterize Pentecostals and Charismatics the world over. Pentecostal and Charismatic spiritualities are expressed in liturgies that often take on the characteristics of the host culture and are not unaffected by older religious traditions that have permeated that culture.

We might say that a fundamental, common Pentecostal spirituality can only be described with difficulty because of the diversity of Pentecostalism throughout the world. It might be more accurate to say that there are different Pentecostal spiritualities. But even when western scholars describe a singular 'Pentecostal spirituality' as the experience of God through the Spirit, this transcends cultural boundaries and provides an authentic, yet flexible encounter with God that is meaningful in its different cultural expressions. This makes a comparative and contextual study of Pentecostal spiritualities, or Pentecostal experiences of the Spirit in different parts of the world absolutely essential.

Finally, in this discussion of the important role of Pentecostal and Charismatic pneumatology we must not lose sight of what has always been a central part of the work of the Spirit: to bring honour to the Lord Jesus Christ. From the beginning, classical Pentecostals declared their faith in strong Christological terms: 'Jesus Christ the Saviour, Sanctifier, Healer, Baptizer and Soon Coming King'. This was the 'full gospel' that was proclaimed in the storefront churches, halls, tents, stadiums and on street corners. Although the experience of the Spirit was that which distinguished them

---

[40] Albrecht, *Rites in the Spirit*, pp. 39, 149, 238.

from the older churches, for the vast majority of Pentecostals and Charismatics the world over, the presence of Jesus Christ as Lord is always the focus of their worship and central theme of their proclamation. Like other evangelicals, they declare that Christ is the one who by his Spirit transforms the lives of Christians in a 'born again' experience and makes them useful in this world in the service of God and humanity. We can only understand Pentecostalism's theology of the Spirit in this light.

Mission, evangelism and eschatology

THE MISSIONARY SPIRIT

Pentecostalism has probably been the fastest growing religious movement in the twentieth century and it is now found in almost every country in the world. One of the reasons for this must surely be because it has always had a strong emphasis on mission and evangelism. From the beginning, Pentecostals and Charismatics have been involved in these activities, but this has always issued from their strong pneumatology. Indeed, the first Pentecostals believed that the Spirit had been poured out on them in order to engage in the end-time harvest of souls that would accompany the preaching of the 'full gospel' throughout the world. Their efforts were grounded in the conviction that the Holy Spirit was the motivating power behind all such activity, and their Spirit baptism had given them different languages of the world, as the first issue of the Azusa Street newspaper declared:

A minister says that God showed him twenty years ago that the divine plan for missionaries was that they might receive the gift of tongues either before going to the foreign field or on the way. It should be a sign to the heathen that the message is of God. The gift of languages can only be viewed as the Spirit gives utterance. It cannot be learned like the native tongues, but the Lord takes control of the organs of speech at will. It is emphatically, God's message.[1]

The fact that most of the early missionaries did not and could not speak the languages of the people to whom they went did not deter them, for they were not motivated by the tongues they had been given, but by the Spirit who was in them. Pentecostals place primary emphasis on being 'sent by the Spirit' and depend more on what is described as the Spirit's leading than on formal structures. People called 'missionaries' are doing that job because the Spirit directed them to do it, often through

---

[1] *The Apostolic Faith* 1:1 (Los Angeles, September 1906), p. 1.

some spiritual revelation like a prophecy, a dream or a vision and even through an audible voice perceived to be that of God. In comparison to the 'Missio Dei' of older Catholic and Protestant missions and the 'obedience to the Great Commission' of evangelical missions, Pentecostal mission is grounded first and foremost in the conviction that the Spirit is the motivating power behind this activity. Pentecostal leader J. Roswell Flower wrote in 1908, 'When the Holy Spirit comes into our hearts, the missionary spirit comes in with it; they are inseparable. . . . Carrying the gospel to hungry souls in this and other lands is but a natural result'.[2] The heart of Pentecostal missions is the experience of the power of the Spirit. This mission has not always been clearly formulated or strategized, as Pentecostal missionaries got on with the job in a hurry believing that the time was short. Declared *The Apostolic Faith*, 'This is a world-wide revival, the last Pentecostal revival to bring our Jesus. The church is taking her last march to meet her beloved'.[3] Their mission activity was grounded in this premillennial eschatology and so reflection about the task was not as important as action in evangelism and mission. Their mission theology was a theology on the move and theirs was an action-oriented missions movement from the start, conducted in the face of strident opposition from 'mainline' Churches and missions, and often with intense, sometimes hostile rivalry and infighting between the different Pentecostal organizations themselves.

Donald McGavran at Fuller Theological Seminary, followed by Peter Wagner, were among the first to ask missiological questions about Pentecostal church growth; and their 'Church Growth' school has had an important influence on US Pentecostal missiologists. One of the first of these was Paul Pomerville, who says that obedience to the written command of the Great Commission is the emphasis of most evangelicals but is not the main motivation for mission for Pentecostals. The Holy Spirit poured out at Pentecost is a missionary Spirit, the church full of the Spirit is a missionary community by nature and the church's witness is the release of an inward dynamic. But it was not only a collective experience of the Spirit; the individual experience that each of God's people had with the Spirit was also the key to the expansion of the church. The centrality of the Spirit in mission has been a consistent theme in Pentecostal studies. The Pentecostal movement was a missionary movement made possible by the Spirit's empowerment.

---

[2] *The Pentecost* 1:1 (Indianapolis, August 1908), p. 4.
[3] *The Apostolic Faith* 1:1 (September 1906), p. 4.

CONTEXTUALIZATION OF LEADERSHIP

As we have seen, early Pentecostals believed that in Spirit baptism they had been given foreign tongues to preach the full gospel to the ends of the earth. Although missionaries from the West went out to the Majority World in independent and denominational Pentecostal missions, the over-whelming majority of Pentecostal missionaries have been national people 'sent by the Spirit', often without formal education or training. This is a fundamental historical difference between Pentecostal and 'mainline' missions. In Pentecostal practice, the Holy Spirit is given to every believer without preconditions. As a result, the rigid dividing line between 'clergy' and 'laity' and between men and women did not develop in Pentecostal churches. Even more significantly, they encouraged the appointment of national pastors and evangelists to build up congregations and reach out to the community.[4] This was one of the reasons for the rapid transition from 'foreign' to 'national' church that took place in many Pentecostal missions.

Until recently, Pentecostals have not had a tradition of formal training for 'ministers' as a class set apart. They have always fiercely defended the principle of the priesthood of all believers. The Spirit speaks equally to each believer regardless of gender, education or social status, and so each Pentecostal believer is potentially a minister and missionary of the gospel.[5] The first Pentecostal leaders (with some exceptions) tended to come from the lower and uneducated strata of society and were trained in an apprentice-type training where their charismatic abilities were recognized and encour-aged. Unfortunately, the emphasis on self-propagation through evangelism and church growth has sometimes resulted in Pentecostals being inward looking, triumphalistic and seemingly unconcerned with or oblivious to the serious issues of their socio-political contexts, especially where there were oppressive governments. The Argentine scholar José Míguez Bonino asks of Pentecostals if the 'global challenge of missions . . . can be ideo-logically diverted from a concern with the urgent challenges of situations at home'.[6] Pentecostals need to heed these warnings, although they are starting to recognize the social implications of the gospel and this fail-ure in their mission strategies. The church not only has to evangelize the nations but also to love its neighbours and this is a vital part of its mission. Gary McGee observes poignantly that 'many Pentecostals who survive in

---

[4] Willem A. Saayman, 'Some Reflections on the Development of the Pentecostal Mission Model in South Africa', *Missionalia* 21:1 (1993), 43.

[5] Klaus, 'National Leadership', p. 226.

[6] José Míguez Bonino, 'Pentecostal Missions is More Than What it Claims', *Pneuma* 16:2 (1997), 284.

Third World poverty and oppression may long for a more forthright witness, one that presses for economic, social, and even political change'.[7]

Pentecostal missions are quick to raise up national leaders who are financially self-supporting and therefore the new churches are inculturated much quicker than older mission churches had been. The pioneering work in this regard of AG missiologist Melvin Hodges and his widely influential book *The Indigenous Church* (1953) not only emphasized creating 'indigenous churches', but it also stressed church planting – a fundamental principle of Pentecostal mission strategy. Roland Allen's books on indigenous churches were already circulating in Pentecostal circles as early as 1921, when Alice Luce, an early AG missionary to Hispanic Americans, wrote a series of articles on Allen's teachings;[8] and Hodges was undoubtedly indebted to Allen's ideas in framing his own missiology. But the influence of Hodges on western Pentecostal (especially AG) missions contributed towards their commitment to the raising of national leadership and the establishment of theological training institutes (often called 'Bible schools') and in-service training structures throughout the world. This in turn resulted in the much more rapid growth of national Pentecostal churches. Hodges was a missionary in Central America who articulated what had always been at the heart of Pentecostal growth in different cultural contexts. He said that the aim of all mission activity was to build an 'indigenous New Testament church' that followed 'New Testament methods'. He emphasized that the church itself (and not the evangelist) is 'God's agent for evangelism', and that the role of the cross-cultural missionary was to ensure that a church became self-governing, self-supporting and self-propagating.[9] He thus enthusiastically embraced and enlarged the 'three self' policy of church planting, the main theme of his book, but he introduced an emphasis on 'indigenization' that was lacking in the earlier works on the subject. The foundation for this to happen was the Holy Spirit:

There is no place on earth where, if the gospel seed be properly planted, it will not produce an indigenous church. The Holy Spirit can work in one country as well as in another. To proceed on the assumption that the infant church in any land must always be cared for and provided for by the mother mission is an unconscious insult to the people that we endeavor to serve, and is evidence of a lack of faith in God and in the power of the gospel.[10]

---

[7] Gary B. McGee, 'Pentecostal Missiology: Moving Beyond Triumphalism to Face the Issues', *Pneuma* 16:2 (1994), 280.

[8] McGee, 'Pentecostals and Their Various Strategies for Global Mission', Dempster, Klaus and Petersen, *Called and Empowered*, p. 212.

[9] Hodges, *Indigenous Church*, pp. 10–12, 22.   [10] Ibid., p. 14.

Hodges' views have had a profound impact on the subsequent growth of the AG, who have prescribed the reading of *The Indigenous Church* to future missionaries. But attaining 'three selfhood' does not guarantee real contextualization unless the 'three selfs' are no longer patterned on foreign forms of being church and are grounded in the thought patterns and symbolism of popular culture. Yet, Pentecostalism's religious creativity and spontaneously contextual character were characteristics held as ideals by missionaries and mission strategists for over a century. The 'three self' formula for indigenization was automatically and seemingly effortlessly achieved by many Pentecostal churches long before this goal was realized by older missions. Hodges was able to tap into that fact. For him, the foundation for Pentecostal mission and the reason for its continued expansion is the 'personal filling of the Holy Spirit' who gives gifts of ministry to untold thousands of 'common people', creating active, vibrantly expanding and 'indigenous churches' all over the world.

Unfortunately, Hodges was still a product of his own context, seeing 'missions' as primarily from North America (or elsewhere in the western world) to the rest of the 'foreign' world. This view of Pentecostal missions is reflected in US Pentecostal missiological writing, which sometimes does not go further than an adapted reproduction of the McGavran/ Wagner 'Church Growth' ideology that sees the mission enterprise in terms of procedures and strategies that succeed in the USA. Fortunately, there have been recent exceptions. Hodges, in spite of his remarkable insights, could not escape the concept of 'missionaries' ('us') being expatriate, white people who had left 'home' for 'abroad', in contrast to the 'nationals' ('them') who must (eventually) take over the 'missionaries' work when the ideal of an 'indigenous church' is reached. Hodges sees 'mission' as 'the outreach of the church in foreign lands'.[11] In these and similar writings, the great majority of Pentecostals in the world remain 'objects' of mission and are marginalized. Fortunately, the Majority World Pentecostal and Charismatic churches are now beginning to produce theologians and missiologists who challenge the presuppositions of the past and are not content to follow foreign mission ideologies and strategies blindly.

A DYNAMIC AND CONTEXTUAL MISSION PRAXIS

We have seen that a prominent aspect of Pentecostal and Charismatic faith is that the coming of the Spirit brings the ability to perform 'signs and

---

[11] Ibid., p. 9.

wonders' in the name of Jesus Christ to accompany and authenticate the gospel message. The role of 'signs and wonders', particularly that of healing and miracles, is important in Pentecostal and Charismatic mission praxis and reflection. Pentecostals and Charismatics all over the world see the role of healing as good news for the poor and afflicted. Early Pentecostal newsletters and periodicals abounded with testimonies to physical healings, exorcisms and deliverances. Early Pentecostal missionaries and especially the mass evangelists expected miracles to accompany their evangelism and 'prioritized seeking for spectacular displays of celestial power – signs and wonders, healing, and deliverance from sinful habits and satanic bondage'.[12] The 'signs and wonders' promoted by independent Pentecostal and Charismatic evangelists have led to the rapid growth of Pentecostal and Charismatic churches in many parts of the world but have seldom been without controversy. We need to critically evaluate those evangelistic ministries that lead to the self-aggrandisement and financial gain of the preacher, often at the expense of those who have very little at all to give.

The Pentecostal understanding of the 'full gospel' means that the preaching of the Word in evangelism should be accompanied by 'signs and wonders', and divine healing in particular is an indispensable part of their evangelistic strategy. Indeed, in many cultures of the world, where the religious specialist or 'person of God' has the power to heal the sick and ward off evil spirits and sorcery, the offer of healing by Pentecostalism has been one of its major attractions. In these cultures, a holistic worldview that does not separate the 'physical' from the 'spiritual' is continued and people see Pentecostalism as a 'powerful' religion to meet human needs. For some Pentecostals, especially in the early years, faith in God's power to heal directly through prayer even results in a rejection of all other methods of healing, including medicine. The numerous healings reported by Pentecostal missionaries and evangelists confirmed that God's Word was true, God's power was evidently on their ministries, and the result was that many people were persuaded to leave their old beliefs and become Christians. This emphasis on healing is so much part of Pentecostal evangelism that large public meetings and tent campaigns preceded by great publicity are frequently still used in order to reach as many 'unevangelized' people as possible.

Pentecostals and Charismatics believe that the miracle power of the New Testament has been restored in the present day to draw unbelievers to

---

[12] Gary B. McGee, '"Power from on High": A Historical Perspective on the Radical Strategy in Missions', Ma and Menzies, *Pentecostalism in Context*, pp. 317, 324, 329.

Christ. This is particularly effective in those parts of the world least affected by modernization, secularization and scientific rationalism. The central role given to healing is probably no longer as prominent a feature for western Pentecostalism, but in the rest of the world the problems of disease and evil affect the whole community and are not relegated to private and individual pastoral care or mere clinical treatment. These communities were health-oriented communities and in their traditional religions, rituals for healing and protection are prominent. Pentecostals responded to what they experienced as a void left by rationalistic western forms of Christianity that had unwittingly initiated what amounted to the destruction of traditional spiritual values. Pentecostals declared a message that reclaimed the biblical traditions of healing and protection from evil, they demonstrated the practical effects of these traditions and by so doing became heralds of a Christianity that was really meaningful. Thus, Pentecostalism went a long way towards meeting physical, emotional and spiritual needs of people in the Majority World, offering solutions to life's problems and ways to cope in what was often a threatening and hostile world.[13] But sadly, this message of power has become in many instances an occasion for the exploitation of those who are at their weakest. Theologies of power must also become theologies of the cross.

Contextualization has been a principle hotly debated and sometimes little understood, and it should not be confused with 'indigenization', which assumes that the gospel message and Christian theology are the same in all cultures and contexts, and it tends to relate the Christian message to traditional cultures. 'Contextualization' on the other hand assumes that every theology is influenced by its particular context and must be so to be relevant. It relates the Christian message to all contexts and cultures, including especially those undergoing rapid social change. The style of 'freedom in the Spirit' that characterizes Pentecostalism all over the world has undoubtedly contributed to the appeal of these movements in many different contexts. A spontaneous liturgy, which unlike that of most older churches is mainly oral and narrative, carries an emphasis on a direct experience of God through the Spirit. It results in the possibility of ordinary people being lifted out of mundane daily chores into a new realm of ecstasy. This is aided by the emphases on speaking in tongues, loud and emotional simultaneous prayer and joyful singing, clapping, raising hands and dancing in the presence of God – all common Pentecostal and Charismatic liturgical accoutrements. These practices made Pentecostal and Charismatic worship

[13] Anderson, *Zion and Pentecost*, pp. 120–6.

more easily assimilated into different cultural contexts, especially where a sense of divine immediacy was taken for granted; and these liturgies contrasted sharply with rationalistic and written liturgies presided over by a clergyman that were the main features of most other forms of Christianity. Furthermore, this total participation was available for everyone and the involvement of the laity became the most important feature of Pentecostal and Charismatic worship, again contrasting with the dominant role played by the priest or minister in the older churches. Although many of the newer Pentecostal and Charismatic churches have reinstated the traditional Protestant emphasis on the preaching of the Word by the minister as a central feature, it is still true to say that Pentecostalism allows for a much greater involvement in church services by ordinary members than is the case in older churches.[14]

The appropriation and proclamation of the gospel by national Pentecostal preachers is couched in thought forms and religious experiences with which ordinary people are already familiar. Some of the largest 'Spirit' churches in Africa for example reject key traditional beliefs and practices like polygamy and the use of power-laden charms. Rituals and symbols adapted from both western Christian and African religious traditions (and sometimes completely new ones) are introduced that usually have local relevance and include lively worship and enthusiastic participation by members. Chilean Pentecostal scholar Juan Sepúlveda comments on the ability of Pentecostalism to inculturate Christianity in local cultures:

The rediscovery of pneumatology by modern Pentecostalism has to do mainly with the spiritual freedom to 'incarnate' the gospel anew into the diverse cultures: to believe in the power of the Holy Spirit is to believe that God can and wants to speak to peoples today through cultural mediations other than those of Western Christianity. Being pentecostal would mean to affirm such spiritual freedom.[15]

He says that 'Creole Pentecostalism' is fundamentally rooted in the *mestizo* culture of the peasants and the urban poor and that this feature differentiates this form of Pentecostalism from historical Protestantism as well as from other Pentecostal churches of missionary origin that show a major cultural dependence on their countries of origin.[16] Of course, Pentecostal missions from the West are not exempt from this danger. But throughout the world,

---

[14] Saayman, 'Some Reflections', 47.
[15] Juan Sepúlveda, 'Indigenous Pentecostalism and the Chilean Experience', Anderson and Hollenweger, *Pentecostals after a Century*, pp. 133–4.
[16] Juan Sepúlveda, 'To Overcome the Fear of Syncretism: A Latin American Perspective', L. Price, J. Sepúlveda and G. Smith (eds.), *Mission Matters* (Frankfurt am Main: Peter Lang, 1997), p. 158.

Pentecostal movements create new voluntary organizations, often multi-ethnic, to replace traditional kinship groups. Many Pentecostal churches have programmes for recruiting new members that transcend national and ethnic divisions, and this belief in the movement's universality and message for the whole world is a radical departure from ethnically based traditional religions.

PENTECOSTAL EVANGELISM AND CHURCH PLANTING

Pentecostalism is notorious for its sometimes aggressive forms of evangelism, and from its beginning was characterized by an emphasis on evangelistic outreach, its highest priority in mission strategy. For Pentecostals, evangelism means to go out and reach the 'lost' for Christ in the power of the Spirit. They have an urgent message to proclaim the 'full gospel' of Jesus Christ as 'Saviour, Healer, Baptizer and Coming King'. The Azusa Street revival resulted in a category of 'called' Pentecostal 'missionaries' fanning out all over the globe within a remarkably short time. 'Mission' was mainly understood as 'foreign mission' mostly from 'white' to 'other' peoples and these missionaries were mostly untrained and totally inexperienced. Their only qualification was the baptism in the Spirit and a divine call; their motivation was to evangelize the world before the imminent coming of Christ, and so evangelism was more important than anything else like education or 'civilisation'.[17] Those Pentecostals who did insist on a modicum of missionary training did not require academic achievement as a qualification for acceptance. When the formation of the PMU was announced in Alexander Boddy's periodical *Confidence* in 1909, the qualifications for candidates were the following:

9. Religious Tests. Candidates must be from those who have received the Baptism of the Holy Ghost themselves.
10. Educational Standards. They must have a fair knowledge of every Book in the Bible, and an accurate knowledge of the Doctrines of Salvation and Sanctification.[18]

And that was all – any zealous Pentecostal believer was potentially a missionary. McGee describes the first twenty years of Pentecostal missions as mostly 'chaotic in operation'. Reports filtering back to the West to garnish newsletters would be full of optimistic and triumphalistic accounts of how many people were converted, healed and had received Spirit baptism, seldom mentioning any difficulties encountered or the inevitable

---

[17] Hollenweger, *The Pentecostals*, p. 34.   [18] *Confidence* 2:1 (January 1909), pp. 13–15.

blunders made. Early Pentecostal missionaries were often paternalistic, they frequently created dependency among their converts and so-called 'native workers', and sometimes they were blatantly racist, though there were notable exceptions to the general chaos.[19] As South African missiologist Willem Saayman has observed, most Pentecostal movements came into existence as missionary institutions; their work was 'not the result of some clearly thought out theological decision, and so policy and methods were formed mostly in the crucible of missionary praxis'.[20] Pentecostal missionaries often have a sense of special calling and divine destiny, thrusting them out in the face of stiff opposition to steadfastly propagate their message. But it must be acknowledged that despite the seeming naiveté of many of these early missionaries, their evangelistic methods were flexible, pragmatic and astonishingly successful. Pentecostal churches were missionary by their very nature and the dichotomy between 'church' and 'mission' that for so long plagued other Christian churches did not exist. This central missiological thrust was clearly a strong point in Pentecostalism and fundamental to its existence.

Nevertheless, there are several lingering problems still to be overcome in many Pentecostal missions. Their parochialism and rivalry makes ecumenical co-operation difficult, the tendency towards paternalism among western missionaries creates reluctance to listen to the opinions of nationals and there is a need for greater involvement in the plight of the poor and in opposing socio-political oppression. It is also a characteristic of most forms of Pentecostal evangelism that the proclamation often becomes a one-way affair, without sufficient consideration being given to the religious experience and cultural context of the people to whom the 'gospel' is proclaimed. The result is those innumerable opportunities to connect the Christian message with the world with which the 'convert' is most familiar are lost and the 'Christianity' that results remains rather 'foreign'. There is an urgent need to give special attention to the hitherto neglected area of the relationship between the Christian gospel and the traditional pre-Christian religions that continue to give meaning to people's understanding of life. Demonizing these religions (the legacy of many western Protestant missions) will not help the cause of evangelism and the healthy growth of the church today. These are some of the issues that Pentecostal missions must still address.

---

[19] Allan Anderson, 'Signs and Blunders: Pentecostal Mission Issues at "Home and Abroad" in the Twentieth Century', *Journal of Asian Mission* 2:2 (September 2000), 193.
[20] Saayman, 'Some Reflections', p. 42.

Church planting is a central feature of all Pentecostal mission activity. Thriving Pentecostal churches were established in many parts of the world without the help of any foreign missionaries. These churches were founded in unprecedented and innovative mission initiatives by national workers, motivated by a compelling need to preach and even more significantly, to experience a new message of the power of the Spirit. The effectiveness of these Pentecostal missions was based on this unique message, which was both the motivation for the thousands of grassroots emissaries and their source of attraction. All the widely differing Pentecostal and Charismatic movements have important common features: they proclaim and celebrate a salvation (or 'healing') that encompasses all of life's experiences and afflictions and they offer an empowerment that provides a sense of dignity and a coping mechanism for life. Their mission was to share this all-embracing message with as many people as possible, and to accomplish this, national Pentecostal evangelists went far and wide.

The remarkable growth of Pentecostal and Charismatic movements in the twentieth century cannot be isolated from the fact that these are often 'people movements', a massive turning of different peoples to Christianity from other religions on an unprecedented scale, set in motion by a multitude of factors for which western missions were unprepared. Charismatic leaders became catalysts in what has been called in the African context a 'primary movement of mass conversion'.[21] These movements did not proliferate because of the many secessions from western churches that took place, but because of mass conversions to Christianity through the tireless efforts of national missionaries, both men and women. Throughout the world, these early initiators were followed by another generation of missionaries, learning from and to some extent patterning their mission on those who had gone before. But the growth of Pentecostalism was not the result of the efforts of a few charismatic leaders or 'missionaries'. The proliferation of the movement would not have taken place without the tireless efforts of a vast number of ordinary and now virtually unknown women and men who networked across regional and even national boundaries. They proclaimed the same message they had heard others proclaim and which had sufficiently altered their lives to make it worth sharing wherever they went.

Most forms of Pentecostalism teach that every member is a minister and should be involved in mission and evangelism wherever they find

---

[21] Adrian Hastings, *The Church in Africa 1450–1950* (Oxford: Clarendon, 1994), pp. 530–1.

themselves. Although increasing institutionalization often causes a reappearance of the clergy/ laity divide, the mass involvement of the 'laity' in the Pentecostal movement was one of the reasons for its success. A theologically articulate clergy was not the priority, because cerebral and clerical Christianity had in the minds of many people already failed them. What was needed was a demonstration of power by people to whom ordinary people could easily relate. This was the democratization of Christianity, for henceforth the mystery of the gospel would no longer be reserved for a select privileged and educated few, but would be revealed to whoever was willing to receive it and pass it on.

PREMILLENNIAL ESCHATOLOGY

Early Pentecostals believed that their mission was part of the preparation for the soon return of Christ. The baptism in the Spirit and the tongues that they had received were above all a sign that the last days had come. Their eschatology was premillennial and dispensational, and it fuelled the urgency of their evangelism from the beginning. Evangelistic sermons like those of Maria Woodworth-Etter and the early periodicals were filled with eschatological themes, probably the most prominent part of early Pentecostal preaching and teaching. The belief in the soon coming of Christ overshadowed and motivated all missionary activities, tending to make Pentecostals poor strategists and little prepared for the rigours of living in a different continent and culture. When the end did not come as expected, Pentecostals adjusted and adapted the mission strategies of other evangelicals. Although the Pentecostal 'foursquare gospel' proclaimed the Christological themes of Christ as 'Saviour, Healer, Baptizer with the Holy Spirit and Coming King', the eschatological theme received the most prominence. This 'eschatological hope' dominated the movement in its formative stage and the linking of the 'full gospel' with the 'last days' was a paradigm shift that set the Pentecostal movement apart from the Holiness movement out of which it emerged. The Azusa Street newspaper, *The Apostolic Faith*, was filled with this premillennial topic and reported many prophecies and visions to this effect. This was the motivation behind the emphasis on evangelism 'before the end comes', and the more spectacular signs like speaking in tongues, prophecy and healing were subordinate to and confirmed this emphasis. The 'signs and wonders' that accompanied the preaching of the Pentecostal message were seen as evidence of the 'end time'. It was believed that the new Pentecostal movement was the

'Latter Rain' outpouring of the Spirit in the 'Last Days' to precede the coming of Christ. It was the fulfilment of prophecy, especially that of Joel (2:28–32).[22]

This was an 'apocalyptic vision' that resulted in a particular type of spirituality. The church was, as Steven Land puts it, 'an eschatological community of universal mission in the power and demonstration of the Spirit'. Thus the purpose of speaking in tongues was to facilitate the preaching of the gospel in all the languages of earth. The imminent return of Christ was the primary motivation for evangelism and world mission, which was seen essentially not as converting the world to Christ (evangelism), but as engaging in activity (evangelization) that would hasten the return of Christ in fulfilment of Matthew 24:14.[23] One of the first missionaries from Azusa Street, A. G. Garr, wrote in a letter from Hong Kong in 1909 that 'His banner of love may float over all nations, and that His glorious Gospel may go forth, bringing out a people for His name's sake, that our King may come again'.[24] Classical Pentecostal missions have therefore always been based on a particular eschatological view of salvation history.

The futurist premillennial framework that most early Pentecostals followed (and is still followed by many 'classical' Pentecostals today) was that propagated by the founder of the Plymouth Brethren, John Nelson Darby. The *Scofield Reference Bible* (1909), the most popular Authorized (King James) version of the Bible in use by Pentecostals in the English-speaking world until the 1970s, further promoted this framework. These were the sources of the narrow premillennial dispensationalism that dominated North American Pentecostalism and Fundamentalism for much of the twentieth century and resulted in elaborate and often fanciful interpretations of both future and current world events in popular apocalyptic literature. US Pentecostal theology and political attitudes were profoundly affected by this eschatology, even though there were elements of dispensationalism at variance with Pentecostal practice. Darby taught that the church (which some believed consisted only of Pentecostals) would be secretly 'raptured' to heaven before a seven-year tribulation period in which the 'Antichrist' would rule the world. At the end of this 'Great Tribulation', Christ would come and defeat the Antichrist in the battle of Armageddon and thereafter would rule for a thousand years (the Millennium). At the

---

[22] Woodworth-Etter, *Signs and Wonders*, pp. 483–4; Woodworth-Etter, *Holy Spirit*, pp. 252–9; Faupel, *Everlasting Gospel*, p. 20.
[23] Land, *Pentecostal Spirituality*, pp. 59–63; Faupel, *Everlasting Gospel*, p. 21–2.
[24] *Confidence* 2:11 (1909), p. 260.

end of the Millennium, Satan would be released and eventually defeated, when the great white throne judgement would separate true believers ('the sheep') from those who were not ('the goats'). The result would be either Heaven or Hell for eternity.[25] The teaching was based on a literal inter- pretation of passages in the book of Revelation and other New Testament passages about the end times.

The significance of this teaching for Pentecostals was that their belief in the 'soon' coming of Christ with its impending doom for unbelievers lent urgency to the task of world evangelization. A detailed premillennial eschatology in the Pentecostal movement however would only arise years later when with the increasing institutionalization of Pentecostal denom- inations, a more theological explanation of the imminence of the coming of Christ was felt necessary. Premillennialism has become so widespread in classical Pentecostalism that Steven Land considers it an essential part of its spirituality.[26] Robert Anderson points out that because belief in *xeno- lalia* and Pentecostal expectations of the Second Coming began to fade, eschatology was replaced by speaking in tongues ('initial evidence') as the central feature of Pentecostal ideology in North America. Furthermore, the millennial zeal of early Pentecostalism has been dampened among the more prosperous Pentecostals of today. Land points out that 'upward social mobility is clearly affecting the apocalyptic fervour and urgency as the world looks a little better to contemporary, more affluent North American Pentecostals', and that the eschatological hope and enthusiasm to witness is found 'more nearly in its pristine state among the burgeoning Third World Pentecostals'.[27] The other consequence of the eschatological stress of Pentecostals has been that their belief in the imminence of the end has meant that there is little time for matters of social concern, as it is more important to get 'souls saved'.

However, the various emphases of Pentecostalism by their very nature tended to blur the distinction and tension in eschatology between the 'already' and the 'not yet'. The promise of the Spirit was not only the fulfil- ment of prophecy and the sign of the 'last days', but it was also the tangible evidence that the 'last days' had already come. The kingdom of God was revealed in the present world in word and deed and an 'apocalyptic exis- tence' had become 'existentially palpable by the presence, manifestations

[25] Faupel, *Everlasting Gospel*, p. 29; James J. Glass, 'Eschatology: A Clear and Present Danger – A Sure and Certain Hope', Warrington, *Pentecostal Perspectives*, p. 127.
[26] Glass, 'Eschatology', p. 134; Land, *Pentecostal Spirituality*, pp. 222–3.
[27] Land, *Pentecostal Spirituality*, p. 71; Anderson, *Vision*, p. 96; Cox, *Fire*, p. 119.

and power of the Holy Spirit'.[28] The Last Days had begun to arrive. Some AICs, with their imagery of the New Jerusalem and Zion, not in some distant land but in the present and tangible reality of Africa, accentuated this 'realized eschatology'. Because the new age had already come through the power of the Spirit, its benefits of healing, deliverance and prosperity were now available for the poor, the oppressed and the dispossessed. Cox thinks that Pentecostalism has become 'a global vehicle for the restoration of primal hope', particularly for those estimated 87 per cent of Pentecostals 'who live below the world poverty line'.[29] This is a major reason for different cultural forms of Pentecostalism retaining their attraction for people all over the Majority World.

THE 'WORD OF FAITH' MOVEMENT

The 'Positive Confession' or 'Word of Faith' movement surfaced in US American independent Pentecostal ministries in the second half of the twentieth century and was an indirect development from Pentecostal 'realized eschatology', the ministries of independent healing evangelists like Oral Roberts and A. A. Allen, and the writings of Baptist pastor E. W. Kenyon. Kenyon taught 'the positive confession of the Word of God' and a 'law of faith' working by predetermined divine principles. He taught that healing is a completed work of Christ for everybody to be received by faith no matter what the evidence or circumstances; and that medicine is inconsistent with faith. The development of the movement was stimulated by the teachings of healing evangelists like William Branham and Oral Roberts, contemporary popular televangelists, and the Charismatic movement. It is now a prominent teaching of Pentecostal and Charismatic churches all over the world.

Kenneth Hagin in particular, widely regarded as 'father of the Faith Movement', popularized Kenyon's teaching and said that every Christian should exercise faith to have physical health, material prosperity and success, a teaching supported by selective Bible quotations. Hagin said that it was not enough to believe what the Bible said; the Bible must also be confessed, and what a person says (confesses) is what will happen. A person should therefore confess healing even when the 'symptoms' are still there.[30] Thousands of Hagin's graduates have propagated his 'Word of Faith' message all over

---

[28] Land, *Pentecostal Spirituality*, p. 66.   [29] Cox, *Fire*, p. 119.
[30] H. Terris Neumann, 'Cultic Origins of the Word-Faith Theology within the Charismatic Movement', *Pneuma* 12:1 (1990), 33–4.

the world and Hagin's books, videos and tapes have been sold in their millions. This type of faith teaching, however, although in a less developed form, has been part of Pentecostalism at least since the time of the healing evangelists in the 1950s, especially Oral Roberts and T. L. Osborne, both of whom are often quoted by Hagin and his followers. Kenneth Hagin received a 'revelation' in 1934 based on Mark 11:24, which resulted in his healing of a heart ailment. His teachings are based on the books of Kenyon and emphasize the importance of the 'word of faith', a positive confession of one's faith in healing, despite the circumstances or symptoms. Kenneth Copeland developed Hagin's teaching with a greater emphasis on financial prosperity and formulated 'laws of prosperity' to be observed by those seeking health and wealth. Poverty is seen as a curse to be overcome through faith. Through 'faith-force', believers regain their rightful divine authority over their circumstances.

The Word of Faith movement teaches physical healing and material prosperity usually through special revelation knowledge of a Bible passage (as distinct from 'sense knowledge') – a 'Rhema word' that is positively confessed as true. The teaching asserts that when Christians believe and confess this 'Rhema word' it becomes energizing and effective, resulting in receiving it from God. When people do not receive what they have confessed, it is usually because of a negative confession, unbelief, or a failure to observe the divine laws. Some faith teachers reject the use of medicine as evidence of weak faith and overlook or minimize the role of suffering, persecution and poverty in the purposes of God.

The 'Word of Faith' has been one of the most popular movements in US Pentecostalism. Not only has it been propagated in Charismatic circles, but it has influenced classical Pentecostals as well. Apart from the fact that this teaching encourages the 'American dream' of capitalism and promotes the success ethic, among its even more questionable features is the possibility that human faith is placed above the sovereignty and grace of God. Faith becomes a condition for God's action and the strength of faith is measured by results. Material and financial prosperity and health are sometimes seen as evidence of spirituality and the positive and necessary role of persecution and suffering is often ignored. The Holy Spirit is relegated to a quasi-magical power by which success and prosperity are achieved and the effectiveness of the message is determined by the physical results.

In an independent development, a similar teaching is part of the theology of the pastor of the world's largest congregation, David Yonggi Cho of the Yoido Full Gospel Church in Seoul, Korea. To the fourfold 'full gospel' of the early Pentecostals he has added the 'five-fold message of the Gospel', which includes (1) renewal, (2) the fullness of the Spirit, (3) healing, (4) blessing (his addition) and (5) the Second Coming. In addition, the 'three-fold blessings of salvation' include 'soul prosperity', 'prosperity in all things' and 'a healthy life', taken from the text of 3 John 2, a favourite text of the Word of Faith movement. The good news, Cho declares, is that God meets all the needs of believers including their spiritual salvation, physical healing and other blessings for material needs. But Cho was given this message in the midst of poverty and destitution after the Korean War, to become the foundation of all his preaching and ministry thereafter. The only way to receive the 'three-fold blessings' is to believe that God is a 'good God' and that salvation includes forgiveness of sins, health and prosperity. His doctrine of 'blessings' is, however, not a selfish, individualistic 'bless me' teaching but one intended to bring 'overflowing blessings' to those people around every believer. Prominent 'Faith' teachers like Robert Schuller and Oral Roberts write forewords to Cho's books, and Roberts even suggests that Cho received his teaching on prosperity from his books and tape recordings. The question of to what extent Cho's theology has been influenced by US American Pentecostalism, especially by Oral Roberts, is a matter that needs greater investigation.[31] Cho himself says that in his search for a 'God of the present in Korea' in 1958, he received a revelation of 'the truth of the threefold blessings of salvation, health and prosperity written in 3 John 2' and that this became the foundation of his preaching and ministry since that time.[32]

Some critics have tried to link the Word of Faith teaching with Norman Vincent Peale's 'Positive Thinking', with dualistic materialism and even with nineteenth-century 'New Thought' and Christian Science. However, these arguments remain unsubstantiated and it is probably more helpful to see this movement within the context of Pentecostalism and its healing emphasis. Early Pentecostal preachers like Smith Wigglesworth emphasized faith and wrote words often quoted by Word of Faith preachers as long ago as 1924, 'I am not moved by what I see. I am moved only by what I believe'.[33] But Classical Pentecostals have joined in the accusations of 'cultism', an AG writer Neuman charging Cho, Hagin and Copeland

---

[31] David Yonggi Cho, *Salvation, Health and Prosperity* (Altamonte Springs, FL: Creation House, 1987), p. 8; Cho, *The Fourth Dimension* (Seoul: Seoul Logos Co., 1979), p. 5; Allan Anderson, 'David Yonggi Cho's Pentecostal Theology as Contextual Theology in Korea', *JPT* 12:1 (2003).

[32] Cho, *Salvation, Health*, pp. 11–12.

[33] Smith Wigglesworth, *Ever Increasing Faith* (Springfield, MO: Gospel Publishing House, 1924, revised 1971), p. 30.

with this error and the US AG taking an official position against the teaching while promoting Cho's literature in particular! Neuman concludes that the 'health and wealth gospel' has 'cultic origins', an 'heretical Christology', and has 'devastating effects on human lives and the false portrayal of Christianity it presents to the world'.[34] On the other hand, criticisms of the 'Word of Faith' message have to reckon with the fact that the Bible is not entirely silent on the question of material need, that Christ's salvation is holistic, making provision for all human need and the enjoyment of God *and* his gifts. Salvation means the wholeness of human life, in which humanity has communion with God and enjoys the divine gifts. God desires to bless his children and this blessing seems to include provision for all their needs, but this is nowhere portrayed in the Bible as an irreversible law of cause and effect, as some 'prosperity' teachers indicate. A 'realized eschatology' which always sees the 'not yet' as 'already' is no worse than one that sees the 'not yet' always as 'not yet'. One of the reasons for the emergence of independent and Pentecostal churches in the Third World was that many people there saw existing Christian missions as being exclusively concerned with the 'not yet', the salvation of the soul in the life hereafter, and that little was done for the pressing needs of the present life, the 'here and now' problems addressed by Pentecostals and independent churches.

In their mission and evangelism, Pentecostals proclaim a pragmatic gospel and seek to address practical needs like sickness, poverty, unemployment, loneliness, evil spirits and sorcery. In varying degrees, Pentecostals in their many and varied forms, and precisely because of their inherent flexibility, attain a contextual character which enables them to offer answers to some of the fundamental questions asked by people. A sympathetic approach to local life and culture and the retention of certain popular religious practices are undoubtedly major reasons for their attraction, especially for those overwhelmed by urbanization with its transition from a personal rural society to an impersonal urban one. Healing, guidance, protection from evil and success and prosperity are some of the practical benefits offered to faithful members of Pentecostal and Charismatic churches. These churches have stimulated mission and evangelism in a postcolonial age and in the face of anti-proselytism, while many other Christian churches have lost faith in these activities and are in a state of serious (some think terminal) decline. All this does not say that Pentecostals and Charismatics provide all

---

[34] Neuman, 'Cultic Origins', 49–51, 54.

the right answers, a pattern to be emulated in all respects, nor to say that they have nothing to learn from other Christians. But the enormous and unparalleled contribution made by Pentecostals and Charismatics independently has altered the face of world Christianity irrevocably and has enriched the universal church in its ongoing task of proclaiming the gospel of Christ by proclamation and demonstration.

12

The Bible and the 'full gospel'

PENTECOSTALS AND THE BIBLE

To understand Pentecostal theology properly we also need to understand how Pentecostals and Charismatics read the Bible, which they acknowledge universally as the source of their theology. For most Pentecostals and Charismatics, theology is inseparable from the Bible in which they find their central message. Although identifying to a great extent with the 'evangelical' position on biblical authority, most Pentecostals are not usually preoccupied with polemical issues like the unity and inspiration of the Bible and other theological niceties. Their purpose in reading the Bible is to find there something that can be experienced as relevant to their felt needs. Archer points out that, from the beginning, Pentecostals like the Holiness groups from which many of them emerged read the Bible with 'a thoroughly popularistic, pre-critical, text-centred approach'. They believe in 'plenary relevance', that the Bible contains all the answers to human questions and must simply be read, believed and obeyed.[1]

Some insight into hermeneutical processes can be gained by the work of Latin American liberation theologians. Severino Croatto outlines three aspects of the discipline of hermeneutics, which is not only concerned with the 'privileged locus' of the interpretation of *texts* (the first aspect), but must also take into account that 'all interpreters condition their reading of a text by a kind of *preunderstanding* arising from their own life context' (the second aspect). For him the third aspect is equally important: 'the interpreter *enlarges* the *meaning* of the text being interpreted'.[2] Carlos Mesters says that when 'common people' (such as most Pentecostals) read the Bible, a 'dislocation' occurs and 'emphasis is not placed on the text's meaning *in itself* but rather on the meaning the text has *for the people*

---

[1] Kenneth J. Archer, 'Early Pentecostal Biblical Interpretation', *JPT* 18 (2001), 68; Wacker, *Heaven Below*, p. 71.
[2] Severino Croatto, *Biblical Hermeneutics* (New York: Orbis, 1987), p. 1 (emphases in original).

reading it'.[3] It is mainly in the West (particularly in the USA) where some Pentecostal academics have more closely identified themselves with a 'conservative evangelical' approach to the Bible. There, a greater emphasis is placed on 'correct' biblical hermeneutics (the 'right' interpretation of the Bible) and on written theology. But most Pentecostals rely on an experiential rather than a literal understanding of the Bible and it is therefore not very meaningful to discuss the interpretation of the text alone. Pentecostals believe in spiritual illumination, the experiential immediacy of the Holy Spirit who makes the Bible 'alive' and therefore different from any other book. They assign multiple meanings to the biblical text, preachers often assigning it 'deeper significance' that can only be perceived by the help of the Spirit. Much Pentecostal preaching throughout the world is illustrative of this principle, where narrative, illustration and testimony dominate the sermon content rather than esoteric and theoretical principles.

All Christians enlarge and condition the meaning of the Bible for themselves out of their own life context and experiences with their own inherent presuppositions. Pentecostals generally may be said to have a literalist or 'concordistic' approach to understanding the Christian message. This literalism, which sometimes confuses the Biblical past with the present, has resulted in unconventional expressions of Christianity, such as the snake handlers and poison drinkers in North America who base their practices upon a literal reading of the disputed ending of Mark 16 or the Pentecostal groups who take first century dress codes quite literally and legislate the same for their members (especially for women). This extreme literalism is quite consistent with Pentecostalism's roots in the Holiness and healing movements, where there tended to be the same literalistic, legalistic approach. But Pentecostalism cannot simply be equated with fundamentalism, as preachers constantly interplay Scripture with contemporary life and present the text as a reflection of common experience. Pentecostals may have a 'concordistic' approach in that they take the Bible as it is and look for common ground in real life situations. On finding these correspondences, they believe that God is speaking to them and can do the same things for them. The Bible therefore has immediacy and relevance to life experiences. Pentecostals focus on divine intervention in these daily life situations by constantly emphasizing the miraculous and unusual happenings in the community of the local church.[4]

---

[3] Carlos Mesters, 'The Use of the Bible in Christian Communities of the Common People', N. K. Gottwald and R. A. Horsley (eds.), *The Bible and Liberation* (New York: Orbis, 1993), p. 14 (emphases mine).

[4] Kenneth J. Archer, 'Pentecostal Hermeneutics: Retrospect and Prospect', *JPT* 8 (1996), 64; Suurmond, *Word and Spirit*, pp. 22–3.

Pentecostals and Charismatics usually interpret the Bible in a way that primarily makes use of the normal or customary understanding of the literal words. 'How does the Bible relate to our daily experiences?' is the implicit question behind Pentecostal hermeneutics. This is not slavish literalism – the Bible is not usually read in isolation from a real-life community or the concrete situation in the communities in which Pentecostals and Charismatics are found. Many, perhaps even the majority of Pentecostals are underprivileged workers, subsistence farmers or are unemployed and many are functionally illiterate. In keeping with a strong sense of community, Pentecostals in the Majority World usually read (or rather, *hear)* the Bible in the community of the faithful, during celebrations of communal worship, where it is often directly related to the real problems encountered by that community. This experiential interpretation of the Bible as it is prayed, sung, danced, prophesied and preached in the worship of Pentecostal churches implies an understanding of the Bible from the underside of society, where ordinary people, like people in the basic Christian communities of Brazil, have 'found the key and are beginning again to interpret the Bible . . . using the only tool they have at hand: their own lives, experiences, and struggles'.[5]

How Pentecostals read and interpret the Bible in their daily lives brings us to the third aspect of hermeneutics, the enlargement of the meaning of the text. I have heard Pentecostal and Charismatic preachers who will expound and harangue on one phrase of the Bible for over an hour (and keep the audience spellbound). Probably above all other considerations, the Bible is believed to contain answers for 'this-worldly' needs like sickness, poverty, hunger, oppression, unemployment, loneliness, evil spirits and sorcery. Throughout the world, Pentecostals and Charismatics will tell personal stories of healing, deliverance from evil powers, the restoration of broken marriages, success in work or in business ventures and other needs which are met, usually through what is seen as the miraculous intervention of God through his Spirit. All of these experiences are often backed up, either implicitly or explicitly, by scriptural support, or something that God had revealed. The Bible therefore becomes the source book of miraculous answers to human need as well as confirmation of the reality of 'supernatural' experience. Pentecostals and Charismatics do not separate their understanding of the gospel from their personal experience of the events the Bible describes. In their liturgy, the telling of stories or 'testimonies' is very important, where people are able to relate their experiences of divine intervention and preachers pepper their sermons with real life illustrations

---

[5] Mesters, 'Use of the Bible', p. 9.

in order that the congregation may further participate in the hermeneutical process and bring these experiences into daily life.

The characteristics of Pentecostal and Charismatic hermeneutics are diverse, because Pentecostals and Charismatics come to different conclusions on the meaning of Scripture, despite their formal confessions of faith. They are usually unaware of their own biases and limitations and sometimes have an inadequate hermeneutic for the application of biblical principles to moral issues. They have a pragmatic hermeneutics that selectively decides what parts of the Bible to take literally and then spiritualize or allegorize the rest. They also tend to exegete their experience in their testimonies, preaching and teaching. However, the strength of Pentecostal and Charismatic hermeneutics lies in the serious role it gives both the biblical text and the human experience. There is a distinctive Pentecostal hermeneutics where the role of the Spirit in human experience is an essential part of understanding the biblical text.[6]

THE 'FULL GOSPEL'

Pentecostals use the Bible to explain the central emphasis on the experience of the working of the Spirit with 'gifts of the Spirit', especially healing, exorcism, speaking in tongues and prophesying. The *charismata* of the Spirit are the proof that the gospel is true. However, we must remember that the 'full gospel' is essentially a Christological construct where Christ is centrally Saviour, Healer, Baptizer and Coming King. Pentecostals and Charismatics of all kinds understand this 'full gospel' to contain good news for all life's problems, particularly relevant in the societies of the developing world where disease is rife and access to adequate health care is very rare. 'Salvation' (sometimes called 'full salvation') is an all-embracing term, usually meaning a sense of well-being evidenced in freedom from sickness, poverty and misfortune as well as in deliverance from sin and evil. Healing from sickness and deliverance from evil powers are major themes in the lives of Pentecostals and are seen as part of the essence of the gospel. To support these practices they refer to Old Testament prophets, Christ himself and New Testament apostles who practised healing. In some African independent churches the healing offered to people usually relies heavily upon various symbols, especially sprinkling with holy water, a sacrament providing ritual purification and protection, but most Pentecostals and

---

[6] Gordon Fee, 'Hermeneutics and Historical Precedent: A Major Problem in Pentecostal Hermeneutics', Spittler, *Perspectives*, p. 122; Hollenweger, *Pentecostalism*, pp. 307–21.

Charismatics emphasize laying on of hands with prayer. Symbolic healing practices are also justified by the Bible, where Jesus used mud and spittle to heal a blind person, Peter used cloths to heal and Old Testament prophets used staffs, water and various other symbols to perform healing and miracles.[7]

The majority of people in the world are underprivileged and for them there are no or few state social benefits, which among other things means that efficient medical facilities are scarce and expensive. Sundkler, writing about 'Zionist' churches in South Africa, said that people receive their healing message as a 'gospel for the poor'.[8] Because people believe themselves to be healed, the gospel is seen as a potent remedy for their experience of affliction. Pentecostals and Charismatics relate the gospel directly to their troubles and the process of understanding the gospel essentially begins in the context of felt needs. The cosmology of many societies in the developing world is filled with fearsome and unpredictable occurrences demanding Christian answers. The gospel Pentecostals and Charismatics proclaim seeks to be relevant to life's totality and offers biblical deliverance from the real fear of evil, misfortune and affliction, which are compelling and universal human needs. This understanding of the gospel has to do with salvation from the experience of all evil forces ranged against people's existence. The methods used to receive this deliverance and the perceptions concerning the means of grace sometimes differ, but Pentecostals and Charismatics believe that their message reveals an omnipotent and compassionate God concerned with all the troubles of humankind. Bishops, pastors, prophets, ministers, evangelists and ordinary church members exercise the authority that they believe has been given them by the God of the Bible. Reinforced by the power of the Spirit, they announce the good news of deliverance from sin, sickness and barrenness, and from every conceivable form of evil, including social oppression, unemployment, poverty and sorcery.

The concept of liberation fundamentally affects the Pentecostal and Charismatic understanding of the gospel. In the context of the recent history of the colonized world, ordinary people themselves, without the help of white missionaries (who often represented oppressive former colonizing powers), discovered in the gospel their own freedom from bondage. Particularly since the comparatively recent translation of the Bible into the vernacular, people discovered the relevancy of the Bible, its ability to fulfil aspirations and meet needs and its application to issues often not addressed

[7] Anderson, *Zion and Pentecost*, pp. 137–41.   [8] Sundkler, *Bantu Prophets*, p. 223.

by western churches. Because of this, principal leaders of many African Pentecostal churches are seen as Moses figures, bringing their people out of slavery into the promised land, the new 'City of Zion'. Like the African slaves of the Americas, these Christians see the Exodus event as a deliverance from the old life of trouble, sickness, oppression, evil spirits, sorcery and poverty. In this understanding, it may be idealistic to suggest that paramount in the minds of these Pentecostals are issues of socio-economic or political liberation – this is usually implied rather than expressed. The profound holism of Africa does not allow its exclusion, although the dominant idea is one of religious or spiritual liberation. The new Israel incarnate in Africa is moving out of Egypt towards the new Jerusalem, the Zion of God, where all these troubles will be forgotten. The people of God are the members of this new African church that has been able to discover its promised land for itself. The concept of Zion on earth, the new Jerusalem, a holy place not in some far off foreign land at some distant time in the past, but present here and now, is a prominent theme.[9]

The 'full' or 'foursquare' gospel not only means that Jesus is 'Saviour' who saves people from sin, but also 'Healer' from sickness and deliverer of people from the power of Satan. To this soteriological and Christological emphasis is added a pneumatological and missiological dimension: Jesus Christ is 'Baptizer in the Holy Spirit' who empowers ordinary people to witness to the ends of the earth. To this is added a fourth, eschatological emphasis: Christ is the 'soon coming King' preparing the church for his rule. The 'full gospel' implies a reciprocal relationship between the Bible and the Spirit, for not only does the Bible explain the experience of the Spirit, but also perhaps more importantly, the experience of the Spirit enables people better to understand the Bible. The Holy Spirit is actually drawn in to the process.[10]

The Holy Spirit is the agent of healing and deliverance for Pentecostals and Charismatics. Most believe in divine healing (they usually prefer this term to 'faith healing') and few even admit their doubts concerning it. Pentecostal and Charismatic belief in healing is often based on testimonies of people who have themselves experienced healing and they see this as a direct intervening act of God. The contemporary healing practices did not originate in early Pentecostalism, as the doctrines of 'divine healing' and 'healing in the atonement' were already widespread in the nineteenth-century North American Holiness movement out of which Pentecostalism emerged and

---

[9] Anderson, *Zion and Pentecost*, pp. 141–2.   [10] Archer, 'Pentecostal Hermeneutics', p. 77.

the ideas also existed in early Methodism. The Holiness movement stressed the four elements of a 'full gospel' of salvation, healing, holiness and the Second Coming of Christ.[11] Early Pentecostals added another distinctive element, the baptism in the Holy Spirit, which they usually linked to speaking in tongues. Jesus Christ was declared to be 'Saviour, Healer, Baptizer and Soon Coming King' – to which the Holiness Pentecostals included 'Sanctifier'.

Although it is difficult to generalize about Pentecostal and Charismatic beliefs in such multifaceted movements, we have seen that most believe that the coming of the Spirit brings an ability to perform 'signs and wonders' in the name of Jesus Christ to accompany and authenticate the Christian message. The role of 'signs and wonders', particularly that of healing and miracles, has been prominent in Pentecostal and Charismatic praxis and reflection all over the world since its inception, and one of the most important emphases of its mission and outreach. Sickness, it was assumed, had its origins in the sin of humanity. At the beginning of the twentieth century, there was an expectation that 'signs and wonders' would accompany an outpouring of the Spirit and a belief that healing was linked to the work of Christ on the cross. Healings demonstrated Christ's victory over all forms of affliction, a holistic salvation that encompassed all of life's problems.[12] The presence of these 'signs and wonders' was the realization of the coming of the kingdom of God. For Pentecostals, the 'gifts of the Spirit', especially healing, exorcism, speaking in tongues and prophesying, are proof that the gospel is true and the 'full gospel' contains good news for all life's problems.

HEALING AND EXORCISM

Early Pentecostals stressed that healing was part of the provision of Christ in his atonement, again following a theme that had emerged in the Holiness movement based on such texts as Isaiah 53:4–5 and Matthew 8:16–17. Dayton considers the 'healing in the atonement' idea to have emerged 'largely as a radicalization of the Holiness doctrine of instantaneous sanctification in which the consequences of sin (i.e. disease) as well as sin itself are overcome in the Atonement and vanquished during this life'.[13]

---

[11] Dayton, *Theological Roots*, pp. 22, 115–41.
[12] McGee, 'Power From on High', p. 324; John Wimber and Kevin Springer, *Power Healing* (New York: HarperCollins, 1991), p. 37.
[13] Dayton, *Theological Roots*, pp. 127–30, 174.

British Pentecostal Harold Horton represented the vast majority of early Pentecostals who rejected 'modern medicine'. In his classic publication *The Gifts of the Spirit* (which first appeared in 1934) Horton speaks of 'gifts' of healing 'for the supernatural healing of diseases and infirmities without natural means of any sort'. He says that 'divine healing' is the 'only way' of healing open to believers and 'authorised by the Scriptures'.[14] Many Pentecostals have rejected the use of any medicine, traditional and modern, because its use is viewed as evidence of 'weak' faith. I am not convinced that the triumphs of medical science make alternative forms of healing redundant, as some would have us believe. For much of the world this expertise is largely out of reach and unaffordable. As Claudia Währisch-Oblau has observed in China, the need for healings in Christian ministry is in direct proportion to the unavailability of medical resources and the breakdown of the public health system. Prayer for healing is 'an act of desperation in circumstances where they see few alternative options'. She found that prayers for the sick and healing experiences were common to all the Chinese Protestant churches and that healings were considered 'normal' there.[15] Michael Bergunder shows the prominence of healing in the south Indian Pentecostal movement and my own work has demonstrated the central role of healing in most African 'Spirit' churches.[16] For people who believe themselves to be healed, the gospel is a potent remedy for their frequent experiences of affliction and is good news for suffering people.

Yonggi Cho's teaching on sickness and healing is typically Pentecostal. Physical healing is seen as part of Christ's redemption, sickness is 'from the devil' and a 'curse', and God wants all people healed. Like most Pentecostal preachers, Cho makes extensive use of personal experience or 'testimony' to illustrate his theology. This is particularly noticeable on the subject of healing, when Cho often refers to his own sicknesses and how he was healed, and gives testimonies of people healed during his ministry to them. Cho makes much of the experience of being 'born again' and all his books have a strong soteriological and Christocentric tone. His holistic view of

---

[14] Harold Horton, *The Gifts of the Spirit* (Nottingham: Assemblies of God Publishing House, 1976), pp. 99, 101.

[15] Claudia Währisch-Oblau, 'God Can Make us Healthy Through and Through: On Prayers for the Sick and Healing Experiences in Christian Churches in China and African Immigrant Congregations in Germany', *International Review of Mission* 90:356/357 (2001), 87–8, 94, 99.

[16] Michael Bergunder, 'Miracle Healing and Exorcism: The South Indian Pentecostal Movement in the Context of Popular Hinduism', *International Review of Mission* 90:356/357 (2001) 103–12; Anderson, *African Reformation*, pp. 290–304.

salvation is in common with Pentecostals all over the world and one of the reasons why the Pentecostal message has spread rapidly among people in great need.[17]

Pentecostals and Charismatics today, particularly in the western world, generally have greatly modified views on healing compared to those of their founders. They frequently resort to modern medicine and accept the validity of 'gradual' and 'natural' healing. Rather than declaring that divine healing is for all, most prefer, as Keith Warrington observes, 'to allow for the *possibility* of healing rather than hold to an unconditionally promised gift of healing for all believers'.[18] More credence is given to the idea that God sometimes chooses not to heal, that suffering is part of the divine economy, and more reflection on these and other issues has led to a more realistic and sensitive theology of healing, including a more nuanced view of 'healing in the atonement'. Warrington also points out that the ministry of a healing evangelist has largely given way to that of a corporate healing ministry in the church. This too is expressed in the recent ecumenical consultations, where the church is seen as a 'community in healing'.[19]

Before leaving the subject of healing, we must say a few words about the related controversial practice of deliverance from demons, or exorcism. This has always been a prominent part of Pentecostal and Charismatic praxis (especially in the Majority World), often conducted in the inner rooms and private counselling sessions of Pentecostal and Charismatic churches and exhibiting a wide variety of procedures. Most Pentecostals and Charismatics believe in the biblical position of a personal devil (Satan) and his messengers known as demons or evil spirits. The reality of this dark spirit world and the need for there to be a Christian solution of liberation from it is particularly pertinent in those parts of the world where the unseen forces of evil are believed to be so prevalent. Exorcism, or as it is better known in Pentecostalism, 'deliverance', is regarded as a continuation of the New Testament tradition and was a feature of the ministry of the healing evangelists (particularly William Branham) and those regarded as having a special gift of 'deliverance ministry'. Although its incidence in western Pentecostalism has probably declined, in some parts of the world it has

---

[17] Cho, *Salvation, Health*, pp. 115–56; David Yonggi Cho, *How Can I Be Healed?* (Seoul, Korea: Seoul Logos Co., 1999), pp. 15–20; Cho, *Successful Home Cell*, pp. 41–4.

[18] Keith Warrington, 'Healing and Exorcism: The Path to Wholeness', Keith Warrington (ed.), *Pentecostal Perspectives* (Carlisle: Paternoster, 1998), p. 149.

[19] E. Anthony Allen, 'What is the Church's Healing Ministry? Biblical and Global Perspectives', *International Review of Mission* 90:356/357 (2001), 50; Warrington, 'Healing and Exorcism', p. 151.

become a very prominent activity, such as in Ghana and other parts of West Africa, where 'prayer camps' have been set up specifically for the purpose of providing places for exorcism for victims of witchcraft.[20] There is no agreement as to whether Christians can be 'demonized', opinions being divided sharply on this question among Pentecostals and Charismatics. There are also differences about what constitutes 'demonization'. Some believe that every mishap and illness is the work of Satan or his evil spirits, while others attribute only certain types of mental illness to Satan. Another commonly-held practice related to exorcism is 'spiritual warfare', an intense prayer activity where it is believed (on the basis of Ephesians 6:12 and similar texts) that believers actively engage and resist the 'spiritual forces of wickedness' that take control of individuals, communities, cities and nations. During these times of intense prayer Pentecostals will sometimes fast for several days. In the western world, Peter Wagner and Charles Kraft, former Fuller Theological Seminary professors and 'Third Wave' proponents, have developed sophisticated theories behind the ministry of 'spiritual warfare' and it has also become the theme of some popular Christian fiction. These issues remain controversial and there is no agreement among Pentecostals and Charismatics about the details.[21]

The widely differing Pentecostal and Charismatic movements have important common features. Far from being expressions of escapist behaviour (as some have alleged), they proclaim and celebrate a salvation that encompasses all of life's experiences and afflictions, and they offer an empowerment providing a sense of dignity and a coping mechanism for life. This empowerment motivates their messengers to share this good news with as many people as possible. Thousands of preachers have emphasized the manifestation of divine power through healing, deliverance, prophecy, speaking in tongues and other Pentecostal phenomena. The message proclaimed by these charismatic preachers of receiving the power of the Spirit to meet human needs was welcome in societies where a lack of power was keenly felt on a daily basis. The main attraction of Pentecostalism in the Majority World is still the emphasis on healing and deliverance from evil. Preaching a message that promises solutions for present felt needs, the 'full gospel' of Pentecostal preachers is readily accepted. Pentecostals confront old views by declaring what they are convinced is a more powerful protection against sorcery and a more effective healing from sickness than either the existing churches or the traditional rituals had offered.

---

[20] Onyinah, 'Akan Witchcraft'.
[21] L. G. McClung, 'Exorcism', *NIDPCM*, pp. 624–8; Cox, *Fire*, pp. 281–7.

THE PENTECOSTAL GOSPEL AND CULTURE

The relationship between the gospel and culture, and by implication, the relationship between Christian faith and other faiths, is a much-debated topic, but one seldom discussed by Pentecostals. Lesslie Newbigin points out that every communication of the gospel is already culturally conditioned, but reminds us that the gospel 'is not an empty form into which everyone is free to pour his or her own content', but that the content of the gospel is 'Jesus Christ in the fullness of his ministry, death, and resurrection'.[22] Nevertheless, the expansion of the Pentecostal 'full gospel' all over the world can be partially attributed to cultural factors and the relevance of the encounter between the gospel and different cultural contexts cannot be minimized. Hollenweger sees the 'oral structures' of early Pentecostalism, like that of Christianity itself, to be the reason for its growth, and not any particular Pentecostal doctrine. His list of characteristics of these structures is well known: oral liturgy, narrative theology and witness, reconciliatory and participant community, the inclusion of visions and dreams in worship, and understanding the relationship between body and mind revealed in healing by prayer and liturgical dance.[23] He observes that these are also predominantly African cultural features, evident in the leadership of William Seymour, whose 'spirituality lay in his past'. Seymour's Pentecostal experience meant more than speaking in tongues and included loving in the face of hateful racism. Hollenweger elaborates on these oral structures in Pentecostal music and liturgy, pointing out that spontaneity and enthusiasm, rather than leading to an absence of liturgy, produce flexible oral liturgies memorized by the Pentecostal congregation. The most important element of these liturgies is the active participation of every member in the congregation. Pentecostal liturgy has social and revolutionary implications in that it empowers marginalized people. It takes as acceptable what ordinary people have to give in their worship of God and thereby overcomes the social barriers of race, status and education. This for Hollenweger demonstrates the pervading and continuing influence of the Azusa Street revival upon early Pentecostalism and upon later forms of the movement, especially in the Third World where the majority of Pentecostal adherents now live.[24]

A central conviction of this book is that Pentecostalism is both fundamentally and dominantly a Third World phenomenon. The Pentecostal

---

[22] Lesslie Newbigin, *The Gospel in a Pluralist Society* (London: SPCK, 1989), pp. 142, 152–3.
[23] Hollenweger, 'Black Roots', pp. 36–43.   [24] Hollenweger, *Pentecostalism*, pp. 269–71, 274–5.

emphasis on 'freedom in the Spirit' has rendered the movements inherently flexible in different cultural and social contexts. This has made the transplanting of their central tenets in the Majority World and among marginalized minorities in the western world more easily assimilated. Several scholars have attested to this. Sepúlveda writes that the reason for the dynamic expansion of Pentecostalism in Chile is to be found in its ability 'to translate the Protestant message into the forms of expression of the local popular culture'.[25] Harvey Cox declares that the great strength of what he terms the 'Pentecostal impulse' lies in 'its power to combine, its aptitude for the language, the music, the cultural artefacts, the religious tropes . . . of the setting in which it lives'.[26] This was quite different from the prevailing ethos at the beginning of the twentieth century. Many older missionary churches arose in western contexts of set liturgies, culturally conditioned theologies, highly educated, rationalistic and professional clergy, and patterns of church structures and leadership with strongly centralized control. These factors often contributed to the feeling that these churches were 'foreign' and that people first had to become westerners before becoming Christians. In contrast, Pentecostalism's emphasis on immediate personal experience of God's power by his Spirit was more intuitive and emotional, and it recognized charismatic leadership and inculturated church patterns wherever they arose. In most cases, leadership was not kept long in the hands of western missionaries and the proportion of missionaries to church members was usually much lower than that of the older missions. By preaching a message that promised solutions for present felt needs like sickness and the fear of evil spirits, Pentecostal and Charismatic preachers (who were most often local people) were heeded and their 'full gospel' readily accepted. Churches were rapidly planted in different cultures and each culture took on its own particular local expression of global Pentecostalism.

Based on the spiritual freedom of Pentecostal pneumatology and his insider analysis of Chilean Pentecostalism, Sepúlveda suggests a 'broader definition' of the term 'Pentecostal' that emphasizes its ability to incarnate the gospel in different cultural forms. This contrasts with the fixed and limited definition of white US American classical Pentecostalism, which differs from Chilean Pentecostalism on several significant fronts.[27] Similarly, the AICs are mostly churches of a Pentecostal type that have contextualized

---

[25] Sepúlveda, 'Indigenous Pentecostalism', p. 111.
[26] Cox, *Fire*, p. 259.   [27] Sepúlveda, 'Indigenous Pentecostalism', p. 111.

and inculturated Christianity in Africa. They are an African expression of worldwide Pentecostalism because of both their Pentecostal style and their origins. I have argued for the recognition of African 'Spirit' churches as Pentecostal movements because of their emphasis and experience of the Spirit, and the same could be argued for many Pentecostal-like churches all over the world that do not conform to a western pattern. Pentecostalism in Asia too is clearly quite different from western Pentecostalism and has taken on distinct, culturally relevant forms in Asian societies, using symbols and modes of expression familiar to these peoples. In Majority World Pentecostalism, experience and practice are usually more important than the preciseness of dogma.

In their attempt to apply scientific principles to human cultures and languages, theologians have often assumed that there is somehow a pure 'Message' that is free of cultural constraints and that when the 'purity' of the gospel is affected in some way by cultural adaptations the result is 'syncretism'. This word is often used in a negative way to suggest that the 'gospel' has somehow been corrupted by the culture. But as Sepúlveda points out, 'the concern for preserving the "purity" of the Gospel has always been stronger than the desire to incarnate (or "inculturate") the Gospel in a particular situation'. He says, 'we cannot grasp any meaning without the help of our precious cultural categories', and so '"purity" is not given to us. Some sort of syncretism is inevitable'.[28] And as Yong observes, a fear of 'syncretism' has resulted in Pentecostals importing 'a western brand of Christian spirituality and religiousness into their local arena'.[29]

Some writers have suggested that Korean Pentecostalism has been successful because it has combined Christianity with 'huge chunks of indigenous Korean shamanism', to quote Harvey Cox. Although many different factors account for the remarkable growth of Pentecostal and Charismatic movements in Korea, Cox has suggested two underlying factors: 'for any religion to grow in today's world it must possess two capabilities: it must be able to include and transform at least certain elements of pre-existing religions which still retain a strong grip on the cultural subconscious' and 'it must also equip people to live in rapidly changing societies'. He says that these two 'key ingredients' are found in Korean Pentecostalism. Cox sees Pentecostalism as 'helping people recover vital elements in their culture that

---

[28] Juan Sepúlveda, 'To Overcome the Fear of Syncretism: A Latin American Perspective', Lynne Price, Juan Sepúlveda and Graeme Smith (eds.), *Mission Matters* (Frankfurt am Main: Peter Lang, 1997), p. 167.
[29] Yong, 'Not Knowing', 81.

are threatened by modernization'.[30] However, this view is highly controversial for Korean Pentecostal leaders themselves, who reject the idea that there is any 'shamanism' in their practices and oppose divination and shamanism, like Pentecostals all over the world do. There is certainly no conscious syncretism between Christianity and shamanism in Pentecostalism, but because a shamanistic background pervades Korean society and underlies all religious expressions, both shamanism and Pentecostalism acknowledge and address needs arising from the Korean spirit world. Similarly, conservative Protestant Christianity with its strict moral laws and male domination finds fertile ground in Korean Confucianism. Perhaps it is better to consider Pentecostalism as a culturally contextual form of Korean Christianity interacting with and confronting shamanism; both continuity and discontinuity with the old religion are kept in creative tension. Korea also has the phenomenon of mass urbanization and the Pentecostal and Charismatic churches have provided places of spiritual security and personal communities for people unsettled by the rapid social changes.

The 'gospel and culture' debate in Pentecostalism is well demonstrated by Latin America, where social scientists in particular have given relevant insights to the topic. One of the first outside observers of Chilean Pentecostalism, Lalive D'Epinay saw the movement as a *Haven of the Masses*, reproducing much of the closeness and authoritarian *patron* (landowner) relationships of the *hacienda* (rural agricultural settlements) and appealing especially to the exploited classes who had moved to the cities and were in unstable employment. It represented the transplanting of popular Catholicism into the urban environment and would eventually decline, he maintained.[31] A variation on this view is that Pentecostals were better able to adapt to the urban environment and had made their converts more easily feel at home. Chilean theologian Cristián Parker says that Pentecostalism is a response by 'the peasant sectors' marginalized by the processes of rapid urbanization and technological advance. He supports Richard Niebuhr's thesis that 'sects' (in which he includes Pentecostals and 'Afro-American cults') arise 'in consequence of the deprivation in which economically dominated groups find themselves'.[32] This 'relative deprivation' argument emphasizing external social factors has been a common theme among sociologists and tends to be reductionist. It does not take

---

[30] Cox, *Fire*, pp. 219–22, 224, 228.
[31] Christian Lalive D'Epinay, *Haven of the Masses: A Study of the Pentecostal Movement in Chile* (London: Lutterworth, 1969).
[32] Cristián Parker, *Popular Religion and Modernization in Latin America* (New York: Orbis, 1996), pp. 143, 155.

into sufficient account the numerous exceptions to this process (especially in other parts of the world where Pentecostalism is growing), nor does it acknowledge internal religious and cultural reasons for the growth of Pentecostal and Charismatic movements. Furthermore, the early observers predicted that Pentecostal and Charismatic churches would stop growing in Latin America, but the opposite has been the case.

Both the older Protestant missions and official Catholicism were in many respects anti-cultural, but Pentecostalism is seen as more contextualized than any other form of Christianity. David Martin explains that Pentecostalism expanded in Brazil during a time of rapid population growth and urbanization. Because it was 'fully indigenous' it was 'able to provide an all-encompassing world-view for marginalized people'. It offered 'the fruits of honesty and thrift and a surrogate family, as well as the chance of participation, and a sense of worth, meaning and empowerment'.[33] Pentecostalism has grown among people immersed in popular (not priestly) Catholicism, which has in effect been a preparation for its easier acceptance. That is to say, that even though Pentecostalism was originally mediated in Latin America through foreign agents like Hoover and Francescon, Vingren and Berg, its acceptance by the masses was because of a predilection, a propensity for the religious experiences it offered. Cox surveys differing interpretations of the growth of Latin American Pentecostalism and quotes Brazilian sociologist Francisco Cartaxo Rolim, who sees Pentecostalism as caused by Latin America's class conflict, a movement of popular symbolic protest that 'provides unmediated access to God and healing that comes from prayer' and not from the numerous accretions that accompany folk Catholicism, Pentecostalism's 'staging ground'. Rolim believes that Pentecostalism, just like popular Catholicism, is a form of protest movement against religion controlled by an educated, often foreign elite.[34]

The relationship between Pentecostalism and culture has been examined by Juan Sepúlveda, a Pentecostal theologian in Santiago, whose doctoral research considered the question of the 'indigenisation' of Pentecostalism in Latin America. Sepúlveda says that Chilean Pentecostalism, one of the earliest expressions of the movement in the world to arise independently of North American Pentecostalism, is an expression of 'indigenous Christianity'. Its origins in and separation from Methodism were at least partly the result of a 'cultural clash' between an 'official' culture and a 'popular' culture and that internal factors rather than external social factors resulted in its dynamic growth. In particular, Chilean Pentecostalism was able to

[33] Martin, *Tongues of Fire*, p. 65.   [34] Cox, *Fire*, pp. 177–80.

translate its message into the forms of popular Chilean culture and to spread among the poor masses. Sepúlveda's view reinforces our contention that Pentecostalism's ability to adapt to any cultural and religious context is one of its main strengths. Earlier 'conspiracy' theories about Latin American Pentecostalism as a form of US American imperialism to counterbalance liberation theology have given way to a recognition of the opposite: that Latin American Pentecostalism, especially in Chile, is of local origin and independent development from the USA. Sepúlveda traces the history of Chilean Pentecostalism from this perspective, suggesting that the secession from the Methodist Church occurred because it was primarily a cultural conflict. The 'clash of cultures' was first, between the foreign religiosity of 'objective' dogma versus the local religiosity giving 'primacy to the subjective experience of God'; and second, between a religion mediated through 'specialists of the cultured classes' (the clergy) and a religion with direct access to God for ordinary people communicated through the feelings in the local culture. Sepúlveda illustrates the clash in the difference between the 'official', foreign culture (educated, rational, modern) of the US American Methodists and the 'popular', local culture ('uncultivated', oral, traditional) of the Chilean revivalists. The clash within the Methodist church caused the separation of the Pentecostals, despite Hoover's protestations that he was not creating a national (independent) church. Chilean Pentecostalism's ability to translate the Protestant message into the forms of expression of the local popular culture is shown by the use of nationals in leadership and ministry, and by a dynamic of both confrontation and continuity with popular culture. Both popular *forms* and *meanings* are preserved in Pentecostalism, and in this way it has become an 'incarnation' of the gospel in the culture of the *mestizo* (mixed race Amerindian and European) lower classes. Sepúlveda discusses whether the differences in Chilean Pentecostalism from North American 'classical' Pentecostalism (infant baptism, speaking in tongues seen as one among many gifts, frequent identification of Spirit baptism with experience of conversion, etc.) mean that Chilean Pentecostalism is not truly Pentecostal, as some have suggested. He points to Chilean Pentecostalism's emphasis on the Pentecostal experience of Acts 2 and says that Pentecostalism should be more broadly defined. The rediscovery of pneumatology by modern Pentecostalism results in 'the spiritual freedom to incarnate the gospel anew into the diverse cultures' and means that 'God can and wants to speak to peoples today through cultural mediations other than those of Western Christianity'. The division in Methodism in Chile in 1910 forced the early Pentecostal movement to rely on leadership by Chilean nationals reared in popular Catholicism. The Pentecostal movement was therefore more able to adapt to the prevailing culture. Even the dominant open-air meetings of the movement adapt the traditional practices of religion in the plaza and the use of processionals (while rejecting overtly Catholic practices). Pentecostals process from the plazas to their places of worship, singing songs to the tunes of the music of the masses accompanied by guitars and tambourines. But sometimes a counter-culture is created, an example of which is the IEP, which under Hoover's influence rejected the use of popular music as a 'concession to the world'.[35]

Walter Hollenweger supports the idea that Chilean Pentecostalism was not a theological but a cultural clash, and was 'a valid expression of indigenous popular religion', while the Methodist Church, by cutting itself off from what it considered to be 'anti-Methodist and irrational', also 'cut itself off from the very soil in which a Methodist Church in Chile could grow'. The Pentecostal revival enabled people to become 'liturgically and theologically active on the level of and with the means of their own culture'. The revival lay firmly within the Methodist tradition, a reappearance of the spirituality of Methodism's past – although the missionary leaders denied this. Hollenweger discusses the impact of this autochthonous Christianity upon the ecumenical movement, particularly the 'uneasiness' that western 'historical churches' have with autochthonous Pentecostalism's free and spontaneous liturgy.[36]

The determination of Pentecostals to make a break between the religious specialists (the clergy) and the religious consumers (the laity) symbolically defies a classist society and provides a new identity to those who have been oppressed within an accepting community in the Pentecostal congregation. This experience is then transmitted through narrative and testimony in forms that ordinary people can understand. Andrew Chesnut sees the growth of Pentecostalism in Brazil primarily as a result of its message of healing, which had particular appeal to the victims of poverty-induced illness.[37] But as Cox observes, in all the different interpretations of the causes for the growth of Pentecostals, few will admit 'with Saint Peter' that it is 'evidence of the activity of the Spirit'.[38] This theological, or pneumatological factor is a major reason, perhaps the main reason, for Pentecostalism's growth throughout the world. Although we must acknowledge sociological

---

[35] Sepúlveda, 'Indigenous Pentecostalism', pp. 112–15, 118, 120, 124–33.
[36] Hollenweger, *Pentecostalism*, pp. 117, 124, 126–31.
[37] Chesnut, *Born Again*, p. 168.   [38] Cox, *Fire*, pp. 163–7, 171–4, 177–8.

factors as relevant to the growth and acceptance of Pentecostalism among different peoples, we must see this primarily as Christian revivalist movements that rely on the Holy Spirit to offer holistic and contextual 'here and now' answers in the name of Christ to fundamental problems encountered by people in everyday life.

13

Pentecostal education and ecumenism

PENTECOSTALS AND ACADEMIC THEOLOGY

Most early Pentecostal leaders and some of the most successful Pentecostal and Charismatic pastors in many parts of the world have been those with little or no theological education. In the 1960s, Swiss sociologist Lalive d'Epinay contrasted the remarkably successful Pentecostal pastors in Chile with little or no education and what he called the 'complete stagnation' of the Methodist and Presbyterian churches with their highly educated ministers. This made him 'less confident' in the benefits of theological education and the western training methods which were imposed on Protestants in developing nations and which were simply 'not suitable for the needs in Chile'.[1] Sepúlveda says that because US Protestant missionaries instituted theological education to avoid what they claimed were the 'excesses' and 'ignorant fanaticism' of Pentecostalism, Chilean Pentecostalism now had a 'strong anti-theological, anti-academic prejudice'.[2]

To qualify for Pentecostal and Charismatic leadership, the emphasis usually has been on the spirituality and call of the leader rather than on intellectual abilities or ministerial skills. We have seen how the first Pentecostal training college in Europe provided rudimentary training for missionary candidates, who simply had to have a good knowledge of the Bible and the doctrines of salvation and sanctification and to have 'received the Baptism of the Holy Ghost themselves'.[3] There was no shortage of applications and entrance requirements subsequently became more difficult, including a required two-year training period. More recently, in theological education offered outside their own institutions, Pentecostals and Charismatics

---

[1] Christian Lalive d'Epinay, 'The Training of Pastors and Theological Education: The Case of Chile', *International Review of Missions* 56: 222 (1967), 185, 191.
[2] Juan Sepúlveda, 'The Challenge for Theological Education from a Pentecostal Standpoint', *Ministerial Formation* 87 (1999), 29–30.
[3] *Confidence*, 2:6 (June 1909), p. 129.

often have had to deal with a liberal, modernist and pluralistic theological agenda that often seems to be diametrically opposed to Pentecostal and Charismatic spirituality and its frequent tendency towards exclusivity. A certain tension exists between academic integrity and spirituality, especially when education does not seem to further spirituality. As a result, there has been a tenuous relationship with theological education and Pentecostals have spoken of a 'dead intellectualism' that sometimes 'stifles the Spirit-filled life'.[4] The European university model that pervades education in western societies creates an educated elite that often loses touch with ordinary people. This has affected Pentecostals and Charismatics alike, where the clergy/ laity dichotomy that they shunned has been recreated through an emphasis on the need for a theological qualification before recognizing a calling and gifting for ministry. The doctrine of the 'priesthood of all believers' that spurred on early Pentecostals to great heights of mission and ministry has sometimes been lost in the academic process. Western models of theological education usually do not take much notice of the specific, local, religious, social and cultural contexts that dominate Pentecostal and Charismatic people throughout the rest of the world. Pentecostal leaders assume that leadership training will use western methodologies and they give little thought to understanding how the gospel might be communicated appropriately in different cultures. In the meantime the Third World contexts they live and work in are increasingly becoming globalized, multi-ethnic, pluralistic and urbanized.

However, Pentecostals probably do not exhibit the same enslavement to rationalistic theological correctness and cerebral Christianity that has plagued many of their contemporary Protestants and have not been as thoroughly immersed in western theology and ideology as their counterparts have. Most early Pentecostals suffered from a siege mentality because they were such a small minority and shunned universities. This was to be expected when the European university model that pervades education in western cultures created ivory towers of an educated elite that often had lost touch with ordinary people. Moreover, Pentecostal and Charismatic Bible schools sometimes nurtured a polemical and confrontational approach to academic theology and sought to preserve Pentecostal 'distinctives'. The problem is exacerbated when this approach is exported beyond the western world, is unrelated to Majority World contexts and overly reliant upon foreign personnel. This in turn creates a vicious circle where US American

---

[4] Klaus, 'National Leadership', p. 226.

'religious right' ideology and premillennial eschatological pessimism become 'orthodoxy' in Pentecostal institutions throughout the world. Pentecostal and Charismatic quietism in the face of oppressive regimes, racism and 'ethnic cleansing' is a disturbing feature of its recent history. Sometimes dominant foreign Pentecostal missions with insensitive and imperialistic attitudes have tended to stifle protest and constructive change. These problems are even further aggravated when newly educated Pentecostal pastors in the Majority World have become clones of western forms of theologizing and new initiatives in providing relevant theological education for their own contexts are very few and far between.

The significant changes occurring in attitudes to other Christians and other religions have been pioneered largely by a new generation of Pentecostal and Charismatic academics, where there has been a fundamental paradigm shift. Walter Hollenweger has played an enormously important role by leading the way in this seismic change. He is an example of the 'post-Pentecostal' phenomenon, where he has become an intellectual leader in 'mainline' church theology. His own experience of the tensions between Pentecostalism and the academy led to his resignation from the Swiss Pentecostal Mission and his becoming a theological student in Zürich. Later becoming a Reformed minister, he was subsequently involved in the WCC and ecumenism. His doctoral research on Pentecostalism in the 1960s resulted in a ten-volume encyclopaedic work in German that has never been equalled. More than any other person, Hollenweger was responsible for the gradual recognition in the western academic world of the importance of studies in Pentecostalism and the beginning of serious academic research undertaken by Pentecostals themselves. He has in effect been the creator of an academic discipline and the foremost authority in Pentecostal Studies for four decades. Hollenweger pioneered postgraduate education in Pentecostal Studies and 'intercultural theology' at the University of Birmingham, England from the 1970s onwards, and his graduates were among the leading academics representing the new paradigm shift. Hollenweger himself traces the changes from a disdain for academic theology to the emergence of Pentecostal academics who must be listened to. Most Pentecostals perceived of academic scholarship as anti-spiritual, and their Bible Schools produced a 'crude rationalism' and 'form of fundamentalism'. But theologians from 'mainline' churches themselves exhibited ignorance of Pentecostalism, until recently regarding the subject as 'exotic'. Hollenweger thinks that this is 'probably because its strongest side is its oral theology', which western rationalists cannot easily relate to.

The intellectual climate within Pentecostalism has now changed to include questions of race, the socio-political potential of Pentecostal origins and critical exegesis. Hollenweger says that by putting resources together Christians might solve some of the problems that have plagued the western churches for a long time and discover in the process 'that it is possible to speak in tongues and be a critical scholar'.[5] A significant event occurred in March 2003, when the Walter Hollenweger Centre for Pentecostal Studies was opened at the Free University of Amsterdam. The principal of Azusa Theologische Hogeschool (the former Dutch Pentecostal college), a Hollenweger graduate and Dutch Pentecostal historian, Cornelis van der Laan, became the first Professor of Pentecostalism at a European university. Pentecostal Studies now has a higher profile in several leading European universities than it had during Hollenweger's time, when he often seemed to be a lone voice crying in a theological wilderness.

The role played by academic societies is very significant, not only in their contribution to the promotion of scholarly research in Pentecostal Studies (particularly through their annual meetings and journals), but also in their contribution to ecumenical dialogue. This is especially the case with the Society for Pentecostal Studies, founded at the meeting of the Pentecostal World Conference in Dallas in 1970. Originally a forum for the emerging classical Pentecostal scholars in the USA, SPS has expanded to include members from all over the world (although predominantly US American) and from many denominations, including 'post-Pentecostals'. In 1979 the SPS journal *Pneuma* was launched, the first academic journal solely devoted to Pentecostal Studies, now subscribed to by academic institutions globally and published by a leading academic publisher in Leiden in the Netherlands. Catholic scholars have been involved in SPS almost since its beginning, three of whom have been elected President of the society, Peter Hocken (1986) and Ralph del Colle (2002) and Anthea Butler (2004). The last two Executive Secretaries of the SPS (1989–2003) have been a Catholic (Hocken) and an Episcopalian (Faupel). Although its relationships with classical Pentecostal denominations are sometimes strained and always ambivalent, SPS has become a significant pressure group for change and ecumenical encounter in these denominations. It has encouraged the participation of African American, Hispanic, Oneness Pentecostal and international scholars, and is the first and one of the only places where

[5] Hollenweger, *Pentecostalism*, pp. 195–9, 204–14; Lynne Price, *Theology Out of Place: A Theological Biography of Walter J. Hollenweger* (London and New York: Sheffield Academic Press, 2002), pp. 7–11.

meaningful dialogue between Trinitarian and Oneness Pentecostals takes place. SPS has been followed by other academic societies in different parts of the world, the most notable being the Asian Society for Pentecostal Studies, which has a journal *Asian Journal of Pentecostal Studies* published from the Philippines since 1998 and an annual meeting. Another important journal was launched in 1992 called the *Journal of Pentecostal Theology*, published in England and edited by CGC theologians in the USA. These and other journals have served a similar function to *Pneuma* in promoting quality academic discourse on the Pentecostal and Charismatic movements.

Leading Pentecostal theologians are now suggesting that Pentecostal theology in the twenty-first century needs to be a 'contextual' theology that gives voices to the different forms of Pentecostalism to strengthen and critique the global Pentecostal community. Contextualization assumes that every theology is influenced by its particular context, and must be so if it is to be relevant. It relates the Christian message to all contexts and cultures. The rise of particular 'contextual theologies' like 'liberation theology' in Latin America, 'Black theology' in the USA and South Africa, and 'Minjung theology' in Korea was not met with the same sense of alarm among Pentecostals as was the case among western evangelicals. The fear that this new trend in theology would lead to 'syncretism' and the placing of culture above God's revelation in the Bible did not grip interested Pentecostals in the same way. Many of them, like the Relevant Pentecostal Witness during the South African apartheid regime, were fully in sympathy with the sentiments of the 'contextual' theologians, for they suffered from the same socio-political problems that plagued their sisters and brothers.

Fundamental problems still have to be overcome in Pentecostal and Charismatic theological education. There are flaws in the structures of their Bible schools, partly because they are still western models foisted onto the rest of the world and legacies of the colonial past with its cultural imperialism and ethnocentrism. Pentecostal missionaries from the West thought they knew what kind of training people needed in Africa, Asia and Latin America in order to become ministers after their own model. The alliance between Evangelicalism and white classical Pentecostalism in the NAE in the USA from 1943 onwards had a profound effect on Pentecostal theological education, which was drawn into the evangelical-ecumenical dichotomy pervading evangelical Christianity. Pentecostal training institutions became vulnerable to losing their distinctive experience-oriented spirituality, as evangelical and fundamentalist models of education were bought into wholesale and uncritically. Henry Lederle points out:

It is an irony of recent ecclesiastical history that much of Pentecostal scholarship has sought to align itself so closely with the rationalistic heritage of American Fundamentalism . . . without fully recognizing how hostile these theological views are to Pentecostal and Charismatic convictions about present-day prophecy, healing miracles and other spiritual charisms.[6]

Pentecostal Bible colleges became prime generators of this new Pentecostal fundamentalism and western denominations gave priority to exporting this theological education to the rest of the world. The AG in the USA has been in the forefront of this trend, with half its missionaries and half the budget of the Missions Department committed to theological institutions by 1959.[7] The question is whether this new emphasis was at the expense of spirituality. The rest of the world suffered from this great malaise in theological education, as missionary educators from the West unconsciously shared their presuppositions, paradigms and theological prejudices in the Majority World. Hwa Yung points out that the many theological institutions that had sprung up all over Asia were conditioned by the methodologies, agenda and content of western theology.[8] But this conditioning has not only disturbed the Majority World; western Pentecostalism itself has lost something as a result. Del Tarr speaks of 'the erosion of the sense of the supernatural' and 'the eclipse of the experiential dimension of the Christian faith'. The emphasis on rationalism in western theology led to an 'indifferent attitude towards spiritual experience and power'.[9] This had a profound effect upon Christians in the Majority World for whom this dimension was so vital.

The independence of India in 1949 began a domino-like fall of colonies culminating with South Africa in 1994. The end of colonialism gave rise to a new and strident nationalism and more recently, a new continentalism that emphasizes human dignity. The emergence of an 'Asian Pentecostal theology' is one example of the changing scenario; Pentecostal and Charismatic churches are developing their own theological paradigms that challenge and transform churches throughout the world. Fundamental questions are being asked about the nature of Pentecostal and Charismatic theological education, and SPS devoted its 2001 annual meeting to this theme. The western church in particular, as Cheryl Johns observes, 'has lost sight of the

---

[6] Henry I. Lederle, 'Pentecostals and Ecumenical Theological Education', *Ministerial Formation* 80 (January 1998), 46.

[7] Benjamin Sun, 'Assemblies of God Theological Education in Asia Pacific: A Reflection', *AJPS* 3:2 (July 2000), 230.

[8] Hwa Yung, 'Critical Issues Facing Theological Education in Asia', *Transformation* (October–December 1995), 1.

[9] Del Tarr, 'Transcendence, Immanence, and the Emerging Pentecostal Academy', Ma and Menzies, *Pentecostalism in Context*, pp. 195–222, 206–7.

pedagogical role of the Holy Spirit', but the Pentecostal experience is the 'epistemological key' that 'radically alters traditional forms of theological education'.[10] One of the most important features of this 'spiritual' model of education is total dependency on the Spirit of God. Pentecostals and Charismatics must affirm that the Spirit makes and equips teachers, is an active participant in their development and is the one who enables them to change in a changing world.

CO-OPERATION AND ECUMENISM

The early Pentecostals called themselves the 'Apostolic Faith' and in spite of the implied criticism of established churches, participants in this movement of the Spirit believed that it would sweep over the entire church. William Seymour, in the first issue of *Apostolic Faith* stated that the movement stood for 'Christian unity everywhere'. However, Frank Bartleman saw the erection of a sign 'Apostolic Faith Mission' at Azusa Street as a sign of creating division, a 'party spirit', and declared:

There can be no divisions in a true Pentecost. To formulate a separate body is but to advertise our failure, as a people of God. It proves to the world that we cannot get along together, rather than causing them to believe in our salvation. . . . No wonder the opposition steadily increased from the churches. We had been called to bless and serve the whole 'body of Christ', everywhere. Christ is one and His 'body' can be but 'one'. To divide it is but to destroy it . . .[11]

Such strong ecumenical convictions abounded in the early years. Early Pentecostal figures such as W. F. Carothers, T. B. Barratt and Alexander Boddy were pioneers in ecumenical contacts. Founder of the ICFG, Aimee Semple McPherson, dedicated her Angelus Temple to 'the cause of interdenominational and worldwide evangelism'. These Pentecostals saw unity as *spiritual, invisible* unity and did not initially place emphasis on unity of doctrine; creeds were often regarded as divisive. But Pentecostal denominations developed in isolation from other Christians (and even other Pentecostals) during the first forty years of their existence. The older churches viewed them with various degrees of disdain, amusement and opposition, because Pentecostalism attracted only the economically and culturally deprived classes – or so they thought. The more Pentecostals were marginalized, the more exclusivist they became and the less they had to do with other Christians.

---

[10] Cheryl Bridges Johns, 'The Meaning of Pentecost for Theological Education', *Ministerial Formation* 87 (October 1999), 42.
[11] Bartleman, *Azusa Street*, pp. 68–9.

As Robeck points out, the Pentecostal movement split in less than a century into 'nearly as many different divisions as it took the rest of the church a millennium to produce', and as a result has not lived up to its ecumenical potential.[12]

This changed when white Trinitarian Pentecostal churches in the USA were invited to become members of the NAE in 1943. The AG and the CGC joined this organization, set up in opposition to the ecumenical movement and 'liberalism' within established Protestant churches. With origins in the fundamentalism that had opposed early Pentecostals, the NAE had done an about swing and welcomed them into its midst. From this time on, the main white US Pentecostal denominations were increasingly seen as fundamentalist. Thomas Zimmerman, general superintendent of the AG, became president of the NAE in 1960 and the AG became a bastion of conservative evangelicalism. The 1963 General Council of the AG condemned the WCC as forerunner of 'the Scarlet Woman or Religious Babylon of Revelation'.[13] New Pentecostal and 'Third Wave' denominations emerged in the 1980s and called themselves 'conservative evangelical'.

Nevertheless, Pentecostal Trinitarian denominations began to see the need for worldwide co-operation among themselves. The first Pentecostal World Conference was held in Zürich, Switzerland in 1947 for 3,000 Pentecostal leaders. The second conference was held in Paris in 1949, when leaders came from thirty different countries. Subsequent conferences were held every three years, where Pentecostals were kept in touch with each other and appraised of the latest developments worldwide. The Pentecostal Fellowship of North America was formed in 1948 but excluded both African American and Oneness Pentecostals. This was disbanded in Memphis in 1994, when the Pentecostal/ Charismatic Churches of North America was formed with African American Bishop Ithiel Clemmons of COGIC as Chairperson. Black Pentecostals were now included but Oneness Pentecostals still left out and the interests of Hispanic Pentecostals (the fastest growing sector of US Pentecostalism) were underrepresented.

The entrance of Pentecostalism into older churches in the form of the Charismatic Movement had a more direct impact and ecumenical theologians started to pay attention to positive factors they saw. In 1953, Bishop

---

[12] Cecil M. Robeck, Jr. 'Pentecostals and the Apostolic Faith: Implications for Ecumenism', *Pneuma* 9:1 (1987), 61–8; Robeck, 'Pentecostals and Ecumenism in a Pluralistic World', Dempster, Klaus and Petersen, *The Globalization of Pentecostalism*, pp. 341–2; Veli-Matti Kärkkäinen, *Spiritus Ubi Vult Spirat: Pneumatology in Roman Catholic-Pentecostal Dialogue 1972–1989* (Helsinki: Luther-Agricola-Society, 1998), pp. 64–5.

[13] Steve Durasoff, *Bright Wind of the Spirit: Pentecostalism Today* (London: Hodder and Stoughton, 1972), pp. 87, 99.

Lesslie Newbigin, then Director of the WCC's Division of World Mission and Evangelism and bishop in the Church of South India, recognized Pentecostalism as a 'third stream' alongside Protestantism and Catholicism. Pentecostalism's emphasis was spiritual vitality and should be welcomed by Protestants and Catholics.[14] In 1957 at the IMC assembly in Ghana, John MacKay spoke of the great contribution of the Pentecostal denominations to the cause of mission. But by this time white Pentecostals in the USA were firmly ensconced as 'Evangelicals' who saw themselves in diametrical polarity to 'Ecumenicals' like those in the WCC, and doctrinal agreement with other Evangelicals became increasingly important as a result. Robeck thinks that this new relationship with the NAE, in spite of many positive benefits, was also costly and involved compromise. Pentecostals surrendered a commitment to pacifism, social concern and women's ministry in order to be more acceptable to their evangelical partners.[15] Attempts at ecumenical co-operation and dialogue by people like Donald Gee, David du Plessis and Robeck himself became more difficult and have been largely the work of individuals who have been misunderstood and misrepresented by the denominational Pentecostals of which they are a part.

But this polarity was not always the case. Hollenweger, a dedicated ecumenist himself, points out the ecumenical significance of early Pentecostalism. His monumental study of Pentecostal scholarship, *Pentecostalism: Origins and Developments Worldwide*, has as its main theme the roots of Pentecostalism in almost every conceivable Christian tradition. Because Pentecostalism has Black oral roots, Catholic (and Methodist), evangelical, ecumenical and critical (liberal) roots, there is great potential for ecumenical participation. After showing the ecumenical and reconciliatory nature of William Seymour's ministry at Azusa Street, Hollenweger shows that Pentecostalism began as an ecumenical renewal movement, especially in Europe. He illustrates this with several short biographies. Jonathan Paul, pioneer of Pentecostalism in Germany and former Lutheran pastor, maintained infant baptism together with believer's baptism in his Mülheim Association, he rejected the view of 'initial evidence', worked together with Charismatics in the Lutheran church and even produced the first modern German translation of the New Testament. Louis Dallière was a French Reformed pastor involved in the beginnings of Pentecostalism in France and Belgium. He practised immersion baptism of believers (without rejecting infant baptism) and was founder of the charismatic Union de Prière

---

[14] Lesslie Newbigin, *The Household of God* (London: SCM, 1953), p. 30.
[15] Robeck, 'Pentecostals and the Apostolic Faith', pp. 70–1.

(Prayer Union) within the Reformed Church. But he was 'removed from Pentecostal historiography' because he did not 'come out' of his church and was at variance with the attempts to establish Pentecostal denominations in France, which he saw as sectarianism. Alexander Boddy, an Anglican vicar who practised infant baptism to the end of his life, was 'the unchallenged pioneer' of the early Pentecostal movement in Britain for many years. A lawyer and geographer in his own right, Boddy edited the monthly Pentecostal periodical *Confidence* for eighteen years (1908–26), and hosted annual Whitsun conferences which were ecumenical gatherings of Pentecostal believers. He too was unhappy about the rise of the Pentecostal denominations in Britain in the mid-1920s. Early Pentecostalism in Britain and in many other countries was more like the Charismatic movement within the established churches from the 1960s onwards. The growing gulf between both Dallière and Boddy and the Pentecostal movement was also a social one. Dallière was a refined middle class pastor and Boddy an 'aristocrat' and Anglican clergyman who supported the British war effort, while most early Pentecostals were working class people and conscientious objectors. Gerrit Polman, founder of the Dutch Pentecostal movement, said that the purpose of the Pentecostal revival was 'not to build up a church, but to build up all churches', although his ecumenical vision failed. Other early Pentecostals who demonstrated this ecumenism included Barratt, Durham and Donald Gee, who in the face of opposition from fellow Pentecostals encouraged contact with the ecumenical movement and said that 'the complete answer to modernism is not fundamentalism, but Pentecost in all its fullness'. David du Plessis, better known as 'Mr Pentecost' in ecumenical circles, was the unofficial roving ambassador to 'mainline' churches in the West for Pentecostalism, for which he was 'disfellowshipped' from the AG for eighteen years.

Hollenweger outlines 'four phases of ecumenical development' in Pentecostalism, each phase taking about twenty-five years: (1) the beginning as an ecumenical movement breaking barriers of denomination, race, education and class; (2) locally organized congregations that accept the thought forms of their evangelical antagonists; (3) 'a group of highly clericalized new denominations' are formed; and (4) a return to the 'ecumenical root' with dialogue between Pentecostals, Catholics and ecumenicals. Hollenweger thinks that the ecumenical momentum of the Charismatic Renewal has more recently been dissipated in the move towards separatism in the creation of new Charismatic and 'Third Wave' churches, but says that the ecumenical movement itself is becoming institutionalized and does not have much time for those, like Pentecostals, who will not toe the party line.

Enormous numbers of Latin American Pentecostals are underrepresented in the WCC, but Pentecostals increasingly participate in this organization, which shows more interest in Pentecostals and Charismatics, especially since 1980. The first two Pentecostal churches (from Brazil and Chile) entered the WCC in 1968 and South American Pentecostals have taken the lead in initiating ecumenical contacts.[16] It appears as if Majority World Pentecostals have far fewer 'hang-ups' when it comes to ecumenism than their western counterparts have.

PENTECOSTAL DIALOGUE

In chapter eight of this book we traced the development of the Catholic Charismatic movement, considerably facilitated by Pope John XXIII (who talked of a 'new Pentecost') and the Second Vatican Council, which propagated a renewed emphasis on the gifts and graces of the Spirit. The Charismatics in 'mainline' churches grew from about 4 million in 1970 to 140 million in 1990, the majority being Catholics. Because of this significant movement (one of the strongest sections of the Catholic church) and the fact that it is often an ecumenical fellowship, dialogue with classical Pentecostals has been the consequence, initiated at first by the Pentecostals. Catholic Charismatics accept the Pentecostal experience without its doctrinal formulations. Hollenweger sees the enormous ecumenical implications, particularly as the Catholic Charismatic Movement has developed its own 'ecumenical momentum'.[17]

The first preliminary meetings between a group of Pentecostal leaders (without official sanction from their denominations) and the Catholic Secretariat for Promoting Christian Unity took place in 1970. Since then, there have been four quinquennia (over five year periods), the last taking seven years and ending in 1997. Hollenweger considers the Catholic/Pentecostal dialogue to be 'one of the most important events in the religious scene of our century', in spite of the fact that it was resisted by US classical Pentecostal denominations. He thinks that the four quinquennia suffered from an inadequate critique over the Catholic doctrine of infallibility, a lack of Third World participation and encounter with the oral Pentecostal tradition, insensitivity on the part of the hierarchy, and a too 'evangelical' view of the sacraments by Pentecostal participants. The dialogue has been extensively

---

[16] Hollenweger, *Pentecostalism*, pp. 20, 334–62, 365–6, 369, 370, 377–87; Kilian McDonnell, 'The International Classical Pentecostal/ Roman Catholic Dialogue', *Pneuma* 17:2 (1995), 167.

[17] Hollenweger, *Pentecostalism*, pp. 154–63.

reported on in various issues of the SPS journal *Pneuma* and other journals, several doctoral theses have been written on it, and it is the subject of two books by Finnish Pentecostal theologian, Veli-Matti Kärkkäinen. Because the Pentecostal participants in the dialogue were unauthorized (unlike the Catholics), they were represented at most individual churches, and their churches could reject, tolerate or support the Final Reports in whole or in part.[18] The limited acceptance of the dialogue by Pentecostal leaders has been a major drawback.

Although, as we have seen, Pentecostal contact with the ecumenical movement associated with the WCC has been occurring since the 1950s and Pentecostal involvement in WCC assemblies since New Delhi in 1961, dialogue between the two has been less developed than the Catholic/ Pentecostal dialogue. Part of the reason for this has been the dominance of Evangelicalism in western Pentecostalism and the commonly held belief that the WCC, besides representing the dreaded 'liberal' and 'liberation' theologies (and worse, possibly a sign of the 'apostasy' in the end times!), was a human organization that did not represent true spiritual unity. Some suggest that Pentecostals have more in common with Catholics than with this part of the ecumenical movement. Nevertheless, the WCC and its affiliated organizations have taken a sustained interest in the ecumenical significance of Pentecostalism, a few Pentecostal denominations are members of the WCC and many are in national councils of churches. Most recently, the Korean Assemblies of God has joined the national council, and its current chairman (2003) is a Pentecostal pastor. In the Canberra assembly of the WCC in 1991, the assembly theme 'Come Holy Spirit – Renew the Whole Creation' and the special workgroup on 'Pentecostal and Charismatic Movements' made the participation of Pentecostals particularly important. Seemingly, they were under-represented there, but Section 3 of the Canberra report entitled 'Spirit of Unity – Reconcile Your People' was extremely significant, especially the ten recommendations, outlined by Catholic observer Jeffrey Gros:

1) recovery of the New Testament sense of the Holy Spirit's gifts by all Christians; 2) churches deepen their teaching on the Trinity and the Holy Spirit; 3) WCC recognizes Pentecostal churches and congregations within the rich diversity of the development of Christian history; 4) WCC churches challenged to recognize the appropriateness, if not the universal prerequisite, of the Pentecostal experience in the lives of those touched by it; 5) WCC foster relations between the Pentecostal

---

[18] Veli-Matti Kärkkäinen, *Ad Ultimum Terrae: Evangelization, Proselytism and Common Witness in the Roman Catholic Pentecostal Dialogue 1990–1997* (Frankfurt am Main: Peter Lang, 1999), p. 50, 55; Hollenweger, *Pentecostalism*, pp. 165–80.

movement and other Christians; 6) study the diversity within the Pentecostal movement; 7) foster dialogue between Third World and North Atlantic Pentecostals, with their different ecumenical experiences; 8) WCC invite Pentecostals into all of its programs; 9) Pentecostal theologians be invited more deeply into the Faith and Order movement; and, 10) WCC worship seek to incorporate Pentecostal styles and leadership.[19]

This amounted to an important shift in WCC relationships with Pentecostals. Gros considers this report to have achieved a substantive change in the programmes and attitude of the WCC but that much change needs to take place as far as some of the Pentecostal leaders are concerned. Perhaps even more significantly, the WCC itself seems to have shifted its self-understanding from one of seeing itself as *the* ecumenical movement to the realization that it is only one part of a much larger 'Ecumenical Movement'.[20] The mutual interest and dialogue between Pentecostals and the WCC continues. In preparation for the conference of the Commission for World Mission and Evangelism in 2005, the WCC has initiated several consultations on faith and healing with a significant number of Pentecostal and Charismatic participants from various parts of the world. In one of these consultations in Accra, Ghana in December 2002, a local committee dominated by representatives of the Church of Pentecost hosted the consultation and Pentecostals and Charismatics formed a majority. There are also dialogue meetings taking place regularly between classical Pentecostals and the WCC. These various meetings have brought about a closer understanding between the WCC and Pentecostalism and a greater willingness to co-operate further.

There have been other significant events in the recent history of Pentecostal ecumenism in the USA. In 1993, dialogue between Black and Hispanic Pentecostals began in New York. One of the most important events was the so-called 'Memphis Miracle' of 1994, when in Memphis, Tennessee the all-white Pentecostal Fellowship of North America dissolved itself and was replaced by the Pentecostal/ Charismatic Churches of North America, governed by six white Americans and six African Americans. It adopted as its first resolution a 'Racial Reconciliation Manifesto' entitled 'Pentecostal Partners' in which were contained specific statements supporting further ecumenism. In a penetrating article, Robeck suggests that Pentecostals who do not engage in ecumenical activities and who ignore other Christians are 'arrogant, self-serving and condescending', are in danger of being involved

---

[19] Jeffrey Gros, 'Toward a Dialogue of Conversion: The Pentecostal, Evangelical and Conciliar Movements', *Pneuma* 17:2 (1995), 192–4.
[20] Robeck, 'Pentecostals and Ecumenism', p. 348.

in both sectarianism and proselytism, and 'run an enormous risk of becoming just like their oppressors when they move into majority status', especially in areas like Latin America and Africa.[21]

Identity is both a very important prelude to and an indispensable part of ecumenical commitment. We have to admit in the debate about the definition of 'Pentecostal' and 'Pentecostalism' that it cannot be prescribed. Here we follow Robert Anderson, who observes that whereas western classical Pentecostals usually define themselves in terms of the *doctrine* of 'initial evidence', Pentecostalism is more correctly seen in a much broader context as a movement concerned primarily with the *experience* of the working of the Holy Spirit and the *practice* of spiritual gifts. Kärkkäinen points out that to define Pentecostal identity in terms of doctrine is 'too narrow an approach for Pentecostalism with its accent in spirituality and experience rather than in discursive theology'.[22] A few years ago, Robeck observed that Pentecostals had not resolved the problem of identity and did not agree as to what constituted a 'Pentecostal,' and that this hindered Pentecostals from being truly ecumenical.[23] Adopting an inclusive definition of 'Pentecostal/ Charismatic' will maximize the opportunities for ecumenism.

For several years, scholars have pointed to the ecumenical significance and nature of Pentecostalism. Robeck has been the leading Pentecostal scholar to do this, pointing out that Pentecostals are ecumenical but that they 'just don't know it' and 'are choosy about their ecumenical partners'.[24] Hollenweger insists that the founders of Pentecostalism believed in the international and ecumenical nature of their Pentecostal experience and that the creation of innumerable Pentecostal denominations was contrary to that nature.[25] If we see ecumenism as primarily visible and organizational, then Hollenweger is indeed right. It is true that Pentecostalism's approach to Christian unity has not been at all helpful. Peter Hocken writes

---

[21] David D. Daniels, 'Dialogue between Black and Hispanic Pentecostal Scholars: A Report and Some Personal Observations', *Pneuma* 17:2 (1995), 219; Frank D. Macchia, 'From Azusa to Memphis: Evaluation of the Racial Reconciliation Dialogue among Pentecostals', *Pneuma* 17:2 (1995), 203, 211; Robeck, 'Pentecostals and Ecumenism, pp. 351–4.

[22] Kärkkäinen, *Spiritus*, p. 50.

[23] Cecil M. Robeck, Jr., 'A Pentecostal Theology for a New Millenium', Paper at the 26th Annual Meeting of the Society for Pentecostal Studies, Oakland, California (1997), p. 3.

[24] Cecil M. Robeck, Jr., 'Taking Stock of Pentecostalism: The Personal Reflections of a Retiring Editor', *Pneuma* 15:1 (1993), 39, 44.

[25] Hollenweger, *Pentecostalism*, pp. 334–8, 343–5.

of the unity of the Spirit in the early Charismatic movement, which has been overtaken by divisiveness 'dampening ecumenical optimism'.[26] But the rigid exclusivism that is part of the nature of some forms of Pentecostal and Charismatic self-awareness may be a bigger problem. Pentecostalism is both ecumenical and multicultural, and that is why Pentecostal understanding of who they are is so important to ecumenism. Macchia says that 'perhaps the greatest weakness of classical Pentecostalism has been its failure to realize its potential for ecumenical diversity'.[27] If we are to acknowledge this 'ecumenical diversity' potential, then we should also recognize that this multifaceted movement has as its unifying characteristic an emphasis on the present-day working of the Spirit in the church. The experiences of the Spirit, or what Amos Yong calls the 'pneumatological imagination' is that which exists in Catholic and Protestant Charismatics, classical Pentecostals, neo-Pentecostals, Third Wavers and independent and so-called 'indigenous' Pentecostal-like churches in Africa, Asia and Latin America.[28] This creates tremendous potential for ecumenical co-operation across the divides, as long as the definition remains broad enough to accommodate differences. The Catholic-Pentecostal dialogue began with an agreement in 1970 that the 'Essence of Pentecostalism' was 'the personal and direct awareness and experiencing of the indwelling of the Holy Spirit by which the risen and glorified Christ is revealed and the believer is empowered to witness and worship'.[29] Agreeing on these basics will bring many Christians together. Yong also argues for such a broad understanding, saying that 'the presence and activity of the Holy Spirit' is 'central to Pentecostal-charismatic spirituality' and that the 'essence' of the Pentecostal-charismatic experience is 'the doctrinal symbol of Spirit-baptism'. He interprets 'Spirit-baptism' broadly to include 'a wide range of phenomena, many of which would occur in any Pentecostal-charismatic experience of Spirit-baptism, but none of which would transpire in all of them', and Yong thereby embraces the many diverse forms of 'Pentecostalism'.[30] Macchia says that the Pentecostal experience of *glossolalia* has ecumenical implications, urging him to come out of 'the closet of my Pentecostal piety' to 'discover "Pentecostalism" in

---

[26] Peter Hocken, *The Glory and the Shame: Reflections on the 20th Century Outpouring of the Holy Spirit* (Guildford, UK: Eagle, 1994), p. 73.

[27] Frank D. Macchia, 'The Struggle for Global Witness: Shifting Paradigms in Pentecostal Theology', Dempster, Klaus and Petersen, *Globalization of Pentecostalism*, p. 25.

[28] Amos Yong, *Discerning the Spirit(s): A Pentecostal-Charismatic Contribution to Christian Theology of Religions* (Sheffield Academic Press, 2000), p. 161.

[29] Kilian McDonnell, 'Five Defining Issues: The International Classical Pentecostal/ Roman Catholic Dialogue', *Pneuma* 17:2 (1995), 178; Kärkkäinen, *Spiritus*, pp. 50–1.

[30] Yong, *Discerning the Spirit(s)*, pp. 161, 168–9.

communions other than my own, especially in ways unfamiliar to me'.[31] If the terms 'Pentecostal' and 'Charismatic' are best understood as referring to those movements with an emphasis on the experience of the power of the Holy Spirit with accompanying diverse manifestations of the imminent presence of God, the recognition of the unifying experiences of the Spirit has enormous scope for genuine ecumenical co-operation.

PENTECOSTAL FUNDAMENTALISM

In various parts of the world, Pentecostalism has absorbed various areas of its cultural context, sometimes with very undesirable results. Sometimes identification with fundamentalism limits the freedom of ecumenical understanding. Cox's more serious criticisms of Pentecostalism in his own country are particularly sobering; for some of the traps into which US Pentecostalism has fallen have been exported to other parts of the world. Cox sees Pentecostalism as the fulfilment of the human longing for a direct experience of God and not to be preoccupied with 'abstract religious ideas'. For this reason, Pentecostals are quite unlike fundamentalists, who are 'text-oriented believers'. He contrasts the otherworldliness of early Pentecostals with the this-worldliness of some US Pentecostals, particularly manifested in the 'prosperity gospel'. The early rebellion against creeds has given way to dogmatism and the 'techniques of raptures' have replaced the original message of 'signs and wonders' as a portent of the coming kingdom of God. He shows the changes from pacifists to 'super-patriots' and from a race- and gender-inclusive fellowship to white male dominated denominationalism, and suggests that Pentecostals might be facing a dilemma they may not be able to survive without betraying their origins.[32] These are very perceptive observations that classical Pentecostals need to heed.

Some have done so in various ways. Fuller Seminary and AG theologian Russell Spittler refers to the television scandals of 1987–93 and shows how journalistic jargon used the terms 'evangelical', 'fundamentalist', 'charismatic' and 'Pentecostal' interchangeably.[33] This confusion has also affected theological assessments of Pentecostalism. British theologian Martyn Percy, for example, makes a very wide definition and thinks that John Wimber is

---

[31] Frank D. Macchia, 'The Tongues of Pentecost: The Promise and Challenge of Pentecostal/ Roman Catholic Dialogue', Paper at the 25th Annual Meeting of the Society for Pentecostal Studies, Toronto, Canada (1996), p. 22.

[32] Cox, *Fire*, pp. 5, 15–17.

[33] Russell P. Spittler, 'Are Pentecostals and Charismatics Fundamentalists? A Review of American Uses of these Categories', Karla Poewe (ed.), *Charismatic Christianity as a Global Culture* (Columbia, SC: University of South Carolina Press, 1994), p. 103.

'a pre-eminent contemporary fundamentalist in the "revivalist tradition"', and that Wimber's appeal to 'power' to authenticate his message is characteristic of this tradition. Percy's analysis seems to lack an appreciation of the difference between experiential Christianity (the Pentecostal/Charismatic emphasis) and the more rational, reactionary fundamentalism from which it can be clearly distinguished.[34] Spittler observes that fundamentalism was an intellectual, apologetic, 'argumentative, logical, rational' reaction. In contrast, Pentecostalism 'profoundly distrusted the intellectual enterprise' and focused on 'withered piety', 'collapsed feeling' and 'the decay of devotion'. Instead of arguing about creeds, Pentecostals give testimonies of their experiences. Fundamentalists united in condemning Pentecostalism in 1928, when resolutions by the 'World's Christian Fundamentals Association' said that the 'tongues movement' was 'a menace in many churches and a real injury to the sane testimony of Fundamentalist Christians'. Because of this, they declared that they were:

. . . unreservedly opposed to Modern Pentecostalism, including the speaking in unknown tongues, and the fanatical healing known as general healing in the atonement, and the perpetuation of the miraculous sign-healing of Jesus and His apostles'.[35]

This was clearly and unambiguously anti-Pentecostal. Nevertheless, because many of the early North American (white) Pentecostals came from churches that later became fundamentalist, Pentecostalism was profoundly influenced by fundamentalism. Significantly, Spittler suggests that it is probably in other continents and cultures (where no such identification with fundamentalism exists) that a 'purer Pentecostal theology' might be seen.[36]

Pentecostalism therefore has predated fundamentalism and is essentially different from it. It brought a new *experience* rather than an argument against theological liberalism. Fundamentalism was one of Pentecostalism's harshest critics and it is therefore better seen as a 'fraternal twin' of liberalism and its 'logical end'. In a presidential address to the SPS in 1992, Faupel pointed out that the early Pentecostal critique was directed at 'an emerging fundamentalism'. Subsequent US Pentecostal history was to reverse this early critique and through the creation of Pentecostal Bible colleges, fundamentalism began to shape the movement. Faupel says that seeing Pentecostalism as a 'subgroup of Evangelicalism' is a major concern.

---

[34] Martyn Percy, *Words, Wonders and Power: Understanding Contemporary Christian Fundamentalism and Revivalism* (London: SPCK, 1996), p. 13; Spittler, 'Are Pentecostals Fundamentalists', p. 107.
[35] Cited in Spittler, 'Are Pentecostals Fundamentalists', pp. 108–9.
[36] Ibid., p. 112.

It would result in the movement becoming 'increasingly rationalistic and sterile', being more concerned about correct belief than about a deepening relationship with God and a silencing of the voices of women.[37]

Cox discusses the clash between scientific modernity and traditional religion during the past three centuries 'over the privilege of being the ultimate source of meaning and value', which had resulted in 'an exhausted stalemate'. He points out that although fundamentalists claim to be faithful to the traditions of the past, they are in fact 'all modern by-products of the religious crisis of the twentieth century'. He says that fundamentalism leads to inevitable conflict, but that experientialism takes many forms 'unified by a common effort to restore "experience" . . . as the key dimension of faith'. He says that the struggle between fundamentalists and experientialists is being played out in Pentecostalism. He gives examples of this struggle and the divisions it causes and says that Pentecostals will have to give a much clearer definition of 'experience'. He sees the key to this being in speaking in tongues. But they also need to define 'Spirit', for 'the *experience* they testified to was an encounter with a Spirit who has a purpose not just for them but for the whole world'.[38]

We have underlined the importance of Pentecostal experience over and against that dogmatic rationalism that thinks it has solutions or biblical texts for every problem. Expressed soteriology and lived soteriology are not the same – 'salvation' means different things to different Pentecostal people. The *theory* of Pentecostal soteriology is based on the experience of regeneration or conversion, but this too has different interpretations among Pentecostals, as does the doctrine of sanctification. The experience of salvation has, in different contexts, to do with the liberating experience of becoming human.

---

[37] D. William Faupel, 'Whither Pentecostalism?' *Pneuma* 15:1 (1993), 21, 24, 26–7.
[38] Cox, *Fire*, pp. 71, 299–300, 302–6, 309–11, 313, 315–17, 320.

14

Pentecostals and Charismatics in society

SOCIO-POLITICAL CONCERNS

Pentecostals have not always felt comfortable with relating to the wider society, but this is something that is gradually changing. The history and theology of Pentecostalism certainly makes room for engagement with society, especially because of the freedom brought about by the Pentecostal experience. One of the results of the experience of the Spirit is what I term a 'Pentecostal theology of liberation'. On issues of discrimination or equality on the basis of race, class or gender, Pentecostals and Charismatics have sometimes led the way, but they have also faltered between extremes and capitulated to the prevailing society. Pentecostals have been accused of a spirituality that withdraws from 'worldly' issues like politics and the struggle for liberation and justice, and of proclaiming a gospel that either spiritualizes or individualizes social problems. The result, some say, has been a 'pie in the sky' approach that has encouraged accepting present oppressive conditions or has led to the 'health and wealth' gospel that makes material gain a spiritual virtue.

The dichotomization of church and state into 'secular' and 'spiritual' spheres has continued in recent years. On the basis of Paul's teaching in Romans 13 and related New Testament passages, Presbyterian Charismatic theologian J. Rodman Williams is typical of this approach. He advocates unqualified subjection to all 'civil governments', but that Christians should also be active citizens, be in political office, and serve in the military in a 'just war' (while loving the enemy!). However, the ambiguity of Williams' position and that of many conservative Christians becomes clear when he allows for certain circumstances where civil disobedience is appropriate because of a 'higher loyalty' to God.[1] Actually, the tendency of Pentecostals and Charismatics to fuse the spiritual and the physical in a holistic whole

---

[1] J. Rodman Williams, *Renewal Theology (3): The Church, the Kingdom, and Last Things* (Grand Rapids, MI: Zondervan, 1992), pp. 273, 277, 281–3.

often leads to involvement in social issues. The aspirations for political office show themselves in different and contrasting ways. In the USA, some Pentecostals and Charismatics supported the 'religious right' during the Reagan years and Pat Robertson, a Charismatic Baptist, was a leading contender for the right-wing Republican presidential nomination in 1988. AG Chairman Thomas Trask in 2003 declared that John Ashcroft, Attorney General in George W. Bush's administration was the denomination's 'favourite son'. There have been serious criticisms of the 'prosperity gospel' propagated by certain sections of the Pentecostal and Charismatic movements throughout the world and the so-called 'Americanization' of global Christianity, where it is claimed that the Bible was being used to further economic and political ends. Pentecostals have also been accused of being representatives of colonialism and obstacles to liberation. But the Pentecostal and Charismatic approach to socio-political issues is actually much more complicated and ambiguously involved than these stereotypes suggest. In Chile for example, we have seen how some Pentecostal leaders actively supported the oppressive regime of military dictator Augusto Pinochet, while most ordinary members had socialist sympathies. Benedito da Silva, a black Pentecostal socialist politician in Brazil, is an example of the potential of Pentecostal spirituality in the transformation of oppressive structures. In 1986 da Silva, an AG member, was the first African Brazilian woman to be elected to the national congress and since 2002 she has been a minister in the socialist (Workers Party) government of President Luís Iñácio da Silva ('Lula'). Although she is the exception rather than the rule, Latin American Pentecostals are playing an increasingly important political role and becoming a force for social transformation throughout the region. This seriously challenges the stereotype that all Pentecostals are politically conservative or 'apolitical'. In several West African nations Pentecostals and Charismatics have been an important part of the ruling president's support base. Pentecostals and Charismatics have played an active role in Zambian politics since the rise of 'born again' Charismatic President Frederick Chiluba in 1991 who declared Zambia a 'Christian nation', and Nevers Mumba, Vice President since 2002, is a Pentecostal preacher. In South Africa during the transition to democracy in the 1980s and early 1990s, while most white Pentecostals were still supporters of the apartheid structures, the majority of African Pentecostals (often in spite of the acquiescence of leaders) sympathized with the liberation movements and the African National Congress and some were practically involved in the liberation struggle.[2]

[2] Anderson, *Zion and Pentecost*, pp. 166–72; Paul Gifford, *Christianity and Politics in Doe's Liberia* (Cambridge University Press, 1993), pp. 210, 285.

But even when obvious support for oppressive structures is absent, Pentecostals generally have been regarded as having apolitical attitudes often accompanied by conservative political views and they have not been noted for their socio-political involvement – except for the wrong kind.[3] Political structures are often seen as evil and Pentecostals are exhorted to have nothing to do with them. For similar reasons, most early Pentecostals were also pacifists, believing that the First World War was the fulfilment of a prophecy about the restoration of the ten kingdoms of Rome and the final battle to precede the second coming of Christ. Early Pentecostal periodicals like *The Christian Evangel* and evangelistic preaching during this period carried frequent exhortations on this theme.[4] The danger with some forms of Christianity, Pentecostalism included, is that an emphasis on personal piety can become a sop for a lack of social conscience. Hispanic American Pentecostal theologian Eldin Villafañe points out:

While it is true that Pentecostalism has been recognized as a powerful force in evangelism, world missions, church growth and spirituality, it is equally true that their services and prophetic voices against sinful social structures and on behalf of social justice have been missing.[5]

Cox lists several characteristics of what he calls 'very unattractive political and theological currents' running through Pentecostalism in the USA and highlights in particular the use of tongues speech as 'performance' rather than 'as protest or as prophecy', the new emphasis on 'money – why you don't have enough and how to get more' (more simply put as the 'health-and-wealth gospel'), the theatrical 'glitz and glamour' which he thought had 'defaced the gospel' and the boasting about church growth statistics in what he calls 'a world-wide religious bandwagon'. Cox also discusses purveyors of a 'new demonology' and their 'obsession with demonic spirits and the powers of darkness'. He writes of the 'vivid strain of apocalyptic inventiveness' that 'runs through the popular imagination of millions of Americans', thinking that these ideas might be analogous to what is true of Pentecostalism in other parts of the world – 'absorbing the flotsam and shards of popular piety into their theology', which is Pentecostalism's 'most serious weakness as well as the source of its greatest strength'. This becomes a dangerous obsession when the new demonology is combined

---

[3] Cecil M. Robeck, Jr. 'Pentecostals and Social Ethics', *Pneuma* 9:2 (1987), 104.
[4] e.g. *The Christian Evangel* 'War! War!! War!!!', 54 (Findlay, OH, August 15, 1914), p. 1; 'Prophetic war horses sent out', 56 (August 29, 1914), p. 1; 'War- A fulfilment of prophecy', 65 (October 31, 1914), p. 1; Woodworth-Etter, *Signs& Wonders*, p. 228; Woodworth-Etter, *Holy Spirit*, pp. 249–59.
[5] Eldin Villafañe, *The Liberating Spirit: Towards an Hispanic American Pentecostal Social Ethic.* (Grand Rapids: Eerdmans, 1993), p. 202.

with US Pentecostals' participation in right wing politics. Thus Pentecostalism in the USA might 'lose touch completely with its humble origins and become the righteous spiritual ideology of an affluent middle class'.[6]

These criticisms indicate how Pentecostalism has in so many cases changed from being an 'apolitical' and 'otherworldly' movement to become a supporter of reactionary politics, not only in the USA, but in countries like Guatemala, Chile and South Africa, as the historical chapters have indicated. The reasons for this are complex and some of them can only be summarized here. Pentecostals sometimes cloud the differences between 'moral' issues like abortion and political ones, so that right-wing politicians are seen as having 'Christian values'. Included in this debate is the sensitive issue of 'gay rights', where Pentecostals generally agree with the conservative Christian opposition to homosexual practice. Charismatic Anglican bishops were among those opposed to the ordination of gay bishops in the furore of 2003. Another reason for this about-turn may be the courting of Pentecostals by wily politicians conscious of their emerging significance and perceived 'anti-ecumenical' (read, 'left-wing') stance. Pentecostals have also been influenced by an eschatology that in the past saw Communism (and later, radical Islam) as anti-Christian; they saw support for the state of Israel (and opposition for Palestine) as a biblical duty. Unfortunately, these views have tended to be shared mostly by the wealthy middle class and the political right, which fact has sat uncomfortably with those Pentecostals of more humble status.

All this betrays the ethos of the beginnings in an impoverished black mission at Azusa Street, which defied so many social mores of the time. Pentecostal roots in the socially active revivalist and Holiness movements of the nineteenth century resulted in a commitment by some early Pentecostals to the struggle for social transformation. But in the USA this soon changed. As Robert Anderson observes, although Pentecostalism was 'an oblique expression of social protest' and 'born of radical social discontent', as it became institutionalized it gradually withdrew from the social struggle. A movement designed to protest against the social system that marginalized and oppressed its members soon 'functioned in a way that perpetuated that very system'.[7] But unlike the situation in the USA, Third World Pentecostalism is not white middle class but predominantly a grassroots movement among the poor. Although until recently, Pentecostals have not been involved in much overt socio-political activity in the wider society (with exceptions in several countries), in their own communities there is

---

[6] Cox, *Fire*, pp. 264–75, 281–7, 297.   [7] R. M. Anderson, *Vision*, pp. 222, 229.

abundant evidence of social concern in the structures created for the welfare of members, as we shall see.

The idea that Pentecostals are 'apolitical' or even 'anti-political' was not borne out by my research among African Pentecostals in South Africa. In fact, white Pentecostals in South Africa were among the most politically conservative in the country, sometimes openly supporting right-wing organizations. Being 'political' (in a negative sense) in these circles in the early 1990s usually meant to have sympathy with the liberation struggle. But there was a contrasting political awareness among African Pentecostals that did not differ perceptibly from that of the rest of the African population and African Pentecostals could not be accused of being supporters of the status quo. Almost half of the Pentecostal respondents in a survey taken in 1991 said they would vote for Nelson Mandela and the African National Congress if the election had been held then, which did not differ significantly from the overall population in the research area. During interviews, the question 'Should the church or its members involve themselves in political matters?' revealed divided opinions. There was no clearly discernible pattern linking one or other church with a particular political stance. Many respondents felt that the church should be involved, as Jesus said we should be the salt of the earth and the light of the world. Others were just as adamant that the church should keep out of politics – mostly because the church leaders had said so and not for any particular reason. Some Pentecostals were concerned at the seeming lack of political awareness in their church and especially among their pastors, but notably, people expressed their political convictions quite freely during these interviews.[8]

To give another example from Korea, YFGC pastor Yonggi Cho refers to the years of suffering after the Korean War in most of his many popular books. This was the social context of the beginning of his ministry in the late 1950s, a very important part of his message and the foundation of the theology he developed for a despairing people. He refers to the sufferings of the Japanese occupation, the Korean War and his own poverty, and his gradual healing from tuberculosis. This was a time when many were 'struggling for existence', when he identified himself with the hundreds of refugees on the streets and became 'one of the hopeless'. He mentions the aftermath of the Korean War when people lost families and businesses, had mental breakdowns, and became 'completely possessed by the devil'.[9]

---

[8] Allan Anderson and Samuel Otwang, *Tumelo: The Faith of African Pentecostals in South Africa* (Pretoria: University of South Africa Press, 1993), pp. 58–60.

[9] Cho, *Fourth Dimension*, pp. 9–10, 14, 110; Cho, *Successful Home Cell*, p. 3; Allan Anderson, 'The Contribution of Cho Yonggi to a Contextual Theology in Korea', *JPT* 12:1 (2003).

His ministry began in a poverty-stricken area of suburban Seoul, where he himself was poor and where people were not interested in a message about heaven and hell as they struggled for daily survival. In this situation, the gospel had to be contextualized to meet the starkly desperate needs of the Korean people. Cho's teaching on healing was closely related to the poverty and sickness rampant at that time. His teaching on blessings and prosperity was his theological counteraction to the ravages of the Korean War. For Cho, the message of Christ and the power of the Holy Spirit was a present contextual message that gave hope to a suffering and destitute community. Most of his members in these early years were extremely poor.[10] His views on poverty are clear, again determined by his context:

Poverty is a curse from Satan. God desires that all His people prosper and be healthy as their soul prospers (3 John 1:2). Yet much of the world has not really seen poverty as I have seen it. Especially in the Third World, people live their lives in despair, struggling to survive for one more day. I am from the Third World. I know first-hand what it is not to have anything to eat.[11]

He writes that it is because of his 'oppressed background', that he has been able 'to understand the plight of many oppressed people who have no hope for a future'.[12] It is important to understand that Cho's views on poverty and prosperity come out of his own Korean context of poverty, Japanese occupation and the Korean War, and should not be interpreted within the context of western wealth and materialism. There are passages in Cho's writings that are theologically hard to swallow, such as his teaching that in the kingdom of God there is no poverty.[13] Cho has also been criticized as being unconcerned with social change and structures of oppression. The YFGC, however, has extensive social care programmes of its own and is involved in national relief and economic aid for North Korea. Although the Korean liberation theology known as *Minjung* theology has espoused the concerns of the poor and oppressed, it is to the Pentecostal churches that the poor and oppressed (the *minjung*) flock for relief.

There is an increasing awareness of the potential in Pentecostalism for a politically and socially relevant engagement, particularly because of its tendency to attract the marginalized and working class people. Pentecostal

---

[10] Jeong, 'Formation and Development', pp. 216, 225–7; Cho, *Fourth Dimension*, p. 172; Cho, *Solving Life's Problems*, p. 132; Cho, *Salvation, Health*, p. 11.
[11] Paul Yonggi Cho, *The Fourth Dimension, Volume 2* (South Plainfield, NJ: Bridge Publishing, 1983), pp. 137–8.
[12] David Yonggi Cho, *More than Numbers* (Waco, TX: Word Books, 1984), pp. 23–4.
[13] Cho, *Salvation, Health*, p. 68.

theologian Cheryl Bridges Johns expresses the hope 'that Pentecostalism can both retain and recapture its revolutionary nature as a movement which can change the course of history'. She asks whether it 'can be a catalyst for personal and social transformation'. She cites Brazilian sociologist Emilio Willems, who suggested that Pentecostalism in Latin America was a 'legitimate social protest' and that with its 'emphasis on lay leadership and its democratization of worship services, [it] exists as a classless society, subverting the traditional social order in the language of religious symbolism'.[14] The founder of the Brazilian Pentecostal denomination 'Brazil for Christ', Manoel de Mello, typified the change in approach saying, 'The gospel cannot be proclaimed fully without denouncing injustices committed by the powerful'.[15] These significant changes are to be welcomed, but many Pentecostal and Charismatic leaders still need to be convinced of the need to be more involved in social protest, and that this will not deflect them from their central 'spiritual' focus.

A PENTECOSTAL THEOLOGY OF LIBERATION

Some Pentecostal scholars see the origins of Pentecostalism as the basis for their insistence on the need for a Pentecostal theology of liberation. Cheryl Johns points out that the Wesleyan roots of Pentecostalism gave the movement 'a strong emphasis upon the transforming power of the Holy Spirit for both personal and social critique', while its roots in African American spirituality gave it 'an emphasis upon the liberating power of the Pentecostal experience and an emphasis upon the oral-narrative character of the gospel which involves active participation of everyone'.[16] Juan Sepúlveda shows the possibility of a dialogue between Pentecostalism and liberation theology by drawing attention to four factors common to Pentecostal and base ecclesial communities in Latin America: (1) their origins among the poorest and most excluded sectors of society; (2) a direct and intense encounter with God through the Holy Spirit, thus eliminating every kind of external priestly mediation resulting in either priestly or cultural domination; (3) the role of popular Bible reading, making the message of the Bible accessible to common people; and (4) the understanding of the church as a healing and missionary or priestly community, accompanied by the 'profound

---

[14] Cheryl Bridges Johns, *Pentecostal Formation: A Pedagogy Among the Oppressed* (Sheffield, UK: Sheffield Academic Press, 1993), pp. 9, 19, 58.

[15] Cited in Murray W. Dempster, 'Pentecostal Social Concern and the Biblical Mandate of Social Justice', *Pneuma* 9:2 (1987), 129.

[16] Johns, *Pentecostal Formation*, p. 108.

rediscovery of pneumatology, of the action of the Holy Spirit in the church and in the world'.[17]

South Africa provides a stark case study of the ambiguous role of politics in Pentecostalism. The rapid increase in urbanization and the socio-political oppression of black South Africans between 1960 and 1990 was one of the reasons for the remarkable growth of Pentecostal, 'Zion' and 'Apostolic' churches there during this period. The insecurities inherent in rapid urbanization provide strong incentives for people separated from their roots to seek new, culturally and socially meaningful religious expressions, especially in a society where there was no access to the instruments of social and political power. The increasing disillusionment experienced by black people in South Africa's political system resulted in many of them rejecting European values and religious expressions such as those found in 'mainline' churches. The apartheid government from 1948 adopted a policy of 'non-interference' in the affairs of black churches, which in effect meant encouraging the development of churches that were totally 'independent' of what were sometimes seen as troublesome mission churches. The government saw the development of these separate African churches, most of which were Pentecostal in orientation, as in complete harmony with apartheid ideology, which opposed any sort of social mixing, including integrated churches. These African churches may have gone through a process of progressive depoliticization. Most African church leaders generally took a 'neutral' stance and forbade their members active participation in structured political activities. During my research in the northern Pretoria satellite township of Soshanguve in 1991–95, there was certainly evidence of 'depoliticization' among some Pentecostals, but an even greater degree of political awareness was emerging among ordinary South Africans at that time after decades of press censorship, state propaganda, institutionalized violence and banned political organizations. It appeared that Pentecostals expressed their political convictions more by their participation in trade unions and civic associations than in structured political parties – although over half were also supporters of African nationalist organizations, especially the African National Congress. The political repercussions of the changing South Africa after 1980 were felt throughout Pentecostalism, manifested in agitation for united structures and equality of leadership opportunities. Most African Pentecostals, like all their compatriots in the violently abnormal apartheid society, struggled for recognition and survival, albeit

---

[17] Juan Sepúlveda, 'Pentecostalism and Liberation Theology: Two Manifestations of the Work of the Spirit for the Renewal of the Church', Hunter and Hocken, *All Together in One Place*, pp. 53, 56, 58, 60, 62.

passively. Frank Chikane is an example of the minority of South African Pentecostals who actively struggled against apartheid (see chapter 6). He has been the leading example of Pentecostal involvement in the struggle for justice in South Africa in the face of very difficult odds.[18] As a whole, however, the South African Pentecostal movement, in spite of its witness to spiritual freedom, acquiesced in the midst of the social evils. The original integration and fellowship was short-lived and black people were denied basic human rights in the very churches in which they had found 'freedom' in the Spirit. Many African Pentecostals silently withdrew to independent church movements or to their newfound Pentecostal 'spirituality' that remained 'otherworldly' for the most part. South African Pentecostalism has its roots in a marginalized and underprivileged society struggling to find dignity and identity. It expanded initially among oppressed African people who were neglected, misunderstood and deprived of anything but token leadership by their white Pentecostal 'masters', who had apparently ignored biblical concepts like the priesthood of all believers and the equality of all people in Christ. And yet the ability of Pentecostalism to adapt to and fulfil African religious aspirations was its main strength.

As several scholars have noted in the past, the Spirit of God brings a liberation that is holistic, not only in that which is confined to the 'spiritual' sphere. If freedom is always the result of receiving the Spirit, then true freedom or liberation is an integral part of Pentecostal experience. In studying concepts of power within African Pentecostal churches, African pre-Christian religions and Black Power I have said that the power of the Holy Spirit has more than just 'spiritual' significance. It also has to do with dignity, authority and power over all types of oppression. God loves and desires the welfare of the whole person; and so he sends his Spirit to bestow that divine, liberating ability and strength. Petersen says that Pentecostal beliefs and practices 'affirmed their sense of personal worth and gave them control over their lives by sustaining the individual forced to cope with the insecurities of change'. The empowerment of people who were marginalized and voiceless meant that the movement 'acquired a revolutionary potential'.[19] Harvey Cox also discusses a Pentecostal liberation theology amounting to 'an impressive counterattack' against the 'growing influence of dominion theology'. He cites Villafañe and Dempster, who advocate a Pentecostal social ethic based on a belief in the power of the liberating Spirit.[20] Hollenweger also refers to these two Pentecostal scholars

---

[18] Anderson, *Zion and Pentecost*, pp. 89–96, 166–72.
[19] Petersen, *Not by Might nor by Power*, pp. 31, 35; Anderson, *Moya*, p. 63.   [20] Cox, *Fire*, pp. 295–6.

in his discussion of social ethics and writes of the Pentecostal dialogue with theology of liberation expressed especially in Sepùlveda's work and in Slovenian Pentecostal Peter Kusmic's dialogue with Marxism.[21] Pentecostal and Charismatic experience means much to the possibility of a contextual Pentecostal theology today, but there are very real dangers. Sometimes an overemphasis on success and 'power' results in a failure to identify with the poor and oppressed in their affliction.

RACE, CLASS AND GENDER

Admitting the defining influence of Azusa Street, where in the most often quoted words of eyewitness Frank Bartleman the 'color line was washed away in the blood',[22] means acknowledging Pentecostalism's non-racial character. With reference to this, Cheryl Johns points out:

> The active presence of the Holy Spirit called for a radical equalizing of blacks and whites, males and females, the rich and the poor. . . . Thus, Pentecostalism stood as a contrast to the dominant order of its day. It was a subversive and revolutionary movement, not based upon philosophic ideology nor totally upon critical reflection. It was a movement that experienced through the Holy Spirit God's divine liberation.[23]

The Pentecostals with their offer of full participation to all regardless of race, class or gender, effected what amounted to a democratization of Christianity, a protest against the status quo. Villafañe suggests that Hispanic Americans in their situation of political and socio-economic deprivation have potentially in Pentecostalism a 'wholistic spirituality' that has a broader social dimension, so that the Spirit is able to 'lead and empower all areas of our life'. He acknowledges that Pentecostal spirituality so often has been privatized and individualistic, but that sin is both personal and 'structural/institutional'. The marginalized Hispanic American Pentecostals bear many similarities to the first Pentecostals at Azusa Street, as indeed they do to other Pentecostals in the Majority World. Villafañe points to five 'signs' of the kingdom of God among Hispanic American Pentecostals that should be acknowledged, re-appropriated and shared: (1) they are of 'mixed' race, which 'embodies and witnesses to the shalom of the races'; (2) they share with the Hispanic Catholic culture 'the positive image of womanhood' in the liberating process; (3) their experience of migration has made them a 'bridge' or 'border' people, a 'bilingual and bicultural church' living

---

[21] Hollenweger, *Pentecostalism*, pp. 206–9, 214–16.   [22] Bartleman, *Azusa Street*, p. 54.
[23] Johns, *Pentecostal Formation*, p. 69.

between the rich North and the impoverished South; (4) they are a 'locus where the poor and the oppressed can find liberation'; and (5) they are 'significant role models' who witness to the reign of God.[24]

The souring of relationships and the split between William Seymour at Azusa Street and Charles Parham in 1906 was caused by Parham's opposition to both the ecstatic manifestations at Azusa Street and the inter-racial mingling there. It resulted in racial segregation that still affects US Pentecostalism after a century. Parham's racism blinded him to the effectiveness of these expressions of African American spirituality, his national leadership was abruptly ended and his work subsided to a small group of churches. He remained convinced of Spirit baptism accompanied by known foreign languages until his death and held to the 'superiority' of the white Anglo-Saxons as the chosen nation of Israel and their special place in God's economy. In contrast, Seymour's understanding of Spirit baptism, especially after this painful division, included the dimension of racial equality in the family of God, and a dimension of love for all people that transcended outward manifestations. Because the divisions in Pentecostalism after 1911 were so sharp, Seymour too was to go into obscurity at the end of his life, but was remembered with admiration by people like John G. Lake, who said he was the man who had 'more of God in his life than any man I had ever met up to that time'.[25] Yet Pentecostalism has over the years not provided much theological justification for racial reconciliation and the opposite has often been the case.

The University of Birmingham under the pioneering work of Walter Hollenweger has been at the forefront of recognizing the revolutionary implications of black Pentecostal spirituality for a contextual theology. Hollenweger calls this the 'oral structure' of the origins of Pentecostalism. This, like that of Christianity itself, is the reason for the initial growth of Pentecostalism and not in any particular Pentecostal doctrine. Hollenweger sees the characteristics of the 'black roots' evident in the leadership of William Seymour, whose 'spirituality lay in his past', and whose Pentecost meant more than speaking in tongues, to include loving in the face of hateful racism. Hollenweger sees Seymour as the ideological founder of Pentecostalism rather than Parham. For him, the choice is not a historical but a theological one based on what is considered to be the essence of Pentecostalism. Parham represents a narrow ideology and an emphasis on a religious experience of speaking in tongues, whereas Seymour represents

[24] Villafañe, *Liberating Spirit*, pp. 89, 163, 165, 171, 198–9.
[25] Lake, *Adventures in God*, p. 19; Wacker, *Heaven Below*, pp. 234–5.

'the reconciling Pentecostal experience' and 'a congregation where every-body is a potential contributor to the liturgy'. Seymour's Pentecostalism is 'the oral missionary movement, with spiritual power to overcome racism and chauvinism'. Hollenweger elaborates on the oral nature of Pentecostal-ism in a chapter on Pentecostal music and liturgy. He points out that rather than leading to an absence of liturgy, spontaneity and enthusiasm produce flexible oral liturgies memorized by the congregation. In Pentecostal ser-vices, 'the most important element' in the liturgy is 'the active participation of every member in the congregation'. This liturgy has social and revo-lutionary implications in that it empowers marginalized people. It takes as acceptable what ordinary people have in the worship of God and thus overcomes 'the *real* barriers of race, social status, and education'. So too, Hollenweger thinks that Pentecostal music also has its roots in black music, and has a 'theological mission of reconciliation'.[26]

British Black Pentecostal theologian Robert Beckford is also from Birmingham and he discusses Black Pentecostalism as a culture of resis-tance. He distinguishes between *passive* resistance exhibited by the black church in its institutions in the midst of white oppression and *active* resis-tance that systematically and corporately resists oppressive structures. He says that black faith and black consciousness are opposite responses in Britain and he seeks to integrate them. He identifies the 'culture of resis-tance' in three areas of black church life: (a) gospel music, expressing 'inter-est in both eschatological and existential realities', giving both spiritual and political meaning; (b) 'black talk', particularly its use in 'extempo-raneous, eclectic, corporate and polemical' prayer; and (c) Sunday 'dress-ing up', which allows black Christians to 'express their "somebody-ness" through a visual aesthetic'. He suggests that the use of black language found in 'dread' culture is the basis for 'developing a theology of liberation', because 'dread' (from Rastafarianism) expresses 'self-emancipation and self-definition and freedom'. Speaking of Christ as 'dread', he suggests, 'points us to an existential black freedom' and unlocks the Christ of British black liberation.[27]

Another product of the University of Birmingham, Roswith Gerloff also discusses the implications of Black Pentecostal spirituality. She sees the early Pentecostal movement at Asuza Street as 'the contribution of the African scene' to the universal church, 'an integrated Christian fellowship under

---

[26] Hollenweger, 'The Black Roots', Anderson and Hollenweger, *Pentecostals after a Century*, pp. 36–43; Hollenweger, *Pentecostalism*, pp. 23, 269–71, 274–5, 277–8.

[27] Robert Beckford, 'Black Pentecostals and Black Politics', Anderson and Hollenweger, *Pentecostals After a Century*, pp. 48–59.

black inspiration and leadership' and with 'quite different communication structures from those of white established churches'. It represents in its 'original lived-out pneumatology' a different concept of the power of the Spirit. But she thinks that Black Pentecostalism was 'taken captive by fundamentalist tendencies', but that it is beginning to shake these off. Although black Pentecostals use the same biblical symbolic language and ecstatic expressions as white Pentecostals do, they 'represent quite different realities'. She wonders whether black religion and music have been exploited by white Christian structures. Black Pentecostalism becomes one of the most significant parts of the ecumenical dialogue. Its essential characteristics include its reticulate 'movement organization' that carries its message along existing social relationships, with committed leaders and members, an easily communicable, action-oriented message and resistance against inhuman structures. Gerloff says that the pneumatology of black Pentecostalism is quite different from that of white Pentecostals, who 'distance themselves from the enthusiastic expressions of black and integrated worship and attempt to deprive the Spirit experience of both its bodily and communal manifestations'.[28]

The use of women with charismatic gifts was widespread throughout Pentecostalism. This resulted in a much higher proportion of women in Pentecostal ministry than in any other form of Christianity at the time. This accorded well with the prominence of women in many traditional religious rituals in the Majority World, contrasting again with the prevailing practice of older churches which barred women from entering the ministry or even from taking any part in public worship. Pentecostals, especially those most influenced by North American Evangelicalism, need to beware of limiting and quenching this most important ministry of women, who form the great majority of the church worldwide. Early Pentecostals declared that the same Spirit who annointed men also empowered women. One of the earliest women preachers in US Pentecostalism, Maria Woodworth-Etter, used biblical precedent to defend 'women's rights in the gospel' to be 'called and commissioned' as preachers. She declared in 1916:

It is high time for women to let their lights shine, to bring out their talents that have been hidden away rusting, and use them for the glory of God, and do with their might what their hands find to do, trusting God for strength, who has said, 'I will never leave you'.[29]

---

[28] Roswith Gerloff, 'Pentecostals in the African Diaspora', Anderson and Hollenweger, *Pentecostals After a Century*, pp. 67, 72–4, 76–7, 80.
[29] Woodworth-Etter, *Signs and Wonders*, p. 202.

But the prominence (or otherwise) of women often depended who told the stories. One female African American writer even suggested that it was Lucy Farrow, and not William Seymour, who was the main inspiration behind the Azusa Street revival. But this liberty was grudgingly given in a male dominated society. After its formation in 1914, a third of the AG's ministers and two-thirds of its missionaries were women. But women had no voting rights in the newly formed AG General Council and they could be evangelists and missionaries but not elders. Full ordination was granted to women in the AG in 1935, but with so many limitations that few women sought ordination. Nevertheless, as Cox observes, 'women, far more than men, have become the principal bearers of the Pentecostal gospel to the four corners of the earth'.[30] By 1936, two thirds of the members and half of the preachers and missionaries of US Pentecostal churches were women.[31] The prominence of women was certainly true in the Pentecostal movement in the USA, which to some extent has reneged more recently on its earlier promotion of the ministry of women, whose exploits have been legendary. Florence Crawford left Seymour in 1908 to found the Apostolic Faith (Portland), Marie Brown (née Burgess) started the Glad Tidings Tabernacle in Manhattan, New York, and Carrie Judd Montgomery and Maria Woodworth-Etter held mass healing revivals all over the USA. Probably the most significant US American Pentecostal woman was Aimee Semple McPherson, who single-handedly built the largest Pentecostal meeting place in the world at the time and established a flourishing Pentecostal denomination. Many prominent early Pentecostal missionaries involved in the planting of Pentecostalism overseas were women, including Minnie Abrams (India), Alice Luce (India and Mexico), Mary Rumsey (Korea), to name but a few. More recently Kathryn Kuhlman astounded observers with her healing services in Pittsburgh and Los Angeles in the 1960s and 1970s, in which diseases were publicly identified and incidences of 'falling under the power' or being 'slain in the Spirit' regularly occurred.[32] Women were effectively mobilized into service as ministers and founders during the early days of the Pentecostal movement both in North America and elsewhere, and the ministry of Pentecostal women continues today in many parts of the world.

The early emphasis on the ministry of women, however, formally disappeared later in classical Pentecostal missions and the importance of the experience of Spirit baptism in the lives of female ministers had 'to take

---

[30] Cox, *Fire*, pp. 124–5.   [31] Wacker, *Heaven Below*, p. 159–61, 166–7.
[32] Durasoff, *Bright Wind*, pp. 184–9.

Figure 12. Church of Pentecost women dancing at Easter convention,
Nsawam, Ghana 2003.

second place to the general patriarchal structure of church and society'.[33] Cheryl Johns says that 'the Pentecostal story contains the story of the con-scientization of women', a story 'rich with symbols of freedom, partnership and hope'. She shows how the baptism in the Spirit in early Pentecostalism brought about a new dimension of freedom whereby women preached, spoke in tongues, gave interpretations, laid hands on the sick for healing, became missionaries and led churches and even whole movements. Spirit baptism and the call of God were the only qualifications for the ministry, and this 'pre-empted social norms and accepted patterns of ministry'. Johns says that the Pentecostal manifestations of the Spirit 'served to liberate the people from dehumanizing cultural, economic and social forces'. Many

[33] Saayman, 'Some reflections', 44.

Pentecostals, she continues, 'have been co-opted out of our revolutionary mission and accommodated to culture'. The Pentecostal movement has failed to address social evils, at times choosing to perpetuate cultural oppression – especially in regard to gender, race and caste. And so the order of the day (at least in the USA) is now 'an abundance of "priestly Pentecostalism" which is characterized by a hierarchical male clergy and a high degree of institutionalism'.[34]

SOCIAL ACTION

Much of western Pentecostalism is stereotyped as a middle class 'prosperity gospel' with 'get rich quick' schemes for its members. This view to some extent has been justified since the advent of the Charismatic movement and the FGBMFI with its proclamation of success theology and the alliance between Pentecostalism and fundamentalism in the US 'Religious Right'. The result has been little or no emphasis on Pentecostalism's social critique on behalf of the poor and oppressed, and US Pentecostals have to some extent become identified with conservative Republican politics.[35] But there are enough concerned Pentecostal voices in the West to temper this assessment. Douglas Petersen, now President of Latin America Child Care is one of them, whose 1996 publication is a comprehensive analysis of a Pentecostal social theology. He says that it is precisely because of Pentecostalism's strength among the most disadvantaged or dissatisfied sectors that it is 'deeply involved in its own kind of here-and-now social struggle' with far-reaching implications for social transformation. He criticizes those Pentecostals who 'use their divine empowering and faith building message for self-serving purposes' and 'neglect the social responsibilities that should accompany this phenomenon' and castigates western Pentecostals whose preoccupation with premillennial dispensationalism precludes them from active involvement in programmes of social concern, and who prefer rather to emphasize evangelism and conversion before Christ's imminent return. He warns against a sense of triumphalism and isolation that will result in Pentecostals forfeiting 'the opportunity to participate in radical change or structural transformation'.[36]

Pentecostals in various parts of the world have always had various programmes of social action, ever since their involvement in Ramabai's Mukti

---

[34] Cheryl B. Johns, 'Pentecostal Spirituality and the Conscientization of Women', Hunter and Hocken, *All Together in One Place*, pp. 153–65.

[35] Johns, *Pentecostal Formation*, pp. 79–80; Hollenweger, *Pentecostalism*, p. 7.

[36] Petersen, *Not by Might*, pp. 227, 229, 231.

Mission in India in the early 1900s and the work of Lillian Trasher among orphans in Egypt from 1911. Early Pentecostals were involved in socio-political criticism, including opposition to war, capitalism and racial discrimination. African American Pentecostals have been at the forefront of the civil rights movement. Throughout the world today Pentecostals are involved in practical ways caring for the poor and the destitute, those often 'unwanted' by the larger society. As Bonino observes in Latin America, Pentecostals have developed a social conscience 'not just at a personal and occasional level but in an institutionalized form', including social, medical and juridical assistance, and educational institutions. Bonino also draws attention to a new awareness of the place of social responsibility in the Pentecostal movement, which indicates 'a vision of a society that takes account of the structural aspects of human life [oppression, discrimination, social decay] and sees in them an area for the work of the Spirit'.[37] The Latin American Child Care Service Program in Central America, founded by John Bueno in San Salvador in 1963 is run by the AG and is the largest evangelical institutional programme of social action in Latin America. Also one of the largest networks of evangelical educational institutions in the world, in 1995 it provided education for 67,487 children. Pentecostal congregations also provide welfare services to needy families, the sick, the abused and the aged, as well as role models and surrogate parents for children. Petersen lists several examples of large-scale structured social welfare programmes in the AG in Central America.[38]

In South Africa, some Pentecostals like Frank Chikane were involved in the struggle against apartheid and are concerned to provide for the holistic needs of their members. Some churches form funeral societies, bursary funds for the education of their children, adult education and literacy programmes, and financial assistance for needy members. Some churches have welfare committees responsible for feeding and clothing the poor and destitute. In Soshanguve (a 'dormitory town' near Pretoria) during the early 1990s, when tin shacks started to appear outside formal housing areas, several of these churches were involved in providing regular food and clothing for the so-called 'squatters'. A primary school administered by Tshwane Christian Ministries (an organization directed by Pentecostals and Charismatics in the Soshanguve area) opened in January 1992 and was followed by a home for destitute children. Adult literacy classes and sewing, knitting and domestic science classes were also held under the auspices of these

---

[37] José Míguez Bonino, *Faces of Latin American Protestantism* (Grand Rapids, MI: Eerdmans, 1997), pp. 66–7.
[38] Petersen, *Not by Might*, pp. 120, 137–42, 153.

churches. As anthropologist Martin West points out concerning independent churches in Soweto, so African Pentecostal churches 'meet many of the needs of townspeople which were formerly met by kin groups on a smaller scale in rural areas'. West lists several ways in which the social needs of church members were met in the urban setting of Soweto. The independent church as a voluntary association provides its members with a sense of family, friendship (providing support groups in times of insecurity), protection in the form of leadership (and particularly charismatic leadership), social control (by emphasizing and enforcing certain norms of behaviour), and in practical ways like finding employment, mutual aid in times of personal crisis and leadership opportunities. The churches thus provide for their members 'new bases for social organisation'.[39]

In Latin America, Africa and elsewhere in the Majority World, Pentecostalism remains what Cheryl Johns calls a 'powerful movement of the poor' and as such 'is pregnant with potential for the transformation of society'. She cites Argentinean Pentecostal Susana Vaccaro de Petrella, who states that the Pentecostal experience of the Holy Spirit results in various kinds of social work as 'a true response to the problems of our day' and 'the strong desire both for spiritual renewal and for the liberation that every human being needs so as to live in a climate of freedom, justice and peace'.[40] We must not write off Pentecostals and Charismatics as hopeless, otherworldly, only concerned with private morality and irrelevant as far as society's needs are concerned. They may have only just begun, but an enormous transformation is now taking place.

---

[39] Martin West, *Bishops and Prophets in a Black City* (Cape Town: David Philip, 1975), pp. 196–9; Anderson, *Zion and Pentecost*, p. 170.
[40] Johns, *Pentecostal Formation*, pp. 78, 96.

15

Globalization and the future of Pentecostalism

CHARISMATIC CHRISTIANITY AS A 'GLOBALIZED' PHENOMENON

This book has shown that after only a century since its commencement, Charismatic forms of Christianity now exist in most countries and have affected all forms of Christianity in our contemporary world – however we regard or manipulate the statistics on affiliation. I hope that the book has succeeded in demonstrating the complexity of what we call 'Pentecostalism', in terms both of its origins and of its theological distinctives. As the subtitle of Cox's *Fire from Heaven* declares, religion itself has been 'reshaped' through the 'rise of Pentecostal spirituality'. Whatever our opinion or particular experience of Pentecostalism therefore, it is a movement of such magnitude that Christianity itself will never be the same. The mushrooming growth of Pentecostal and Charismatic churches and the 'Pentecostalization' of older churches both Protestant and Catholic, especially in the Majority World, is a fact of our time. Ghanaian Presbyterian theologian Cephas Omenyo says that the Pentecostal experience is becoming 'mainline' Christianity in Africa, 'not merely in numbers but more importantly in spirituality, theology and practice'.[1] This observation applies to other continents too, as we have seen. With all its warts, wounds and weals, this composite movement continues to expand and increase across the globe. Simon Coleman's recent seminal study of a Charismatic church in Sweden has demonstrated the globalization of Charismatic Christianity by reference to three dimensions: (1) the use of the mass communications media to disseminate its ideas; (2) a social organization that promotes internationalism through global travel and networking, conferences, and megachurches that function like international corporations; and (3) a 'global orientation' or global Charismatic 'meta-culture' that transcends locality

---

[1] Cephas N. Omenyo, *Pentecost Outside Pentecostalism: A Study of the Development of Charismatic Renewal in the Mainline Churches in Ghana* (Zoetermeer, Netherlands: Boekencentrum, 2002) p. 306.

and denominational loyalty and displays striking similarities in different parts of the world.[2] Some of its more flamboyant representatives have been guilty of the grossest forms of corruption and exploitation, but this seamy side of Pentecostalism is not a new phenomenon in the history of Christianity. Some of its ambassadors jet around the world with their message of success and prosperity for all who will believe and support their organizations. Despite these many faults, Pentecostals are among the most enterprising entrepreneurs of the religious world, creatively adapting to changing contexts and making use of the most recent electronic media and advertising techniques. There seems to be no stopping the relentless advance of Pentecostalism, in contrast to most other contemporary expressions of Christianity which seem to be in a state of permanent decline. Anyone wishing to measure the religious temperature of our world must take a hard look at Pentecostalism. The future of Christianity itself and the encounter between Christianity and other faiths is deeply affected by it.

The Pentecostals and Charismatics may not be accused of offering only a 'pie in the sky when we die' Christianity, but there are real dangers in the 'realized eschatology' promises of instant healing, wholeness and prosperity for all. The preoccupation with these earthly concerns often comes at the expense of Christian virtues like humility, patience and peace. The freedom of the Spirit recognized by all Pentecostals often renders them vulnerable to authoritarian leaders who may exploit their members and cause further division. The jet-setting, lavish and sometimes morally lax lifestyles of some of Pentecostalism's most notorious representatives and the wiles of those religious charlatans who present themselves as specialists with miraculous powers and who prey on the weaknesses of unsuspecting and credulous followers betray the attitude of the suffering Servant on the cross and that of his most effective first century disciples.

THE WIDESPREAD CONTEMPORARY APPEAL

To what extent have contemporary forms of Pentecostalism become 'popular religion', in that they present only that which the masses want to hear and omit important fundamentals of the gospel of Christ? The reasons for crowds of people flocking to the new churches have to do with more than the power of the Spirit, although we may not disregard this important pneumatological factor. The offer of a better and more prosperous life often gives hope to people struggling in poverty and despair.

---

[2] Coleman, *Globalization*, pp. 66–9.

Cox suggests that the rapid spread of Pentecostalism is because of its heady and spontaneous spirituality, 'like the spread of a salubrious contagion'. The Pentecostal emphasis on experience touched people emotionally and was spread through testimony and personal contact. Faupel speaks of the 'revival flame' that spread in early Pentecostalism, leaving 'creative chaos in its wake', seen in the fanning out of workers and missionaries from Azusa Street, the role of this mission as a mecca to which Christian leaders came (especially from Holiness churches), the creation of new Pentecostal centres and the spread to the nations of the world.[3] But there is more than 'spirituality' to Pentecostalism; there are real, this-worldly concerns that it seeks to address, and these concerns have had at least as much impact as the 'otherworldly' ones.

Pentecostalism has continued to expand in the Majority World in many different forms. An important aspect only touched on in this study is that of the prophetic churches (especially in Africa), where oracular prophecy fulfils many pastoral and therapeutic functions. Pentecostals and Charismatics believe in the primary function of spoken prophecy as being for 'edification, exhortation and comfort', as an older English rendering of 1 Corinthians 14:3 puts it. African prophetesses and prophets have taken this three-fold function a step further and have become counsellors, pastors and healers at the same time, treating human needs in ways consistent with the worldviews of those who consult them.[4]

Taken as a whole, Pentecostalism was the fastest growing section of Christianity in the twentieth century and one of the most remarkable occurrences in church history. The expansion of Pentecostalism in recent years is so significant that Cox has reversed his well-known position on inevitable secularization and speaks of Pentecostalism as a manifestation of the 'unanticipated reappearance of primal spirituality in our time'.[5] Although North American Pentecostal denominations have been aggressive in their missionary and evangelistic efforts, at least two thirds of Pentecostalism is now in the Majority World and only a quarter of its members is white. Pentecostals and Charismatics have taken on quite different characteristics in different parts of the world largely because their belief in 'freedom in the Spirit' often allows them more flexibility in developing their own culturally relevant forms of expression. In recent years, the greatest increase in Pentecostalism has been in sub-Saharan Africa, Indonesia, the Philippines, South Korea and especially Latin America. The rapidly growing house church movement

---

[3] Cox, *Fire*, pp. 61, 71; Faupel, *Everlasting Gospel*, pp. 210–22.
[4] Anderson, *Zion and Pentecost*, pp. 277–9.   [5] Cox, *Fire*, p. 83.

in China is mostly of an autochthonous Pentecostal type, even though it may not recognize itself as 'Pentecostal' in the western sense of the word. Enormous buildings holding thousands of worshippers reflect the emerging Pentecostal middle class in many parts of the world. Pentecostals in the Majority World, however, are usually and predominantly a grassroots movement appealing especially to the disadvantaged and underprivileged. Many, if not most of the rapidly growing Christian churches in the Majority World are Pentecostal but operate independently of western Pentecostalism. US founded classical Pentecostal denominations, especially the AG, the CGC and the ICFG are rapidly growing in many parts of the world, but the vast majority of their international membership is from Latin America, Africa and Asia.

THE IMPACT OF PENTECOSTALISM ON WORLD CHRISTIANITY

It would be premature to suggest as some have done, that the Charismatic movement has run its course and that we are now in a 'postcharismatic' stage of church history. There are still many vital, flourishing renewal movements within churches all over the world, including renewal within classical Pentecostal churches themselves. It is true to say that in the western Protestant world at least, the label 'Charismatic' no longer sits comfortably with those who would have been considered 'Charismatic' some forty years ago. There are many reasons for this, among which might be the televangelist scandals in the USA, the appropriation of the term 'Charismatic' by the faith and prosperity preachers and the rise of 'Charismatic' independent churches that seem to be accountable to nobody. But there is no escaping the fact that Pentecostalism and its various phenomena are now well and truly at home within the mainstream churches of the Catholic and Protestant world. As a result, the potential for ecumenical co-operation is enormous. More than thirty years ago John V. Taylor said:

I believe the time has arrived when we must take into account all that is positive in the pentecostal movement if we hope to press further forward along any of the various roads of liturgical renewal, inter-faith dialogue, the indigenization of Christianity, experiments in Christian community and group experience, the ministry of healing, especially towards psychotics and addicts, and new approaches to church union.[6]

To these might be added the relationship between theology and spirituality and the ministry of prayer, both of which have formed a major part

---

[6] Taylor, *Go-Between God*, p. 201.

of Steven Land's research.[7] All of these elements are important in considering the value of charismatic experience for the church today, but I will highlight the first three given by Taylor. Renewal in church life has always brought new vigour and vitality that has especially appealed to younger people, and this is usually first expressed in liturgical changes. The Charismatic movement has spearheaded a return to 'Scripture in song' and a new psalmody that has refreshed many older churches. Inter-faith dialogue is possibly a more controversial aspect to consider, but because the Pentecostal and Charismatic movements are so often at the forefront of the encounter with other faiths (to be sure, sometimes antagonistically so), it has lessons for the entire Christian community that are learned in real life contact rather than in the academic ivory towers of our pluralistic western philosophers and theologians. Although often unconscious of this fact, the Pentecostal churches have absorbed so much of the religious and cultural context into their Christian faith that they have much in common with other faiths. In his pioneering work, Amos Yong writes of 'discerning the Spirit' in other faiths and makes a distinct Pentecostal contribution towards a pneumatological theology of religions.[8]

This brings us to the aspect of indigenization that occurs in Pentecostalism, which I have preferred to call 'contextualization'. There is a lot more work to be done in this area, but I have tried to show that Pentecostalism with its flexibility (or 'freedom') in the Spirit has an innate ability to make itself at home in almost any context. It has continued to expand in the Majority World in many different forms. Pentecostals and Charismatics have taken on quite different characteristics in different parts of the world largely because their belief in 'freedom in the Spirit' often allows them more flexibility in developing their own culturally relevant expressions. Cox says that our age suffers from an 'ecstasy deficit' and that the restoration of the spiritual gifts enables people to become aware of 'deeper insights and exultant feelings'.[9] However, if these experiences are merely for personal, 'spiritual' gratification then the emphasis on spiritual gifts is detrimental to a healthy and holistic Christian life and becomes merely a 'passionate expression of self-concern'. But if the spiritual gifts enhance an individual's sense of belonging to a community, meet felt needs and bring a greater awareness of and love for both God and one's neighbour, then the emphasis

---

[7] Land, *Pentecostal Spirituality*, pp. 165, 220.
[8] Yong, *Discerning the Spirit/s*; Amos Yong, *Beyond the Impasse: Toward a pneumatological theology of religions* (Grand Rapids, MI: Baker Academic, 2003).
[9] Cox, *Fire*, pp. 83, 86.

on the Spirit is surely to be welcomed.[10] Pentecostals and Charismatics are realizing that the work of the Spirit extends beyond personal piety and private experience of charismatic gifts; the Spirit is the Creator Spirit who renews the earth and is concerned about all of this world's needs. This holistic approach to the role of the Spirit will remove the suspicion that Pentecostalism is only a privatized and individualized religion unconcerned about the wider needs of society and the whole creation.

The reason for the very existence of Pentecostals is their conviction in the power of the Spirit working in the church. We have not discussed in any length the Pentecostal ecclesiology implicit in their view of the church being primarily a gathering of local believers rather than an institution, nor have we considered in any detail the ramifications of a stress on 'church planting'. There are many dangers in this latent ecclesiology, not least of all the rampant individualism that creates a proliferation of new 'churches', some of which are no more than a handful of people. But this is a feature of this postmodern age and in Pentecostalism the Spirit is the one to whom credit is given for almost everything that takes place in all church activities, whether large or small, weird or sensible. As far as ecclesiology is concerned, there is a tension between charisma and institution in Pentecostalism and between different forms of baptism. The lines between those who belong to the church and those who do not are not as clear as some Pentecostals might think, as they are influenced by different contexts in different ways. The role of women in the church has also changed significantly. All of these issues must be thoroughly dealt with if Pentecostal theology is to become truly relevant to its context.[11]

An emphasis on receiving a conscious experience of the Spirit is a fundamental characteristic of the different kinds of Pentecostal and Charismatic churches. The spiritual worldview of most societies is a personal, inter-related universe in which a person as a living force is dependent upon all other forces for survival. The emphasis on receiving the power of the Spirit, a power greater than any other power threatening this survival is really good news. In the early twentieth century, Pentecostals discovered that the biblical doctrine of the Spirit was not as detached and uninvolved as academic theology had often projected, and that the human need for religious involvement was met there. The pervading Holy Spirit in Pentecostalism gave Christianity a new vibrancy and relevance. The biblical concept of the Spirit makes an experience of divine involvement possible in

---

[10] Taylor, *Go-Between God*, pp. 220–1.
[11] Hollenweger, *Pentecostalism*, pp. 248–50, 253–6, 258, 261–8.

real terms, which absorbs the whole Christian life and not just the 'spiritual' part of it. This often results in a release of emotion, a catharsis that has a purifying effect. Criticisms of Pentecostal and Charismatic churches with their emphasis on the Spirit and their emotionalism are often missing the point. These churches (like many older ones) are naturally limited by their humanness and for this reason sometimes need correction. But they have demonstrated that it is at least as important to practise theology as to theorize about it. In many parts of the world there are a myriad of needs that will seldom be met by old-fashioned, rational, and rather impotent, philosophical Christianity. The innovative Christianity of many Pentecostal and Charismatic churches takes seriously the popular worldview with its existential needs. It is specifically in the various manifestations of the Spirit in these churches that we can see their valuable contribution to a practical and contextual theology.

THE FUTURE OF CHARISMATIC CHRISTIANITY

If Pentecostalism is still the fastest growing religious movement of our time, then what about its long-term future? Here, it is risky making predictions. Social scientists generally claim that when any religious movement leaves the 'charismatic' phase and becomes institutionalized, its rate of growth slows markedly. Some have suggested that Pentecostalism has now entered this phase and will eventually be overcome by modernity and secularization. But other, more convincing to my mind, recent studies show that the opposite is the case. If the statisticians are to be believed, then there are no signs that the growth of Pentecostalism is abating. It has become one of the most significant expressions of Christianity in the past century, flexible and resilient enough to adapt to and be at home with both modernity and its elusive successor, post-modernity. There are signs that in countries where its most remarkable growth has occurred, as Pentecostalism has become more of a preferred option for the middle class than for the poor, so the numbers of new members have declined. South Korea is one example of this. But Pentecostalism's ecclesiology is such that even within the same denomination (as the example of the recent Pensacola revival in the USA has shown in the AG), there is the possibility of renewal and transformation under the working of the Spirit.

The old 'full gospel' message of 'Jesus Christ the Saviour, Healer, Baptizer and Soon Coming King' still rings loud and clear in Pentecostal churches throughout the world. These theological emphases render them 'conservative', as does their biblical literalism. We have seen that despite the similarities, this does not amount to a form of fundamentalism, because Pentecostalism emphasizes the intuitive and emotional through the revelations and freedom of the Spirit rather than following a slavish biblical literalism.[12] Sometimes this freedom results in division and schism, but even this has the effect of mobilizing new people in the service of the 'full gospel' and the building up of churches. This book has tried to point out the potential within Pentecostalism for ecumenical co-operation and social transformation. This cannot be achieved by a reversion to fundamentalism, for the result of this is that there will be as many versions of 'truth' as there are thousands of movements. But the experience of the Spirit is the unifying factor that transcends petty differences and brings people together.

The enormous growth of Charismatic Christianity in Asia, Africa and Latin America also means that it may continue to expand and influence all types of Christianity there and further afield. Increasingly, these influences and interconnections have become both global and heterogeneous. In creative ways Pentecostals and Charismatics have promoted a globalized Christianity that has not lost touch with its local context. As Coleman observes, ideas originating in the USA have been 'subject to constant forms of cultural appropriation, repackaging, and redissemination into the transnational realm'.[13] This has become a phenomenon that preserves both global and local characteristics, making it possible to speak at the same time of 'Pentecostalism' and 'Pentecostalisms'. So at least for the foreseeable future, the continued vitality of Charismatic Christianity is probably assured. The whole Christian church may be thankful that this is the case, for it may mean the salvation of Christianity itself in the next century from decline and eventual oblivion.

---

[12] Coleman, *Globalisation*, pp. 24–6; Cox, *Fire*, p. 15.   [13] Coleman, *Globalisation*, p. 36.

Bibliography

Adhav, Shamsundar M., *Pandita Ramabai*, Madras, India: Christian Literature Society, 1979.

Albrecht, Daniel E., 'Pentecostal Spirituality: Looking Through the Lens of Ritual', *Pneuma* 14:2 (1992), 107–25.

    Rites in the Spirit: A Ritual Approach to Pentecostal/ Charismatic Spirituality, Sheffield Academic Press, 1999.

Allen, E. Anthony, 'What is the Church's Healing Ministry? Biblical and Global Perspectives', *International Review of Mission* 90:356/357 (2001), 46–54.

Anderson, Allan, 'The Prosperity Message in the Eschatology of Some New Charismatic Churches', *Missionalia* 15:2 (1987), 72–83.

    Moya: The Holy Spirit in an African Context, Pretoria: University of South Africa Press, 1991.

    Bazalwane: African Pentecostals in South Africa, Pretoria: University of South Africa Press, 1992.

    'The Gospel and Culture in Pentecostal Missions in the Third World', *Missionalia* 27:2 (1999), 220–30.

    'Signs and Blunders: Pentecostal Mission Issues at 'Home and Abroad' in the Twentieth Century', *Journal of Asian Mission* 2:2 (2000), 193–210.

    Zion and Pentecost: The Spirituality and Experience of Pentecostal and Zionist/ Apostolic Churches in South Africa, Pretoria: University of South Africa Press, 2000.

    African Reformation: African Initiated Christianity in the 20th Century, Trenton, NJ & Asmara, Eritrea: Africa World Press, 2001.

    'Stretching the Definitions? Pneumatology and "Syncretism" in African Pentecostalism', *JPT* 10:2 (2001), 98–119.

    'The 'Fury and Wonder'? Pentecostal-Charismatic Spirituality in Theological Education', *Pneuma* 23:2 (2001), 287–302.

    'The Newer Pentecostal and Charismatic Churches: The Shape of Future Christianity in Africa?', *Pneuma* 24:2 (2002), 167–84.

    'The Word of Faith Movement', Chris H. Partridge (ed.), *Encyclopedia of New Religions*, London: Lion Publishing 2004, 90–4.

    'The Contribution of Cho Yonggi to a Contextual Theology in Korea', *JPT* 12:1 (2003), 87–107.

and Hollenweger, Walter J. (eds.), *Pentecostals after a Century: Global Perspectives on a Movement in Transition*, Sheffield Academic Press, 1999.

and Otwang, Samuel, *Tumelo: The Faith of African Pentecostals in South Africa*, Pretoria: University of South Africa Press, 1993.

and Tang, Edmond (eds.), *Asian and Pentecostal: The Charismatic Face of Christianity in Asia*, Oxford, UK: Regnum, 2004.

Anderson, Robert M., *Vision of the Disinherited: The Making of American Pentecostalism*, Peabody, MA: Hendrickson, 1979.

The Apostolic Faith, Los Angeles, CA, Nos. 1–13 (1906–08).

Archer, Kenneth J., 'Pentecostal Hermeneutics: Retrospect and Prospect', *JPT* 8 (1996), 63–81.

'Early Pentecostal Biblical Interpretation', *JPT* 18 (2001), 32–70.

Asamoah-Gyadu, Kwabena J., 'The Church in the African State: The Pentecostal/Charismatic Experience in Ghana', *Journal of African Christian Thought*, 1:2 (1998), 51–7.

'Renewal within African Christianity: A Study of Some Current Historical and Theological Developments within Independent Indigenous Pentecostalism in Ghana', PhD thesis, University of Birmingham, UK, 2000.

Badcock, Gary D., *Light of Truth and Fire of Love: A Theology of the Holy Spirit*, Grand Rapids, MI: Eerdmans, 1997.

Barrett, David B. and Johnson, Todd M., 'Annual Statistical Table on Global Mission: 2003', *International Bulletin of Missionary Research* 27:1 (2003), 24–5.

Kurian, George T. and Johnson, Todd M., *World Christian Encyclopedia* (2nd Edition), Vol. 1, New York: Oxford University Press, 2001.

Bartleman, Frank, *Azusa Street*, South Plainfield, NJ: Bridge Publishing (republished), 1925, 1980.

Beckford, Robert S., 'Towards a Dread Pentecostal Theology: The Context of a Viable Political Theology Within Black Pentecostal Churches in Britain', PhD thesis, University of Birmingham, 1999.

Bennett, Dennis, *Nine O'Clock in the Morning*, Plainfield, NJ: Bridge Publishing, 1970.

Berg, C. L. and Pretiz, P., *The Gospel People of Latin America*, Monrovia, CA: MARC, 1992.

Berg, Mike and Pretiz, Paul, *Spontaneous Combustion: Grass-Roots Christianity Latin American Style*, Pasadena, CA: William Carey Library, 1996.

Bergunder, Michael, 'Miracle Healing and Exorcism: The South Indian Pentecostal Movement in the Context of Popular Hinduism', *International Review of Mission* 90:356/357 (2001), 103–12.

Berryman, Phillip, *Religion in the Megacity: Catholic and Protestant portraits from Latin America*, New York: Orbis, 1996.

Blair, William N. and Hunt, Bruce. *The Korean Pentecost and the Sufferings Which Followed*, Edinburgh: The Banner of Truth Trust (republished), 1977.

Bloch-Hoell, Nils, *The Pentecostal Movement*, Oslo: Universitetsforlaget and London: Allen & Unwin, 1964.

Blumhofer, Edith L., *The Assemblies of God: A Chapter in the Story of American Pentecostalism* (2 Vols), Springfield, MO: Gospel Publishing House, 1989.

Restoring the Faith: The Assemblies of God, Pentecostalism, and American Culture, University of Illinois Press, 1993.

and Balmer, R. (eds.), *Modern Christian Revivals*, University of Illinois Press, 1993.

Spittler, R. P. and Wacker, G. A. (eds.), *Pentecostal Currents in American Protestantism*, University of Illinois Press, 1999.

Bonino, José Míguez, 'Pentecostal Missions is More Than What it Claims', *Pneuma* 16:2 (1997), 283–8.

BRIDGE: Church Life in China Today (ed. Deng Zhaoming), various issues 1985–1993. Hong Kong: Christian Study Centre on Chinese Religion and Culture.

Brouwer, S., Gifford, P. and Rose, S. D., *Exporting the American Gospel: Global Christian Fundamentalism*, New York: Routledge, 1996.

Bundy, David D., 'Pentecostalism in Belgium', *Pneuma* 8:1 (1986), 41–56.

'Louis Dallière: Apologist for Pentecostalism in France and Belgium, 1932–1939', *Pneuma* 10:2 (1988), 85–115.

'Thomas Ball Barratt: From Methodist to Pentecostal', *JEPTA* 13 (1994), 19–40.

'Historical and Theological Analysis of the Pentecostal Church in Norway', *JEPTA* 20 (2000), 66–92.

Burgess, Stanley M., 'Pentecostalism in India: An Overview', *AJPS* 4:1 (2001), 85–98.

and van der Maas, Eduard M. (eds.), *New International Dictionary of Pentecostal and Charismatic Movements*, Grand Rapids, MI: Zondervan, 2002.

Calley, Malcolm J., *God's People: West Indian Pentecostal Sects in England*, London and New York: Oxford University Press, 1965.

Cargal, Timothy B., 'Beyond the Fundamentalist-Modernist Controversy: Pentecostals and Hermeneutics in a Postmodern Age', *Pneuma* 15:2 (1993), 163–88.

Cerillo, Augustus Jr., 'Interpretative Approaches to the History of American Pentecostal Origins', *Pneuma* 19:1 (1997), 29–52.

Chesnut, R. Andrew, *Born Again in Brazil: The Pentecostal Boom and the Pathogens of Poverty*, New Brunswick, NY: Rutgers University Press, 1997.

Cho, David (Paul) Yonggi, *The Fourth Dimension*, Seoul, Korea: Seoul Logos Co., 1979.

The Fourth Dimension, Volume 2, S. Plainfield, NJ: Bridge Publishing, 1983.

More than Numbers, Waco, TX: Word Books, 1984.

Salvation, Health and Prosperity: Our Threefold Blessings in Christ, Altamonte Springs, FL: Creation House, 1987.

How Can I be Healed? Seoul, Korea: Seoul Logos Co., 1999.

(with Harold Hostetler), *Successful Home Cell Groups*, Seoul, Korea: Seoul Logos Co., 1997.

The Christian Evangel (eds. E. N. Bell and J. R. Flower), Plainfield, IN, Findlay, OH and St. Louis, MO, Nos. 1–80 (1913–15).

Clarke, Clifton R., 'Faith in Christ in Post-Missionary Africa: Christology among Akan African Indigenous Churches in Ghana', PhD thesis, University of Birmingham, 2003.

Clayton, Allen, 'The Significance of William H. Durham for Pentecostal Historiography', *Pneuma* 1:2 (1979), 27–42.

Cleary, E. L. and Stewart-Gambino, H. W. (eds), *Power, Politics and Pentecostals
in Latin America*. Boulder, CO: Westview Press, 1997.

and Sepúlveda, Juan, 'Chilean Pentecostalism: Coming of Age', Cleary and
Stewart-Gambino, *Power, Politics & Pentecostals*, 98–113.

Coleman, Simon, *The Globalisation of Charismatic Christianity: Spreading the
Gospel of Prosperity*, Cambridge University Press, 2000.

Colletti, Joseph R., 'Lewi Pethrus: His Influence Upon Scandinavian-American
Pentecostalism', *Pneuma* 5:2 (1983), 18–29.

Confidence: A Pentecostal Paper for Great Britain (ed. Alex. A. Boddy), Monkswear-
mouth, Sunderland (1908–26).

Conn, Charles W., *Like a Mighty Army: A History of the Church of God 1886–1976*,
Cleveland, TN: Pathway Press, 1977.

Corten, André and Marshall-Fratani, Ruth (eds.), *Between Babel and Pentecost:
Transnational Pentecostalism in Africa and Latin America*, Bloomington, IN:
Indiana University Press, 2001.

Cox, Harvey, *Fire from Heaven: The Rise of Pentecostal Spirituality and the Reshaping
of Religion in the Twenty-first Century*, London: Cassell, 1996.

Creech, Joe, 'Visions of Glory: The Place of the Azusa Street Revival in Pentecostal
History', *Church History* 65 (1996), 405–24.

Croatto, Severino, *Biblical Hermeneutics*, New York: Orbis, 1987.

Culpepper, Robert H., *Evaluating the Charismatic Movement: A Theological and
Biblical Appraisal*, Valley Forge, IN: Judson Press, 1977.

Daneel, Inus (M.L.), *Quest for Belonging*, Gweru, Zimbabwe: Mambo Press,
1987.

Daniels, David D., 'Dialogue between Black and Hispanic Pentecostal Scholars:
A Report and some Personal Observations', *Pneuma* 17:2 (1995), 219–28.

Dayton, Donald W., *Theological Roots of Pentecostalism*, Metuchen, NJ: Scarecrow
Press, 1987.

Dempster, Murray W., 'Pentecostal Social Concern and the Biblical Mandate of
Social Justice', *Pneuma* 9:2 (1987), 129–54.

Klaus, B. D. and Petersen, D. (eds.), *Called and Empowered: Global Mission in
Pentecostal Perspective*, Peabody, MA: Hendrickson, 1991.

Klaus, B. D. and Petersen, D. (eds.), *The Globalization of Pentecostalism: A
Religion Made to Travel*, Oxford: Regnum, 1999.

Dunn, James D. G., *Baptism in the Holy Spirit: A Re-examination of the New
Testament Teaching on the Gift of the Spirit in Relation to Pentecostalism Today*,
London: SCM, 1970.

'Baptism in the Spirit: A Response to Pentecostal Scholarship on Luke-Acts',
JPT (1993), 3–27.

Durasoff, Steve, *Bright Wind of the Spirit: Pentecostalism Today*, London: Hodder
& Stoughton, 1972.

Edwards, Joel, 'Afro-Caribbean Pentecostalism in Britain', *JEPTA* XVII (1997),
37–48.

Ervin, Howard, *Conversion-Initiation and the Baptism in the Holy Spirit: An Engaging Critique of James D. G. Dunn's Baptism in the Holy Spirit*, Peabody, MA: Hendrickson, 1984.

Evans, Eifon, *The Welsh Revival of 1904*, Bridgend, UK: Evangelical Press of Wales, 1969.

Farah, Charles, 'A Critical Analysis: The 'Roots and Fruits' of Faith-Formula Theology', *Pneuma* 3:1 (1981), 3–21.

Faupel, D. William, 'Whither Pentecostalism?', *Pneuma* 15:1 (1993), 9–28.

The Everlasting Gospel: The Significance of Eschatology in the Development of Pentecostal Thought, Sheffield Academic Press, 1996.

Flames of Fire (with which is incorporated Tidings from Tibet and Other Lands) (ed. Cecil Polhill), London, Nos. 1–53 (1911–17).

French, Talmadge L., *Our God is One: The Story of Oneness Pentecostalism*, Indianapolis, IN: Voice & Vision Publications, 1999.

Frodsham, Stanley, *With Signs Following: The Story of the Pentecostal Revival in the Twentieth Century*, Springfield, MO: Gospel Publishing House, 1946.

George, A. C. 'Pentecostal Beginnings in Travancove, South India', *AJPS* 4:2 (2001), 215–37.

Gifford, Paul, *Christianity and Politics in Doe's Liberia*, Cambridge University Press, 1993.

African Christianity: Its Public Role, London: Hurst, 1998.

Goff, James R., *Fields White unto Harvest: Charles F. Parham and the Missionary Origins of Pentecostalism*, Fayetteville: University of Arkansas Press, 1988.

Gros, Jeffrey, 'Toward a Dialogue of Conversion: The Pentecostal, Evangelical and Conciliar Movements', *Pneuma* 17:2 (1995), 189–202.

Harper, Michael, *As at the Beginning*, London: Hodder & Stoughton, 1965.

Hedlund, Roger E. (ed.), *Christianity is Indian: The Emergence of an Indigenous Christianity*, Delhi: ISPCK, 2000.

Hilborn, David (ed.), *'Toronto' in Perspective: Papers on the New Charismatic Wave of the Mid 1990s*, Carlisle, UK: Paternoster/Acute, 2001.

Hocken, Peter, *The Glory and the Shame: Reflections on the 20th-Century Outpouring of the Holy Spirit*, Guildford, UK: Eagle, 1994.

Hodges, Melvin L., *The Indigenous Church*, Springfield, MO: Gospel Publishing House, 1953.

Hoehler-Fatton, Cynthia, *Women of Fire and Spirit: History, Faith and Gender in Roho Religion in Western Kenya*, Oxford University Press, 1996.

Hollenweger, Walter J., *The Pentecostals*, London: SCM Press, 1972.

Pentecost Between Black and White, Belfast, UK: Christian Journals, 1974.

Pentecostalism: Origins and Developments Worldwide, Peabody, MA: Hendrickson, 1997.

Hong, Young-gi, 'The backgrounds and characteristics of the Charismatic mega-churches in Korea', *AJPS* 3:1 (2000), 99–118.

Hoover, Willis Collins and Hoover, Mario G., *History of the Pentecostal Revival in Chile*, Santiago, Chile: Imprenta Eben-Ezer, 2000.

292 Bibliography

Horton, Harold, *The Gifts of the Spirit*, Nottingham: Assemblies of God Publishing House, 1934, reprinted 1976.

Hosack, James, 'The Arrival of Pentecostals and Charismatics in Thailand', *AJPS* 4:1 (2001), 109–17.

Hunter, Harold D. and Hocken, Peter D. (eds.), *All Together in One Place: Theological Papers from the Brighton Conference on World Evangelization*, Sheffield Academic Press, 1993.

Jehu-Appiah, Jerisdan H., 'The African Indigenous Churches in Britain: An Investigation into their Theology with Special Reference to the Musama Disco Christo Church and the Church of the Lord (Brotherhood)', PhD thesis, University of Birmingham, 2001.

Jeong, Chong Hee, 'The Formation and Development of Korean Pentecostalism from the Viewpoint of a Dynamic Contextual Theology', ThD thesis, University of Birmingham, UK, 2001.

Jeong, JaeYong, 'Filipino Pentecostal Spirituality: An Investigation into Filipino Indigenous Spirituality and Pentecostalism in the Philippines', ThD thesis, University of Birmingham, UK, 2001.

Johns, Cheryl B., *Pentecostal Formation: A Pedagogy Among the Oppressed*, Sheffield Academic Press, 1993.

Johnstone, P. and Mandryk, J., *Operation World: 21st Century Edition*, Carlisle, UK: Paternoster, 2001.

Kalu, Ogbu U., 'The Third Response: Pentecostalism and the Reconstruction of Christian Experience in Africa, 1970–1995', *Journal of African Christian Thought* 1:2 (1998), 3–8.

Kärkkäinen, Veli-Matti, *Spiritus Ubi Vult Spirat: Pneumatology in Roman Catholic-Pentecostal Dialogue (1972–1989)*, Helsinki: Luther-Agricola-Society, 1998.

Ad Ultimum Terrae: Evangelization, Proselytism and Common Witness in the Roman Catholic Pentecostal Dialogue (1990–1997), Frankfurt am Main, Germany: Peter Lang, 1999.

'"From the ends of the earth to the ends of the earth" – the expansion of the Finnish Pentecostal Missions from 1927 to 1997', *JEPTA* 20 (2000), 116–31.

Pneumatology: The Holy Spirit in Ecumenical, International, and Contextual Perspective, Grand Rapids, MI: Baker Academic, 2002.

Kay, William K., *Pentecostals in Britain*, Carlisle, UK: Paternoster, 2000.

Kelsey, Morton, *Tongue Speaking: The History and Meaning of Charismatic Experience*, New York: Crossroad, 1981.

Klaus, Byron D. 'National Leadership in Pentecostal Missions', Dempster, Klaus and Petersen, *Called and Empowered*, 225–41.

Koch, Kurt, *The Revival in Indonesia*, Baden, Germany: Evangelization Publishers, 1970.

Kydd, Ronald A. N., *Healing Through the Centuries: Models of Understanding*, Peabody, MA: Hendrickson, 1998.

Lake, John G., *Adventures in God*, Tulsa, OK: Harrison House, 1981 (reprint).

Lalive d'Epinay, Christian, 'The Training of Pastors and Theological Education: The Case of Chile', *International Review of Missions* LVI: 222 (1967), 185–92.

Haven to the Masses: A Study of the Pentecostal Movement in Chile, London: Lutterworth, 1969.

Land, Steven J., *Pentecostal Spirituality: A Passion for the Kingdom*, Sheffield Academic Press, 1993.

Larbi, E. Kingsley, *Pentecostalism: The Eddies of Ghanaian Christianity*, Accra, Ghana: Centre for Pentecostal and Charismatic Studies, 2001.

Lederle, Henry I., *Treasures Old and New: Interpretations of 'Spirit-baptism' in the Charismatic Renewal Movement*, Peabody, MA: Hendrickson, 1988.

Lee, Jae Bum, 'Pentecostal Type Distinctives and Korean Protestant Church Growth', PhD thesis, Fuller Theological Seminary, Pasadena, CA, 1986.

Lee, Hong Jung, 'Minjung and Pentecostal Movements in Korea', Anderson and Hollenweger (eds.), *Pentecostals after a Century*, 138–60.

Lee, Young Hoon, 'The Holy Spirit Movement in Korea: Its Historical and Doctrinal Development', PhD thesis, Temple University, Philadelphia, PA, 1996.

Ma, Wonsuk and Menzies, Robert P. (eds.), *Pentecostalism in Context: Essays in Honour of William W. Menzies*, Sheffield Academic Press, 1997.

Macchia, Frank D., 'Tongues as a Sign: Towards a Sacramental Understanding of Pentecostal Experience', *Pneuma* 15:1 (1993), 61–76.

'From Azusa to Memphis: Evaluation the Racial Reconciliation Dialogue among Pentecostals', *Pneuma* 17:2 (1995), 203–18.

MacRobert, Iain, *The Black Roots and White Racism of Early Pentecostalism in the USA*, Basingstoke, UK: Macmillan, 1988.

Martin, David, *Tongues of Fire: The Explosion of Protestantism in Latin America*, Oxford, UK: Basil Blackwell, 1990.

Pentecostalism: The World Their Parish, Oxford, UK: Blackwell, 2002.

Maxwell, David, '"Delivered from the Spirit of Poverty": Pentecostalism, Prosperity and Modernity in Zimbabwe', *Journal of Religion in Africa* 28:4 (1998), 350–73.

McBain, Douglas, *Fire Over the Waters: Renewal Among Baptists and Others from the 1960s to the 1990s*, London: DLT, 1997.

McClung, L. Grant Jr. (ed.), *Azusa Street and Beyond: Pentecostal Missions and Church Growth in the Twentieth Century*, S. Plainfield, NJ: Logos, 1986.

McDonnell, Kilian, *Catholic Pentecostalism: Problems in Evaluation*, Pecos, NM: Dove Publications, 1970.

'Five Defining Issues: The International Classical Pentecostal/ Roman Catholic Dialogue,' *Pneuma* 17:2 (1995), 175–88.

'The International Classical Pentecostal/Roman Catholic Dialogue', *Pneuma* 17:2 (1995), 163–88.

McGee, Gary B., *This Gospel Shall be Preached: History of the Assemblies of God Foreign Missions to 1959*, Springfield, MO: Gospel Publishing House, 1986.

(ed.), *Initial Evidence: Historical and Biblical Perspectives on the Pentecostal Doctrine of Spirit Baptism*, Peabody, MA: Hendrickson, 1991.

'Pentecostal Missiology: Moving beyond triumphalism to face the issues', *Pneuma* 16:2 (1994), 275–82.

'"Latter Rain" Falling in the East: Early-Twentieth-Century Pentecostalism in India and the Debate over Speaking in Tongues', *Church History* 68:3 (1999), 648–65.

McKay, John, 'When the Veil is Taken Away: The Impact of Prophetic Experience on Biblical Interpretation', *JPT* 5 (1994), 17–40.

Menzies, Robert P., *Empowered for Witness: The Spirit in Luke-Acts*, Sheffield Academic Press, 1994.

Mesters, Carlos, 'The Use of the Bible in Christian Communities of the Common People', N. K. Gottwald and R. A. Horsley (eds.), *The Bible and Liberation*. New York: Orbis, 1993, 119–33.

Moltmann, Jürgen and Kuschel, Karl-Josef (eds.), *Pentecostal Movements as an Ecumenical Challenge, Concilium 1996/3*, London: SCM Press, 1996.

Montgomery, Jim, *New Testament Fire in the Philippines*, Manila: C-Grip, 1972.

Nagasawa, Makito, 'Makuya Pentecostalism: A Survey', *AJPS* 3:2 (2000), 203–18.

Nelson, Douglas J., 'For Such a Time as This: The Story of William J. Seymour and the Azusa Street Revival', PhD thesis, University of Birmingham, UK, 1981.

Neumann, H. Terris, 'Cultic Origins of the Word-Faith Theology Within the Charismatic Movement', *Pneuma* 12:1 (1990), 32–55.

O'Connor, Edward, *The Pentecostal Movement in the Catholic Church*, Notre Dame, IN: Ave Maria Press, 1971.

Ojo, Matthews A., 'The Church in the African State: The Charismatic/Pentecostal Experience in Nigeria', *Journal of African Christian Thought*, 1:2 (1998), 25–32.

Omenyo, Cephas N., *Pentecost Outside Pentecostalism: A Study of the Development of Charismatic Renewal in the Mainline Churches in Ghana*, Zoetermeer, Netherlands: Boekencentrum, 2002.

Onyinah, Opoku, 'Akan Witchcraft and the Concept of Exorcism in the Church of Pentecost', PhD thesis, University of Birmingham, UK, 2002.

Padwick, T. John, 'Spirit, Desire and the World: Roho Churches of Western Kenya in the Era of Globalization', PhD thesis, University of Birmingham, 2003.

Pandrea, Rodica, 'A Historical and Theological Analysis of the Pentecostal Church in Romania', *JEPTA* 21 (2001), 109–35.

Peel, J. D. Y., *Aladura: A Religious Movement Among the Yoruba*, Oxford University Press, 1968.

The Pentecost, Indianapolis, IN (August 1908).

The Pentecostal Witness 1, London (July 1924).

Perriman, Andrew (ed.), *Faith, Health & Prosperity: A Report on 'Word of Faith' and 'Positive Confession' Theologies*, Carlisle, UK: Paternoster, 2003.

Petersen, Douglas, 'The Formation of Popular, National, Autonomous Pentecostal Churches in Central America', *Pneuma* 16:1 (1994), 23–48.

Not by Might nor by Power: A Pentecostal Theology of Social Concern in Latin America, Oxford, UK: Regnum, 1996.

Pinnock, Clark H., *Flame of Love: A Theology of the Holy Spirit*, Downers Grove, IL: InterVarsity Press, 1996.

Poewe, Karla (ed.), *Charismatic Christianity as a Global Culture*, Columbia, SC: University of South Carolina Press, 1994.

Pomerville, Paul A., *The Third Force in Missions: A Pentecostal Contribution to Contemporary Mission Theology*, Peabody, MA: Hendrickson, 1985.

Price, Lynne, *Theology Out of Place: A Theological Biography of Walter J. Hollenweger*, London and New York: Sheffield Academic Press, 2002.

Sepúlveda, Juan and Smith, Graeme (eds.), *Mission Matters*, Frankfurt am Main: Peter Lang, 1997.

Ramabai, Pandita, 'Stray Thoughts on the Revival', *The Bombay Guardian and Banner of Asia*, Bombay, India, 7 November 1905, 9–10.

Ranaghan, Kevin and Dorothy, *Catholic Pentecostals*, New York: Paulist Press, 1969.

Randall, Claire, 'The Importance of the Pentecostal and Holiness Churches in the Ecumenical Movement', *Pneuma* 9:1 (1987), 50–60.

Rasmussen, Ane Marie Bak, *Modern African Spirituality: The Independent Spirit Churches in East Africa, 1902–1976*, London and New York: British Academic Press, 1996.

Redemption Tidings 1:2 (October 1924), 1:4 (January 1925).

Riss, Richard M., *A Survey of 20th-Century Revival Movements in North America*, Peabody, MA: Hendrickson, 1988.

Robeck, Cecil M. Jr., 'Pentecostals and the Apostolic Faith: Implications for Ecumenism', *Pneuma* 9:1 (1987), 61–84.

'Pentecostals and Social Ethics', *Pneuma* 9:2 (1987), 103–7.

'Taking Stock of Pentecostalism: The Personal Reflections of a Retiring Editor,' *Pneuma* 15:1 (1993), 35–60.

'Pentecostal Origins from a Global Perspective', Hunter and Hocken, *All Together in One Place*, 1993, 166–80.

'Pentecostals and Ecumenism in a Pluralistic World', Dempster, Klaus and Petersen, *The Globalization of Pentecostalism*, 338–362.

Saayman, Willem A., 'Some Reflections on the Development of the Pentecostal Mission Model in South Africa', *Missionalia* 21:1 (1993), 40–56.

Sanders, Cheryl J., *Saints in Exile: The Holiness-Pentecostal Experience in African American Religion and Culture*, New York: Oxford University Press, 1996.

Schoffeleers, Matthew, 'Ritual Healing and Political Acquiescence: The Case of the Zionist Churches in Southern Africa', *Africa* 60: 1 (1991), 1–25.

Sepúlveda, Juan, 'Gospel and Culture in Latin American Protestantism: Toward a New Theological Appreciation of Syncretism', PhD thesis, University of Birmingham, UK, 1996.

'The Challenge for Theological Education from a Pentecostal Standpoint', *Ministerial Formation* 87 (1999), 29–34.

'Indigenous Pentecostalism and the Chilean Experience', Anderson and Hollenweger, *Pentecostals After a Century*, pp. 111–34.

Shaull, Richard and Cesar, Waldo, *Pentecostalism and the Future of the Christian Churches: Promises, Limitations, Challenges*, Grand Rapids, MI and Cambridge, UK: Eerdmans, 2000.

Shelton, James B., *Mighty in Word and Deed: The Role of the Holy Spirit in Luke-Acts*, Peabody, MA: Hendrickson, 1991.

Sherrill, John L. *They Speak with Other Tongues*, New York: McGraw-Hill, 1964.

Smail, T., Walker, A. and Wright, N., *Charismatic Renewal: The Search for a Theology*, London: SPCK, 1995.

Snaitang, O. L. (ed.), *Churches of Indigenous Origins in Northeast India*, Delhi: ISPCK, 2000.

Spittler, Russell P. (ed.), *Perspectives on the New Pentecostalism*, Grand Rapids, MI: Baker, 1976.

Stoll, David, *Is Latin America Turning Protestant?*, Los Angeles: University of California Press, 1990.

Stronstad, Roger, *The Charismatic Theology of St Luke*, Peabody, MA: Hendrickson, 1984.

Suenens, Leo J. Cardinal, *A New Pentecost?*, London: DLT, 1975.

Sundkler, B. G. N., *Bantu Prophets in South Africa*, Oxford University Press, 1961.
Zulu Zion and Some Swazi Zionists, London: Oxford University Press, 1976.

Suurmond, Jean-Jacques, *Word and Spirit at Play: Towards a Charismatic Theology*, London: SCM, 1994.

Suzuki, Masakazu, 'A New Look at the Pre-war History of the Japan Assemblies of God', *AJPS* 4:2 (2001), 239–67.

Synan, Vinson (ed.), *Aspects of Pentecostal-Charismatic Origins*, Plainfield, NJ: Logos, 1975.
The Holiness-Pentecostal Tradition: Charismatic Movements in the Twentieth Century, Grand Rapids, MI and Cambridge, UK: Eerdmans, 1997.

Tari, Mel, *Like a Mighty Wind*, London: Coverdale House, 1973.

Taylor, John V., *The Go-Between God: The Holy Spirit and the Christian Mission*, London: SCM, 1972.

Teraudkalns, Valdis, 'Pentecostalism in the Baltics: Historical Retrospection', *JEPTA* 21 (2001), 91–108.

Things New and Old (ed. A. E. Saxby), London, Vols. 1–4 (1921–5).

Turner, Harold W. *History of an African Independent Church (1) The Church of the Lord (Aladura)*, Oxford, UK: Clarendon Press, 1967.
Religious Innovation in Africa, Boston, MA: G. K. Hall, 1979.

van der Laan, Cornelis, 'The Proceedings of the Leaders' Meetings (1908–1911) and of the International Pentecostal Council (1912–1914)', *Pneuma* 10:1 (1988), 36–49.
'Discerning the Body: An Analysis of Pentecostalism in the Netherlands', *JEPTA* 14 (1995), 34–53.

Villafañe, Eldin, *The Liberating Spirit: Towards an Hispanic American Pentecostal Social Ethic*, Grand Rapids, MI: Eerdmans, 1993.

Wacker, Grant, 'Are the Golden Oldies Still Worth Playing? Reflections on History Writing Among Early Pentecostals', *Pneuma* 8:2 (1986), 81–100.
Heaven Below: Early Pentecostals and American Culture, Cambridge, MA and London: Harvard University Press, 2001.

Wagner, Peter, *Look Out! The Pentecostals are Coming*, Carol Stream, IL: Creation House, 1973.

Währisch-Oblau, Claudia, 'God Can Make us Healthy Through and Through: On Prayers for the Sick and Healing Experiences in Christian Churches in China and African Immigrant Congregations in Germany', *International Review of Mission* 90:356/357 (2001), 87–102.

Warrington, Keith (ed.), *Pentecostal Perspectives*, Carlisle, UK: Paternoster, 1998.

Watt, C. Peter, *From Africa's Soil: The Story of the Assemblies of God in Southern Africa*, Cape Town: Struik, 1992.

West, Martin, *Bishops and Prophets in a Black City*, Cape Town: David Philip, 1975.

Wigglesworth, Smith, *Ever Increasing Faith*, Springfield, MO: Gospel Publishing House, 1924, revised 1971.

Wilkerson, David, *The Cross and the Switchblade*, New York: Random House, 1963.

Williams, J. Rodman, *Renewal Theology (2): Salvation, the Holy Spirit, and Christian Living*, Grand Rapids, MI: Zondervan, 1990.

Willis, Avery T., *Indonesian Revival: Why Two Million Came to Christ*, S. Pasadena, CA: William Carey Library, 1977.

Wilson, Everett A., *Strategy of the Spirit: J. Philip Hogan and the Growth of the Assemblies of God Worldwide 1960–1990*, Carlisle, UK: Regnum, 1997.

Wilson, Mark W. (ed.), *Spirit and Renewal: Essays in Honor of J. Rodman Williams*, Sheffield Academic Press, 1994.

Wimber, John, *Power Evangelism: Signs and Wonders Today*, London: Hodder & Stoughton, 1985.

(with Kevin Springer) *Power Healing*, New York: HarperCollins, 1987.

Wiyono, Gani, 'Timor Revival: A Historical Study of the Great Twentieth-Century Revival in Indonesia', *AJPS* 4:2 (2001), 269–93.

Womersley, Harold, *Wm F. P. Burton: Congo Pioneer*, Eastbourne, UK: Victory Press, 1973.

Woodworth-Etter, Maria, *Signs and Wonders*, New Kensington, PA: Whitaker House, 1916, reprinted 1997.

The Holy Spirit, New Kensington, PA: Whitaker House, c. 1918, reprinted 1988.

Yong, Amos, '"Not Knowing Where the Wind Blows . . .": On Envisioning a Pentecostal-Charismatic Theology of Religions', *JPT* 14 (1999), 81–112.

Discerning the Spirit(s): A Pentecostal/Charismatic Contribution to Christian Theology of Religions, Sheffield Academic Press, 2000.

Beyond the Impasse: Toward a Pneumatological Theology of Religions, Grand Rapids, MI: Baker Academic, and Carlisle, UK: Paternoster, 2003.

Index

Abraham, K. E., 127
Abrams, Minnie, 37, 125, 174, 193, 274
African Independent Churches, 11, 12, 13, 32, 67, 103, 104–106, 107–108, 111, 112–114, 197, 232, 237, 268
African Israel Church Nineveh, 113–114
Aladura churches, 4, 118–121
Albrecht, Daniel E., 204
Anderson, Robert Mapes, 14, 166, 256, 264
Anglicans, Episcopalians, 31, 91, 95, 105, 112, 124, 144, 145, 147, 148, 152, 153–154, 155, 159, 252
Anglo-Israelism, *see* British Israelism
Anim, Peter, 116–117, 118
Apostolic Church (various), 100, 101, 116, 140, 268
Apostolic Church of Great Britain (and related), 36, 88, 93, 96, 104, 116, 117, 121, 142, 143, 177
Apostolic Faith, Apostolic Faith Mission (USA), 39, 40, 41, 43, 51, 58, 60, 92, 134, 146, 249, 274
Apostolic Faith Mission of South Africa, 105, 106–107, 108–109, 110, 141, 177, 181
Argentina, 6–7, 58, 59, 64, 68–69, 70, 74, 155, 158, 162, 174
Assemblies of God (non-USA), 69, 71–72, 75, 76, 77, 78, 80, 92, 94–95, 96, 97, 98, 101, 109–110, 114, 116, 118, 126, 127, 128, 130, 131, 137, 138, 140, 142, 143, 164, 177, 254, 262
Assemblies of God (USA), 42, 46, 47, 51, 52–54, 58, 59, 68, 75, 76, 78, 79, 80, 100, 104, 111, 112, 115, 126, 129, 130, 131, 139, 140, 146, 149, 150, 158, 193–195, 209–210, 223, 248, 250, 252, 258, 274, 277, 282, 285
Australia, 31, 141–142, 143
Azusa Street revival, 36, 39–45, 54, 57, 61, 83, 84, 90, 104, 109, 115, 124, 137, 166, 167, 170–172, 173, 174, 175, 187, 188, 189, 190, 191, 206, 217, 218, 235, 251, 264, 270, 271, 272, 281

Babalola, Joseph, 118, 177
Bahamas, 80

Bakker, Jim, 150
Baptism in the Spirit, *see* Spirit baptism
Baptists, 31, 32, 36, 85, 92, 95, 96, 98, 99, 101, 133, 148, 150, 153, 154, 155, 157, 220, 262
Barratt, Thomas B., 64–65, 84–85, 86–88, 91, 99, 124, 145, 188–189, 249, 252
Bartleman, Frank, 36, 37, 46, 61, 166, 167, 170, 187, 249, 270
Bays, Daniel, 133, 173
Beckford, Robert S., 272
Bennett, Dennis, 144, 147–148, 152, 154
Berg, Daniel, 46, 58, 71, 97, 174, 239
Berg, George, 124
Bergunder, Michael, 170, 232
Berlin Declaration, 89
Bethel churches, 130, 131
Bhengu, Nicholas, 109, 177
Bloch-Hoell, Nils, 166, 167
Blumhardt, Johann, 24, 30
Boddy, Alexander A., 36, 84, 91–92, 93, 94, 96, 99, 145, 214, 252
Bonnke, Reinhard, 58, 89, 109
Bosworth, F. F., 53, 193
Branham, William, 58, 145, 157, 220, 233
Brazil, 58, 63, 64, 69–74, 97, 158, 169, 171, 174, 262
Brazil for Christ, 72–73, 267
Bredesen, Harald, 147, 148
British Israelism, 33, 35, 92, 93, 142, 271
Brownsville Revival, *see* Pensacola
Buntain, Mark, 126
Burma, *see* Myanmar
Burton, William F. P., 93, 110, 182

Canada, Canadians, 43, 49, 68, 76, 80, 81, 109, 112, 113, 114, 115, 126, 162–164
Catholic Charismatics, Catholic-Pentecostal Dialogue, 13, 74, 75, 78, 101, 128, 132, 144, 147, 150–152, 153, 154, 155, 156, 195, 246, 253

Ceylon Pentecostal Mission, The Pentecostal Mission, 127, 128, 129
Cherubim and Seraphim Society, Eternal Sacred Order of, 118
Chikane, Frank, 109, 269, 277
Chile, 64–67, 68, 69, 70, 84, 85, 145, 162, 171, 174, 239–241, 243, 262
China, Chinese, 11, 12, 13, 42, 49, 58, 90, 129, 132–136, 173, 175, 176, 179, 182–183, 232, 282
Cho, David (Paul) Yonggi, 2–4, 137–139, 158, 159, 173, 221–223, 232–233, 265–266
Christ Apostolic Church, 5, 116, 118–121, 177
Christenson, Larry, 148, 152, 154
Christian Assembly, Little Flock, Local Church, 133, 135–136
Christian Congregation, 70–71, 72, 97
Christian Outreach Centres, 142, 143
Christian Revival Crusade, 142, 143
Church of God (other than Cleveland), 59, 76, 77, 80, 109
Church of God (Cleveland and related churches), 47, 51, 52, 54–55, 76, 77, 78, 80, 81, 95, 109, 110, 125, 138, 143, 146, 247, 250, 282
Church of God of Prophecy, 54, 55, 80, 81, 95
Church of God in Christ, 8–9, 42, 47, 51, 52, 194, 250
Church of Pentecost, 116–120, 255, 275
Colombia, 74
consequence, doctrine of, *see* 'initial evidence'
Congo, Democratic Republic of, 104, 106, 110–111, 178, 182
contextualization, 38, 76, 104, 113–114, 122, 124, 175, 197, 198–199, 201, 203, 208–210, 212–214, 223, 236, 238, 239, 242, 247, 266, 270, 271, 283
Cook, Glenn, 41, 48, 188
Cook, Robert, 125, 127
Copeland, Kenneth, 146, 158, 221, 222
Côte d'Ivoire, Ivory Coast, 115–116, 175
Cox, Harvey, 44, 61, 62, 104, 166, 171, 200–201, 202, 236, 237–238, 239, 241, 258, 260, 263–264, 269, 281, 283
culture, gospel and, 235–242

Dallière, Louis, 96, 145, 153, 251, 252
Dayton, Donald W., 166
Deeper Life Bible Church, 161
deliverance, *see* exorcism
Denmark, 86–88
Dhinakaran, D. G. S., 127
dispensational, dispensationalism, *see* premillennialism

Dowie, John Alexander, 31–32, 34, 35, 89, 105, 106
du Plessis, David, 94, 108, 146–147, 154, 251, 252
Duncan-Williams, Nicholas, 158, 161
Dunn, James D. G., 192–193
Durham, William, 41, 45, 50, 56, 61, 70, 71, 174, 252

ecumenism, 67, 68, 73, 75, 98, 99, 146, 152, 245, 249–251, 253, 254–255, 258
education, theological, 208, 243–249
Elim Pentecostal Church, 36, 93–94, 95, 114, 117, 142
El Salvador, 76
El Shaddai, 132, 155
Episcopalians, *see* Anglicans
eschatology, 29–30, 33, 94, 171, 217–220, 263
Ethiopia, 49, 115
Ewart, Frank, 46, 48
evangelism, 206, 214
exorcism, deliverance, 197, 201, 211, 228, 230, 231, 233–234

faith message, *see* Word of Faith
Faith Tabernacle, 117, 118, 121
Faupel, D. William, 32, 60, 62, 166, 171, 246, 259, 281
Fee, Gordon D., 193, 194–195
Fiji, 142
Filadelfia Church (various), 84, 85, 88, 96, 97
Finished Work Pentecostalism, 45–50, 83, 191
Finland, Finnish, 83, 85, 86, 111, 112, 114, 129
Finney, Charles, 28
Fletcher, John, 25, 26
Foursquare Church, *see* International Church of the Foursquare Gospel
France, 24, 96, 153, 251
Francescon, Luigi (Luis), 46, 58, 68, 70, 97, 174, 239
Freidzon, Claudio, 6–7, 69, 162
Full Gospel Business Men's Fellowship International, 145–146, 148, 156, 157, 276
fundamentalism, 218, 258–260

Garr, Alfred and Lillian, 57, 124, 128, 218
Gee, Donald, 91, 94, 251, 252
gender issues, 273–276
Gerloff, Roswith, 272–273
Germany, German, 24, 30, 35, 88–89, 145, 148, 152–153, 251
Ghana, 104, 116–118, 121, 158, 161, 175, 177, 255
gifts of the Spirit, *see* spiritual gifts
glossolalia, *see* tongues
God is Love Pentecostal Church, 72, 73

Guatemala, 76–77
Guti, Ezekiel, 161

Hagin, Kenneth E., 86, 146, 158, 163, 220–221, 222
Haiti, 79, 80
Harper, Michael, 153–154
Harris, William Wade, 115–116, 175
Haywood, Garfield T., 48–49, 53
healing, 19–25, 30–33, 58–59, 108, 145, 177, 201, 210–212, 220–221, 228–234, 266, 280
health and wealth gospel, *see* Word of Faith
hermeneutics, 225–234
Hocken, Peter, 154, 246, 256
Hodges, Melvin, 75, 209–210
Hollenweger, Walter J., 13, 43, 44, 53, 88, 104, 166, 168, 196, 235, 241, 245–246, 251–253, 256, 269, 271–272
Hong Kong, 57, 124, 129, 134, 175
Hoover, Willis C., 64–66, 75, 84, 145, 162, 174, 193, 239, 240, 241

Idahosa, Benson and Margaret, 158, 161
India, 35, 36–37, 42, 57, 58, 64–65, 124–128, 145, 155, 169, 170, 171, 173–174, 176, 179, 181, 232
Indian Pentecostal Church of God, 127
Indonesia, 59, 130–131, 281
Indonesian Revival, 130–131
initial evidence, 10, 34–35, 39–45, 53, 60, 65, 94, 189–195
International Church of the Foursquare Gospel, 46, 52, 56–57, 72, 75, 77, 131, 139, 143, 194, 249, 282
International Pentecostal Holiness Church, 47, 55, 59, 67, 77, 92, 114
Irving, Edward (Irvingite movement), 24, 32, 35, 189
Italy, Italians, 68, 70, 83, 97–98, 174
Ivory Coast, *see* Côte d'Ivoire

Jamaica, 79, 81
Japan, 42, 49, 140–141
Jesus People, 149
Jeffreys, George, 36, 90, 91, 92, 93, 94, 96
Jesus Family, 133, 135
Jesus is Lord Church, 131
Johns, Cheryl Bridges, 267, 270, 275, 278

Kärkkäinen, Veli-Matti, 254, 256
Kenya, 104, 111–114, 161
Keswick Convention, 26, 28–29, 30, 32, 83, 91, 141
Kimbangu, Kimbanguist Church, 106

Kivuli, Daudi Zakayo, 113–114, 122
Korea
    South Korea, 1–4, 35, 37–38, 85, 136–138, 139, 145, 158, 159, 169, 171, 172, 173, 221–223, 232–233, 237–238, 254, 265–266, 281, 285
Korean Pentecost (Revival), 37–38, 136, 145, 172
Kuhlman, Kathryn, 156, 162, 274

Lalive d'Epinay, Christian, 166, 167, 238, 243
Lake, John G., 40, 58, 106, 107, 177
Land, Steven J., 196, 203
Latter Rain Movement, 51, 85
Latvia, 98–99
Lekganyane, Engenas, 107–108, 177
Liberia, 58, 104, 115, 175
Li Changsoo (Witness Lee), 136
Little Flock, *see* Christian Assembly
Local Church, 136
Lugo, Juan, 79
Lutherans, 46, 86, 88, 89, 145, 148, 152, 251
Luz del Mundo, 75, 78

Macchia, Frank, 257
Malaysia, 128, 129–130, 134
Mango, Alfayo, 112–113
Mason, Charles H., 8, 47, 51, 52, 53
McDonnell, Kilian, 151
McGavran, Donald, 207, 210
McGee, Gary B., 174, 208
McKeown, James, 116, 117–120
McPherson, Aimee Semple, 46, 56–57, 58, 72, 93, 131, 141, 249, 274
Menzies, Robert P., 194, 195
Methodists, 24, 25–26, 27, 28, 33, 37, 59, 64–65, 84, 136, 137, 145, 147, 148, 150, 154, 173, 231, 239, 240–241, 243, 251
Methodist Pentecostal Church, 13, 64–65, 174
Mexico, Mexican, 56, 59, 77–79, 97
missiology, 168–172, 183, 206–224, 248
Montanism, 19–20, 24
Mülheim Association, 89, 91, 251
Myanmar, Burma, 129

National Association of Evangelicals, 53, 55, 56, 57, 145, 247, 250, 251
Netherlands (Holland), 89–90, 252
New Zealand, 141, 142, 143
Ni Doushen (Watchman Nee), 135–136
Nigeria, 4, 5, 104, 117, 118–121, 158, 160, 161, 169, 171, 177
Norway, Norwegian, 68, 83, 84–85, 88–93, 111, 171

Oneness Pentecostalism, 13, 46, 47–51, 53, 74, 75, 76, 77, 78, 130, 134, 140, 192, 246, 250
Osborne, Tommy L., 58, 59, 77, 145, 221
Otabil, Mensa, 158, 161
Oyedepo, David, 158, 161

Parham, Charles F., 33–35, 39, 40–41, 44–45, 51, 57, 60, 61, 62, 76, 167, 190, 191, 193, 271
Paul, Jonathan, 84, 88, 89, 91, 100, 145, 251
Paul, Ramankutty, 127, 128
Pensacola Revival (Brownsville), 164, 285
Pentecostal Assemblies of Canada, 49, 68, 80, 81, 109, 112, 113, 114
Pentecostal Church of God, 52, 56
Pentecostal Church of Indonesia, 130, 131
Pentecostal Holiness Church, *see* International Pentecostal Holiness Church
Pentecostal Mission, *see* Ceylon Pentecostal Mission
Pentecostal Missionary Union, 58, 90, 92, 93, 94, 110, 128, 140, 178, 179, 181–182, 190, 214
Pentecostal World Conference, 88, 94, 146, 250
Peru, 75
Petersen, Douglas, 276
Pethrus, Lewi, 84, 85, 87
Philippines, 131–132, 155, 281
Pinnock, Clark H., 193, 195
pneumatology, theology of the Spirit, 14, 19–25, 26, 27, 28–29, 34–35, 39–45, 133, 134, 187–205, 206–208
Poland, 100–101
Polhill, Cecil, 91, 92, 93, 94, 96, 181, 190
Polman, Gerrit, 89–90, 91, 252
Pomerville, Paul A., 172, 207
Portugal, 74, 79, 83, 96–97
positive confession, *see* Word of Faith
Prayer Mountain Movement, 137
premillennialism, 29–30, 33, 94, 171, 217–219
Presbyterians, 24, 31, 37, 70, 133, 136, 137, 145, 147, 148, 152, 173, 189, 192, 243, 261, 279
prophecy, 19–25
prosperity gospel, *see* Word of Faith
Puerto Rico, Puerto Rican, 59, 78, 79–80, 97

Quakers (Society of Friends), 23–24, 113

Ramabai, Pandita, 37, 64–65, 124, 125, 173–174, 193, 276
Ranaghan, Kevin, 151, 155
Reformed churches, 26, 28–29, 30, 89, 145, 148, 153, 245, 251
Restoration Movement, *see* Shepherding
Robeck, Cecil M., Jr., 250, 251, 255, 256

Roberts, Oral, 55, 58, 59, 145, 146, 150, 156, 157, 220, 221, 222
Robertson, Pat, 150, 156, 262
Roho churches, 112–114
Romania, 83, 84, 100
Russia, 24–25, 35, 83, 98, 99–100

Sandford, Frank, 32–34, 35
Sanford, Agnes, 147
Scott, Douglas, 96
Sepúlveda, Juan, 213, 236, 237, 239–241, 243, 267
Seymour, William J., 34, 35, 39–45, 46, 47, 48, 51, 57, 60, 61, 62, 167, 172, 188, 190, 193, 235, 249, 251, 271, 274
Shakarian, Demos, 145, 146, 156
Shepherding (Discipling) restoration movement, 155, 156–157
Sherrill, John, 149, 151
Simpson, A. B., 29, 31, 33, 34
Singapore, 129–130, 134, 159
Society for Pentecostal Studies, 49, 154, 246–247, 248, 259
South Africa, 42, 58, 74, 104, 106–110, 141, 145, 146, 155, 158, 163, 171, 177, 181, 229, 247, 262, 265, 268–269, 277–278
South Korea, *see* Korea
Spain, 79, 97
Spirit, doctrine of, *see* pneumatology
Spirit baptism, 14, 26, 27, 28–29, 34–35, 39–45, 133, 134, 187–195
Spirit of Jesus Church, 49, 140
spiritual gifts
    gifts of the Spirit, 19–25, 27, 228, 231
spirituality, 195–205
Sri Lanka, 128
statistics (discussion), 10–14, 104
subsequence, doctrine of, 26, 192–193
Suenens, Cardinal Léon Joseph, 151, 152
Sung, John, 129
Swaggart, Jimmy, 150, 158
Sweden, Swedish, 24, 35, 58, 68, 71, 72, 75, 78, 85–86, 111, 114, 115
Switzerland, 30, 88
Synan, Vinson, 194

Taiwan, 134, 136
Tanzania, 114
Taylor, John V., 187, 193, 195, 282
Thailand, 129
Third Wave, 158–159, 195, 252
Tomlinson, A. J., 47, 54, 80
tongues, speaking in, glossolalia, 10, 19–20, 21–24, 27, 29, 34–35, 36, 37, 39–45, 53, 60, 94, 189–195, 228, 231

Toronto revival (blessing), 157, 162–164
Torrey, R. A., 28–29, 88
True Jesus Church, 13, 49, 133–134, 140

Uganda, 114–115, 161
Ukraine, 83, 84, 100, 169
United Kingdom (Britain), 7–8, 24, 28–29, 32, 35–36, 74, 81, 83, 91–96, 145, 153–155, 157, 159, 164, 169, 171, 252, 272
United Pentecostal Church, 49, 52, 74, 75, 80, 81, 129, 143
United States of America, 8–9, 24, 26–30, 31–35, 39–62, 69, 72, 75, 76, 78, 79, 84, 112, 126, 131, 143, 144, 145–152, 167, 169, 170, 182–183, 244, 246, 247, 250, 251, 255, 258, 264, 276, 282
Universal Church of the Kingdom of God, 73–74, 97

Venezuela, 63, 74, 75
Villafañe, Eldin, 263, 270–271
Vineyard Association, 7–8, 95, 157, 158, 162, 163, 164, 195
Vingren, Gunnar, 46, 58, 71, 72, 97, 174, 239

Wacker, Grant, 166, 167, 168
Wagner, Peter, 195, 207, 210, 234
Warrington, Keith, 233

Welsh Revival, 35–36, 83, 91, 172
Wesley, John, 25–26, 28, 30, 191
Wigglesworth, Smith, 93, 96, 141, 142, 146, 222
Wilkerson, David, 149, 151, 158
Williams, J. Rodman, 192, 261
Wimber, John, 7, 158, 162, 163, 164, 195, 198–199, 258
women in ministry, *see* gender issues
Woodworth-Etter, Maria, 31, 48, 58, 162, 217, 273, 274
Word of Faith ('prosperity gospel'), 85–86, 150, 157–158, 159, 220, 258, 262, 263, 266, 276, 280, 282
World Council of Churches, 67, 68, 73, 75, 98, 99, 146, 152, 245, 250–251, 253, 254–255
World Pentecostal Conference, *see* Pentecostal World Conference

Yoido Full Gospel Church, 1–4, 137–138, 221–223, 265, 266
Yong, Amos, 201, 202–203, 237, 257, 283

Zambia, 104, 110, 262
Zimbabwe, 104, 110, 161
Zion Christian Church, 32, 107–108, 177
Zionist churches, Zion cities, 31–32, 105, 106–108, 110, 229, 230, 268